KRISTI

Arboretum footbridge, Seattle, Washington

KRISTI
So Thin Is the Veil

PETER BEAULIEU

A Crossroad Book
The Crossroad Publishing Company
New York

The Crossroad Publishing Company
16 Penn Plaza – 481 Eighth Avenue, Suite 1550
New York, NY 10001

Copyright © 2006 by Peter and Kristin Beaulieu

Printed in the United States of America

The text of this book is set in 10/13 Goudy Old Style.
The display face is Nuptial.

The sketches throughout the text are by the author.

Cataloging-in-Publication Data is available from the Library of Congress.

ISBN-10: 0-8245-2398-9
ISBN-13: 978-0-8245-2398-5

1 2 3 4 5 6 7 8 9 10   12 11 10 09 08 07 06

To our Laura and Mark
and families and friends of their generation —
in anticipation of the New Springtime

"From life to greater Life. I know this with a certainty.
I've just had a long talk with Jesus — my best Friend."
— Kristi —

"We shall see that the tears of this century have prepared the ground
for a new springtime of the human spirit. . . . "
—John Paul II, at the United Nations in New York, 1995

" . . . to lead people out of the desert, towards the place of life,
towards friendship with the Son of God."
—Benedict XVI, first homily at St. Peter's Basilica, 2005

All royalties from this true story are donated
to those needy mothers who reverence the right to live
of their needy and unborn daughters and sons.

Contents

Introduction

But Oh for the touch of a vanished hand,
And the sound of a voice that is still!
— Alfred Lord Tennyson

Near the end of her ordeal with cancer, my dear wife, Kristi, lost the use of her hand for writing. Earlier she had lost most of her voice. *"Pray for me,"* she whispered, *"that I can simply offer this up . . . like my voice."* As a wife and mother Kristi was a gift of inner smallness and gentleness. And when the hugeness of cancer entered our life, even this was carried along by her consistently sweet disposition. This intruder was carried along until Kristi's "dear Lord" touched and reclaimed her with His total healing.

And with this total healing, both the disease and Kristi slipped from our sight.

Farther back to a time long before we met, I recall a family vacation of my teen years on the ocean beaches of Oregon. The gray clouded sky and the boulder jetty mingled with the constant ocean spray. Sea birds circled overhead. On that melancholy beach I considered the words in Tennyson's poem "Break, Break, Break" that captured in poetry the loss so irreversible. And now alone again, here I was walking the beaches, when these words came drifting back to meet my hollowed soul.

11

The veil has fallen across our marriage, and now Kristi is gone from me. Where now is her hand in mine, and her voice with mine?

The first days after Kristi's death, I was suspended over the edge of an inner abyss. Facing me was desperation. Was it possible in some small way to still hold hands with Kristi — even through the veil? I was not then quite in shock, and the question was real. How total is the loss? What is memory? And what of our presence one to another? Is there a hidden path around the edges of the veil and the closing circle of despair?

Slightly more practical a question eventually showed itself: How to move on, but still without letting go? The path, I discovered so slowly, is that the only way to hold on to Kristi, to the spouse lost, is to loosen the imagination — the mental images of moments past. If death has a purpose, it must be to teach us to know the difference between our migrant imaginations and an enduring reality not of our making.

Even when she was with us and the cancer was with her, Kristi reposed and even rejoiced in the certainty that she was moving through the veil "from life to greater Life." The Communion of Saints, so much a part of Kristi's story that follows, is the full and enduring gathering even now of all of God's people, present *and* past. With all of her heart, Kristi was happy here but also eager to join this full communion instead of lingering here a while longer.

In my more accepting moments, I was to learn that this gathering shines through so very thin a veil falling between those partially living "here" and those fully living "there" in eternity.

And so I have learned that in death the one lost is not to be found trailing behind in fading and shattered images. Kristi is now in front of me, and resplendently and solidly beyond the finite grasp of mere imagination. Knowing this, the "memory" becomes not only the ability to recall the past, but part of our *presence* toward the redeemed and fully real person. The person lost lives in fullness no longer confined in our speck-like minds. Space and time cannot contain this. We are more likely to connect all of the dots in the star-filled heavens. We cannot contain the mystery, but it can and does hold us.

The key is in suspecting deeply what Christ must have meant at the Last Supper. He offered the bread and wine and said to His disciples, "This is my body, which is being given for you; do this in *remembrance* of me" (Luke 22:19). Memory is a rejoining, it is the re-membering and the presence, rather than only the mental imagination of things past. And His presence is real, not simply therapeutic. And "do this" is an action spoken eternally from the mouth of the One who is unchanging and ever new, and in whom all things find their very being. The infinite Presence and His finite act of consecration are contained within each other. His eternity creates and then enters our time.[1] Our remembrance is an anticipation of things hoped for, a memory of the future.

In this re-membering is an intimacy and a gentleness of self-forgetfulness greater than any power or any limitation we might imagine. Even in the Our Father, I have heard, the correct translation of "Thy will be done on earth as it is in heaven" is really "Thy will be done in time, as it is in eternity." In some of her simplest gestures Kristi was deeply in touch with this presence of All to all.

This book, in part, is an effort by a wandering spouse to understand some of this simple truth about the gestures, all of the little things.

Hints were given to me along the way. Scattered here and there like flower petals. On one quiet afternoon during our final months of home hospice care, Kristi was especially saddened. It was the thought that our life together was coming to an end — that "it is all over." I think my response to Kristi's words — at this shared moment of exquisite sadness — remained beyond words and unspoken. I do not remember actually saying what I knew. The moment was lifted away in a larger silence.

But at that moment, as we sat together on our sun-streaked back lawn, I discovered within myself that in death Kristi was not really slipping away from me. I discovered that she — the total she — would rest in the sacred heart of our Lord Jesus Christ, and that His heart, which touches so silently into our shared history at a particular time and place, excludes no one, not yesterday, today, or forever. *We would be parted, but not separated.* This communion is not merely psychological; it is more than poetry or elaborate denial. It is a mystery, and He has a name and a face.

In the months and then years following Kristi's death, she has helped me find the truth about our "moment of sadness" when we first really saw that it was all over. In these pages, Kristi has helped me rediscover what I saw only schematically and left unsaid on that quiet afternoon. Inside of the sadness and the pain, and not around it or beneath it, is an eternal joy.

For me, of course, the bittersweet sadness continues. Had I been forewarned by a reading from Emily Brontë's "Remembrance," I might not have attempted this book, this indulgence "in Memory's rapturous pain...." Over a year was to pass before I could consistently remember with any confidence what I knew then so abstractly, but with certainty. We truly will be together again, more so than before.

Even now, Kristi nudges me, *"Why so many words to say something so simple?"*

In Kristi there was such sweetness. Everyone who met her could see it. And in the gesture of a moment this sweetness spoke more than any book, including this one. With Kristi even I lived in a cheerful and sacramental universe — a holy universe that was at once five hundred years behind our modern mind-set and perhaps as many years again ahead of its time. Here and now, and without

even knowing it, Kristi was among those chosen souls who eternally
are part of the awaited New Springtime of the human spirit.

The veil that now divides all of us from the departed is personal
mortality — it is death. And death is not an abstraction, not an
idea like "humanity" or "the future," or even "the past." It is only
in a time so rootless as ours that even the mystery of death — such
a colossal disrespect for each human person — would become the
subject of owners' manuals. We have manuals on how to operate
grief. There is the denial, then the anger... then adjustment... we
are told. For those who might feel undernourished by this shallow-
ness, a sentimental and possibly spiritual section might be thrown
into the manual (but one usually not so incisive as to jeopardize
sales in these fickle times).

The simple reality for me now is that I will never absorb what
has happened. There are no words.

My words here are more like the stones framing a well, and the
well has no bottom. In its details Kristi's story is remarkable, and not
easily believed. Parts might read as fiction, but they are not. And
while her story of consistent serenity through cancer is not unique,
it is still gifted and it is true. Revealed in Kristi is the Communion
of Saints — each member so totally personal and so totally surrendered within each other, even to the point of vicarious suffering
for one another. This is a gathering that is real. It is a gathering of
such density that Kristi is even more real now than the veil that
conceals her.

Is this degree of presence true, and can we, Kristi and I, in some
way even now hold hands through the veil?

I now live with this certainty. I have this certainty because of
our marriage itself, an unwritten proof overlooked by so many. True
marriage partakes of eternity; true marriage really is all or nothing. If
we listen to the Soul within our soul, we find that marriages are not
only indissoluble, but that they are also *indestructible*, least of all by

death. And so, our life together endures and carries me now toward our awaited full reunion. With Kristi received into His hands, *we* are halfway there.

These pages are partly my poor effort to record how I grew from near panic into this confirmed certainty. Kristi has guided me both in what we became before she died and in what she helps me to see now. And possibly in what I am to do here and in the remaining time that is given.

Throughout our marriage our woven paths — this dance — played out in different ways. Professionally, I pursued an education and niche career in planning for cities and regions, somewhat allured by a puzzle-solving mentality. There can be spiritual poverty in this calculus. We often cannot really tell what actions are doing good, all things considered, but we at least can tell what things are doing direct harm. Kristi, better than I, was more lighthearted and consistently present to the person directly in front of her. Up until the end, Kristi still wondered anew how my preoccupation, my career and professional vocation, actually affected real people. The puzzle held no fascination. For her, it was important to notice even those people we meet casually, when all too often we are brushing past to do something else. The grocery store clerks miss and mourn her. Kristi asked me to come with her during those last months when she dropped in on her hairdresser on a sunny afternoon to say good-bye.

How does our busyness of even professionalism affect real people? The lesson might be to always search for ways, in our organizations and in our compact world, to see each other not only as individuals, but as full *persons.* Persons first, each toward the other, within the heart of God. Not groups alone, but also not simply individuals within any kind of system. In all of this noise, to never lose touch with the mystery of the real person in front of us. Hubris and economics are not enough to solve the "puzzle" when each of the human parts, without exception, is another self of infinite value. Not a key, but a foundational truth, is to first do no direct evil even in the hope of accomplishing good.

In the desolation following Kristi's death I have sometimes wondered why anyone does anything at all. Is it only our fear of true silence, or footloose appetite for having over being? Toward the end Kristi expressed amazement even at how the body keeps trying to move on when there is nothing left. What we do is part of who we are. It simply must be more than the work of a tool-wielding animal. It must be love, rather than an appetite for "progress" or a nod toward careerism, or the energy of the game and pride of life. It must be more than an escape from boredom, or even the use of our inner talents to fashion a better world for ourselves and possibly for others. The goal, finally, might be compassion enough to reduce duress in the world such that we do not leave each other in such a bind as to choose evil over truth, whether this is on the scale of individual persons or entire nations. And beyond our goals and measurement, if we had eyes to see we would know that each act leaves a mark that is everlasting, because it is human and resurrected.

Cardinal Ratzinger (now Pope Benedict XVI) cut to the chase in some follow-up work to the most recent gathering of the entire Church to deepen itself and only then to step up to the needs of the modern world (the Second Vatican Council — 1962–65). He proposed that what the world desperately needs is not better management, but more saints.[2] This is not because saints see farther than the rest of us into the practical puzzle of this world. The puzzle is not mathematical. Instead, it is through these hidden and ordinary saints that God's grace still enters us, especially when we are puzzled in the world.[3]

In ordinary days the closest connection between my workaday world and Kristi's personal touch came when we stood side by side in witness with others. We stood across the street from abortion clinics. In the mother of each unborn child we see duress. And in the child we see beyond the statistic of one and to a personal universe. Near the curb, we place ourselves in a prayer space, an open cathedral for the twenty-first century — a cathedral without walls. This is the place where any one or two or more can be totally present for another, if only for a moment. One does not save the world, and yet each one touched is a world.

In the bigger picture, the picture of one to another, hearts might be touched and changed. In this way, in this "sacrament of the present moment," Kristi lived and was a *witness*. I tried to keep up. This was part of her day-to-day gentleness. By any lesser yardstick she did very little that the world would ever notice. In her own estimation, she was a very small person, a "peewee."

Kristi's path was also one of family affection and harmony. This harmony sprung from heartfelt acceptance of His will, even and especially if it is terminal cancer. Acceptance — not resignation. Her way, finally, was to find joy in the Lord and in others, and then to offer up her own cross for these others. Kristi was very simple in the end, transparent. Single-heartedness: this is a hidden path to wholeness and to holiness.

This reaching out from spiritual smallness into our still smaller world of sophisticated barbarity is the leading edge to the New Springtime of the human spirit. The Springtime, or the "second spring," ties us intimately to one another, and perhaps especially to the radiance of the littlest among us:

> The First Spring was the springtime of Advent, presaging the summer of the Incarnation and the first Christian civilization. The Second is the springtime of the children of the Blessed Virgin, of her saints, especially the saints of spiritual child-hood, saints like St. Therese. The Second Spring — whenever

it comes — is therefore the springtime that presages the Second Coming of Our Lord. . . . Perhaps we may add, that the blood of the Holy Innocents of our century, poured out in wars and pogroms and clinics the world over, has surely watered the ground that will blossom in the century to come.[4]

Now well over two years after Kristi's death, the feelings of panic and self-reproach, borne of my own inner agitation, are lifting. If it is true that grieving for a spouse consumes one month for each year of marriage, then the timing for us is about right. But the path is always different. Kristi left me two months before our twenty-seventh anniversary. In a dream after so long, finally without distortion of imagination, Kristi stood before me in a favorite outfit. She said, "*I had such a wonderful life with my dear Peter.*"

At last, I can repose in all of the memories of things past. And I finally view the grieving and the fog from the outside. And I see Kristi clearly, without obstacles, less in mental pictures now and more apart from the anxious churning of an imagination under attack. Even my demons are finally exhausted and expelled.

Of the present and the future, I know where Kristi is.

But what does the Communion of Saints actually look like? This term refers not only to our union here and now through the other sacraments given to us by the Soul of our souls, and especially the Eucharist, but also to the undivided gathering of persons both here *and* beyond. As with any other friend or neighbor, we can also ask for the gentle intercession of the saints departed. All are part of the full Communion of Saints.

This is the teaching. But what does this gathering look like when viewed from *within a marriage,* with the partners parted on opposite sides of the veil? What does the gathering "in heaven" look like when the view is ripped open by the death of one spouse and not the other? The conversation of marriage is changed, not taken away; the partners are parted, but not separated. Instead, it is in our separation from everything else that the everlasting togetherness, through the resurrected Christ, is assured.

This story of Kristi, all of it true, is a glimpse with one corner of the veil lifted a small bit from time to time. Kristi and I write these pages for our family, and for the neighbors and parishioners. We also write it for the clergy and those in the medical profession who stood by us in our need. We write for others unknown to us, both living and dead, whose prayers shielded us over the years in ways that are known now to Kristi but that cannot be seen by me this side of the veil.

Before her release of total healing, Kristi guided all of us to pray *"in thanksgiving for the path that is given to each one of us, whatever it may be."* And now — with Kristi yet so near — I look back over the two years and more since her death. And I am spun about by the entire fourteen years since the cancer was first detected. From this treading of the path given to us comes our story. Not the closing chapter of our past, this writing is more the beginning of a future, and a future that is everlasting. We write in anticipation of a New Springtime of the human spirit. This will come, one person and one family at a time.

In these pages, Kristi and I hope to visit with three groups or audiences. First, we join grieving spouses whose faith might be shaken and who by our story might be nudged a small step toward steadfastness and some measure of reassuring joy. And next are those looking for convincing inspiration while dealing with serious illness or hospice care, and the temptation toward an easy way out. We also feel ourselves part of a more general gathering interested in a personal story for this time of encounter between the life of Christ within each of us and, on the outside, an uprooted postmodern world.

Astonishment at the fullness of the resurrection accounts for our selected title: *Kristi — So Thin Is the Veil.* Kristi peered one way through this veil as she stood before our living room window, one year to the day before the first day of hospice care and final months of our ordeal began:

> *I worry about you; I don't want to leave you alone.*
> *And Laura and Mark. But for me, it's a win-win.*
> *From life to greater Life.*[5] *I know this with a certainty.*
> *I've just had a long talk with Jesus — my best Friend.*

Chapter One

Our Vow
to One Another

From the Camas Prairie

Born four minutes before her identical twin, Kristi entered the world in 1949 in a large public hospital in Chicago. Kristi and Kerry were exact replicas of each other — each was five pounds five ounces, and each was nineteen inches long. After a quick two years the growing family moved farther west through Denver. In 1951 Kristi's father, Dr. Richard E. Orr, finally returned to his childhood home in Cottonwood, Idaho, on the Camas Prairie, and settled there with his wife, Jeanne, and the first four of seven children. This farming village nestles in a shallow gully fifty miles south of Lewis and Clark's 1805 route westward on the Clearwater River. The prairie life, he judged, would be the most nurturing place to raise his family in a world both promising and threatening.

I was born five years earlier than Kristi, a few minutes after my own identical twin brother (I was a full six ounces heavier). The place of our birth was Hanford, Washington, now a ghost town about one hundred miles downstream from where the Clearwater empties into the Snake River. The Snake flows west to join the Columbia, the last leg of the Lewis and Clark trail. Hanford is twenty or thirty miles upstream of where the Snake loses itself in the larger river in their shared westward path to the Pacific.

From the earliest years the Orr twins, Kristi and Kerry, were inseparable. This special bond is marked best by one of countless instances. At the age of seven, Kerry came down with appendicitis and was taken to a hospital fifty miles north in Lewiston. I remember Kristi telling me, decades later, how separated and abandoned each felt, with Kristi on the lawn outside the hospital and Kerry's sad little face framed by the second floor window. The fever hung on, but then immediately dropped once the twins were placed together again.[1] The attending physician finally suspected the non-clinical cause of the fever and offered a room in his home where the twins could be together for Kerry's recovery.

July 6 is the date of Kristi's birth, the feast day for St. Maria Goretti. In 1902, in her sweetness and devotion, twelve-year-old Maria resisted unto death rather than yield to the lust of an older neighbor boy. Canonization as a martyr and a saint came in 1951. Present for this event, after having spent twenty-seven years in prison, was her repentant assailant. On her deathbed many years before, Maria had already forgiven him. After two millennia, martyrdom for a life both higher and deeper within remains a theme for individuals and for untold numbers in the twenty-first century. We are recalled to other times only thought to be less enlightened and more primitive than our own. Little Goretti always was one of Kristi's favorite saints and dear friends.

In 1973 and only weeks after we had met, Kristi invited me — a "new friend" — home to visit her family for Christmas. When asked by her father on the phone, "What is *her* name?" Kristi answered, *"His name is Peter."* And so, our story begins. . . .

The Orr home rests on a gentle slope of high ground in west central Idaho overlooking the Camas Prairie and the Salmon River Canyon to the south, a short four miles east of Cottonwood (founded in 1862). Cottonwood is a close-knit farming community with a population of eight hundred and something. In the following years we checked the sign at the edge of town whenever we made our regular visits. On that prairie I discovered extended families and a fabric of family histories. The generations live side by side in a richness that contrasts with the abruptness of my own hometown experience in Richland, a wartime boomtown located in the flat expanse of eastern Washington.[2]

Unlike the new Richland, Cottonwood breathed continuity. As a farm community it offered a close sympathy with the seasons. The Camas Prairie is wheat and cattle country, edging into higher forests and forested gullies. Homes with the same family names, most often German, are marked by scattered signposts on the back roads. If I was at first a bit too romantic about this treat to village America, I also was to learn about the all-too-human details. These details included a small town traffic ticket collected on an unpaved back road, which I probably should have framed under glass.

The prairie drops off sharply to the south from the Orr home. Here the Salmon River flows west to join the larger Snake River. Farther south the peaks of the Seven Devils Range rise to over nine thousand feet to form a snow-capped part of the distant horizon. Not quite visible across the Snake River to the west are the alpine peaks of the Blue Mountains and the glacially formed Lake Wallowa, which was to become a mecca for large family reunions in the early 1990s.

The much smaller Buffalo Hump Mountain, a local landmark, is closer and a bit to the southeast. This point and others are still the subject of a proudly remembered history of settlement and occasional Indian battles. To the right of the Hump and twenty miles from the Orr house is White Bird Canyon. Looking across from the higher prairie, and with a sweep of the outstretched hand, family members would trace for me the northeasterly path followed by Chief Joseph on his unsuccessful flight in 1877 toward LoLo Pass and safety in Canada under the British monarch, Queen Victoria.

And straight to the east is the very small town of Dixie. Dixie exchanged gas lighting for electric power only in the late 1970s, and at the same time received its first telephone service. All of this was part of the memory of the families distributed in small communities and proud farmhouses on the prairie.

At the center of the Cottonwood community is the Benedictine Abbey of St. Gertrude (dedicated in 1924). This large, dark, stone-block structure is fronted by two red-domed towers. The twin towers are visible several miles away as from east to west they survey the full sweep of the prairie. The nuns came to this country to escape a feared expulsion by the government from their convent, St. Andrew's at Sarnen in Switzerland. They settled at their permanent new home in Cottonwood in 1907, only eight years before Kristi's father was brought into the world, possibly by his own father, Dr. Wesley Orr.

From the Orr home the abbey can be reached on foot from above and behind through the pine forest. A shorter walk up the hill from the abbey leads to the convent cemetery, tucked away in a small clearing behind a crumbling white picket fence. The several rows of simple white slab markers are connected to a small orchard and the abbey grounds by a winding trail marked with fourteen small shrines at eye level, each housing one of the Stations of the Cross. These markers are a reminder of Christ's steps between His "trial" and His crucifixion for each of us. At the foot of the hill is a replica of the Marian statue found at Lourdes in France. In the early days of the abbey this shrine was blessed on the Feast of the Assumption (August 15), and it still might be the site of daily devotions and sometimes Vespers and Compline prayers. The community has prayed the Liturgy of the Hours every day since their arrival to the Pacific Northwest in 1882.

Six miles west of Cottonwood and again visible from the higher ground of the Orr home is the small country village of Keuterville.

Here we find a half dozen homes and a restaurant complete with post office and a sociable tavern attached. Facing south from the opposite side of the single crossroad, and rising above the prairie and the few gathered rooftops, is the broad white steeple of Holy Cross Church. Holy Cross is the first of several small churches built across the prairie (1886). One has to squint to see any changes in this postcard village between my first visit in late 1973 and even now and an early history book photograph taken two generations earlier on Easter Sunday in 1912.[3]

The white church is modest outside and within. The three aisles and seating and kneelers can handle perhaps 250 people. The interior features carved woodwork, railings, a creaky floor, and a few brightly painted statues, and on the walls the familiar Stations of the Cross. At the front to the left of the recessed altar is the Pietà in bright blue and white. In red and white robes, Christ rises above the tabernacle, and Sts. Therese and Joseph take their positions to the right. The black robed and nearly lifesize St. Benedict stands with Bible and chalice in hand, slightly above eye level along the left wall overlooking the communion rail.

In front and at the center behind the altar is a traditional carved backdrop housing the tabernacle. The lighted red tabernacle candle is suspended from above, reassuring that the consecrated Host — and the Lord of all history and of each soul in history — is truly present within. The incarnation does not segregate reality into the spiritual and the material as does the human mind. In the incarnation He became a servant... "enlarging our humanity without diminishing His divinity."[4] So, too, the Real Presence. Living, not passive, "the same yesterday, and, yes, today and forever" (Heb. 13:8).[5]

In the consecrated Eucharist His courtesy toward his flock, if we can call it this, sets aside forever the total hiddenness of a God we cannot see. And in the Eucharist, more completely than in the

Holy Cross Church, Keuterville, Idaho. "At the front to the left of the recessed altar is the Pietà."

Scripture, the prairie families find the ever-new center of the entire gathered Church.[6] The Church is the gathering of all those who *do not* say, "This is a hard saying…who can listen to it?" and then walk away (John 6:60).[7] The Church is the gathering at both the table and the foot of the cross and then at his startling resurrection and personal presence toward us.

What of religious devotion to Christ, and particularly this most special devotion? What of the Eucharist that He gives to us, obliterating any distancing in the passage of time? It is He we find truly present, and not merely our thoughts of Him. Some modern psychology dismisses this accessibility as yet another example of ritualized behavior by the simple and harmless in an uncertain world. Such shaping by the mind comes up short.

It is the Source of existence that revealed itself to Moses ("I am who am"), and now Christ is His hand touching us ("I *am* the way and the truth and the life"). Here is the depth of Calvary once and for all, yet also renewed and distinctly present to each of us at our different time and place. Even many within the Church in the West step back, centering themselves more on the diluted gospel of social work alone, or some other lesser meaning than His Real Presence. Much better to choose *any* ideology we might conjure up than to genuflect before the self-revealing wellspring of life eternal. Much easier to conjure up more external and manageable truths and to dismiss as simply one idea among many the majestic fabric of His Presence.

For this prairie community and the Church as a whole, Christ is the center of each heart and of all history. To discount His singular sacrifice, re-presented at the Mass, as simply one of a succession of communal meals would be to trivialize the unifying abyss of his Cross. With God there is no time or space. The passion and resurrection are simultaneous in this sense, and mysteriously contained within each other. Baptism, too, is both death and resurrection. To miss this kind of depth-within-depth would be to trivialize our own radically free and, yes, crucified response, which draws us together, each toward the other, as his Mystical Body. "Do you not know that you are the temple of God and that the Spirit of God dwells in you?... [For]... this temple you are" (1 Cor. 3:16–17). The repose of complete self-acceptance depends not on self-transcendence, but first upon being truly loved by Another, and knowing it. This, rather than any achievement or self-definitions of our making.

We might notice an almost explosive manhood and fatherhood in the upper room on the eve of the passion, in that first instant of consecration. Christ declines to be maneuvered by human stupidity and the indifferent flow of events. This is not the saccharine Christ of cheap art or the hollowed "historical" Christ of the Jesus Seminar. Eternal and closer to us is He than even our imagination or deepest thoughts about Him. At the Mass he calls each of us to discover the givenness of our togetherness, as an image of His own self-giving. Subtracting time from the picture, as we are free to do when we accept Christ's divinity, we see that His passion, death, and resurrection are inseparably the same event. So too, in the Eucharist "now." "I am the food of grown men.... You will not change me into yourself, as you change food into your flesh, but you will be changed into me."[8]

The human mind in our own time is slow to notice or recall such "religious" things. The lens we have ground for ourselves is more nearsighted, often open only to the light that comes through physical data and the senses. And even this is carefully filtered. We are factual toward all things except the anomaly of the resurrection.[9] We enjoy the seeming safety of our more measurable and instrumental approach to the world and to each other. We paint by the numbers and miss the splendor and the calling. We might be able to deal with the *idea* of resurrection — sanded down as simply another word for springtime — but we will not allow ourselves to be astonished by the actual resurrection in person. Might this Real Presence of Christ toward us be the most "radical" and refreshingly untamable event in all of human history, past or future? More than an idea: a fact? And a fact not teased from Scripture, but Wisdom surely reflected there.

Inseparable from God's self-revelation to man is the included revelation of man to himself. Each of us is the embodiment of a soul called to communion with Him who is the Soul of our souls — and therefore with each other. It is almost as if He confers our existence as persons upon each of us, through each other.

Compared to this taproot of personal and fully human independence and *communion,* might it be the managed secular fundamentalism of our time that is the more stifling "organized religion"? We settle too easily for a hollow restlessness today and the inordinate need for self-definition through individual and measured achievement. The radical substitution of our estranged objectivity in place of the Spouse fully in our midst finds a recent voice in such men of bare *ideas* as René Descartes and Immanuel Kant. A sympathetic harmony between the inner self and the full world of being is no longer allowed.[10] In our self-isolation we paint a distanced God of Deism in our own image (God the watchmaker), and in this pride we name our construct the Enlightenment project.

Shaping the mind of the "conservative" Catholic is the total self-giving of Christ as He is re-*presented* on the altar by the Spirit He has given. Eternity enters time as more than an idea, and in the same moment leavens us from within. The Eucharist is both symbol *and* that which is symbolized. In addition to everything else that theologians might say, this is the point where the symbol-building mind beholds directly the totally gratuitous and living source of all that is. Our personal encounter with unconditional friendship which can be touched. Friendship bounding our common experience in the world, and not barricaded away by it. Within His sacramental presence Christ assembles and informs us and his full Communion of Saints, past and present. This communion, too, both deepens and transcends time as we experience it. This is the burning love of the sacred heart of Jesus embedded in the now unbloody sacrifice of the Mass, a center that is equally accessible from across all points of geography and human history.

The obstacle to seeing this Real Presence, and our distancing from God (both), come from ourselves. In the Mass it is this mysterious reflex from within ourselves that is overcome. The doctrinal precision of the Real Presence — carefully worded at the time of the Reformation — might be taken less as a definition imposed than as a poem unveiled. It is the poem of His heart and is His heart. The Real Presence is a covenant; it is a divine love song personally present — even to us here and now. Through Christ is given to the Father all honor and glory, and we are invited. He is the first and the last line of the poem of creation, the alpha and the omega that rhymes with every line and point in between. With Christ in the Eucharist we have both the poem *and* the Poet. It is all an unconditional gift, all of it. "A morsel of bread is more real than the universe, more full of existence, more full of the Word — a song overflowing the sea, a mist confusing the sundial — God in exile."[11] And not only is the Lord truly present, but all of Him is there. Nothing is left behind as if held back in reserve. This is the symbolic meaning of the crucifix.

Christ's "passion" is not confined to the misery of His final hours leading up to a final and freely accepted crucifixion. His passion is his lifelong self-donation in our world as part of His eternal self-donation to the Father. His heart is nuptial, not simply conceptual. His heart is mirrored in every marriage of one spouse to another. Each marriage reflects the eternal and inner life of the Trinitarian God. Even in this life, we already live within Him. We are, more than we know, strangers in a strange land, but not strangers to each other. To blink here in a nod toward self-sufficiency — we call it pride — is both a moral defect and a profound violation against the real. The real is our groundedness in a creating God, in whom we are equal in truth, without exception.

Kristi's single-hearted devotion to her "dear Lord" in the sacrament of the Eucharist would have much to do with the light in her eyes under the changing circumstances in coming years.

In addition to the Cottonwood church and tabernacle, on the Camas Prairie there is also a hospital for a different kind of healing. Kristi's father, Dr. Richard Orr, was a surgeon and the only doctor for many of the surrounding communities. For him the medical vocation and profession had to do primarily with patients and their doctors, not merely large organizations and pharmaceuticals. Each and every time before picking up his scalpel for surgery, he prayed that the Lord would guide his hand. Apart from the abbey itself, Dr. Orr was one of the foundation stones for the community.

On at least one occasion he averted a medically recommended amputation. For over twenty uninterrupted hours he labored alone over a single patient, a father with several dependent children, to successfully piece together a hand severely mangled in a logging accident. Part of the Orr family story also tells how as a young navy doctor on a destroyer in the heavy seas of the Atlantic, he strapped himself and his patient together to a rolling mess room table to successfully complete an emergency appendectomy.

Dr. Orr set a high standard of watchfulness, protection, and guidance for his family as well as his patients. When the girls were still young, the family sometimes visited the single theater in the larger farming center of Grangeville fifteen miles south of Cottonwood. On one such occasion, even in the dark he caught the eye of one of his girls as the hand of a nearby viewer drifted in the direction of her knee. Kristi described the explosion as Daddy jumped the seats to collar the man who was caught completely off guard. With arms locked the doctor dragged the figure up the aisle and threw him out the double doors into the street and the full light of day.

This decisiveness revealed character and clarity in a world of gray. It reminds me of a similar eruption of holy rage from my own father. While very different from each other, in some ways the two men were much the same. For me, too, came a defining moment when I knew from my own father how the world really works. It was a lazy Saturday. The phone rang. My high-school-age older brother was calling to report that his employer was refusing to give him his final paycheck. Tom had worked conscientiously all summer at a downtown service station.

I was only a few steps away when Dad shot a phone call back to the employer to deliver an unambiguous message. And then I was sucked with him into the family car — "Get in the car, Pete. We're going downtown. . . . " Arriving at the station, the largest one in town, we found that the office and garage doors still were open, but the complex was strangely silent and totally deserted. On top of the cash register was an envelope, and inside the envelope was the full payment in cash.

As with Kristi in the theater, in the air for me that day was a palpable sense of truth. The French author Bernanos gets at this: "In order to become a holy man, don't you think, you must first of all be a man?"[12]

In Cottonwood, the doctor's medical practice was shared with his father, Wesley, until his death in 1969. The apparent cause of death was the strain of successfully giving mouth-to-mouth resuscitation the night before to a choking victim in a restaurant. The doctor (Wesley) was eighty-nine and still fully in the harness. At the time Kristi was halfway through college and visiting in Japan as part of a language program at the Language Institute of Odawara near Tokyo. Years later she would tell me more than once how saddened she was to not be home with the family for Granddaddy's funeral.

Kristi's father, like his father before him, intended to never retire. But he was able to continue the practice only to the age of sixty-two (until 1977) when he was placed on permanent disability. He suffered a nearly fatal aneurysm near the base of the neck. A day or two before, a young homeward-bound child had been rushed to his hospital. The boy, barely ten, had been severely mauled by a domesticated dog, half shepherd and half wolf. Given the massive extent of the neck injuries, there was very little Dr. Orr could do. When he was hospitalized for the aneurysm Kristi flew from Seattle to be with Daddy. From the timing, I have always felt that this permanent disruption of his vocation was triggered by his emotional and then physical reaction to this brutal medical case.

For me, Kristi's absence meant four days alone at home in Seattle. This is one of the very few times that we were apart. I took a few days off from work to care for our daughter, Laura, then barely two years old. Late one evening Laura and I skipped regular bedtime. It seemed a better time for a ride on the swing. The sun was long down and the sky offered an unusual display of stars, the same canopy I will always remember from long nights in the navy in the South Pacific. It is probably part of my nature to think about loneliness under such a vast sky. But there is another vision that I wanted for our little girl: "Laura, those stars look far away; don't they look lonely? But look again; each one of those stars is a little friend for you." Up and down she swung, into the starry night. This was a magical and treasured moment, and despite her very young age, Laura remembers it too.

With his forced retirement the table conversations at Dr. Orr's home were no longer influenced by an active involvement in the medical profession. He was a robust and intensely interested man in so many ways, but the doctor's underlying health became increasingly uncertain. Kristi sometimes would talk to me about his weak heart and how this had intruded during the summer so many years

before when she was only ten (1959). An infrequent family vacation had taken them to Priest Lake in the Rocky Mountain foothills
north of Spokane in northeastern Washington. Here, at the age of
forty-four, Kristi's father suffered his second heart attack. His first
had been ten years earlier. Most of the family returned home, but
the doctor remained for two months in a Spokane hospital, and this
divided the family throughout the summer.

Years later after his forced retirement the doctor remained active
in new ways, partly as an intent bird watcher. And, as an amateur
painter, he noticed the nearly infinite variety of hues on the prairie
under each season and each time of day. In 1980, he noticed and recounted to us how the bluebirds farther south strangely disappeared
from their sanctuary one or two days before the famous eruption of
Mount St. Helens a distant three hundred miles due west.

Kristi's father was a remarkably sensitive, professional, and toughly
principled man, nearly venerated by his family. He tended very much
toward the serious side, but at the same time he was a man of uncommon tenderness and affection. Kristi's mother, Jeanne (Quiring),
was a more buoyant complement to her spouse. During most of the
first twenty years following his retirement, she provided most of the
family income. She was from a prominent Kansas family and likely
would have left her mark on the theater. Her talent and flair con-
tributed to her occasional theatrics at the kitchen table during the
long family conversations. Her own mother, Laura, had died without
any loss of patience after two painful years of extensive bone cancer.
Our daughter is named after Kristi's grandmother.

The banter between the doctor and Jeanne from one end of the
kitchen table to the other was fuel to keep the table talk going for
hours at a time. Kristi and I always sat side by side, the doctor on
my left and Jeanne on Kristi's right. Jeanne could be counted on to
tease the doctor about his serious streak. Of his worrying, he would
tease back, "Someone has to do it, and it's a cinch you'll never get

to it." I picked up this line for my own use at our home in Seattle and sometimes would extend the comment with the mock dismay of a perfectly obtuse husband, "Besides, if I don't do it, it might not get done at all...."

On the Camas Prairie, the kitchen table discussions sometimes extended from one meal to the next. Topics ranged widely as the family continually renewed and deepened itself in this way. Almost any topic was fair game if one was well prepared, but there was always a common flavor in the background. This little something, or rather this taste that was never lost, was a nearly extinct sense of wonder and fidelity. This is difficult to define, but it was this — the sense that there can be certainty of knowledge without pride of knowledge. This came to a head from time to time, for example, with the question of physical evolution. We noted that a believer has the freedom to either believe that the physical side of the human person evolved naturally, or not. The atheist surrenders a similar freedom to admit even the possibility of the truly spiritual informing the physical. The broader view notices a discontinuity of divine freedom at the beginning as well as for each human soul in history; it is less linear than is evolutionary thought, which presumes to stand by itself only on our feet of clay — more right-brained than it is right-wing fundamentalism. Beyond the level of physical facts, we have wonder and perhaps reverence — and a bent knee toward an underlying passion to communicate being (*wonder* is the first gift of the Holy Spirit: "fear of the Lord").

More than once the doctor recalled the spiritual conversion of the famous physician Alexis Carrel, whose eyes were opened by an event he witnessed at Lourdes in southwestern France, the site of Marian apparitions that took place in 1858. Lourdes, of course, is the most visited place of pilgrimage in the world, the site of numerous documented and undocumented cures from all manner of illness.

As a fashionable religious skeptic, Carrel had accompanied from Paris his invalid and bedridden patient who was judged by other physicians as too deteriorated even to travel. At Lourdes Carrel found himself documenting her very abrupt and permanent cure.[13] Carrel jeopardized his medical career by publishing his findings, and later he wrote another short book entitled simply *Prayer*. In this tiny volume this modern physician wrote, "The power of prayer is the greatest power in the world."

In addition to Kristi and Kerry, there were five other brothers and sisters. The oldest son in the Orr family was Dick. He was senior to Kristi and Kerry by three years. Dick had been stationed with the Air Force in Thailand in the late 1960s while I was with the navy in the Tonkin Gulf. Cherie, three years older than Dick, is supremely gifted with a voice judged by her university trainers to be worthy of the Metropolitan Opera. She was to sing at our wedding and again many years later at Kristi's funeral.

Then, in order, were the younger brothers and sister, Pat, Mike, and Lori. At age ten, Lori's very first comment to me was a direct, "Are you taking good care of my sister?" And I said, "yes." Especially during his long-hair phase, the youngest son, Mike, was fond of cautiously quoting Scripture to his father, from St. Paul, "Fathers, do not nag your children, lest they lose heart" (Eph. 6:4). In later years Pat would spend part of his career managing the Country Haus restaurant in Cottonwood, a favorite gathering place for the community and for our family celebrations.

It was in April of 1974, on the side yard overlooking the prairie, that I asked Kristi's father for Kristi's hand. He welcomed me as "a member of the family." I was to have Kristi as my wife and to be part of this family that in less than one year had come to mean so much to me.

During all of our ten-month courtship, Kristi and I often read together. I remember reciting Robert Frost's "The Road Not Taken," a

poem I had treasured and memorized in high school. And I had always liked Edgar Allen Poe's sonorous "Annabel Lee": "And neither
the angels in Heaven above, nor the demons down under the sea,
can ever dissever my soul from the soul of the beautiful Annabel
Lee." (Little did I realize how prophetic this line was to be for me
in future years.)

On Sunday afternoons during our courtship Kristi often made
a small cake that we could share, and then we would stroll in the
neighborhood near her apartment, at the edge of a small town north
of Seattle. On one such Sunday afternoon, I read an undistinguished
but original poem. The lines had been inspired a month or two
before we met by one of those unusual events of nature. I had been
visiting my identical twin brother, John, and his wife, Kath, in the
rose garden section of Portland, Oregon.

Under the clear autumn blue sky I strolled the neighborhood, and
one very large oak tree caught my eye. Still clinging to the branches
were the leaves of purest scarlet. A few steps forward, and the leaves
fell all at once, *upward*. Not leaves, but birds. And as they flocked
out of sight into the blue, the tree suddenly stood completely bare,
reaching up against the sky, every perch abandoned. Not a single
leaf remained. Kristi seemed to admire my amateur poem.

Resurrection

Do we ever open the eyes of our soul to notice,
The painted leaves of autumn are also the green?
Like us, they freely mingle their joys and sorrows,
The autumn of veiled dreams with the springtime . . .
of eternal giving.

How, like us, they let go so easily . . .
And how only then can they soar?
How, in this, each leaf is all leaves,

And all the spiraling seasons are one . . .
And the vagrant colors of autumn are eternal.

And do we notice (with Blake)
That the universe lies hidden
In each grain of sand . . . and "eternity in an hour"?
And do we see the silent center of it all:
The silent leaf of autumn . . . Suspended?

And do we then notice with a shiver,
That time is but a façade, the burden of small hearts . . . ?
The world is a forest and we dance among the trees,
In the light and in the shadow,
In laughter and in tears . . . in autumn, together.

And then, before us, with leaves of scarlet,
With leaves now falling *upward* . . .
Yes, birds taking flight —
The whole and the part are all a single dream,
Given from the heart of God.

In her own readings Kristi was much more familiar than I with Aleksandr Solzhenitsyn. Friends noted that this was an unusual reading for a young lady. "Don't let her get away," they said. We talked about *The Gulag Archipelago*. Kristi also valued highly *The Abolition of Man* by C. S. Lewis, and Blaise Pascal's *Pensées*. She had been deeply touched and would repeat to me over the years Pascal's familiar insight, "the heart has its reasons, which the reason cannot understand."[14]

One short book Kristi and I read together was Romano Guardini's *End of the Modern World*. Guardini surveys the flight in recent centuries from heartfelt religious insight. Then he looks into the Western flirtations with substitutes: nature, personality, and culture, and finally the resulting mass society and our amoral use of economics and technology. Looking a few years ahead toward our slightly more modern times he writes:

> Loneliness in faith will be terrible. Love will disappear from the face of the public world (Matthew xxiii, 12), but the more precious will that love be which flows from one lonely person to another, involving a courage of the heart born from the immediacy of the love of God as it was made known in Christ.[15]

It is good for man — male and female — to be a family, masculine and feminine and husband and wife, and to be *not* alone.

Holy Cross Church served as the canopy for our exchange of marriage vows on October 12, 1974. Hundreds came from the surrounding communities and other more widely scattered homes. But who was this "Peter" that Kristi had brought home for Christmas in 1973 and then was to marry less than one year later?

Downstream to the Columbia

Kristi's Cottonwood on the Camas Prairie differed from the wartime boomtown of Richland, where I was raised. In the early 1940s Richland fully displaced such a farming community with a planned town twenty or thirty times its original size. And my actual birthplace of Hanford, north of Richland (and thirty or forty miles north of where the Snake River meets the Columbia), disappeared altogether. For decades it has been only a desolate spot on the map marking the outer walls of the only surviving structure, a typical pre–World War II schoolhouse. An aerial photograph *National Geographic Magazine* captures the desolate mood perfectly. Hanford was evacuated almost overnight and then disappeared behind the "barricade" surrounding the Hanford Nuclear Reservation.[16]

Outside the fence and downstream was the bedroom community of Richland, population twenty-five thousand. Here was a planned bedroom city without a past, attached to the secret and abrupt nuclear industry. Unlike Cottonwood with its idyllic Benedictine abbey on the hill, Richland's churches were simple shed-roof military constructions. The Catholic Church differed from the others in the fact that it lacked the standard steeple. It featured instead a small statue nested below the ridge line and dedicated to Christ the King, the name selected for this mission parish.

Along the Columbia River there was much to bring out the sense of adventure in a growing boy. The setting brought the richness of the seasons. My teen years were spent in our second home on the north edge of town, barely a quarter mile from the Columbia. At this point the river is a mile wide due to the McNary Dam completed in 1953 some fifty miles downstream. With the later completion of the entire system of dams on the Columbia, the last free-flowing stretch is confined to the thirty of so miles beginning at Richland and extending upstream past my birthplace of Hanford.

On Saturday mornings in the autumn, the thrill for me and my identical twin brother, John, was to be the first explorers to the willow-lined riverbank. In the early fog it was possible to reach the shoreline in time to startle the migrating ducks as they slept. As we arrived at the edge of the river, the entire darkened shoreline seemed to slide outward and finally take flight, heading for the safety of the barren islands half a mile distant and midway to the other side. In those days naturalists working from aerial photographs placed the annual number of ducks in the millions.

But in addition to this sense of nature's abundance, there was also the sense of emptiness under the vast desert sky and starry nights. It was possible in the earliest years for Dad to stop the car late at night at the edge of town and to listen to the serenade of the coyotes under the full moon. Of this smallness and our common human loneliness,

C. S. Lewis captures something fundamental. He writes that only people can look into the stars and, from this, feel diminished by our own infinite smallness. Animals simply see lights in the dark. We are teased and perhaps frightened by the immensity. The stars can seem to stare back at us, sightless and with chilling indifference. Lewis says that our sense of smallness and estrangement comes not from the stars, but from a spirituality within ourselves.[17]

I felt this smallness at a very early age and in at least two ways. One was the sense of being poised in time at the edge of a totally new town that had no past. Time was an edge, rather than a fabric as in Kristi's Cottonwood. Not more than half a mile away from our first house there stood a few concrete block-shaped irrigation weirs in the shade of what were to me enormous poplar trees. The small structures marked key points in the eroded pattern of irrigation furrows. At the age of four, with a bundle of wild asparagus in each hand, I wondered who had been here before, and "where did they go?" "Farms," my mother said, "these used to be farms, but they're gone now." As at Hanford, after some fifty years on the map, in March 1943 the residents of the original town site were given a few weeks to evacuate by the same Manhattan Project that had brought us and all of the new families from all over the country.[18]

In these earliest years, I also felt the immensity of space — the evening breeze blowing out of a dense purple sky to the west. This sky rose over the rounded and treeless "Badger Mountain" a few miles from our first home. Safe inside the house, I looked up from a large living room chair. I recall noticing once or twice that the coziness was separated by only a few inches of wood from the void and sometimes the eerie howling of the desert wind.

The simplicity of the evening sky and the vastness of the wind have their own special beauty, but the emptiness also speaks to us and can leave an impression even at an early age. Is the void empty or full? A vacuum or a grace? Does God exist outside of our minds,

and does He really touch us? However obscurely, the middle case —
the mere *idea* of God — even then seemed to me unstable. Ideas
alone are hollow. Deeper within each of us is a nearly incapacitating
emptiness and nostalgia for . . . God. Modern humanism, a reasoned
compromise of ideas rinsed clean of all belief, is more of a cocoon
spun only from ourselves, at best a cosmetic for a deeper and stark
insufficiency. It does not answer the deepest question about the stuff
around us and about the human heart: "Why anything . . . instead
of nothing?"

At this early age I could not formulate this question, but I think I
felt it.[19] As a human question, the dependence of things on *something
else* forced itself upon me a few years later. This jolt came unexpectedly at the age of not quite eleven. It was on a warm spring evening
in June (I remember it as ten minutes after six in early June) that I
heard an abrupt "pop" like a very loud and deep firecracker. From
an upstairs bedroom in a neighbor's house, John and our friend and
I ran in the direction of this excitement. But it was far too early for
the Fourth of July.

Instead, it was a suicide.

It happened only a few houses away, in an alley parking lot
surrounded by an empty field. The gun lay across his ankle and
extended right palm. "Both barrels," they said the next day in the
paper. For a moment I stood there alone, looking into what was left
in the driveway. Stretched out at my feet was a man in his early
twenties dressed in blue. Looking up was a face, but with only part
of a head, and this was still slamming up and down on the pave-
ment. The tear in the fabric of a cozy summer evening was absolute.
A solitary woman fifty or a hundred steps away dropped her running
garden hose as she rushed to the closest house to find the father of
the fallen man. In another direction a family in full view continued
a picnic at their backyard table, unaware that the universe had been

shattered, and disbelieving as I pointed back to where I had stood only seconds before.

John and our friend were soon beside me in the driveway again. Uncomprehending, I heard one of us remark, "Quiet, he might hear what we say." Perhaps it was even my own voice that I heard. I wondered with a calm urgency, Where is his soul? Is there really a soul? Years later I was intrigued to learn that the French philosopher and mathematician René Descartes had also paused at this riddle, this fit between the physical and the spiritual. (He solved this urgency in a curious way by locating the soul in the pineal gland.) And he derailed the following generations of academics into asking these questions each within his own mind, rather than first within communion with one another. Beneath the cerebral solitude is there not a deeper mutuality of one to another, a fundamental communion that cannot, must not, be swept aside, and that is truly said to be in the image of God?

Even then I noticed the coincidence of the blood and naturally red hair. Then looking up into the sky, I recorded that the streaked cumulus clouds in the blue evening sky had also turned red from west to east. For several minutes the entire universe, it seemed, was red on blue. Peel away the surface ... is creation really only a hollowness like what was before me? Are the stars scattered only randomly like the little red mounds now under my feet and scattered over much of the driveway? A face covering and expressing only part of a hollowed head. Is eternity no more than an echo rattling around in our craniums and that disappears once the music stops, if not before?

At home I did not speak much of this abyss that had thrust itself in my path. Nor did I understand. I did ask my mother how does one choose — *nothing?* "Why would anyone choose *nothing*," I asked? The conversation was repeated but short, and I acted satisfied, but no answer seemed to touch the question. I was told how duress can sometimes seem too much and drive some to end it all. But in front of me, far enough out, was a kind of inexplicable drop-off in my mind. Nothing?

Are there only atoms after all? Of the disconnect between thought and matter someone more sophisticated might ask if there really is any qualitative difference between thought and the activity of neurons, and the mathematics of quantum mechanics.[20] Complexity, but nothing more? Is all chance; is the entire universe hollow too?

Years after the suicide I would be struck to find how Voltaire, at the site of the Lisbon earthquake in 1755 where fifty thousand perished, rethought the problem of evil and for him an ever-more-distant God. Closer to our own time, in Algeria and under a beautifully clear blue sky, the sixteen-year-old Albert Camus witnessed the randomness of a small boy being crushed by a bus. The atheist Camus pointed to the crowd of onlookers and then to the sky: "You see, heaven is silent."[21] Even the Christian writer C. S. Lewis gravitated into atheism at first. He was broken by the fact that despite his childhood prayers his mother still died of cancer when he was only nine, and later he was hardened further by his experiences in the trenches of the First World War.

For all of us, the religious question ultimately comes not through power structures from the past, but immediately from our center deep within. Deeper than even the question or the questioning. We are either grounded, or we are not.

Two years later I would be reminded of this event by particular black- and-white photographs in *Life Magazine* at the periodical display in my public junior high school. These were close-up street scenes of the carnage from the uprising in Budapest in 1956. I clearly recall pointing to one and turning to a seventh grade classmate. "This is something I have seen in color," I announced. The immensity of the twentieth century was at the doorsteps of all of us through the daily media. And part of this immensity accounted for the existence of my hometown and for the "barricade" a few miles to the north.

And all of this is prelude to the brutality and victimization routinely available today to the young generation as we enter the convoluted twenty-first century. One need think only of the persecutions and mutilations in the Sudan and many other parts of Africa, child slavery or prostitution abroad, or even the lucrative California pornography industry, bankrolled in part through any number of mutual funds and stock market packages. It is said that without grace, the entire world is a ghetto.

Still, the future was buoyant for all of us in those days, and the universe was a wonder. But here now was a dull note, the front edge of weighty questions usually reserved to adults who are also unprepared. At an early age I had found a small dark shelf — the possibility of *nothing* — at the back of my soul. It was not so much that I was afraid; it was more a very stunned perplexity, and the sense that there is something huge out there that experience and reason alone cannot bridge. I clearly remember assuming that in coming years I might begin to understand in some way.

I dwell on this experience here because of a quite different and wonderful and defining childhood experience that Kristi had at about the same age. Several years into our marriage, Kristi confided to me that in her early teens — and maybe she also was eleven or ten — there was a sublime moment when she suddenly felt cradled by the immense wonder that she did "exist as *a person.*"

We had been talking about the pristine "intuition of being" mentioned by some philosophers. Behind all of our ideas is the fact of mutual existence, that our personal existence is a gift, nothing less. This is more than the groping of philosophers. Kristi had this secret intuition at an early age, and she treasured it fondly. I asked if it had ever happened again. And she said to me — I think I remember this correctly — that it had never left her. Part of our story together, Kristi's and mine, was this difference between us. Part of me was drawn or driven to work out questions of faith while Kristi seemed to jump over the difficulties with a purer and more genuine and gifted faith that "never had any need for that."

Instead, gentleness.

But Kristi said, too, that she always liked listening "to the kinds of things that Daddy has to say" and that sustained and refreshed us together over the years. And again, these conversations at the Camas Prairie kitchen table served as a kind of ongoing seminar on these enduring questions. Early after our marriage, over the breakfast bowls, from the head of the table, the doctor posed this mind-stretching thought: "What is the nature of evil, that the Second Person of the Trinity would have to undergo the passion?"

One inadequate response to the originality of this question is Deism. A single God, yes, but one *without* a Trinitarian inner life of openness to His creation and to each of us in our deepest need. Over the years I have only wondered more at the doctor's question. Perhaps wonder is the complete response. What is it about each person and our inner life that our merely(?) human transgressions and our potential have this kind of weight? What is it about Christ that He is closer to us than we are to ourselves? We struggle with these things, as He suffers *for* us. It is not the nature of our transgression that victimizes even God in our history, but rather His own voluntary hold-nothing-back love, which He *is*.

In my early years my serious readings began with the first social encyclical letter, Pope Leo XIII's *Rerum Novarum* (*New Things: On the Condition of the Working Class*, 1891). Leo's message on the sacred worth of each person within current history warned against both the atheistic state and the mechanistic market, and even anticipated the Communist Revolution of 1917. Following this first letter a dozen such formal encyclicals have looked into the energies and events of our recent century.

Dry reading, yes, but I think much of the Church's verbiage is independently captured for us in a single poem. Inspired by Millet's famous painting *The Man with the Hoe,* an obscure Oregon-born school principal named Edwin Markham penned this poem by the same title in 1899. Peering into the darkened eyes of Millet's brutalized dirt farmer, he wrote:

> O masters, lords and rulers in all lands.
> ... How will it be with kingdoms and with kings —
> With those who shaped him to the thing he is —
> When this dumb Terror shall rise to judge the world,
> After the silence of the centuries?

The Church's social teaching reduces to the irreducible dignity of each human person, and to a kind of peace that is more than political. This peace is capable of touching all the nooks and crannies of our imperfect world and of our world within.

So I studied the encyclical *Rerum Novarum* with absorbing interest during my sixteenth summer.[22] To think that enduring *personal* values actually relate to concrete and *global* events! Truth is not simply subjective opinion to be marginalized and crushed by the forces of history.[23] Beyond igniting and feeding my fascination, this opening also helped me to deal with additional photographs I happened across in my junior year of high school (1960–61). During our lunch period, my friend Eric and I occasionally sneaked back into the library of our public high school. We flipped through the pages of a large tabletop photographic history of World War II. Included were shots of Auschwitz and the many other concentration camps as they were found on their day of liberation. Six million Jews and possibly a million or two others, including Christians. Without speaking we wondered, "How can this be?" (Eric was to remain a lifelong friend. When we regained close contact after many years,

he was working in cancer research in Seattle. Kristi always regarded
him as the "perfect gentleman.")

Jumping past my undergraduate years at the University of Washington, on a clear autumn night in 1968 I had my first inkling that
Kristi might come into my life. This was five years before our paths
actually crossed. I had graduated from the University of Washington and after a summer job in Seattle had completed five months
of Officer Candidate School in Newport, Rhode Island. I was in the
western Pacific as a junior officer on an aircraft carrier (the USS
Hornet). After a scheduled month on tour in the Tonkin Gulf the
ship was again silent, twisting slowly at anchor in the lights of Hong
Kong harbor.

It was my turn to pace the midwatch on the blue-carpeted
quarterdeck. To help pass the time I rolled things over in my mind,
and sometimes I would recite the prayer of St. Francis, "... Where
there is doubt, let me sow faith.... For it is in dying that we are
born to eternal life." Such a leap. The ship rotated ever so slowly,
and gliding before me were the night colors of this amazing city.
Still thirty years would pass before the end of the British colonial
period. Illuminated high-rises stepped up the base of the romantic
and darkened Victoria Peak. A red neon advertisement for "Sanyo"
from Japan, several stories high, caught my eye. Lighted reflections
scattered across an almost glasslike harbor under a starlit sky. I felt so
diminished as I looked back on my abrupt transition to the military
from family and student life, half a world away.

Then, there it was. For the smallest part of a second, flashing
before my attention and slightly above my angle of vision was a
map of the state of Idaho.

The image was barely detailed enough to intrigue me with a spot
marked in the west central part of the state. Where had this come
from, this flash? I continued my pacing, but now in my solitude
I was buoyed by the distinct notion that it might be interesting,

socially, to take a trip to find that spot on the map of Idaho. I would be released from the navy in two years. I might take another long drive, I thought, as I had done to Colorado and through the Southwest during my last month before entering the navy. A few months later, on another street corner, this time in Singapore, I bought a piece of jewelry for my future wife — wherever she might be. Not knowing the important details, I selected a universal color scheme for this cosmetic ring, a blue star sapphire in a gold setting rather than silver. Green or blue eyes, or possibly brown. At sea one could still dream.

It was during this port call in Hong Kong that I witnessed one of those unforgettable moments that engraves the deeper questions into one's mind and memory. It was a sunny Sunday morning. I strolled into the city down a gently winding road from the top of Victoria Peak. The city and its harbor, speckled with ships from all over the world, were arrayed before me. Higher up, in the quiet morning air I had heard a single hammering cadence from a shipyard far away, lifting up from somewhere in the harbor like a distant church bell.

Bordering the path on my left a waist-high rock wall snaked its way toward the city. Behind it there began a series of cemeteries, each following the other. All were woven together by a canopy of spreading branches from what I remember as oak trees. Strung like beads along this descending path I found a succession of world religions: Muslim, Confucian, Hindu, Buddhist, Catholic and Anglican, and Zoroastrian and Jain at the lower edge where the path trailed off into the dense market alleys and roadways of the city.

After the first half mile, and just before the markets, the path ended near a confluence of three other narrow streets. At the center was a small wide area in the sidewalk and what appeared to be a solitary human figure. Resting on a square pallet with a tiny wheel at each corner, in this marketplace corner of world history, was a tormented deformity with a face. Twisted into a shiny bronze pretzel was the figure of a man wearing only a blue cloth. His chin rested on the pallet only a few inches above the ground, and his back and legs arched up behind his head. Both feet came down from different directions on either side of his ears.

Next to the pallet was a beggar's cup. At a short but safe distance, I halted motionless. I was sure I could actually *hear* ringing in my ears from the tormented expression of his face. The pealing of bells broke the spell. Only a few steps up the hill to the right were two small Western churches. At this moment the congregations in their bright-colored clothes began filing out into the midmorning sunlight. I watched. Amazed, I followed with my own eyes the small groups and individuals as they filed down the sidewalks, passing on either side of the human soul who cried out in silence.

So this is who we are, I thought. It was not that so many passed him by, or that not even one stopped, but that so many found ways to look casually and even artfully elsewhere. Perhaps they had left many donations on many previous weeks until this had become too routine. . . . I was new and left my donation, knowing it was nothing; I did not really give. (I do remember leaving paper, but the currency exchange rate in those days was seven to one.) I recall that I barely glanced into his eyes.

And I recall distinctly feeling at the time the certainty that simply ending it all probably had not even entered the mind of this human figure. It seemed too Western an idea. It was only his body that was twisted. And I see now how this innocent victim on that sun-filled Sunday morning was, in person, a sermon to the rest of us.

Is it through the eyes of this man with a tin cup that we will judge ourselves when Christ returns from the right hand of the Father?

Months later and one day before our departure from the Tonkin Gulf (April 15, 1969) for the West Coast of the United States, a navy reconnaissance plane was shot down over international waters far to the north near the coast of North Korea. Ours was one of four carriers and over two dozen other widely assigned ships that were assembled on the run into Task Force 71. This formation, the largest navy task force assembled since the Korean War, was dispatched to the Tsunami Strait separating the mainland from Japan. In a hasty wardroom meeting the intelligence officer briefed the officers about the aircraft caves of North Korea — we faced a fifty-percent chance, he reported, of being attacked within twenty-four hours by jets armed with tactical nuclear weapons.

For nearly a week our ship and the entire task force were in black-out conditions. Beneath the cloud cover we were lost to the world. The crew was poised around the clock in a condition of readiness one level short of general quarters. But the days passed. As the crisis abated a Japanese plane with the news media broke through the cloud cover and discovered us. It was probably with the help of the U.S. media that a photograph of the *Hornet* was misidentified and displayed on the front page of dozens of newspapers as the nearby nuclear carrier *Enterprise*.[24]

Because of this incident, my ship berthed for only one night in Yokosuka, Japan, before steaming east on schedule to Long Beach, California. And it was on that balmy spring evening in Japan, and unknown to me at the time, that identical twins Kristi and Kerry actually visited the *Hornet*. They were completing their six-month program teaching English to small children and businessmen in the nearby Language Institute in Odawara. Their visit was at the invitation of an onboard enlisted man from their hometown. His family operated the single gas station at the center of Cottonwood. Kristi and Kerry must have turned a few heads as they toured parts of the ship. This crossing of our paths would serve as a most unlikely conversation piece for Kristi and me on our first lunch date still more than four years into the future.

We finally met in October of 1973. This time Kristi was spending a few weeks in Seattle, where I was now living. Such a glow. A modest five feet four inches tall, she wore her blue plaid skirt and a petite, dark blue wool sweater. It was clear to everyone that here was a princess with a "dynamite smile." Kristi's long and full dark hair matched her dark eyes as they gave off their special inner light.

My God, what an angel, but she is probably attached, I thought. But there was magic in the wind and within the month, by mid-December, we were seeing each other almost every evening. (In my delight I sketched an idyllic brick foot bridge near the shores of Lake Washington and gave this to Kristi for her apartment wall. This drawing, our special path through the forest, was later to remain in our living or dining room throughout our marriage, and appears on the opening pages of this book.) After the first few weeks Kristi accepted my self-invitation to drive with her over the Cascade Mountains to her home for Christmas break. I suggested analytically that if I came along I would be there to chain the tires if need be.

With the mountain pass safely behind us, and driving through eastern Washington, we detoured for a short break a few yards off the road. This spot marked the barren northern edge of the Hanford Nuclear Reservation — a desert expanse of over five hundred square miles. Fifteen miles farther east (and still off limits) was the abandoned town site of Hanford, where I had been born twenty-nine years earlier. And here the Columbia River divided the flat sagebrush setting on the north bank from an immense basalt escarpment one mile to the south on the far side. This setting is as it has been for twelve thousand years. In prehistory the ice-locked Lake Missoula broke through at a point farther upstream in what is now Montana, dramatically marking the end of the most recent Ice Age.[25] The wall of water is known to have been eight hundred feet deep here as it flooded its way downstream the final two hundred miles to the Pacific.

At our special little place we stood beside the remaining bottom tiers of a solitary log cabin. The remains of light snow covered shaded parts of the ground, and the blue sky was as clear as Kristi's soul. "Being with you makes the sky a little bluer, and the snow a little whiter."[26] The magic of this gesture, a few simple words, and then a smile. The vision before me was to be tested but unchanged in the years ahead. The same curled lower lip and slight tilt of the head has graced all of Kristi's photographs. During that first visit to Kristi's home I was already able to tell one twin from the other, even in the earliest baby picture that "no one ever gets right." There is a mystery here, how even identical twins can be so alike, and yet so completely individual.

At this time and during our courtship I still was a graduate student living in a subdivided three-storied house not quite a mile north of the campus. In grander times this house had been home to the founder of Trans World Airlines. On a postcard-type Sunday afternoon in the spring of 1974, I watched Kristi still a block away as she approached up the partly shaded sidewalk. My dream was dressed in a white pantsuit with a lighthearted overlay pattern of blue circles. With full dark hair flowing, she passed toward me through patches of light and shade on the tree-lined street. By this time our songs were "Love Is a Many Splendored Thing" and "Mona Lisa," both as performed by Nat King Cole. On that sunny day we canoed the University of Washington Arboretum and the shores of Lake Washington.

And on that day, *the decision* made itself. On the following day we met at noon for lunch and I surprised Kristi with a white bouquet. "Look into the flowers," I hinted. After many attempts, on one flower petal I had delicately penned the simple petition "Marry me!" There was a pause for searching.

"Oh yes!"

Kristi jumped, and then slipped into that angelic smile. I remember on Kristi a beautiful pink dress, and in my soul the flight of eagles.

A Threesome

For where two or three are gathered together . . . there am I in the midst of them.   —Matthew 18:20

An astounding glimpse into our future path together, Kristi's and mine, was given on the day before our wedding on October 12, 1974. It happened in the prairie church of Holy Cross in Keuterville. In the late afternoon we stood together near the church railing rehearsing the wedding ceremony. My bride-to-be wore a knit wine-colored dress suit with white trim. The carved wood backdrop to the altar rose up behind a very short Fr. Rath. He recited the parts of the ceremony we would repeat together the following day.

"In sickness and in health, in good times and in bad. . . . " At these words I paused. A picture flashed in front and slightly above me. I saw a hospital bed. The angle of view placed me standing at the head and at what would be a patient's right side. I was looking diagonally to the opposite foot of the bed. I saw specialized bedside equipment. The bed was empty with the top edge of the sheet folded back in waiting. This instantaneous image was not photographic, but it was distinct and I could easily paint it even today.

Hospital beds happen to other people, I protested. And then within myself, I questioned: "Is this Kristi's bed, or mine?"

And there was a *response;* this was Kristi's bed. There now began more of a speedy dialogue than a simple visual premonition. Within myself came the second of several questions: "When?" And at this, a large figure "20" appeared above the bed. Twenty years from our wedding is so short, I observed. I would be only fifty years old, and any children we have might still be in the house. "This is too early," I thought, and I asked a third question, "Is this the end, is Kristi to die in a hospital only twenty years into our marriage?"

The figure "23" replaced the "20." With this I knew that the worst period of hospital confinements would be lifted after a three-year interval. There would be a release, for a while. The bed and numbers gave way to a new picture. I saw a downward curve from left to right, marked by a series of eight dots (years) and set against a red and black checkerboard backdrop. I think I also saw a half-drawn bedside curtain at the left of the new image. I asked a hopeful question, "Might we have seven or eight better years together . . . ?" I thought of Kristi and me growing a little older together, normally. Even as I tugged, my attention seemed to be guided back to the few dots nearest the center of the curve. The sense was that there might be three or maybe four years, not eight, and that I was to stop pushing for more certainty about future events.

I wanted more time, but now the experience seemed to intensify more deeply within. Now a question came toward me, more from the outside. It was about my self-certainty. Did I truly mean the words I was to repeat the next day, during the marriage vow, "in sickness and in health"? Would I be there for Kristi until the end — and would I accept Kristi leaving me through the veil, shortly after I turned fifty-seven?

My response to the questioner within myself came in rapid stages. It was layered. I was not at all single-hearted. My first thought was self-centered. Perhaps I did not want to handle this. But above this, or deeper, I also weighed the question. And in rapid succession I discovered and said four final things. I knew that "fifty-seven is better than fifty" and said that I would not look elsewhere — that "Kristi is the one." Then, that it was "better me than anyone else," and finally, as for the years alone that would follow, however many: "I will find a way."

All of this, the entire dialogue, passed in a flash. The clock on the church wall to the right of the altar must have shown no passage of time. At most a second or two of conversation.

After the nearly twenty-seven years, midway through hospice care (in the spring of 2001), Kristi and I sat quietly together on the davenport. On the opposite wall were pictures from our wedding day. *"That was the happiest day in my life,"* she said. More silence. In one picture, Kristi is beaming in her wedding dress. She pauses on a landing that drops a few more steps into the living room of her Cottonwood home. In the other, a close-up, we face each other with a white wedding bouquet nested between us. And now I told Kristi about the fleeting dialogue so many years before. *"You never told me about this,"* she wondered. This was true. But I had never kept this memory as a secret. It was more that the secret kept itself. It was too vivid to ever be lost, and yet too brief and too light to force itself back into my mind and life.

Shortly after Kristi's death I was to be questioned for the first time about this moment. Standing with me in an antique store in Portland, Oregon, was my twin brother. John asked about this pause at our rehearsal almost thirty years before. The pause, he remembered, lasted "only one second or two," but he revealed now that this was just long enough to draw a remembered chuckle from a few family members. "Were you having second thoughts," he joked to lighten the current moment. . . .

All of this is possibly not as unusual as it might seem. I cannot explain it, but I still see the mental pictures and remember the questioning *and* the answers from outside of myself. In truth, my decision the day before the wedding was no more than the marriage vows exchanged by any other spousal couple, but with some of the details revealed.

As with the map of Idaho that I "saw" overhead in Hong Kong harbor, this is inexplicable, a little treat, a gift. Evangelicals might call this a word of knowledge or a locution. I knew nothing then of such things. Even our meeting was inexplicable. Life is a gift, and there is a personal Giver. In our managed and mismanaged lives and world, gifts still find us. These moments, these tiny windows into the wonder before all of us, are shining gems in a splendorous mosaic. Above the clutter, this is still an enchanted universe and a design. The key is not to encompass much, but to live deeply, to notice the moments, and to reverence flowers and each other. To touch one another and not let go. This is marriage, eternity in an hour.

I see now. My treasured Kristi was entrusted to me by Another. And after so many years I begin to suspect that in His infinite goodness, to each of us, He leads gently, as a shepherd. . . . I begin to suspect that His first offer was to come for Kristi when I would be fifty, not fifty-seven. This was too heavy. He respects us, we who are in His image, and we are to do the same for each other. This is the natural law.

Our wedding day fell on a crisp and clear autumn day on the prairie. My mother wore a green silk brocade dress she had made from fabric I had purchased in Japan during my service in the Navy. In her wedding party, Kristi's three sisters wore autumn orange gowns sewn by a friend of the family. Cherie sang a spellbinding "Ave Maria" and "Sunrise, Sunset." Kristi's identical twin sister, Kerry, was her maid of honor, and my identical twin, John, was my best man. Lori was a bridesmaid. Kristi's three brothers were among the ushers.

The church was filled with family friends and so many others from the prairie whom I had never met. The reception was held at the Orr family home on the hill overlooking the entire prairie and the church and Keuterville village farthest to the west. From the top of the hill and all across the prairie could be heard the pealing of a school bell salvaged from the first Cottonwood schoolhouse. The day before, I had helped Kristi's father mount the bell in the garden a few steps from the house.

Attending the wedding and reception was the patriarch of the extended family, Cherie's father-in-law, George Seubert. He had moved to the prairie as a child in 1895 and was to live until 1996 and his one hundred and third year. In the crowded house George and his wife beckoned Kristi and me aside. "Remember," he offered, "in marriage it is the little things that count." Outside again, from a balcony overlooking the yard and prairie to the south, the revered, aging, and very German Msgr. Verhoeven offered a toast, " . . . that their troubles may be only little ones."

I have since found a gift tape recording with comments made by others of the family and by guests. Included are remembrances of Kristi in her childhood. From a former baby sitter: "Oh, she was cute, she was really cute, an awfully nice girl. She was never in a fight with her brothers and sisters. She was the sweetest little kid. She is just as sweet as she is pretty."

From another, "She's a nice girl, a great girl." One guest recalled an earlier encounter with rattlesnakes during an afternoon of swimming on the Salmon River. "Kristi takes all these things in stride, completely unruffled. Just as cool and calm as a cucumber. She's always in perfect control. Really, it's amazing."

For all of us, this wedding and all of our special moments are more than simply spots that disappear into the stream of time. More likely the reverse is true. Points in time hold our nostalgia for God within the larger moment of His eternity.

Chapter Two

Into His Presence

. . . and yet [men] leave themselves unnoticed; they do not marvel at themselves.
— St. Augustine

New Horizons

Courtship and marriage opened new vistas for both of us, together. There was more from Kristi's idyllic past. And the family conversations around the kitchen table on the hill above the Camas Prairie were always something to relish and look forward to. I was to learn that three years before we met, in 1971, the St. Gertrude's Benedictine Academy in Cottonwood closed its doors. To some this is remembered as a turning point on the prairie, even larger than the completion of the new highway a few years later.

Kristi had spent twelve years in its classrooms and fondly recalled noon periods of playing softball on the spreading lawns. (A few of the nuns were stern about the girls not playing ball with the boys, and Kristi was always hurt by the implications, which she did not even understand at the time.) The decision to close the Academy was probably due to many reasons, but Kristi's father, who valued the nuns highly, sometimes attributed this action to a lack of inner will ("bone marrow") rather than to, say, external economics.

Another likely influence following the Second Vatican Council was a greater and perhaps misunderstood new sense of personal vocation by some of the nuns. Community life among religious almost everywhere suffered widespread erosion. And then there was the papal request in 1961 for religious orders to voluntarily release up to 10 percent (more was not asked) of their numbers to meet the enormous needs in Latin America. Finally, there was the trendy new look in theology. This included the influence of such writers as the French Jesuit Pierre Teilhard de Chardin, whose poetic and evolutionary vision (his pantheism) and inventive vocabulary were often mistaken for advanced theology.[1]

What might have been a fairly routine event, transfer of a school building to new and public ownership, marked a shift in community focus on the prairie. This high school — in an overwhelmingly Catholic community — had been served for most of a century by the Benedictine community of nuns. The Academy had attracted outside boarders from around the Northwest, even one or two from my class in Richland. The nuns also had cared selflessly for Dr. Orr's patients at the local St. Mary's Hospital, as one or two still do.

The history of the Benedictine order reaches back fifteen hundred years. This beginning is one thousand years before other Church investments like the Academy, across large parts of Europe, were actually confiscated by the emergent nation-states of Europe, part of the fallout from the complex Reformation in the sixteenth century.

St. Benedict — whose balanced motto is to both pray and labor "*Ora et labora*" — is a patron saint of Europe and of the remarkable experiment called the West (proclaimed as such by Pope Pius VI in 1964). Enlarged outward from itself by faith, the receptive human mind is not so self-sufficient and self-absorbed as to reject belief in things hoped for and things eternal. The truth is always more than anything we might do. On this dual foundation — the eagle's joined wings of faith and reason — the West was once a rare marriage of engaged action *within* reverence and recollectedness. Benedict knew

St. Gertrude's Benedictine Monastery. "*The history of the Benedictine order reaches back fifteen hundred years.*"

that fully human action comes within a deeper silence, a reverence toward the wonder of creation and the ultimate mystery of a Creator.[2] Without this recollection our actions often become an addiction and a neurosis — a frenzied enterprise to contrive a more material kind of unity. The social contract theories of politics comes to mind (Hobbes, Locke, Rousseau). But with reasoning faith, the universe is not so hollow. We find that the unity we seek has been already *given* from the very beginning as a gift within, both older and newer than anything we might fabricate.

Eventually we find authentic humanism best revealed in the simplest actions of a Blessed Mother Teresa in the streets of Calcutta, rather than in any or all of the titanic Western ideologies of the nineteenth and twentieth centuries. And missing more and more is this silence of inner stillness. Missing is attentiveness to being. Missing is even the suspicion that the premodern world was also capable of being touched by a deep freedom, a freedom larger than we find in our amplified web of organized noise and noisy choices. To both pray and (then) to labor is to have our actions surrounded from within by something larger than ourselves. We are told that in the Latin, the word "obedience" — much out of favor these days — translates as "to listen deeply" (in the sense of "abiding," 1 John 4:12–16). We are larger than our compartmentalized doings in this "world" — this spherical piece of real estate and oversubscribed resources. For labor to be leavened by prayer is to "breathe with both lungs," as the expansive vision of Pope John Paul II gently reminds us. By comparison, how much of our self-directed "doing" has become a sort of ritual? How much of our culture has become a ritualized silencing of the voice within — the "internal eternal" that so fascinated St. Augustine? (At what point does the Protestant Ethic, by itself, become a disconnected cult, a fertile ground for autonomous decision making over discernment and, with reference to the smallest among us, for abortion, which is even state supported, in contradiction to a deeper culture of life?)

With the loss on the prairie of the Academy in 1971, some saw the two hands of St. Benedict being pulled loose from the prairie community. Kristi completed her Academy high school years in 1967 as class salutatorian, and then she earned a double major in English and French and a teaching certificate. Her first two college years were spent at the short-lived Mackinac College on Lake Superior in Michigan on the island by that name. Costs were covered by work at the dining tables in the historic and picturesque Victorian buildings that served as a campus.[3] After a final two years at Whitworth College in Spokane, in 1971 Kristi graduated magna cum laude and winner of the Dean's Cup. During these college years she also earned a summer scholarship to study at the Hoover Institute on the campus of Stanford University. One class was taught by the politically controversial physicist J. Robert Oppenheimer. Early in his career Oppenheimer had directed atomic energy research under the Manhattan Project at Los Alamos, New Mexico (1942–45). (By coincidence, he accounted in large part for the existence of my home town of Richland in eastern Washington and its sister city of Oak Ridge, Tennessee.)

As another part of their college years, for six months in 1969, Kristi and Kerry briefly taught business English at the Language Institute of Japan. Their stay in Japan brought them to Tokyo and a few miles south to Odawara. Here they quickly befriended the many students in business suits, classrooms of laughing children, and the nearby parish priest, Fr. Arthur Breslin. Breslin endured loneliness as an orphan and then heard the call to become a Columban priest. In this calling he followed the missionary vocation of his Irish forerunners, the first Columbans, who ventured to the European Continent back in the fifth century at the time of St. Benedict.

Years later Kristi and I enjoyed Breslin's occasional visits with us in Seattle while our Laura and Mark were still quite young. Breslin's last visit in 1982 came after several months of recovering from many years of burnout so common among missionaries. Looking younger on this visit and so much more alive again, he was really a new person. His was an imposing figure at six foot three, dark hair combed straight back, and housing an excellent Irish brogue.

Breslin and I sat alone for a few minutes at the kitchen table. In his hand was a small copy of "Evangelization in the Modern World," which clearly gave consoling meaning to his lifetime in Japan so far from his Irish homeland. In part, it reads:

> What matters is to evangelize man's culture...always taking the person as one's starting point, and always coming back to the other relationships of people among themselves

and with God. Above all the Gospel must be proclaimed by witness.... They radiate in an altogether simple and unaffected way their faith in values that go beyond current values, and their hope in something that is not seen and that one would dare not imagine.... Through this wordless witness these Christians stir up irresistible questions in the hearts of those who see how they live: why are they like this?[4]

Leaning toward me and looking deeply into my eyes, he gave this personal edition to me and then recommended that I also read Vincent Cronin's *Wise Man from the West,* the true story of Matteo Ricci in China during the sixteenth century. I preserved his next remark:

I am convinced of the tremendous power of prayer.... My path, which may be "too simple," as you might say, is this: to each day find myself a little closer to Christ. (Of his marvelous inner peace, he said) I cannot give *this* to you. You must get it from ... the same One who gave it to me.

Breslin had discovered that "there is no need for heroic deeds." After so many years he was at peace with his secret and longtime fear that he would not have been able to stand up to persecution as did his forerunners in the early days of missionary Japan.[5] He also said that he valued the contemplative Thomas Merton, who stressed holiness in the ordinary things. Merton suggested that the path to sanctity for a poet, for example, is to write good poetry, not "holy" poems. Breslin also treasured St. Therese and the "Little Way" of holiness achieved through the most ordinary of things done with special love.

Breslin was the first to really impress Kristi and me with a lesson we would come to need. This lesson is to keep one's eyes on the eyes of the Lord — like Peter as he placed his feet on the waters — and to not look back and to not look down.

After Japan, Kristi and Kerry were off to Europe together (1972–73), Kristi as a governess in Paris, first for two small boys, François and Christian, and then for a small girl, Julie. Except for a few very close visits together, Kerry spent most of her time in Marseilles. For Kristi, the domestic positions gave her a roof and covered the costs of living during her year and a half studying French language and authors. The schools both were within walking distance, the Alliance Française and the Sorbonne, where Kristi earned a fifth-year diploma of French Language and Civilization (June 1973). Her diary for this period records visits to plays and restaurants, a side trip with a family to Normandy, and a tour of Italy and northern sites with her parents and her own family when they visited. Kristi records pleasant evenings studying or relaxing with her host families, and regular visits to Notre Dame Cathedral.

Some of the days were drab, but the recovery was always buoyant toward another "beautiful day!" Almost every page tells of new friends, and some of them became very close. Of Irene from Rome, she felt the very special affection of a very close "sister." Kristi writes, "... A precious thing — friendship." One diary entry in January 1973, addressed to no one in particular, claims my heart: *I would love to get married!*"

When we finally did meet in the fall in Seattle, Kristi was looking for a position as a bilingual secretary (French and English). The Canadian consulate quickly hired her for what was probably the only job match in the entire area. After our wedding less than a year later in 1974, Kristi remained at work with her new friends.

It was Kristi's income that helped enable me to finish my last year of graduate school. I was studying for a doctoral degree through the College of Architecture and Urban Planning at the University of Washington. My five-member supervisory committee and class

selections came mostly from the larger campus. For part of my
dissertation research I selected the city-state of Singapore and its
larger regional setting to serve as a case study. With mixed Chi-
nese, Malay, Muslim, and European populations, it might give a few
clues on political and economic questions affecting dozens of new
nation-states (actually multi-national pre-states) derived from the
European colonies after World War II.

At the beginning of my classes, in 1972 (still one full year before meeting Kristi), I sat in the office of my prospective committee
chairman, Dr. Harold Amoss. An anthropologist, he had settled
into community participation work in the United States and ended
up in the college where I was enrolled. At our first meeting, my attention was drawn to the stark concrete wall behind Amoss's desk
(the blunt architectural style is aptly named "Brutalism"). On it
was a large mural of the historic Khyber Pass linking Afghanistan
and Pakistan. "Of course," he said as he watched my eyes, "I am
most interested in things Islamic." Amoss's original field of specialization had been Afghanistan, but he was agreeable to work with
me and was quick to offer several valuable theoretical and practical
suggestions.

During one coffee shop session, Dr. Amoss wrapped up his pensive remarks on colonial Britain's probes into central India. Three
or four students had gathered and listened in. His was an honest
and unexpected remark on the deepest human experience. After
a pause he switched gears completely: "I don't know if God actually talks to people." Speaking among friends Amoss had put his
finger on the enormous anomaly behind the Western experience,
fully understood. Modern social science knows nothing of this. The
comment reached above and beyond what one expects to find on
secular campuses. Does God talk to people? Out of the vast and
deep silence, is there a verb spoken to and within each of us and
who is not ourselves, singular or collective, but the very word of

God? Is there a God who is more than an idea squeezed from our meager experience and our probing minds, and who freely discloses Himself to us in some gifted way — who whispers Himself to us? In the years ahead I would return again and again to the freedom in this: "Eye has not seen nor ear heard, nor has it entered into the heart of man what things God has prepared for them who love him. *But to us God has revealed them through his Spirit*" (1 Cor. 2:9–10).

Of all the committee comments that I was to receive in the coming two years on my dissertation drafts, one such edit seemed to hit this nerve again. The marginal note challenged whether the sum of human thought might be simply a closed monologue. In the draft I had proposed or assumed that the ultimate criteria for judging the flow of history must come, finally, from outside of the events under review. History is, but history is not God. There must be more to the human experience than constant change. This sounds dry enough, but it is the watershed insight and fully human fact that had happened in (and defined) the West. This something more means that man, and each person, emerges from an inner freedom that is more than individual subjectivity. We are radically more than the sum of circumstances or statistics or even private impressions or the flow of events. Truth is more than what is.

The marginal note on my draft asked, "Why must this be so?" Was this note an assertion that everything is reducible after all to "social science?" I felt challenged to either prove or abandon my different premise. From the times and from some of our class reading, perhaps falsely I thought the reviewer to be a neo-Marxist who would not and could not accept my view. His analysis consistently and almost predictably trended toward the economic, and yet his syllabus was broad enough, and he was one of the more encouraging and challenging professors of my academic career. A good man and scholar.

I was too cautious in my response to his marginal note, too skit-tish on this secular campus, and admittedly too poorly equipped, and a bit concerned about maintaining research focus. I felt myself too much a stranger in a strange land. But I do remember decid-ing that I would permit myself the "religious" question (Karl Marx had called it the "question of contingency"[6]) even in my academic exercise, and see what I might learn.

Near the end of one challenging academic quarter, I was re-warded by a poignant moment at the tail end of one of this professor's classes. We were dealing broadly with political and eco-nomic events in Southeast Asia and other Third World countries. The themes reached into Europe and our past as well. To my sur-prise my professor, a non-Christian, defended the monasteries of the West as conduits of scholarship and centers of thought. This matter-of-fact notion seemed indigestible to a large segment of the class.

We also had had some far-ranging discussions about the use-fulness of myths, especially modern ones. On the practical side we were asking about a possibly utopian myth. We asked, if nature were fully harnessed to human appetites by technology and politics, might there be no limit to what it can pull? From our upper third floor, my professor helped us search for a contemporary answer to the human condition. On this day the class was particularly engaged and then silent. A student presenter had posed the stereotyped Marx-ist dream: What if wealth were technologically expanded and then distributed equally to all by a new political machinery imposed by "us" instead of "them"? Our professor did not feel bound to this dream. Personal appetites finally have no limits and at least some key resources must be finite in some limiting sense. So, how long was an unbounded spiral between appetite and consumption really sustainable?[7] In working the math, our professor also searched his own soul. With one foot on the seat of his chair he peered between the window mullions of this Tudor Gothic citadel and ventured: "The purpose of social science is to offer people *hope*."

Breaking the spell was a sudden response from below — the howling on cue from the ground floor. It was a student's German shepherd tied to a bike rack. Such an exquisitely timed rebuttal, then more silence. Our professor waited and then announced his premise a second time, repeating himself word for word: "The purpose of social science is to offer people hope." Again the spell was broken by what I now chose to imagine as the howling of wolves circling in on all of our failed agnostic formulas. Here was a direct equivalence between the vulnerability of the modern world and that of medieval Paris, where manuscript chronicles tell us during some winters perhaps a half dozen people would be eaten by wolves in the very streets of the city.

The earlier coffee table conversation with Dr. Amoss ("I don't know if God talks to people") recalls another encounter in the same coffee shop. I would tell of this to Kristi during our year of courtship. On one slow afternoon I had joined a fellow student nursing a coffee cup alone at his table. "I haven't seen you for a while. Where have you been?" I asked. Tom was Czechoslovakian (a Czech from Prague, rather than a Slovak). He had been an exchange student in Bergen, Norway, during the Soviet invasion of his homeland in 1968. Now, in 1974, at the table in front of me, he wore even longer shoulder-length hair than I remembered and peered pensively into his coffee mug.

Tom's story took nearly an hour to unfold, but I made the time. I learned that he had been gone six months. He had flown to north Africa with the intention of slipping back into Prague to visit his parents and sister. But in Morocco he was notified long-distance and warned by other exiled refugee contacts centered in Paris. For his failure to return from Bergen in 1968, he already had been tried in absentia by the Czech authorities and sentenced to three years in prison. He would be taken immediately upon crossing the border. His entry visa was subtly marked for his arrest (it was printed on ivory paper instead of white).

Deciding not to return yet to the United States, he hitchhiked for six months, first across north Africa and through the Middle East and Afghanistan, and then south into India and east to the foothills of Tibet. With a friendship that crosses language barriers, a farmer offered him a corner on the pounded earth floor of his family's small hut. There Tom entered the cadence of the seasons. Time and calendars — the governing mathematics of our times — disappeared for Tom. After several months it was only with great effort that he recalled our world, a world so preoccupying, that he had left behind.

But against the timeless backdrop of the Himalayas Tom decided to make his way back to Seattle. In the coffee shop, I was the privileged first person Tom spoke with upon his return. I was the spellbound listener, like the speaker in Coleridge's *Rime of the Ancient Mariner.* Tom was still in his travel clothes. He wore the hand-sewn leather and fur parka he had bought on a snowy night southbound on a mountainous trail through Afghanistan. His T-shirt was clean. A worn toothbrush projected from a side pocket.

At this table I found a window into the surprising stories that await us behind the faces we avoid on city streets and in rest homes. One can only guess at the worlds that disappear when the elderly slip away unheard, perhaps reduced to numbers in an equation of medical costs and benefits. In later years, the nineties, Kristi regularly volunteered to visit the rest homes and usually had a story for me following her visits with shut-ins in the parish. Not unusual stories or even long ones, but little treasures and tragedies mixed together.

In social science we might find the confidence of achievement and even self-fulfillment. But we will not find the total confidence of self-abandonment, not unconditional hope. So what then is worthy of human hope? What, truly, is our origin and our end? Is there a truth above the laws of change and deeper than our own doing, our artifact of history? Good management is not enough.

The inner dimension of the human person and the person in community are the secret of those historical anomalies that we call saints. To suspect (as they do) a source of hope higher than social science or politics involves a degree of freedom that is always more or less countercultural.

One mentor for me on this riddle of faith (a faith not without reason) was a historian. Not a member of my dissertation committee at the university, he was a friend of two or three years, always with a challenging perspective or two on Western history, Fr. Gerard Steckler, S.J. In Steckler I found even then a reflective squint taken in by neither the ideologies attached to late Western progress ("chronological snobbery"), nor by the opposite pseudo-religious faith-iness (ranging from individualistic fideism to academically fashionable Gnosticism.)[8] Steckler suggests that "hope is a theological virtue" rather than an attitude.[9] This is a very radical proposition, as radical as the resurrection. And the resurrection explains a second lesson I have tried to take to heart. On prayer, he was probably the first to counsel us that we must pray for concrete needs. Otherwise prayer does not really lift us out of ourselves. Vague prayer is only an exercise in consciousness-raising.

Two years after Kristi's and my wedding, the historian Steckler joined us in our home for dinner, and we considered the eternal destiny of *each* human person, through *and* yet above (or larger than) all of history. This startling view — personal fidelity to this truth in Person — always brings with it the risk of being cornered into martyrdom in an imperfect and aggressive world. Each of us is a potential Maria Goretti. This is so even if the surrender is only our graceful acceptance of something so common (and total) as our personal and natural deaths. Scrape the surface, and what "hope" can we expect from the social sciences as each of us faces the fundamental events of human existence — life and death?

Asked his view on another point of human freedom, that of priestly celibacy, Steckler had a clear and off-handed response. The religious simply decide to "grow in a different direction." Celibacy, he suggested, is openness of the total person toward boundless hope, hope for eternity.[10] The distance from eternity for each of us is measured in only a few minutes or perhaps decades. We are all equal in this, we are all the same age. This eternity is the face of God. Whenever we forget this, he said, history becomes a downhill slide into a menu of ideologies, as in recent centuries.

Kristi and I found ourselves standing together at the living room window and facing into a magnificent red sunset above our glimpse of the distant Olympic Mountains to the west. Steckler would depart for a year of teaching in Florence, and we were sorrowed by this coming separation. His response was typically blunt and potentially consoling: "There is no separation in the Communion of Saints." I was struck by this, the insight that our experience of separation in space and time is less real than our *being* together, which is not seen with the eyes or even with the imagination. This communion is a concrete and transcendent fact expanding from within — something we discover to be true from the beginning and not something that we construct in any way.

My graduate years at the university (in 1972–75) were among the happiest and most fulfilling of my life. These were marvelous years, and I enjoyed sharing the last two with my fiancée and then wife. After our first year of marriage our dear Laura Kristina entered the world. Laura's birth, this miracle of a particular new life and daughter, overwhelmed me. I actually helped coach Kristi through the birth (bedside coaching by the husband can be a potential complication in case of emergency and was not entirely acceptable to Kristi's consistently professional father in Cottonwood). Laura was born on July 28, 1975, in Providence Hospital, a few blocks south from the oldest standing Catholic church building in Seattle. The massive brick and twin-towered Immaculate Conception Church crowns one of the seven hills that shape so much of the city, rising in silhouette against the distant Cascade Range to the east. Along its interior left wall, the church houses a replica of the Grotto of Lourdes in France. On Laura's first day I visited the Grotto to simply light a candle.

The remaining summer weeks brought us the light magic of sunny walks and threesome visits to one park or another. About this time, Kristi and I also briefly considering the attractions of a job offer in Alaska, but we decided to make our permanent home in the Seattle area. On silken summer evenings we listened to recordings of Murielle Mathieu, a voice from Paris. And the Camas Prairie community was only a day's drive away. Holidays frequently had us on the road crossing through eastern Washington, and the prairie experience grew into a seasonal symphony of changing colors and moods. In central Idaho and eastern Washington, brilliant spring greens give way each summer to the light ochre of wheat ready for harvest. Then come the rich browns of late autumn and, on the prairie, the pastel blue and pink tones of the late afternoon sun streaking through clustered pines and across the winter snows. Year after year, we thought those pilgrimages would last indefinitely, driving past the twin towers of the abbey toward the Orr home on the far side of the hill — a family sanctuary in view of the Salmon River canyon due south and our Keuterville steeple to the west.

As the kitchen table conversations continued, I was to learn that Kristi's family tree reached in several directions. Her father was Irish on his mother's side and English from his father. Kristi's mother is

partly German from her father and Scotch, Irish, and English on
her mother's side. The German ancestors came indirectly to the
United States, passing through Russia in the 1880s. Along the way
they helped introduce the famous Russian red wheat to the Kansas
prairie where Jeanne was raised.

Dr. Orr was raised in Cottonwood and then studied medicine
at the prestigious Northwestern University in Chicago. He taught
anatomy briefly at New York University. As a physician, Kristi's father guided his family with references to very concrete stories (such
as Alexis Carrel's). But as long as I knew him, he also struggled with,
and was encouraged by, the prayer in Scripture offered by the father
of a boy possessed: "Lord, I believe, but help me in my unbelief"
(Mark 9:24). The doctor found a resonance between this profession
of faith and the similar tension we see in the doubting St. Thomas
even until he pointed his fingers into Christ's side. Serving the spiritual within the physical was part of the doctor's own experience as
he tended in each case to the entire patient.

The human questions, and especially the religious question, were
as natural as the food we ate together at the table. Rarely did a
meal pass without a challenging foray into some aspect or other of
philosophy or theology, or politics, or current Church personalities
and events.

Along these lines, Kristi's father often gave us books as gifts. The
first and most valued was Malcolm Muggeridge's account of Blessed
Mother Teresa and her Missionaries of Charity in Calcutta — *Something Beautiful for God* (1971). Another was Robert Jastrow's *God
and the Astronomers* (1978).[11] Others were heavier reading, Cardinal
Joseph Siri's *Gethsemani: Reflections on the Contemporary Theological
Movement* (1981), and Mortimer Adler's *Ten Philosophical Mistakes*
(1985). The doctor enjoyed telling of Adler's encounter with a critic
after one talk to a packed audience. Adler's philosophy, with its attention to the radical *existence* of concrete things as they are in

themselves, apart from mathematics and our *ideas* about things, sounded a lot like the ever-new insights articulated by the medieval Catholic mind St. Thomas Aquinas. When challenged why he embraced Aquinas without also being a Catholic, Adler replied, "Madam, I may be unsure in my faith, but I have not lost my mind."

Siri's work also fit into the larger and ongoing discussion. An important table theme during these Cottonwood years, even a preoccupying one, was the turbulence within the Church following the Second Vatican Council (1962–65).[12] Siri took issue with the intrusion of philosophical historicism, the idea that God is reducible to truth and that truth is finally a human idea that evolves. This notion displaces a theology that maintains a clearer distinction between nature and thought on the one hand, and the total gift of God's self-revelation and His divine grace. One must decide, within one's own lifetime, whether Christ is a fact and a Person in history but not of history, or whether truth is relative and more ambulatory — a matter, finally, of simply being on the right side of history.

Around the table we held to lively and therefore "orthodox" fidelity, although as amateurs and onlookers into the intricate and not trivial debates of theologians. (Kristi's entire story in these pages turns on her single-hearted and humble submission to her "dear Lord" in the sacraments, *rather than* the subtle sophistication of many published thinkers.)

Whittaker Chambers, especially through his *Witness* (1952), also had an honored place at the table. During the Cold War, the formative moment in Chambers's life was not, as many assume, his famous testimony against Alger Hiss in the case prosecuted by the future President Nixon. As Chambers himself says, truth came to him in his personal rejection of alternative paths to happiness — the atheist path of the Communist Revolution and the more productive path of the West when even it becomes ethically uncommitted.

Dr. Orr stressed that Chambers first saw through the grip of atheism not by scholarly argument, but by simply noticing the intricacy of something so simple as his sleeping daughter's ear. In a shaft of light, this moment of insight at the bedroom door unveiled for Chambers the mystery of conscious design and of exquisite love acting above and then throughout the universe from beginning to end. For all families, one compelling argument for the existence of God is children. May this always be so.

Celebrating this gifted universe was another selection from Chambers, a letter written later in his life (1954) and read at the kitchen table:

> The enemy — he is ourselves. That is why it is idle to talk about preventing the wreck of Western civilization. It is already a wreck from within. That is why we can hope to do little more now than snatch a fingernail of a saint from the rack or a handful of ashes from the faggots, and bury them secretly in a flowerpot against the day, ages hence, when a few men begin again to dare to believe that there was once something else, that something else is thinkable, and need some evidence of what it was, and the fortifying knowledge that there were those who, at the great night fall, took loving thought to preserve the tokens of hope and truth.[13]

Here was the discovery that relics, things we can see and touch, are necessary for us to sustain within the truth and to keep beauty alive. And here is the possibility that relics are more than an anesthetic for the cruelties and suffering of history. The reason we preserve relics is not to help us escape into our imagination, but instead to help keep our imaginations from wandering into political fantasy.

As the doctor looked up from Chambers, I glanced toward the prairie framed by the kitchen window. I was surprised to feel so

deeply and simply that the surrounding forests were more than potential two-by-fours or even a beautiful setting for a family home. I
felt that the very cell structure of the tree rings harbored living memories reaching back to the radically original message of Christianity.
The world of tree rings and the abiding presence of a changeless God
were here long before tribes herded themselves into larger language
groups and then political domains defined by gunpowder and the
printing press, and finally (or fleetingly?) nation-states harnessed
to economic theories and machines. Human constructions come
and go.

The secrets of the forest were old long before we divorced His
eternal presence and His self-disclosure (His "revelation") from our
shivering gift of reason. The Psalms speak of the "everlasting hills,"
and at this transporting moment I glimpsed from within what this
inspired poetry means.

On one of these visits to the prairie, Kristi's father took me alone
closer to the forest farther up the hill behind the house. He found
again a spot in his memory. There seemed to be a solemnity about
our being there. Between us at the edge of the clearing we inspected
a stump. Many years before, a large pine tree had fallen. But during
the intervening years a second tree had grown up from within the
stump of the first. And this second tree had been cut off at nearly
the ground level. From the center of both enclosures there projected
a third tree — yet a new pattern of tree rings. In later years after
my father-in-law's death in 1996 I tried to return to this unusual
marker, but now it was hidden. The forest edge is blurred with
a new growth advancing toward the prairie below, but the forest
remembers. I never asked, but I sensed that this might be the secret
place where Dr. Orr had buried a sorrowful miscarriage from the
early years of his marriage to Jeanne.

Later, during Kristi's and my visit to France in 1999 (chapter 4)
I would feel another sympathy touch me from another forest. This

*On the edge of the clearing near Kristi's home. "There projected a third tree —
yet a new pattern of tree rings."*

would be for the contradictory mingling of Christian symbols with
the pagan gargoyles of the forest as they peer down from the ledges
of Notre Dame Cathedral in Paris. Is it only our pride that tells us
these gargoyles are less valid than the collective totems or ideologies
of the fading modern world? We nod before the gaping grin of market shares and the hubris of technology. Only with difficulty do we
discard our own gargoyles, the collective myths of the twentieth
century: Socialism, Fascism, Communism ... and now situational
pragmatism or moral relativism.

   At the table on the prairie we would wrestle with these idols and
the divorce of secular society from the deeper stirring in the human

heart.[14] Finally, the world still is enchanted — and this sense of enchantment brings us close to reverence, what the Church identifies as the first gift given to us by the Holy Spirit (sometimes "fear of the Lord").

For twenty years of family visits the kitchen table renewed the family bond within the challenge from a higher truth and an ultimate glory. At the time of Chambers's letter, in 1954, no one could foresee the collapse of the Berlin Wall in 1989. No one could see the collapse of the entire Soviet Union in 1991, an event in history equivalent to the dissolution of the Roman Empire over a much longer period. We know now that Chambers also wrote before globalization — our new interconnectedness in economics, ethnic nationalism, and terrorism — which has followed the abrupt end of the Cold War.

Islam, a religion and a political ideology rolled into one, infested by a rogue terrorist threat to all, rolls us back several centuries. The Enlightenment project, too, has its limits. Picking up table talk themes, the post-Christian West is faced with not only a clash of geographically separated Western ideologies and nation-states at home (the world wars), but now with a possible collision between *post*-civilizations. If so, some of the underpinnings are *theological* even more than they are cultural or economic. Within the West, the trial might involve also our descent into agnosticism in a new and geographically footloose form. This is our own Consumerism, the flat-earth cult of *having* over *being.*

If it were possible, our little table talk today would surely find its way to this new landscape and the reshaping map of the European continent. We would notice the allergy of the new European Union toward any charter recognition of its Christian roots. Our consistent question would be whether or not the new unity includes a closer tie to what is beyond ourselves, and therefore to the sacredness of each human person — as this is revealed through Trinitarian Christianity.

And so we would surely talk again around the table of the fully human institution of the family itself.[15] More than a transitional social grouping, the family is the litmus test for judging anything proposed by contemporary social science or by a totally time-bound notion of human history. An efficient and tired world forgets that together we are to be a new creation, and are already more than what we know.

In all of our kitchen table conversations, my father-in-law's views showed us two recurring poles in his thinking. One was the intricacy of moving from sound philosophical foundations to actual situations. This is much like diagnosing a real patient beyond the few numbers on the chart at the foot of the bed. As he might have said, doctors treat patients, not x-rays. And the other pole was the sinewy tough-ness simply to see that in the convoluted political world, the thing that is most often missing is not yet another layer of complexity. Missing is a more instinctive sense of rightness, and the courage to go with it — what he called "bone marrow." Of so many political riddles, the doctor would finally demand: "Don't you think some of this bunk just gets down to a question of bone marrow?"

On the neighborhood scale, I recall one afternoon in the mid-1980s we searched the roadway as it wound its way up the two hundred yards from the bottom of the hill. The question was this: If we knew that a notorious rapist and stalker was approaching, at what point would we repel him with necessary force? Considering hypothetical doubt, and yet for the protection of our families, when would we shoot? How far toward or into house and home might he be allowed to come? Into this situation came the thinking of a European intellectual and realist whom we will consider more later (the Austrian Erik von Kuehnelt-Leddihn). His view was very much in line with traditional and fog-free moral theology: anyone has the right to be a pacifist, to offer his own neck to the knife of an assailant, but no one has the right to stand aside and offer the necks of his family or of others. The fireman does not negotiate with the fire.

On one early visit to the prairie the doctor showed me on his bedroom wall a framed original sketch. It depicted a hand with thumb and fingers projecting a scalpel. The Latin inscription at the bottom read, *Primum non nocere* (First, do no harm). His professional and personal ethics were irreconcilable with the pragmatism which by now had infiltrated at least parts of modern medicine. Pragmatism has become a slippery calculus that now justifies even abortion and euthanasia — not what we *ought* to do, but what we can do. For many years this doctor, so intensely committed and proud of membership in his profession, felt himself betrayed and forced to withhold his annual dues from the American Medical Association. This was as much a matter of clear-eyed reason accessible to all as it was a matter of faith. In more and more ways, the Golden Rule is no longer on the gold standard.

To my eye the drawing of hand and scalpel carried an unintended double meaning. Moving from the hand farther up the wrist there was a sharp ending to the drawing, still well inside the frame's edge. This rendering gave the appearance of a hand that had been severed, possibly that it had severed itself with the very scalpel it was still holding.

No topic seemed off limits at the Orr table. For starters, during my first visit to the prairie I was directly asked over dessert what I thought of the trendy B. F. Skinner, and whether his ethic of conditioning and rejection of human moral freedom was widely accepted on secular campuses like the University of Washington. And often before us was the drift of medicine into bureaucracy and away from the realness of each patient — away from the concrete and spiritual person. I know that sometimes the doctor wondered a bit even about the mixed blessing of his new St. Mary's Hospital building in town, built in 1965. The new facility had been funded with a federal grant, with the strings attached that would take ever more of his direct attention and time away from his patients. Voices on telephones far removed from the patient would scan printouts and averages to determine medical protocols (a little as military commanders sometimes dining in London once supervised faraway life and death in the trenches of World War I).

In the mid-1970s we noticed under new federal laws the redefinition of doctors and patients. Doctors became "health care providers," and the rest of us became "health care consumers." Even we saw then how this market wording would first divide and then dehumanize both. And during his visits with us in Seattle in the 1970s, Kristi's father was startled and disgusted to see the difference between his patients' billings in a rural hospital and the billings from his counterparts in our metropolitan area. Often he did not charge at all if the family could not pay. The complex of marketing, fragmentation, specialization, and so on added up mostly to only one thing even in his mind, "greed." This can be active greed, but more likely it is something else, the sedative of routine complexity that allows and then invites the multiplication of specialized niches and the compounding of costs. The country doctor was most scandalized that the doctor-patient relationship was succumbing to the way of so many things modern: dollars, bureaucracy, and anonymity. His personal and individual service and his small hospital were always very highly regarded and in time the hospital was to be recognized as one of the top ten small hospitals in the United States.

For me, the most transfixing family moment at the Orr kitchen table came in 1985, twelve years after my first visit. On a late afternoon I found myself standing alone facing my father-in-law across the kitchen table. The rest of the family had already moved into another room. The doctor surely had been thinking about how, over time, even the closest families might drift apart. Even on the prairie, time can erode families as well as bond them.

Centered on the table between the two of us he had placed two generous jiggers of his favorite Scotch. He gripped and raised the drinks, one for himself and the other he extended to me. Beneath his full eyebrows, his dark and unblinking eyes shot out and seemed to penetrate through to the back of my head. And he extracted from me a promise.

My father-in-law, who years before had welcomed me into the family, now said only two words, "To family."

"To family," I promised, and we drank together. Nothing else was ever said of this, but I never forgot.

Our son, Mark, was born to Kristi and me on June 3, 1978. As with Laura three years earlier, I was there again to help coach Kristi through the birth. Mark was only five when he discovered the wonderful workings of his own mind. On a gravel beach on the east shore of Vancouver Island in British Columbia, he tottled along with me, his small and trusting left hand in my right. On the previous day he had asked a question to which a simplified explanation of the moon and the tides was the answer. Today a new piece of information had to do with how gravity holds even the water in its place. Then came this, "Daddy, I know where the waves come from! See, the moon pulls the water up first, and then the gravity pulls it back down again." I supported this particular conclusion. A silence followed, and then came the ageless delight of Archimedes' cry, "Eureka!": "Hey, I can figure things out!" I shall always treasure Mark's entry into the world of figuring things out, and the fact that I was there to hold his hand in mine and to be held by his. After all, even Galileo never warmed up to the idea that the sun and moon influenced the tides.

Two years later, in another small way proportioned to his world, Mark seemed to sense the enormous riddle also at the root of St. Thomas Aquinas, whose niche is Western thought was to find a synthesis between faith and reason (at the University of Paris, responding to Arabic translations of Aristotle). Thomas maintained that within the finite human mind truth is still not contradictory, while the Arab Averroes held that two genuinely contradictory *concepts* can both can be true. The latter view discounts the gifted power of the human mind and its ability and calling to know things deeply as they are. This is done by making meaningful *judgments* between our own spun-off ideas about these things (a broader approach than the scientific method alone, which is confined to and explores the universe at its physical level).

Of this kind of riddle, the difference between imagination and reality, Mark asked me simply, "Daddy, why can't two numbers both be bigger than each other?" I do not recall how I answered our seven-year-old.

Kristi delighted in all of the little daily events and achievements of our children. I recall my special moment with Mark on the beach, but the privileged role of mother is to be more consistently there every day, to share an entire fabric of such daily threads. During the summers their tans darkened from daily visits to Richmond Beach, strung between the bluff and Puget Sound, only three miles from our Seattle area home. Piano lessons took place in the home, and there were the school classes and Laura's artistic talent from a very early age. I still have many of her very original drawings of rabbits and dogs, and sometimes hybrid creatures of her own invention.

Sitting beside me in the car on one Monday Scout night in 1989, Mark, at the age of eleven, abruptly announced a decision, "I am going to do it." And then as a fresh new member of the Boy Scout troop he explained that he intended to advance to an Eagle Scout. This achievement and his additional qualification for a private pilot's flying license both came during his high school years. As with Laura before him, Mark's high school years slipped by quickly. The summer of 1996 after his high school graduation Mark entered the

Marine Corps Reserves, a few weeks before following his sister to Franciscan University in Ohio.

While both of the kids were still growing up, from time to time we fitted some special performances into our family schedule. The Pacific Northwest Ballet trained in the renovated hilltop structure in Seattle where Laura's kindergarten Montessori school was located. (The school shared space with many other groups in the former Home of the Good Shepherd, which previously had provided safe haven for unwed mothers). In 1980, when Laura was five, the troop gave a very special classroom performance of *Peter and the Wolf* for the children. Over the years we also managed to take in several larger Seattle stage plays. These included *Les Misérables, Annie,* the Pacific Northwest Ballet's nationally celebrated production of the *Nutcracker,* and *The King and I* with the visiting Yul Brenner in the lead role.

Kristi's favorite movies included those based on the novels of Jane Austen, and I think that her favorite actor was eventually Anthony Hopkins in his more thoughtful roles such as C. S. Lewis in *Shadowlands.* She was very touched by the movie portrayal of Mitch Albom's *Tuesdays with Morrie* (1997), the very popular and true story of the final life-filled months of a victim of Lou Gehrig's disease. Maureen O'Hara was a favorite in her spirited role opposite John Wayne in *The Quiet Man.*

Music was part of Kristi's inner being. While she was growing up in Cottonwood it had been common during holidays, especially Christmas, for the family to gather in song around the polished black mini-grand piano. And during the earlier years of our marriage while our kids were still entering piano recitals at our St. Mark's Parish grade school, between 1984 and 1986, Kristi gave herself to weekly professional voice lessons. This meant daily practices in our second home. She had already been in the church choir, and when still pregnant with Mark had even performed a wonderful solo for

Christmas season. Kristi was the darling of the generally older choir, with her floor-length scarlet robe and long dark hair.

Often on Saturday afternoons when I returned from a run through the neighborhood, as I passed through the back gate under our mountain ash, I would be greeted by Kristi's sweet voice. From out of the kitchen came Oscar Hammerstein's "Make Believe" from *Showboat,* or at other times, "Why Do I Love You," or "Till There Was You" from the *Music Man,* or even selections from Puccini's *La Bohème.* In the house our ears were also tuned to our favorites, such as Plácido Domingo, and in the nineties, Gregorian chant and such pieces as vespers from Hildegard von Bingen.

The rigor of serious singing was a challenge for Kristi. Now from the taped recordings of Kristi's weekly training sessions, I find Kristi's instructor, Eve, sometimes saying, "You are not realizing your voice." And, "If you feel comfortable and wonderful, it is not working." But on the lighter side, there were one or two summer evening social events for all of the voice students. In the summer of 1985 the students met east of Lake Washington at a yard party hosted by the instructor. Here Kristi and I met the distinguished Rabbi Raphael Levine, a well-known ecumenical figure in the region.

Levine was probably best known for his books and television talk show series (*Challenge,* 1960–74) conducted with a Catholic priest and a Protestant minister. He first came to the United States from Poland at the age of eight, and during the first years of the Second World War returned again from England. On his hand-carved walking stick was the motto, "To love is to live," which he enjoyed explaining to me on that balmy evening when I nudged him to do so.[16]

Kristi's last recital came the following year. The four of us arrived early, and Laura, Mark, and I found our chairs in the front row. The duet selection was from Mozart's *The Marriage of Figaro.* Kristi's dark hair was hidden under a high white wig. This flair was

Jefferson County Courthouse, Port Townsend Washington

complemented by the same pink floor-length gown she had worn as maid of honor at Kerry's wedding a full fifteen years earlier. At this final recital she let go more than ever before.

Kristi "realized her voice," and her entire personality.

Gliding across the floor Kristi gave her own life to the part. Light danced in her dark eyes, and her sweet smile touched even those in the back of the hall. Applause was spontaneous and unrestrained. After returning home to take pictures under the evergreens in our back yard, I smothered with kisses my treasure still clothed in her storybook dress, dark eyes sparkling under her fantasy white wig.

Throughout all of the eighties and early nineties our day trips sometimes took us west beyond Whidbey Island and across Puget Sound to Port Townsend on the northeast corner of the Olympic Peninsula. The Peninsula features the faceted and snow-crowned Olympic range, bounded on the west by the Pacific coast rain forests. At its strategic corner location Port Townsend marks the northwest entry channel into all of Puget Sound. In its early years of the late 1800s the town had aspired to become the capital of the new Washington State. As San Francisco was being rebuilt from its famous earthquake and fire, Puget Sound was the market for lumber. This surge of activity lifted this small town to become one of the busiest seaports in the United States at the time, second only to New York City.

The Victorian homes and brick-towered courthouse remain a popular destination in the Northwest. Picturesque military housing units, two rows facing each other across a large marching field, are now open to summer groups. Deserted concrete military bunkers still search the passage today as modern container ships slide within view of our favorite eastside beaches to and from the Pacific Rim ocean ports of Seattle and Tacoma.

Port Townsend was especially important to Kristi for family reasons. During most of the summers of Kristi's college years, her family had been able to break free of the hospital schedule long enough to try their hand at sailing in the sound. A port call at Port Townsend was the highlight of this whole period and these special family times together. In the following years around the kitchen table, Kristi's father still would search his memory for the lines of a favorite poem tied to the freedom he found in sailing. He relished "Sea Fever" by John Masefield, especially the last two lines: "And all I ask is a merry yarn from a laughing fellow-rover, / and quiet sleep and a sweet dream when the long trick's over."

North of Port Townsend and at the extreme northwest entrance to Puget Sound is the San Juan Island group, a world unto itself. The boat landing to the major island (San Juan Island) is on an east-facing bay where it is protected from the seasonal Pacific wind and weather. During one visit on the west side, we followed a forested side road to a small clearing a few miles south of Roche Harbor. We found ourselves facing a large and secluded moss-covered mausoleum. Seven classical Doric columns rose in a circular pattern to meet a shared ring-shaped cornice at the top. One of the columns was incomplete. This seventh column projected down two or three feet from its capital, and then by design was broken off in space. Surrounded by this structure were six empty concrete chairs — separate crypts for deceased members of a one-time prominent Island family. The chairs faced each other blankly and faceless in stunned silence across an empty and moss-covered concrete table. They seemed to be touching nothing here or hereafter.

The plaque explained that this cultic design symbolized the incompleteness of any and all human endeavor throughout all of history. It also proclaimed the earthbound nature of all such striving, confined as it was believed to this side of an eternity that does not exist. We were left with the eerie feeling of a closed world. A closed world in a flat universe only partly human, because it points to nothing beyond itself. How absolutely different this symbol is from the octagonal symbolism of much Christian architecture. The additional eighth side (found especially on bell towers and baptismal fonts) opens the closed circle to a larger world beyond any horizon. This Christian symbol is open to (and by) the resurrection on the eighth day of the week. It witnesses to a personal eternity beyond the veil and not of our making. Beyond self-generated optimism, however courageous, it restores a more grounded hope that is indestructible even by death.

Surrounding the site of the seven-sided mausoleum temple we felt some additional symbolism. The cleared original west view to the ocean horizon is now closed off and swallowed by the forest. In barely a century the cult of the forest clearing is again unable to escape the encroaching shade.

Closer to Seattle is yet another and different side trip. This road took us to the historic Port Gamble mill town and its lovely cemetery on an open hill. This entire town is on an elevated bluff overlooking the north end of the sound where it divides into the main unit bordering Seattle and Tacoma to the southeast, and the narrower Hood Canal (a long glacial scar two miles wide) passing to the west. The San Juan Islands are fifty miles north across the water. The white picket fence around the cemetery recalls the Victorian period, quaint and simple — or so we imagine — and so dear to Kristi.

We always stopped at the fence for the view and a picnic, and sometimes even dozed on the grass within, between the historic marker stones. These hideaway naps in the cemetery came to be an inside joke for the family. On one calm summer day, Kristi remarked that *"this would not be a bad place to wait for eternity."*

In the summer of 1995 on our last trip together as a family to Cannon Beach in Oregon, we noticed a swallow's nest. Tucked under the eave outside the kitchen window of our rented cottage, it gave us something special to inspect over breakfast each morning. As we watched during the next few days, the two baby swallows ventured out from their haven, and then one day were gone. The nest was empty.

Kristi watched all of this intently. This natural passage seemed to give comfort as her mind wandered to Laura's college years and Mark's graduation from high school in the coming year. Transitions like this always come so quickly and nearly break the heart, the letting go of precious moments always so fleeting and incomplete.

Kristi's heart always went out spontaneously to children. To her each one was precious, like the birds in the nest. In the early eighties, Kristi found a place as a volunteer librarian at the parish school. "These beautiful children hold up their books so carefully, with their big eyes poking over the edge of the desk!" Later in the mid-1990s, her favorite assignments as a part-time substitute teacher with the public school system had been with the youngest grades. These salaried assignments helped cover the costs of braces and high school tuition at Bishop Blanchet High School in north Seattle.

It was only a matter of time, probably, before the small lace-like gold cross around Kristi's neck would become an issue at the public school. It was a very neutral religious souvenir from our trip together to New Orleans in 1994. One of the children — a troubled child from a broken home — had asked Kristi about it, and on that lonely playground that day had seen that there is love in the universe. Perhaps it was unrelated, but Kristi came home aching for all the children of an agnostic world, anesthetized at best by all of the television shows that our consumer culture has to market. She continued to wear the cross. And I am lifted each day when I glance at a detail in the individual staff picture taken during this period in late 1995. Kristi wore her subversive Christmas earrings.

A few years earlier, when Laura and Mark were younger, Kristi had enjoyed volunteering as a spelling assistant in a parish program. Created and led by a published former school superintendent (parishioner Dr. Ted Glim), the program routinely produced state champions. Glim created a challenging program based on etymology rather than word lists alone. The young children and mentors like Kristi had the rare excitement of being exposed to some twenty-eight different languages.

At some point along the way Kristi was strongly attracted to a more needy set of children. She learned that hospitalized children recover more quickly if they are simply held. The prestigious

Children's Orthopedic Hospital in Seattle had her attention, but Kristi was deterred from volunteering. At first she was afraid that she would become too attached, and then she found that simply to hold these special children she would need nursing credentials. Now the moral challenges and pressures of emerging frontiers of medical ethics were set aside: "*I wish that I had gone into nursing.*"

Instead, after her formal education, Kristi had put in the time and effort it took to earn a real estate license and then a two-year certificate in travel from the nearby community colleges. These achievements involved typically conscientious work on Kristi's part. Later when she put herself into her part-time work, in her heart she longed for something else and even a different kind of world than we are given. The business world placed a premium on a market orientation that really was not part of Kristi's makeup. One cannot do real estate part time. If things had worked out differently for us, she would have liked to run a friendly bed and breakfast with quaint furnishings and Victorian wallpaper.

For my part, during the eighties I worked long days and a four-day week to be more with the family and to fit in my hobby of freehand drawing. While some of my work was better than others, I could always count on Kristi admiring my efforts and the results. Such a plum to me.

Kristi asked for so little. A quiet corner of the world was just fine. We always had dinners together as a family. In this way we tried to continue the exceptional sense of gathering about the table she had known in her upbringing. It was not the same, but I do particularly remember Mark and Laura taking repeated delight in our occasional readings especially from Lewis Carroll's *Jabberwocky.* And they showed a more polite interest in my original and unforgivable shaggy dog stories. After the kids were gone, a sandwich night out was every bit as good for Kristi as a trip to a classy waterfront restaurant. Now the windowsill above the kitchen sink sustains me, decorated as it is with little pewter collectibles from so many anniversary dinners, and tiny sea shells and other little nothings from our years of family outings.

Like most husbands, I ask if there was ever a spouse like Kristi, who took so much sheer delight in the simple and genuine things — our children, a sunset and autumn leaves, the early Seattle cherry blossoms in February, a surprise snowfall, or a simple stroll in the neighborhood? After high school Kristi also enjoyed Michigan and Japan and Paris. She loved them all, but in the last several years of our marriage Kristi often repeated to me of our home in Seattle, *"There is nowhere else in the world that I would rather live than here."*

We liked the setting in the Pacific Northwest. Surveys show that the residents of Washington and Oregon are quite content trying to find themselves on the ski slopes, and that these are the two most "unchurched" states in the Union. It is easy to lose oneself in the blessings.

For Kristi, the setting was wonderful, but at the center there was the life within:

> Men go to gape at mountain peaks, and the boundless tides of the sea, the broad sweep of rivers, the encircling ocean and the motions of the stars: and yet they leave themselves unnoticed; they do not marvel at themselves.[17]

Pilgrims in a Strange Land

> *Like the sun rising in the Lord's heavens, the beauty of a virtuous wife is the radiance of her home.*   — Sirach 26:16[18]

What would we see if we marveled in wonder at ourselves as much as at the rest of nature? The ones who marvel the most are the saints. If we wondered more, might a few more of us have a chance to be numbered among those who marvel in this way? One such was Therese of Lisieux. About her, Kristi's favorite little saint, the biographer Ida Friederike Gorres wrote this: "The hidden holiness that exists in the Church is a story in its own right. There are probably dozens of people like this ... but no one pays them much attention."[19] Therese, the Little Flower, is our model of simplicity and trust in an increasingly agitated world.[20]

I find myself wondering how much in married life Kristi's inner portrait came to resemble her little friend Therese. Kristi, too, was single-hearted. Was Kristi guided in small steps toward being one of those dozens to whom we pay such little attention?

Yes, I think, and this gentleness came from Kristi's very personal devotion to her "Dear Lord" in the Eucharist. And I think now that in late 1986 our pastor, Fr. Ted Sullivan, made this path more possible for Kristi and others. This help came to our St. Mark's Parish when he instituted the devotion of Perpetual Adoration. In this devotion parishioners can return at any time, day or night, to keep watch at least an hour with Him — the full and Real Presence of Christ in the tabernacle. At first Kristi and I selected a Monday afternoon hour near the time we picked up the kids from school. As the family schedule shifted we moved into Monday evening, and then continued this weekly island of reflection and devotion into each following year. Sullivan, who died in 1988, thought that the parish would do well to keep this going for even three years. But as I write, the devotion continues, now in its eighteenth year.

Kristi's friendly spirituality might have been nudged along in yet another way in the spring of 1988 when my uncle Otto on my mother's side passed through Seattle for the first time. (This was still more than a year before Kristi's cancer was detected.) Otto was attending a Lutheran ministry conference at Seattle Pacific University and then planned to visit my parents in eastern Washington. A career parochial school teacher in Dayton, Ohio, he was a late voca-tion to the Lutheran ministry. He was also the most recent vocation in the unbroken string through each generation on my mother's side of the family. This record spans a full seven centuries, the Catholic priesthood at first and then, since the mid-sixteenth century, the Lutheran ministry.

With Otto's white beard and ready smile, we simply and totally enjoyed each other. Otto was very enthusiastic about a new ministry he told us about within the Catholic Church. Contact with this ministry had given him a new peace. What he told us was completely new to us, the "healing of memories." This level of healing surely overlaps any good psychology, but psychology is not the full explanation. This ministry was something he said he encountered during a summer conference conducted in the Midwest at Franciscan University in Steubenville, Ohio.[21]

We also compared thoughts on a more familiar book, the autobiographical *Seven Storey Mountain* by the Trappist monk Thomas Merton. A discussion group on Merton had been part of Otto's path into the ministry. In the late sixties this early work of Merton had absorbed my attention as well. His story was important side reading while I finished the fifth year of an undergraduate program in architecture at the University of Washington.

Our time with Otto was magical. From the moment I picked him up on the street corner and drove him home, we loved each other's company. Kristi's hospitality and banana bread, her genuine presence toward guests, played through the evening. This hospitality would bring us into close contact with several other special people as well throughout our marriage — wayfarers and friends in a strange land. When Kristi sometimes took a good look and wondered if she was "doing enough," part of my answer was to praise her one-on-one special hospitality. There is this from St. Paul: "Look on the needs of the saints as your own; be generous in offering hospitality" (Rom. 12:13).

After three hours we looked about and only then realized that we had never moved beyond the living room. It was now too late to continue, and I had to chauffeur Otto back to his group for the night.

The following year Otto's visit and his contact with the "healing of memories" opened the door for me into a new freedom and peace. His visit was not an accident. Four days after my father's sudden death in October 1988, I received a remarkable peace in *knowing* that he was safe and healed, and that *now* he is filled with inexpressible happiness and an even more boundless devotion to his family. This point of knowing was a gifted and decisive moment and carried me through the grieving and beyond. This knowledge came through the single healing prayer offered by another. It came as a flash of lightning (Matt. 24:27; Luke 17:24) but in a silence without thunder, and will always be with me. It is a peace that in a single instant is His total power and total gentleness, both together, and each within the other. Breslin's words return to me, "I cannot give this [His peace] to you. You must get this from . . . the same One who gave it to me."

It is enough to say here that Kristi also shared in a deepened way a belief in the boundless touch of grace in our lives. *Nothing* is impossible with God. Both of us now understood that prayers for concrete and impossible needs are answered in concrete ways and that one can point with wonder to a certainty larger than any of our questions or our questioning.

The onset of Dad's passing was hinted five years earlier in 1983 when he suffered a moderate stroke. On the following evening I was with my mother in Richland. In the earliest morning hours I woke to find her frightened and wandering the house in the dark. I dressed and sent Mom back to bed with the reassurance that I would visit the hospital and find a way to get into the intensive care unit. Dad was still in rough condition. I sat with him in the dark. He permitted and then appreciated a foot rub to help pass the endless night. We talked as he stared upward, all wired up to the machines.

After perhaps two hours it drifted to this: "Do you believe in God?" I asked. Dad paused at this, and then said, "I suppose." He gestured to his chin, and I thought he meant to reject artistic images of a personified god made in our image and likeness with beard and all.

I looked for words. A Christian message came back from a bulletin board display (actually a magazine quotation from the Koran) from my junior high school years: "To save one person is to save the universe." Surely this wording goes back to Christian roots. Then followed the silence, and against the backdrop of occasional misunderstandings my father asked in the dark for a clear reassurance from his son, "Am I a universe?"

And I said "yes." Yes, each of us can rest in the promise, more vast and personal than natural selection and quantum mechanics, that we are more than an accident.

This was an important time together. It was followed by a few more heart-to-heart chats walking the neighborhood. The last was five years later only a few months before his sudden death. By then all of the workday battering and resentments that can come with working under high stress (on the Hanford Nuclear Reservation) and even with subtle social stratification (imagined or otherwise) had been reduced to uncomplicated forgiveness. He would not have used this word, but he did say to me from his heart, "It doesn't matter any more."

I have always felt myself especially fortunate and graced that I drove to the hospital at three o'clock in the morning in 1983. And that Kristi and I and the kids happened to pass through town in the summer of 1988 for what was to be our last visit. Dad died on October 13, 1988, the afternoon following Kristi's and my fourteenth wedding anniversary. It was over a glass of wine during our anniversary night out that I had mentioned to Kristi how our families were aging — and that "things might change in the coming year."

Our life together with cancer began a short year after Dad died, in late 1989. From this point, Kristi and I and our family were protected through the prayers of our assistant pastor and special friend, Fr. "Thomas" (he asks that I not use his name). It was through his powerful healing prayer the year before at the time of my father's death that my burden of fear for him was lifted most profoundly.

Ten years before we met, at a conference in Dublin, Fr. Thomas had caught the attention of Sister Briege McKenna.[22] At that meeting McKenna sensed and informed Fr. Thomas that he was among those favored to have the healing gift recorded in Scripture. Upon reflection he discovered that, yes, there was a pattern of beneficiaries who had returned to him over the years to say "thank you." As with me, very specific benefits coincided with his intercession for each of them.

This kind of giftedness seems to me to be linked to an unusual degree of openness and dedication to God's will. When His healing works, it is through those who have found a single-heartedness unalloyed by personal desires. The healing involves a willingness to surrender all in order to take up the cross, not for oneself, but for others. Fr. Thomas's devotion to the Eucharist — the banquet and the cross combined — was arresting. In comparison to the Real Presence, he once told us that he would not walk across the street to see the more dramatic and sometimes authentic workings of the Spirit that one often hears about. It was under his guidance in 1990 that Kristi and I began reciting daily a very simple novena to the Holy Spirit and another to St. Therese, always for "complete healing and recovery."

Under Fr. Thomas's guidance at St. Mark's, Kristi joined others who help shut-ins take part in communion. She was one of "Christ's little angels," as he called them. The angels traveled in pairs after Mass to carry the Eucharist to those unable to get out. After Kristi's death, Sharon, Kristi's usual companion, remarked to me, "She had such special contact with each of the rest home people when giving them communion. I just marveled."

In addition to Fr. Thomas, we were blessed with other very special friends, all clearly on their own pilgrim paths to their personal place in eternity. The very unlikely story of one of these began with a phone call that Kristi made in early 1995. Approaching the Lenten season, Kristi thought it might be good to have a three-day retreat at St. Mark's Parish. Such an event would not be worth pursuing unless a visiting retreat master could be found, and this was not likely on so short a notice.

To take the lead in something like this, especially when not asked, was not Kristi's way. But this is what she did. *"Should I see if Fr. Stephen Barham can come?"* Three years earlier we had been impressed with Barham's message and his booming voice and laughter (very amusing to some, and probably just as irritating to others). More round than he was tall, he usually would introduce himself with a rhetorical question: "We are temples of the Holy Spirit. Why bother with a mere church when you can have a basilica!"

The Right Reverend Stephen Barham was a convert from the Assembly of God congregation and explained that he now was an Archimandrite in the Melkite Greek Catholic Order.[23] This is part of the Byzantine Rite Catholic Church, in full union with Rome (our more familiar Roman or Latin Rite), and not to be confused with the culturally similar but separated Orthodox Churches.[24] In his position, Barham was equivalent to an abbot, for example, for a Benedictine monastery.

At the 1992 conference, Barham told of his physical healing — through prayer alone — from medically incurable cancer. This had happened fifteen years earlier. Barham told how he had returned from India with severe intestinal symptoms, dysentery he thought. Back in the United States a complete checkup revealed that it was cancer. The tumor was already fully metastasized throughout his entire abdominal area. Beyond the reach of any treatment and with a prognosis of only six months to live, Barham sought prayer with a prominent evangelist.

As he told it, a few weeks after his diagnosis and during the fourth prayer session, he felt an intense heat passing through his body. He returned to the cancer center and at his insistence the attending physician reluctantly reordered a second full set of diagnostic tests. This time the results were "negative" (meaning clean) on every count. Barham's story of his healing is compelling, although possibly not formally documented with the rigor given to the officially recognized cases at Lourdes.[25] Barham did mention that his investigating physician, driven by his own personal experience with Barham's case, later converted from his agnosticism. As I had learned on the Camas Prairie, this also had been the case with Alexis Carrel, another physician, when he was faced with an earlier patient and similar evidence of a cure at Lourdes.

Barham blamed his cancer on his own tendency toward trying too much to control his own little world: "I gave cancer to myself!" For a while Kristi imagined that this kind of physiological trigger might also apply to us. There was in Kristi a mild rigor toward details and a tendency to internalize. She only wondered at this aloud once, and we knew together that things most usually are not this simple, especially in dealing with the myriad causes of cancer. Breast cancer hits one of every six women.

At the same 1992 conference, where we heard Barham testify to the Spirit for the first time, another speaker, Fr. Louis Camelli, suggested three certain signs to help discern whether it is the Spirit who is working in our lives, or (more likely) whether we are falling into fantasy or deception. First, he said, we are to understand that no circumstance is beyond the touch of the Holy Spirit. Otherwise there is no God. Second, actions of the Holy Spirit in our lives are concrete and specific, not abstract and conceptual (which would be more comfortable to our narrowed and rationalist mind-set). He does truly know us and intervenes concretely in history and in each of our lives. The spiritual and the material are not divorced in the way that we have come to divorce church and state. In a real sense, each person, without exception, *is* such an intervention by God, made in His image and likeness. Are we totally blind to the wonder? From each of us, then, effective prayer is prayer said for the concrete, and from the inside out of our very specific situation, not more safely for generalities. A prayer for only generalities can manifest a lack of trust that there can be gifted answers to our real needs.

And third, we must wait for His concrete action to come in His own time. To a nonbeliever this sounds facile. But we must wait in trust for Him to guide the pieces of our lives and likely the lives of others into His particular answer for all of us. In his remarks, Barham punctuated this third point of confident patience with his immense laugh, "The Lord is never late...but He is never early either!" In this sense of waiting on the Lord, Kristi and I sometimes sensed together a hidden freedom that was larger than our cross and larger than any circumstance. There was, too, the leap involved in knowing that prayers even can be answered retroactively. We can pray with confidence even for what appears to us as a past situation. As past events occur, they still can take a needed shape in anticipation of our later spoken petitions, even before we recognize these needs. God is not bound by our knowledge or our time. In our trust we should not be bounded by our small field of vision. We are human and forced to work in such finite contexts, but this does not apply to His healing.

In all of his evangelization, Barham was always quick to explain that spiritual healing does not diminish real personal responsibility and even guilt. But healing does go beyond "sin" to get at our deeper festering and predispositions. These can be lurking scars that injure our will, intellect, and heart and that lead us to close down toward specific sins. In the healing there can be the letting go of hidden weeds within our souls, perhaps some injury or craving for preemptive self-justification, or perhaps a lingering resentment or even a self-satisfaction, or perhaps an enormous abuse of long ago — all of these obstacles to transparency.

Following his own gifted physical healing, Barham found that for the benefit of others he had received the same gift. This new healing ministry amounted to a new and less convenient calling for Barham. It accounted for his shoestring-budget Apostolate for Catholic Truth and Service and his committed calendar to visit parishes such as ours. Barham was a widely sought witness and speaker. In 1991 he had been the keynote speaker for the First International Congress on Catholic Families in Manila, Philippines.

Kristi wanted this priest to visit our parish for Lent in 1995. By now the reality of special spiritual gifts was something we had come to accept. From the living room I encouraged Kristi to make the call to Barham's number in Fresno, California. What could be the harm in asking? And after a day or two of hesitation Kristi picked up the phone. I heard the give and take of only one side of the phone conversation. After several minutes Kristi emerged from the kitchen with a sweet look of surprise and success.

Barham's secretary had answered, but at first said that his schedule was always booked solid at least six months out. Reservations should be made one full year in advance. Then, this: "Oh, here is a reservation in three weeks that has been canceled. Funny, I didn't notice this before." But then the secretary explained further, "This still is not possible. Fr. Barham is out of the country, in Papua, New Guinea, and he has to approve all reservations. He is out of touch and will not be back in time to approve this."

Then something more: "Oh, wait, let me answer another call," then "You won't believe this, but Fr. Barham is on the other line! He is calling long distance to see if he has any incoming calls." In less than a minute he agreed to visit Seattle and St. Mark's Parish and said he would be with us in three weeks. Yes, Kristi was successful and surprised.

Our pastor at this time, Fr. Ed Norris, was a sinewy six feet three, and at the age of sixty-three could still be seen on early mornings swimming for exercise far into the cold waters of Lake Washington. He avoided the middle of the lake, he explained, for fear of being hit by a boat. During his seminary years he had excelled for over ten years at the high hurdles, and would have appeared as scheduled on the Olympic team for Ireland if his bishop had not caught up with him first. For many years, through Project Rachel, Norris had been active as an understanding ear and counselor to mostly young girls recovering from the lasting trauma of abortion. His heart always went out to these "little darlings," victimized as much by big medicine and misplaced compassion as by themselves or itinerant boyfriends. Victimized is too weak a term. There must be a deeper sense of personal betrayal under duress, sometimes even at the hands of close family members.

Now Norris, too, was suffering from cancer. He had been under a stout chemotherapy treatment for leukemia for several months, but he was still active in his vocation. His long white hair, combed back and now thinned by the treatments, was still largely intact. He teased me as a lector, and a bald one, that soon he might look more like I do. I hoped he might be luckier.

It was about this time that Kristi also organized a simple calendar with rotating lead voices to continue the rosary after daily Mass in the Church. At the end of this fifteen-minute prayer the parishioners who take part now added a perpetual novena prayer for cancer victims such as Norris and many others (this prayer continues to this day). The Novena to St. Peregrine (the cancer saint) for his intercession ends with this: "... that by imitating him and by the help of his prayers, we may believe more fully in Your healing help, bear the suffering of this life without wavering, and come with joy to the peace of heaven." Also about this time, a small Thursday evening prayer gathering with Norris had to be discontinued. Norris no longer had the energy to lead us through the Liturgy of the Hours, and without him it was not the same.

During his less than three years with us, Norris won the hearts and respect of his new parish. Not a great administrator (and this shortcoming can be a virtue!), he was man enough to choose Marian devotion over the more excessive post–Vatican II paperwork. On very special occasions immediately after Mass, he would mount the lectern. Rising to his full stature, from under his snow-covered temples he would boom out in his Irish brogue "Danny Boy." On Mother's Day, it was a ballad to his mother. The parish was always spellbound until he finished, and if there was a dry eye among us, I could not see it.

Norris hesitated before permitting the Barham retreat, but the chancery office had already signaled its okay. He gave his own nod to this possibly controversial Lenten event with a "healer." At the end of the third and final evening retreat Mass, at least five hundred parishioners and visitors came forward for Barham's one-on-one prayers. He prayed beneath his breath, in tongues, with eyes tightly closed in contemplation. Side by side the parishioners and visitors completely encircled the base of the freestanding sanctuary platform, about one hundred at a time.

First in line was our cautious but needful and now willing pastor, the beloved Fr. Ed Norris. Of the several hundred seeking healing *through* Barham on that special evening in St. Mark's, at least four out of every five would drop to the floor. Nothing like this had ever happened at St. Mark's. Norris, the first in line, was visibly affected, but remained standing. As Barham turned away toward others, the three immediately beside Norris fell back at once and hit the floor. Recruited as a catcher for the first time, I had a close look at what was happening. There might be a few attention seekers, but four hundred? So many times I noticed a subtlety in the prayer encounter. There was the consent to be receptive as Barham faced each of them, often without any touch at all. In so many cases a very light but distinct twitch signaled something special and mysterious as the person involved was released and then tilted backwards *completely* relaxed. Many remained motionless on the floor for several minutes, some even longer.

Kristi was among those who slipped to the floor in "dormition" (1 Cor. 12:4–12). It was five or six minutes before she awoke with her angelic smile. This happened frequently enough at later healing Masses. I always positioned myself to be the one to catch my Kristi and ease her down. I became accustomed to sitting beside her and simply waited for my bride to wake up. It was always with the same modest smile.

In late 1993, a little over a year before Barham's visit, Kristi had experienced dormition for the first time, but this was with other family members. When she returned to Seattle at the end of the weekend in Spokane, she told me about this. I did hear her words, but could not fully get it at the time. So Kristi did not really tell me everything. One of those present had claimed to receive a "word of knowledge" about Kristi: "Kristi is a flower that the Lord is pleased to crush." I heard of this particular comment or message (termed a "locution") only indirectly and after Kristi's death nine years later.

What kind of Lord is this? But then: "For whom the Lord loves, he chastises; and he scourges every son whom he receives" (Heb. 12:6). We are consoled to know that the Lord chastises those whom He loves, and I see now that Kristi was so chosen. My crushed flower.

In the Catholic Church our understanding of dormition differs from the fundamentalist Protestant notion of being "slain in the Spirit." For us, from the beginning as we read in Scripture, the event is seen as a very simple hug and a resting in the Spirit. The Holy Spirit first formed His gathering of followers at Pentecost fifty days after the resurrection. Christ is the one thing entirely new under the sun within our shared earthly history. We do not wait for something more. In the indwelling we find the ragged-edge appearance of eternity and power into space and time, and the historical beginning of the Church. The same grace of Pentecost is received now through the sacraments instituted and sustained by the resurrected Christ and passed from His hands by the acting of the same Spirit. The human hands we see in the consecration and at the Mass today are those of His "unworthy servants," dedicated and ordained to this *service* by the unbroken laying on of hands in ordination. This is not possessiveness; rather, it is totally the opposite.

Within the Church, any additional and special experience of the Holy Spirit, such as dormition, is understood as simply activating or strengthening a grace already received sacramentally, communally, and equally by all at baptism and confirmation. Dormition is a call to witness this new life of the Church as a whole. It is not a singling out for personal merit or attention. Barham commented that dormition touches some on a given day, and not others, and most never. In this sense it means almost nothing. No significance is to be attached to this. Besides, he counseled, "Seek the Healer, not the healing! And know that you are already healed two thousand years ago — by His stripes we are (already) healed. Do not beg for healing as if it is withheld and still to be done. Claim even now a piece of the resurrection!"

The working of grace remains a mystery to our finite minds. The Spirit is a mystery, or better, *the* Mystery, and He blows where He will.

At the end of our special Lenten evening with Barham, I was responsible for emptying and locking the church. Turning to the front doors I found that a middle-aged couple from a city thirty miles to the south had entered. As the last of the crowd left, they stood together under the dimmed entry lights. They stopped Barham and thanked him for prayers offered for them during a visit five years earlier. In a single evening, his prayers had totally reversed a long path of alcohol addiction and abuse within their family. I heard them say that there had been not even one relapse in the entire five years that followed.[26]

Like the tenth healed leper in Christ's time, even now there are at least some who return to give thanks. Some remember and are astounded enough to show gratitude. Of the others, maybe it really is ingratitude, or possibly it is resentment on the morning after that asks why we should be thankful for what was rightfully ours all along. We become dull and ungrateful. And maybe it is a form of inertia and disbelief, as if nothing that happens to us is so real as to merit real engagement of any kind, least of all gratitude. The failure to return gratitude — at its root is this our inability to sustain amazement? Is it an inability to see with the eyes of the heart, and in this way to be like little children?

As part of his short stay in Seattle, Barham was a dinner guest at our home. He said that any healing passing through his hands also leads him. This guidance comes in small steps, each step inviting and requiring a response. He was one of us. As with the rest of us, the unveiling of our real need comes in layers, in small steps, and only then is the very particular contact with the Spirit sometimes able to get through to us. Barham mused that he must give his own "yes" at each step if only to see what the next step might be. Respectful love from even the Divine Physician guides and responds only in a freedom that is a mutual belonging, and even nuptial. This is our docile and created freedom being invited and drawn toward uncreated and infinite freedom. This is healing far beneath the surface. Beneath one's own failings and hesitations, and the failings of others toward us, is a personal worthiness to be unwrapped and discovered. Our deepest worthiness is our truest selves, but comes from beyond ourselves. There is a healing. And yet, Barham asked, "Pray for me . . . those who are placed in the service of this gift are sometimes inclined to doubt even more."

The morning of Barham's departure we picked him up at his waterfront motel. At almost the last minute, and at our hurried invitation, one of Kristi's friends met us there. There was just time enough in the lobby (!) for Barham to enter within himself and to pray over her. She was scheduled for a biopsy the following day to see whether a recently found lump was malignant or benign. During the prayer a visual image occurred in her mind (and, she said, it possibly resembled a lump) and then diminished in size and disappeared. We were to learn the following week that the biopsy was not performed because the lump, confirmed in earlier tests, could no longer be found (and has not returned in the following ten years).

At the airport we waited together, Barham and Kristi and me. Over a snack breakfast he added something about the healings in biblical times and recorded by St. Luke in the Acts of the Apostles:

Biblical healing did not occur simply to validate the teachings in the Gospel, and then end.[27] Rather, He lives! He intervenes even now. Rationalist priests are always dumbfounded when they see this Life acting in their own parishes today. They are influenced too much by the excesses of historical criticism, and have read too much of the rationalist Harnack (who in the nineteenth century, and like the Jesus Seminar today, sought the historic Christ stripped of his miracles) and even parts of the Catholic biblical expert Fr. Raymond Brown.

Carried too far, historical criticism decapitates the presence Who surrounds us on all sides even today, and Who even lives within His Church, and Who from within is the Soul of our souls.[28] Barham also mentioned that from his studies, it was clear that the three "kings" in the Christmas story (a misnomer for three wise men) really did search for a Messiah. He suggested that even the Isis resurrection myth of Egypt might have been a corruption of the original and earlier Hebrew prophecy. Some evidence exists that even Plato, with his theory of transcendent ideas that free us from materialism, was actually keying off his own hearing of the older Hebrew revelation "I am who am."[29]

This was a fascinating conversation. These insights lift the veil and reassure us that revelation is not simply one of several equivalent myths, but as C. S. Lewis discovered, "the heart of Christianity is a myth which is also a fact."[30] We paused and wondered together. I asked, what might have been the course of history if as a young man Muhammad had been taught differently about Christ? What might have happened if he had heard from an orthodox Christian about Trinitarian Christianity, rather than from a Nestorian about a more terrestrial Christ?[31] Christ as both God and Man, fully both, and less confined by our human minds, would not have been flattened so easily into the sequence of prophets lengthened forward by Muhammad toward himself as the last in the line: "There is no God but Allah, and Muhammad is his prophet."

If Christ is not divine, then his suffering has no meaning above the historical moment. And if he is only divine and not Man, then our own suffering is not transformed and remains only a private torment.[32] The God of all monotheism (Christian, Jewish, Islamic) is revealed in Christ to have an *inner* life that we call Trinitarian, and that by adoption incorporates ourselves as well — if we will it and if in our given freedom we live and act within the truth of His freedom. This action is most put to the test when we are weakest, as when we are called to surrender to terminal illness as the mysterious path permitted by Him to some of us.

How rich we were, Kristi and I, as her hospitality extended to Otto, and then to Thomas, and now to Barham. Another acquaintance, extending over ten or fifteen years into the late 1990s, was a continental intellectual from Austria. This was Dr. Erik von Kuehnelt-Leddihn, a scholar and linguist. He was not a houseguest, but regularly visited Seattle on speaking tours. Kristi's father had read some of his work and even had written to him on one occasion. At the kitchen table in the late seventies, Dr. Orr had showed me the carefully saved handwritten letter he received in return.

During his 1998 visit to Seattle, Erik reported having been a recent guest at a gathering of Islamic scholars in Muscat, Oman, on the Arabian Sea. Without advance notice, they turned to him and asked his opinion, as an outsider, why the Islamic world was barely the shadow of its former self. At one time the Muslim world had been so superior in so many ways — philosophy (as evidenced by the translation and transmittal of Aristotle to St. Thomas Aquinas in twelfth-century Paris), medicine, astronomy, and mathematics. Why had the Muslim world been eclipsed in recent centuries?

Erik could have pointed to social and economic reasons. He might have noted the breakthrough in the West, so far missed in Islam, that allowed parallel and more open explorations into both faith and reason, and then more distinct paths (but now fatefully divorced paths) of a waning religious culture and a system of increasingly brittle secular states.

Pointing deeper, Erik announced to the poised and crowded hall, "It is because you do not respect your women." He felt that personal growth and cultural creativity depend upon each other, and on a primary sense of relationship with others. And, especially as in any marriage, they depend upon self-transcendence and forgiveness. Erik knew that where this engagement fails at the personal level, cultures, also grow stale. In his mind, the transcendent human person was equally the key to families, cultures and civilizations. The world's problems were traceable, ultimately, more to theological errors than to secular miscalculations. We in the West might also take this message very much to heart as we look back on our own disfigured cultural history and trends today, especially including the expanding export of Hollywood pornography.

For Erik, the French Revolution was a distinct watershed. With the full rupture of faith and reason in the streets of Paris, ongoing martyrdom or slaughter of the human person to ideology was assured. To him, Auschwitz, the Gulag, and the concentration camps of Pol Pot (a Sorbonne graduate) are all cut more or less from the same cloth as the Revolution of 1789. Even World War II, he said, was best understood as a collision between offspring of the Revolution: Fascism, Socialism, and Communism. In 1988 Erik passionately reported the words of the French delegate to the new European Parliament. The delegate implored the Assembly to not celebrate the bicentennial of the French Revolution in 1989, because (quoted Erik) "It had been not only a sanguinary orgy but, in addition, bears co-responsibility for the Russian and German revolutions in 1917 and 1933 respectively."

Beneath his critique of the political left, and beneath even his conservatism, Erik was more than a "conservative." Eyebrows lifted when in a single sentence he described himself at once as a "rationalist, monarchist, liberal, and anarchist," all this without any sense of contradiction. The folly of modern-day conservatives, too, he would point out, is the notion that reason alone is enough.

As a working approach to the human person, he favored mixed government. And, quite out of step with nation-state democracies, each with a single identity and fully armed, he advocated a more central European experience — *multi*-national states (housing our differences under a roof that is shared). On this practical side, Erik thought the solution to the riddle of governance in an imperfect world was qualified mediators (historically, monarchs as coordinators) over democratic collectives, parties, and post–World War I nation-states. He deplored and feared the tendency toward populist amateurs who now have "more power than 125 Genghis Khans!" He resented the destruction of the monarchical option at Versailles, all in a Wilsonian quest to "make the world safe for [only?] democracy" in one or two forms.

Erik's political critique, he explained, was human and therefore was based ultimately in theology rather than sociology or even philosophy. Erik's thinking traced back far before our side trip into the Enlightenment and the Revolution and their unprecedented consequences in the twentieth century, "the most barbaric century in all of history." He never wavered from an early thesis validated in our own time: "Indeed, there is no 'compelling argument' not to slit anybody's throat except the Commandments given on Mount Sinai."[33] Erik also was fond of quoting Dostoyevski, "If there is no God, everything is permitted."

Even his early works were in full agreement with the premise developed later in John Paul II's encyclical letter in 1993 on moral theology. Here John Paul II reminds us, and teaches, that authentic human freedom is not the flat-earth license to calculate and manipulate, that it is instead freedom *for* the truth about oneself and God.[34] The common good is not simply the total of all special interests. When quizzed by a small Seattle audience in 1998, Erik surprised many by clearly supporting the emerging European Union.[35] But, he added, "The Union needs a mission; we need a task before us ... not simply fatness defending itself!"

We can speculate on this point. If the Union walks away from its Christian roots, attaching itself to only the classical heritage of Greece and Rome, then on the big stage we should notice this divorce. We might see this denial in combination with an eventual and separate reunion on a different level of the Catholic and Orthodox Churches, a goal of the Second Vatican Council. The European Union, as a secular political collage, would straddle the Western border of *this* future and deeper communion from one thousand years before the Reformation and the blip in history of nation-states and state-dominated religions and finally secular and predominantly economic fabrications. The pattern of the past five hundred years — smaller secular nation-states with their domesticated national religions as departments of state — would be (as we say) history. Is modernity obsolete?

The New Springtime of the human spirit will come when we reconnect to the prepolitical depths of presence to one another, one people at a time, and one person at a time, as in marriage. This stirring will again elevate human dignity to a waiting splendor that we can barely remember. Whatever the political map, the reunion of persons is not a throwback. It is a mutual witness to the full dimension, from within, of the physical and spiritual "person." The person is not merely a subjective and subjugated individual.

For his part, Erik's thinking was original and complex, and a topic of frequent prairie conversations. At root, it was partly a defense of fatherhood. And in this it was also a defense of woman and of the right of children to their childhood.

Kristi's particular liking to his talks in Seattle probably came from his attention to the pivotal role in the West of the Revolution in France and to his attention to real people. In a few phrases, such maligned figures as Marie Antoinette and her young son are brought to life before they are put to death. All of this deepened even more Kristi's appreciation for having lived and studied for a year and a half in Paris.

During all of the nineties, the years of Thomas, Barham, and Erik, Kristi and I could be found at "charismatic" Masses. These are Masses open in a deliberate way to the healing that is always available at any Mass. We shared a growing freedom that in our better moments it is possible to pray as if it mattered. And we can do this with an unlimited confidence of being heard. Such prayers are answered. On one such occasion, in January 1997, it struck me to place myself in proxy for a cousin in southern Oregon. After six weeks, she still remained in a deep coma following a crippling and nearly fatal traffic accident. It was on this same day, perhaps even at the same hour, that the coma simply lifted. There is always the possibility of coincidence, but a Christian has no right to attribute everything to coincidence!

Spring of the same year found us at a Marian conference across the state in Spokane. As we tidied up to join the morning session it was already clear that something serious and medically wrong was happening to Kristi. A drilling headache was the primary symptom: *"It feels like nails are being hammered into my right eye."* We knew nothing then of shingles and the critical need to diagnose and treat it in the first twenty-four hours. Kristi was set on hearing the opening session and dismissed my urging to visit (yet another) emergency room. By this time our first bout with cancer was eight years behind us.

During the first intermission, a woman unknown to either of us approached from the upper bleachers. On the cleared main floor she faced us across the emptied next row of folding chairs: "I do not know what this means, but Mary says that you will. She has given me a message for you: 'Thank you for coming to me during this, your time of thorns, and (you can) know that the fragrance is as sweet as the fresh summer grasses.'"

Did this mean anything to us? Kristi thanked the woman for having the thoughtfulness to risk sharing something a bit strange with total strangers. The shingles was truly a "time of thorns," and in some mysterious way, as with all human suffering, this was a real participation in Christ's crown of thorns. We both had arrived at the point of knowing dimly that all human suffering takes part in the actual suffering of the one Christ, and that each step in our path is in His footsteps. The very special communication from Mary was *"too personal"* Kristi told me, and she asked me to keep it between us. I marvel at her simple *"Thank you"* and modest reserve over such a gifted (and equally crucified) moment.

For those so afflicted and so gifted, might it be an embarrassment at being so selectively gifted to suffer with Him? But who would appreciate or believe it? It must surely be that heaven itself is also an intimately personal and total fulfillment. We read that Christ, when he performed His miracles, often urged the chosen to tell no one. (Theologians tell us the reason was to ensure that the transfiguration and the crucifixion would not be separated in our minds.) There is a difference between enthusiasm and faith. More than a call for secrecy, this modesty of the sublime might also be an encouragement to simply treasure these moments of personal transparency and healing in an enlarged heart within. The soul is larger than the world, and it is sometimes quite enough to remain silent.

From the series of charismatic Masses, a sweet memory returns to me now. This was another one of those times when I was sitting beside my reclining wife on the floor, alongside several others who were also in dormition. Kristi had hesitated at first to go forward. *"Isn't that silly,"* Kristi remarked upon waking, *"I was worried about my wig falling off."* While we never really regarded ourselves as charismatic, there was not much room in Kristi for fakery there. Looking back on our entire marriage I can add with total confidence that Kristi was incapable of telling a fib. She did not know how to do it.

There was yet another close friend, another pilgrim in a strange land. For all of our married life we knew him, and he was charismatic. But at the same time, he was so ordinary and domestic, for example, in his enjoyment of afternoon tea and good food: "There are many ways to fast besides passing up good food, or at least I hope this is so." His inner peace simply went out to others. This was Fr. Joseph ("Jack") Fulton. Fulton's affection for steam trains and for trolleys was legendary. His father, who died when Jack was only two, was a prominent structural engineer in New York, and Fulton's family tree this side of the Atlantic traced back to Robert Fulton himself and even into the early 1700s.

I first met Fulton when I arrived at the University of Washington in 1962. He was a refreshing counterpoint to some of what I found on campus. As a freshman I was overly distracted by the darkness I found in such writings as Thomas Hobbes's *Leviathan* and Jean Jacques Rousseau's *Social Contract*. Their general message was that the transcendent person is at best an individualized bundle of tendencies making the best of it within the larger flux of history.

Yes, a society can be constructed from theories with our bestial tendencies held in check by either the hammer or consensus. In academia in the sixties a new radicalism mingled with the established influence of a more cerebral brute stalking on all fours — Jean Jacques Rousseau, Charles Darwin, Sigmund Freud, and Karl Marx. In our declining post-Christian era, the riddle of human life seems to be reduced once again to the politics of romantic collectivism, biology, consumer appetites, or simply power. In an introductory psychology class an aging professor pondered aloud to a room crowded with unsuspecting underclassmen, "Each of us is a chemical sack worth not more than ninety-eight cents on the open market." As often as we suffered this refrain I hoped it was meant only to be provocative, but was never quite sure. The class was too large to admit to any discussion, and I usually arrived late in the back row. Back at student housing I listened in on a midnight argument between two night owl students on this same theme. Larger than the argument, there was something consoling in the finality of a firm self-assertion, "Okay, *your* thoughts may be nothing more than electronic impulses, but I know that in *me* there is more than this!"

During the ten-minute bells between classes I sometimes had a long run across brick walkways from one lofty podium to the next. On one afternoon I rushed from the psychology class to another in political science. Arriving at the second door, I nearly crashed into an exiting professor of anthropology. In his hands he carried an open box at chest level. Here I was, a ninety-eight cent agitated bag of chemicals suddenly staring face to face into a lecture prop — the cranial ridge and vacant eye sockets of a gorilla skull. I was a speechless as the gorilla. The moment in the back alley at the age of ten returned to me — hollowness with eyes. It all fit together in a distorted way — the artificial English Tudor architectural façade concealing a spiritual vacuum in at least of few of the classrooms, and the rush from one fragmented and tax-funded academic specialization to another.

My bookish turmoil was calmed at least once each week by simply sitting for a few minutes in the presence of the peace-filled man Fr. Fulton.[36] The opportunity was his Monday night Bible studies at the Newman Center[37] at the north edge of campus. Fulton's worn black briefcase usually carried at least three versions of the Bible: Douay-Rheims, King James, and the original Greek New Testament. In his personal testimony he told how he had converted in his early twenties from devout scriptural Methodism to the religion of the Real Presence. The lead-in for this redirection extended over several years. His curiosity began during his early teens after he moved to Seattle from his beloved Brooklyn.

At the age of thirteen, in 1925, Fulton sneaked for the first time into Blessed Sacrament Church one mile north of campus. The Seattle church, a monumental brick design, is regarded as the finest example of Gothic revival west of the Mississippi River. As part of the neighborhood, this rising structure gathers together the low-slung single family homes in a manner compared by many to Chartres in France. This design quality has survived completion of the new freeway in the early sixties, which eliminated one fourth of the parish neighborhood and homes. The single steeple at the southeast corner was still under construction and it was this that first caught Fulton's eye. In his autobiography Fulton writes how intrigued he was then by the mixture side by side of people in suits and in work clothes, all attentive to something outside of themselves that was going on at the altar.[38]

During his undergraduate years he and a few respected scholars on campus, including a professor or two, were a part of what could be called a "mini–Oxford Movement."[39] This enlightenment yielded a scandalous conversion here and there, including Fulton's. Professor Herbert Cory, one of his mentoring professors in classics, published his story in his learned *Enlightenment of a Freethinker.*[40] He concludes and summarizes with a selection from Francis Thompson's "Hound of Heaven." Fulton graduated from the university in classics in 1934 with the top student honor, the President's Medalist award. One year later, Cory and his wife, Mary, were sponsors for Fulton's baptism into the Catholic Church.

I sometimes escorted Fulton on his mile walk from the church to the Newman Center next to the campus. On one of these journeys he opened my eyes in a new way. It was an offhanded remark, "Oh look, Peter, at the flowers. Every flower is a symbol of God's great love for each of us." Looking down I noticed tiny flowers in one of the small terraced rock gardens so common in Seattle. We usually walk by such insignificance as we rush along from one arbitrary place to another. But this time the world receded for a moment as a setting for these flowers alone, these gentle witnesses. Of course they were purple. Fulton's favorite color was purple, the color of penitence overcome by mercy and trust.

This was my first really deep appreciation of living symbolic vision. Not mere biology or even landscape design, but symbols pointing through and beyond themselves to a groundedness Who is inexhaustible and unconditional generosity and giftedness. In this instant I discovered that while there are things to be known by investigation, there are also different ways of knowing. The human mind and heart are made to be more than a receptacle for physical discoveries filtered at arm's length through outward measurement and the scientific method.

Fulton was gifted with this symbolic vision, this ability to see not only with the eyes, but *through* the eyes. It must have been on this walk that Fulton also looked ahead and remarked, "Peter, you must remember that when I die, I want to be buried in white, because that will be the day of my homecoming." And then, "All of my life has been a waiting to see my father." (Fulton's natural father died when Jack was only two.) Fulton was so approachable and yet seemed to be delightfully from outside of our time and place. Within him was a special, indefinable inner light and freedom. And as for the rock garden — if we do not give Him honor, "the stones will cry out!" (Luke 19:40).

During my navy years after graduation, Fulton sometimes wrote, and on one small card was this: "Blessed Sacrament Church is still full of young people. I love them all and hope they will find some peace and joy and real experience of God." And later, in 1974, in his wedding card to Kristi and me, he added, "May you shine with the beauty of the Lord through all your life together." We continued to keep in touch. After our wedding our first home was an upstairs apartment in the University District, across the street from the back of Fulton's Blessed Sacrament Church. Throughout all of our married life Kristi and I frequented Fulton's parish, often for the Saturday afternoon sacrament of confession. The peace of these visits was always visible on Kristi's face, increasingly in the later years. And as they were growing up, Laura and Mark always joined us in this family tradition.

Blessed Sacrament Church, Seattle, Washington. "Blessed Sacrament Church is still full of young people."

From time to time we invited Fulton for dinner. His earliest visit was late in 1974 when he joined us as a couple for our first Christmas. He found his chair and gave one of his famous readings of Charles Dickens's *Christmas Carol.* Even while in the seminary in the Bay area in the thirties, Fulton had been on the air weekly as a reader for the local Dickensian Society. But his favorite novelist was Sir Walter Scott, and in 1982 he visited Scotland to mark the 150th Anniversary of Scott's death. With his delightful and trusting manner, within two weeks he was on (Presbyterian) Scotland's national television to give his personal testimony of faith. He mentioned the Sunday afternoon food kitchen set up in the basement of Blessed Sacrament (this continues). Wherever Fulton went he touched large numbers of people with a kindness that did not come from him alone.

Once in the early nineties we invited Fulton to pray in tongues at our dinner table, and he did. The belief is that this kind of prayer is a direct joy of the soul and that it bypasses translation into our languages: "For we do not know what we should pray for as we ought, but the Spirit himself pleads for us with unutterable groanings"(Rom. 8:26). As to what his groanings meant, Fulton said he did not know: "The interpretation of tongues is given to others." Within the Spirit we are persons, but no longer separate.

On two or three special occasions Kristi prepared a simple lunch instead of dinner, and then Fulton and I would prowl through old bookstores, in his words "looking for treasures." Missing from his impressive Scott collection were only the biography of Napoleon and a book of poems. I kept my eyes open over the years. In 1985 I found an early two-volume edition of the *Life of Napoleon Buonaparte* by "the Author of Waverly." Published in 1832 (the spelling is a publisher error), this find was marked down and still within my price range. Mark and Laura each presented him with a wonderfully yellowed and crisp volume. Kristi listened from the kitchen as she put the finishing touches on another special dinner. Fulton drew the two volumes to his heart and, with crossed arms and eyes lifted upward and closed, he announced, "Now I can die and go to heaven!"

In the summer of 1995 Fulton joined us for dinner again, this time with Kristi's visiting parents. It was a profoundly peaceful evening, after which Fulton simply announced, "Mary has been here with us this evening." He did not mean this to be taken in any way other than literally.

In November 1997 Fulton was hospitalized for a short period, and at his advancing age he never fully recovered. From his bed he gave part of his published testimony to me orally, one-on-one.

Nearly thirty years earlier, Fulton had been changed suddenly. At one point in an annual luncheon with a group of evangelicals, he found himself giving a small group report to the entire assembly. As he recounted it to me:

> I do not know what happened. Everyone rose up clapping after I spoke. I was changed in four ways. I found that I loved *everyone*, without exception. And then I found that Jesus is *within* me. Christ is only his title; Jesus is His name. Third, I knew that the resurrection is *real*. And fourth, the *power* of the Holy Spirit filled me, and I could see that rather than a record, it [Scripture] was a message . . . to me. I could see with St. Paul that all of it is true, for me. Looking at each line, I knew that, why yes, this is how it is, and that that [line] too, is really true.

Fulton often spoke in wonder and delight of a special Scripture passage he had too easily dismissed during his entire lifetime of study: "For our Gospel was not delivered to you in word only, *but in power also,* and in the Holy Spirit" (1 Thess. 1:5). "It's true — it's really true!" he would announce of the incarnation and the resurrection, with full conviction, with a wonder both seasoned and childlike, and with a radiant joy. By now he was eighty-five (and as an aside, since his pastoral assignment in 1965 he had discontinued doctoral work on his favorite Greek poet, Pindar).

Still visiting in his hospital room, I mentioned the biblical gift of physical healing, and Barham's cancer experience more than fifteen years before. From his bed Fulton held out and inspected his own outstretched hands. "To think," he wondered, "that I might heal others with these hands!" He was amazed and open to this wonder too. A second or two passed, and then a very contented conclusion: "Ah, but that is not my gift; my gift is that I love *everyone*." Fulton was in person what political sensitivity only pretends to be.

In February 1998 a weakening Fulton called while I was still at work, and Kristi picked up the phone, "Can Peter visit me? I need him." We had a quick dinner and I was with Fulton that same evening. I found a seat in his makeshift new room on the ground floor of the priory of Blessed Sacrament Church. He could no longer climb steps. We talked and laughed a little at his calendar of cats. He prayed with me for Kristi. On December 12, the Feast of Our Lady of Guadalupe, he died suddenly. I remember that his hooded Dominican burial gown was black, but it did cover a white inner robe.

In the spring of 1999 I retrieved Fulton's unmarked and discarded family photo album at a parish rummage sale. I had been guided, it seemed, to this obscure Saturday morning nonevent for this very purpose. Rescued at the price of ten dollars, this album was treasured as a relic in our home for nearly three years. Here were the original sepia photographs of Fulton's dear mother, of his father who died two years after Fulton was born, and of the beloved brownstone childhood home in Brooklyn. Also his 1934 university diploma and collectibles from his later ordination into the Dominican priesthood in California. After these three years, and shortly after Kristi's death, I was introduced to Fr. "Gus" Hartman, the regional archivist for the Dominican Order. By then I was able to part with this irreplaceable record — to hand it on. I felt the confidence that my role in recovering the album was complete.

Always exceptionally ecumenical in spirit, Fulton said that in converting he did not leave behind what he had had as a devout Protestant. He often said that he found it fulfilled in the Real Presence, in the Mass, and in the tabernacle of his new spiritual home. Fulton was devoted intimately to Our Lord fully present in the Eucharist, the Blessed Sacrament. It was this more than anything else that attracted him as a teenager to the Gothic church tower rising

in north Seattle. It was this that brought him fully into the Church
and that gave to him the peace that so consistently passed through
him to so many others of all faiths.

Another happy coincidence...Fulton directly influenced the
Seattle oncologist who was to be such a strength and guide for
Kristi and me for over a decade beginning with Kristi's first cancer
operation in late 1989. During our many visits over the years with
Dr. Doug Lee, he usually found time to close his office door for
a few minutes. As a person, not as a medical specialist, he prayed
humbly with us to the "Divine Physician." We followed with him:
"...that You heal your devoted Kristi, either with the medication,
or around it." When asked, he told us that he and other doctors
in the Seattle area, mostly Protestant like himself, had learned from
Fulton how to pray in a very special way with any patients who
might be receptive.

From others, also during the nineties, we learned more of the
power recommended to us, "...If two of you shall agree on earth
about anything at all for which they ask, it shall be done for them by
my Father in heaven" (Matt. 18:19). The number two, rather than
one, ensures that prayer is free of self-absorption. It is necessary to
let go, even at the imagined risk of personal embarrassment. There
is the need for this degree of inner silence and real inner trust. This
self-abandonment *is* the prayer. The fact that there are two or more
provides the mysterious and needed entry point for the incarnate
Christ himself to be present, extending to us the intimacy which is
the triune God — one God in three "persons," Father, Son (now
"like us in all things but sin"), and Holy Spirit.

The year after Fulton died, in the autumn of 1999, we visited the
Camas Prairie once again. Time permitted a special family outing
into a new piece of back country. In three cars the extended family
made its way south and across the Salmon River canyon a few miles

downstream from where Lewis and Clark labeled this the River of No Return. A road without guardrails wound its way up the south wall to the remote plateau shown on the map as Joseph Plain in the Wilderness Area and distantly visible from the Orr kitchen window. I had heard the name for twenty years, but had never made the trip. The few inhabitants, tucked away here and there, are local legends of self-sufficiency. On this single drive, we counted at least two dozen deer.

I treasure and marvel now at the memory of Kristi as she was at the clearing we selected, sitting on a fallen pine log beside her twin sister. As they sat together, so close, so relaxed in quiet conversation, Kristi turned and called gently to me: *"Peter,"* with such a sweet and expectant smile. *"Look at the sun!"* Over their heads to the southwest, the afternoon sun was still bright. I guarded my eyes, but Kristi turned and simply continued to face the sun directly. *"It's dancing,"* she said. Later I was given more of a description. The sun appeared *"with a suspended host in front, and pulsing."*

Without injury to her eyes, Kristi might have actually seen something a bit similar to the event predicted and then reported at Fatima, Portugal, on October 13, 1917. Do such things happen even now? The Fatima event was witnessed in varying degrees by some seventy thousand people and was prominently covered in the local secular press. (The reporting *Daily News* had the largest newspaper circulation in Portugal at the time.) The vision at Fatima came in the last of a series of apparitions of Mary to three peasant children. On this occasion she spoke of the need for prayer and conversion, and she warned of the consequences of the atheistic Communist Revolution in faraway Russia, an event that had not yet taken place. Mysteries we do not understand, but I know that on that afternoon (August 15, the Feast of the Assumption) Kristi was delightfully happy for an unnatural period, looking into the sun.

Courting the Courts

> *Each family is a beacon of light which must illumine the Church*
> *and the world for the end of this millennium and as long as the*
> *Lord allows this world to exist.*   — John Paul II[41]

Another light memory comes to me now from a bit earlier at our
Seattle dinner table. Kristi was particularly troubled by theological
turbulence within the Church that she loved so much. This was
still a year or two before the wide publicity on sexual abuse and
mismanagement (in 2002), especially within much of the Church in
the United States.

Efforts now to tar all of the hierarchy with the same brush, even
within the Church, would have distressed my wife greatly. *"And
if these things bother me so much,"* she wondered of earlier tension
points, *"think how it is for them* [the large majority of clergy who are
faithful]." And then, *"I am just* [searching for words] *. . . a plum, just a
little peewee!"* This endearing self-evaluation did not drop unnoticed.
How accurate and simple: "Peewee plum." Sweet and humble, a
most dear wife in so many ways, my treasure. (She was also quite
capable of making me squirm when I needed it.)

Mingled with this lightness of heart was a remarkable presence
between Kristi and her unseen friends. At the table, a recurring
prayer for others was that "Mary will wrap her mantle over the
shoulders" of someone or other Kristi might name. Sometimes she
mentioned that she had asked angels to go to the assistance of one
family member or another. She recognized spiritual powers greater
than the human mind. And there was the certainty more solid than
the floor under our feet that these petitions were heard. Kristi found
names for our angel guardians (as we also should *name* the unborn),
and there was no doubt in her mind that this particularity was also
accurate. Most memorable in retrospect was the familiarity in all of

this between Kristi and her friends, spirits unseen and yet touching the world of the ordinary at our kitchen table.

This nickname "peewee" stuck for a while on a note card or two. On Kristi's fifty-first (and next-to-last) birthday, this whimsical e-mail arrived from my office to her at home:

> My little peewee, My plum,
> My traveling companion on the road of life;
> The other half of my self, my better half,
> My sainted wife . . . Happy Birthday.

Kristi, in her careful humility, was so reluctant to judge others. Overly reluctant, I sometimes thought, and this could be a point of passing friction. I think she must have learned earlier and well the falsehood of some of her own first impressions, and she remembered. We sometimes disagreed on the fine line between "judgment" of the heart, which is to be avoided, and simply noticing the obvious actions of others. "It is not judgment to simply see the obvious," I would say, a bit perturbed. But I did not fully appreciate the depth of what was sometimes going on there. I think now that one could ask which is the greater fault, consistent gentleness toward others, although not fine-tuned enough, *or* more self-satisfied wit combined with a more flippant disposition? This question answers itself.

As husbands especially, we often need reminding to think twice about feminine "irrationality." Georges Bernanos captures something that all young couples might ponder together to their benefit. He says that "when women talk they talk to each other, but when men talk they talk about what they talk about." Great potential, there, for charged misunderstandings. Or, as a newlywed friend once summarized to me: "*It* wouldn't matter so much to me, if *it* didn't matter so little to her. . . ." On our wedding day the oldest couple at the reception and on the prairie had shown us this mysterious tangling together of respect and disrespect with the seemingly little things. Their words again: "In marriage it is the little things that matter."

On judging others, Kristi would simply smile, calmly aware of how passing curiosity can be already a participation in something that is either untrue or unjust. For her, insignificant remarks often touched a deep chord. At the least, our willing ear amplifies in a way what usually is not necessary to hear. The itching ear is so often wired to a larger will to put things in their place, the will to dominate at least a little, if only within our minds. Kristi's manner was instinctively to have no ears for the random comment.

What did others sometimes think of Kristi's manner? During our last year together she once wondered aloud about this. She rose from our kitchen table, *"How can they know what is in my heart?"* I did not ask what this was about, but there was a barb from something recent. Do unto others. . . . From Kristi it was often *"Peter, we must pray for . . . ,"* and I would be informed who was on her mind. The selection was sometimes quite direct or simple, perhaps people carried daily into all of our homes by a probing and even voyeuristic news report. At other times it was a public figure or a notorious entertainer whom she had "spiritually adopted" for a prayer or two or sometimes much longer.

Kristi's habit of silent restraint especially included an occasional prayer for all priests. But if she had not been retrieved from this veil of tears when she was, Kristi would not have minimized the current sexual abuse scandal (the molestation of mostly older boys by some who have been ordained into the priesthood). She would have been most troubled by the lifelong damage to all of the direct victims and others — including the Church itself, which also has been invaded in a way.[42] Were Kristi still with me, we would need to take a walk or two through the forested neighborhood.

Part of the broader story, we read, is neglect in the Church and its schools to clearly teach, in season and out of season, the moral dynamic or "natural law" found within each of us.[43] Even in 1971 the sweep of future events (much wider than the scandal) was apparent. "The present moment of history, with all its challenges...is not the time to forget the primacy of life or the supremacy of the person...What fundamentally distinguishes 'perversion' — as homosexuality, lesbianism, and bestiality — from bisexual relationship is precisely its fundamental lack of relationship to the transmission of life and its consequent inevitable fact and sense of natural frustration."[44] The author, even then, connected the dots between personal respect and our anemic culture of consumerism and planned obsolescence that would eventually find a place even for euthanasia.

The nuns of Kristi's youth in the late fifties might have been off base to discourage mixed noontime baseball on the lawn of the Academy, but perhaps they did correctly sense the magnitude of the enemy we now face. Looking to Christianity as a whole, we find the landmark action taken a decade or two earlier at the Lambeth Conference in 1920 by the Anglican community now in such disarray. At Lambeth (the highest-level structure of Anglican governance), the Anglicans were the first denomination to approve a compromise admitting contraception — what the defeated minority still rejected as late as 1948 as the "world of Aphrodite."[45]

A *culture* of life, larger than simply its morality, radically affirms the nature of the human person. It really does stand as a sign of contradiction and authentic freedom *for* the truth (not *from* restraint). In a way, contraception cuts the last remaining thread to what from the beginning is an enchanted universe embodied in the human person. At the center, the spouse becomes ordinary (and as in pagan times, finally a "partner" indistinct sexually from oneself). The miraculous wine of Cana reverts back to water.

Is it not the broad springtime of the human spirit which comes to us in the refreshing "theology of the body"? This theology recalls an "original innocence" that runs deeper than our tendency to render things and persons too ordinary, ever now and then, and deeper still than even our radical pretentiousness. The "original sin" is less the transgression than it is living the spiritual dullness that precedes and follows — our pretentious authority and "knowledge [conceptual and experiential] of good and evil."

And so we settle for the inkling that even the act of creation can be owned, a possession that can be instrumented. It is our catastrophic loss that we place having over *being* — as in being in love. How long until we ourselves are owned by test tube protocols?

The theology of the body proposes, in season and out of season, that the physical body and body language are by their nature an unambiguous communion and even a direct path for a grace. With the human person, the Creator finds His inner and Trinitarian creativity to be not only "good," but "very good." What an astonishing teaching to uphold that marriage is a "sacrament" to be mutually conferred by the spouses on each other.

Kristi and I happened across a remarkable line: The " . . . theology of the body — constitutes a kind of theological time bomb set to go off, with dramatic consequences, sometime in the third millennium of the Church."[46] In the third millennium — "perhaps in the twenty-first century" — the time bomb will surely restore the inviolate unity of the person, male and female, and with this the unity also of our threatened families. Especially in marriage we and *all* of creation are consistently nuptial, not mechanical or mathematical or divorced from the spirit in the mold of Descartes and the Enlightenment.

The gentle breeze of this new and deeper enlightenment of rediscovered communion will touch everything, but also and especially families.[47] It might be that this culture shift among "ordinary" families will restore from within large parts of our atomized and minutely organized and abused society. Creatures of the state, the courts now presume to reduce and redefine marriage as even less than a mere biological combination. The family — more original than even the idea of the state — is colonized by the media as is the state itself and its courts. In our electronic culture, how far is the family now, legally, from its role as a "sanctuary of life"?

Within a culture of life — this New Springtime — some foresee a more winnowed core of believers and a much-reduced Church, but one of resilient fidelity, a flourishing sign of contradiction.[48]

This sign is more enduring than any denial of the fully human person, whether in this third millennium . . . or the tenth. Whether written on papyrus or on legal paper or even electronic disks.

On the big screen of history, marriage spirituality is a second path to be fully discovered, alongside monastic community and spirituality. Separated by barely fifteen hundred years, complete recognition of these two complementary paths — celibacy often with sacramental ordination, and sacramental marriage — will always offer two paths of fresh hope for the single-hearted:

> Not only is the eros between human beings the basis that permits God to impress his own agape on the human person; the encounter face to face between man and woman is also the basis that permits the possibility of such face-to-face encounter between God and humanity. . . . The Trinitarian love is the only ultimate form of love, both the love between God and men, and that between human persons.[49]

Single-hearted. It is the deepest nature of things that we are dealing with unity, not duality: "Do you not know that your body is a temple of the Holy Spirit within you, whom you have from God, and that you are not your own?" (1 Cor. 6:19).[50] On this inner unity the universe of the person and of the family, too, will thrive under the stars long after we are free of incestuous legal precedents relayed from one court to the next, rationalization masquerading as reason.

Bernanos gives encouragement. He finds genuine spirituality especially in a world that is untidy. What von Balthasar says of Bernanos also applies to the stature of each marriage in the world today. Bernanos found fault with the "individualistic mysticism of interior ascent that is more influenced by Neoplatonism than by the Gospel and that strongly colors both the Patristic and the Scholastic periods. Even in our own day it occasionally is allowed too much weight in the Church's mystical theology. . . . For him [Bernanos], mysticism means, pure and simple, being evicted out of all shelteredness, *not only* of the world *but also* of a supernaturally and ecclesially secure existence in faith, to be cast out into the abysses."[51]

It is necessary to be a man before one might be a holy man. It is necessary to be a woman before one might be a holy woman. And it is necessary for this twofold person to be one without inner contradiction before they might become a holy family. In radically secularized Europe we now witness abrupt population decline (partly offset by problematic immigration), what George Weigel terms "demographic suicide."

Earliest writers recorded the impression given by the Christians:

> They marry and have children like everyone else, but they do not abandon their children. They share the same table, but not the same bed. They live in the flesh but not according to the flesh. They live on earth, but, in fact, they are citizens of heaven.[52]

Sometimes as Kristi faced out the opened front door into the yard, she remarked to me how deeply she felt about all this, "*Sometimes I see how strange the world has become, and how much like a stranger I feel.*"[53] And how much like a refuge and "*sanctuary*" for her our home had become. In one of her cards Kristi wrote, "*No matter how uncertain the world around us is, it's nice to know that we are certain.*"

It was at irregular times, usually as we sat together at our kitchen table, that we rediscovered some of the little things that matter. I might remind Kristi of something that she already knew intuitively. We belong to a "city" that does not pass away. In the sacraments and in marriage we belong to an eternal city that will long outlast the ups and downs of media reports on our doorstep and even the full length of all earthly history.

Decades after the fact, Kristi recalled to me an early experience during her two years at Mackinac College in the revolutionary (but nothing new) late sixties. For a routine speech, she chose to present to her circle of classroom friends her ideas about all of this and specifically on the flat-earth "casualness" of the contraceptive mindset already so entrenched on campus. Facing her friends with only a smile and inner light, Kristi proposed the marriage alternative to free love.

I tried to visualize the classroom reaction. Is it possible today to light your candle without having someone else blow it out? Probably a few were patronizing, or at least uncomprehending.[54] Looking back on this with me and how stiff she might have sounded, Kristi mused of herself: *"O Kristi, they must have thought I was a goody two shoes."* How different Kristi's message is from the polite and calculated silence we find today in the classrooms of at least a few professors of carefully footnoted moral theology on many campuses still working to redefine the Catholic label.

From private recreational sex to the ritualized cleansing of state-sponsored abortion — this is the imposition placed on some forty states by the U.S. Supreme Court in its inventive 1973 ruling of *Roe v. Wade*.[55] From doing what we believe, to believing what we do.

Culturally, what is it that accounts for the great divide in our society in *what* we see? To answer this, we might wonder first at *how* we see. Since Descartes especially, we are more interested in our ideas than we are about reality itself as it presents itself to us.[56]

Of this strained kind of logic, the writer G. K. Chesterton gives us a clue: " . . . his mind moves in a perfect but narrow circle. A small circle is quite as infinite as a large circle; but though it is quite as infinite, it is not so large. In the same way the insane explanation is quite as complete as the sane one, but it is not so large. . . . [the] most unmistakable mark of madness is the combination between a logical completeness and a spiritual contraction."[57]

As the child is removed from the mother, the mother is amputated from her own maternity. It takes a lot of energy, constant vigilance, to not notice this. To favor the abortion industry over the innate rights of the most helpless and innocent, and their often isolated and uninformed mothers, endangers all others as well. Extending its logic, The United States Supreme Court announces that the abortion *rite* implies an underlying option to redefine not only the child as a nonperson, but all of reality. The 1992 ruling in *Casey v. Planned Parenthood* imposes a "right" to define the entire universe as we please, instead of reverencing or at least acknowledging what we find. The lofty ruling finds that "at the heart of liberty (as protected by the due process clause), is the right to define one's own concept of existence, of meaning and of the mystery of human life." It is this arbitrary (though scrupulously footnoted) mentality that now spawns the broadening "culture of death."[58]

In her classroom presentation Kristi simply proposed greater authenticity toward a universe that is both gifted and reasonable through and through. The marvelous poetry of Kahlil Gibran speaks to this with uncomplicated simplicity and grace toward the universe within each of us. In *The Prophet,* he might have captured this transparency in a single sentence: "But let there be spaces in your togetherness, and let the winds of the heavens dance between you."[59] In her characteristic transparency, Kristi was suggesting that we let the first of these spaces be the time before the promise —

the courtship before the personal and public promise of marriage.[60] And of children, Gibran writes in *The Prophet:*

> Your children are not your children.
> They are the sons and daughters
> Of Life's longing for itself.
> They come through you but not from you,
> And though they are with you yet they belong not to you.[61]

Through and through, in Kristi was gentle innocence and a pure kind of quiet courage. Light your candle, or at least protect it from being snuffed out by the winds that blow. Is this courage? Years later, as Kristi faced her own death, she claimed to me that she certainly was not courageous. Of herself she said: "*I am nothing.*" But what else than courage was this unguardedness before one's peers in any classroom in the late sixties (and what else her inner calm and tender resolve in the nineties)?

Kristi was not falsely complicated. Women save men from their overly complicated selves. Kristi seemed to be so directly in touch with the real and, therefore, also so capable of being easily hurt. A word here or a word there — or maybe the lack of a word. The eternal feminine. Kristi's was a soul of instinctive and unconscious defense of the blueness of the sky, and the whiteness of snow, and of single-heartedness and strength over any kind of power.

As part of this same breath, she also was to witness on the streets to the real existence of children conceived but not yet born. In the autumn of 1998, we were invited by friends (Matt and Georgene) to meet with other witnesses for the unborn, still in search of a name. Proposed was communication with the Helpers of God's Precious Infants,[62] a new kind of counter-cultural gathering of volunteers on street corners in many cities here and abroad. The silent across-the-street witnessing by the Helpers does not involve demonstrations, nor is it even political. An oddity in our highly politicized era, it is more cultural than political; it is prepolitical.

In their prayerful presence, the Helpers are deeply cultural, re-discovering a missing point of reference for our world of organized noise. This kind of sidewalk witness is perhaps the front edge of the New Springtime of the human spirit, like the hilltop refuge of St. Benedict himself in the equally disjointed times of sixth-century Europe. The casting of such witness as "narrowly" Catholic would be as uncomprehending as dismissing prayerful groups of Holocaust protesters — had there been some — as religious sectarians.

In the New Springtime we will see again most clearly with our own eyes. We will see that apart from the legal gloss, in abortion it is the *concrete human person* who is abused directly, and not merely his rights, which are so easily redefined in the courtroom. Recent centuries have moved us in a circle from the divine right of kings to the now regnant *defining rite of judges* . . . and probably a similar deifi-cation of the arithmetic (sic for democratic) process as the source of truth.

Kristi admired the work of the first prominent ex-abortionist doc-tor, Bernard Nathanson. In her reading she found that even in 1983 he disclosed that the "anti-Catholic warp was a central strat-egy, a keystone of the abortion movement. . . . The more vigorously the church opposed, the stronger the appeal of the anti-Catholic line became to the liberal media, to the northeastern political es-tablishment, to the leftist elements of the Protestant Church, and to Catholic intellectuals themselves."[63] For over seventeen years (the U.S. Supreme Court issued a final and unanimous ruling in favor of the defendant in February 2006) the courts even examined whether punitive action against dissenters was warranted under the Racketeer Influenced Corrupt Organizations (RICO) Act. As the least regulated industry in the country, the abortion network points promiscuously beyond itself to find "racketeers. . . . "

As "racketeers" the Helpers find themselves standing together in the good company of Galileo and his telescope! The unborn child is as real as the tiny moons of Jupiter that opened his eyes. Today, the shoe is on the other foot. Today the new evidence of the sonogram and fiber optics and elementary embryology reveal the human *universe* of an unborn child, as he or she recoils independently from vacuum dismemberment and extraction. To those who see nothing and who legislate from the bench a "right to define one's own concept of existence" (as this pertains to others!), in their silent prayers the Helpers whisper back with the famous stargazer: "Nevertheless, it moves!"[64]

One of the abortion "clinics" in Seattle that has attracted vigil attention is located within the shadow of St. James Cathedral in the central area. Always courting political support, in December 1997 the operators of the clinic held an open house for state legislators. During the Christmas season, as others in Seattle were collecting about the manger of mother *and* child, the clinic placed on display the bottled and preserved fetal remains of their "service" to mother *over* child.[65]

Kristi wanted to visit the site with a few others who later became the Helpers. And we did. We recalled to each other, from the Gospel of John: "The hour is coming for everyone who kills you to think that he is offering worship to God" (John 16:2). The Helpers have witnessed regularly at this central Seattle site ever since. Over the years this gathering and presence on the sidewalk has been quiet; it has remained a nonevent for anyone angling for photo opportunities. Kristi and I stood vigil with others here in the central area on selected Saturdays, and during the week she sometimes visited another site nearer our home when her declining strength allowed.

Witnessing, so important in Kristi's unobtrusive life, offers a simple act of presence for those mothers who might be encouraged by knowing that they really are not solitary and alone.

Kristi wrote for prayer support to dozens of religious institutions in our state, including some cloistered houses of prayer. Her chosen little task was no more nor less than to invite them to join in this prayer intention for the unborn and equally for their mothers, and for ourselves. All of us have cut corners in one way or another. And so, when the Helpers stand witness for others, they stand at the foot of the cross — rather than not. Occasionally a mother accepts help for herself and her unborn child. And sometimes a year or two later a proud mother *and* her child in arms return to join the group if only for a few minutes.

In all of this darkness of spirit and then the witnessing, history is sometimes on the side of the witnesses. Kristi was devoted to Our Lady of Guadalupe, the symbol of how Christianity lifted the Aztec native Americans in Mexico from their cult of human sacrifice.[66] In our own day, not so different as we might think, we are again called to be simply present, at least in silence and prayer. One by one: "Rachel mourns her children, she refuses to be consoled because her children are no more" (Jer. 31:15).

Perhaps it was providential that the clinic's message, shortly before Christmas in 1997, was so bizarre. For the benefit of state legislators the operators actually displayed the preserved and de-personalized fetal remains of their work. (Reportedly the event was smaller than hoped for.) An ancient myth held that St. Nicko-las (a real figure of the fourth century) not only distributed gifts freely, but on one occasion also resuscitated children murdered by an innkeeper — and then pickled in brine. Brine yesterday, formalde-hyde today. The myth of yesterday speaks as a prophecy across the centuries now to our commercialized and disposable culture. St. Nickolas, himself abducted as a seasonal stock market icon, rises anew not so much as a dissenter *against* the flat-earth culture of over-commercialization and death, but as a witness *for* a culture of life.[67] Small wonder that as a "religious" symbol he will soon be illegal, while all things marketable are not.

Did You See His Eyes?

A friend recounts an experience with Kristi in the early 1980s. The two of them were receiving donations for single red roses in the back of St. Mark's Church. The single red rose is a "pro-life" symbol of each human person and his or her personal and prepolitical right to live. Facing Kristi and her friend was a scornful figure in cowboy boots. He sneered a bit at the roses and the one-sided stare down began. How could anyone be so foolish as to affirm this mere opinion to others, and to sell roses?

Without a flinch Kristi continued to arrange the flowers. In her light and perky way she simply floated above the impending confrontation, *"Well, this is what we are doing."* Totally disarmed by witness over innuendo, the inquisitor suddenly changed his tune, "Well, okay," and then turned away.

During most of the eighties Kristi also scheduled a bus to help parishioners stand with thousands of others on the capitol steps in Olympia. This annual event takes place on the anniversary of the U.S. Supreme Court's 1973 decision to remove state restrictions on abortion. John Paul II's more recent *Gospel of Life* challenges all of us with a *"grave and clear obligation to oppose them by conscientious objection."*[68] This higher affirmation lifts us from our grayness of spirit — our default into a spreading indifference. (I was sure that the reading called for "civil disobedience," but Kristi — God bless her — corrected me on my inaccuracy.)

As part of witnessing in person, Kristi's modest way was to donate financially at least a little each month to her chosen causes. Her three favorites were a local pregnancy aid center, a well-known Manhattan home for street youth, and an orphanage in the Middle

East served by the Catholic Near East Welfare Association. Over the years the pictures and names assigned from the orphanage changed, but always with her special personal touch Kristi kept track and mentioned them by name in our usually hasty family prayers.

Near the end of 2000, still a few months before events turned us toward home hospice care, Kristi decided to make a special visit into downtown Seattle. She wanted to find a street person and one not likely to visit a shelter, to give him *face to face* what he needed to eat. She was excited about this very little street project. I suggested that we turn this into a family event and meet first for lunch along the Seattle waterfront. Then I could show her where to look. We bought a small book of food gift certificates.

Several hard-luck figures had spaced themselves evenly over the next hundred yards on the walkway above the edge of Elliot Bay, each with a predictable cardboard sign. How does one know which one, if any, is genuine? Fr. Norris had once advised me, "You would never find me down there, but your heart will tell you." My heart does not often speak clearly to me, or else I am unable to hear it. "That one," I suggested, as I stood off to the side. He had caught my eye earlier in the week.

Kristi, so trusting of me, approached and leaned forward toward the bundled, bearded, and seated young man. She did not hurry by and did not look over or past him. Instead their eyes met. Several seconds passed. There was a wonder as Kristi straightened and returned the few steps to my side. Of this one, Kristi asked me, *"Did you see his eyes?"* I did not. *"That was Jesus Christ!"* Kristi was astonished.

More than once she mentioned this encounter to me and to others, with an undiminished sense of wonder. Christians sometimes talk of seeing Christ in our neighbor. This was more. I do believe that something remarkable happened on that small piece of waterfront when my wife looked into the eyes of this fellow traveler, another stranger in a strange land. He must have been amazed too, this time especially to receive not only a handout, but also if only for a moment, his full dignity not as an individual, but as a person worthy of a kind gesture. How far into his soul and her own had Kristi seen? How visible is the Soul of our souls in those around us?

I know now that the sentinel on the hill, the Benedictine contemplation that has been lost in the West, has a contemporary meaning. It is the silence, which when lost through the Enlightenment project resulted in the wars of the twentieth century as Europe came crashing to the ground. It is the silence without which we dehumanize each other, even before we think. It is even the silence that came on that nanosecond of silent purity at the very front edge of the Big Bang. It is that silence hovering over the edge of human conception when forty-six chromosomes and sixty thousand genes of the genome become a person distinct from all others. It is the silence of our freedom, when we then decide whether to notice the silent scream of the sonogram or the obvious facts of elementary embryology. By a reflex of will, not knowledge, we *depersonalize* this thing from the beginning, and then we calculate the economics of embryonic stem cells and tissue harvesting from abortions. This is the Original Sin in modern language, a crisis of our time and our culture. Our blindness is even more disconnected than "moral relativism"; it is more like moral graffiti — random markings with no consistent and rooted patterns at all. Only action.

But with God it is different, both within time and before and after time, and are we not in His image and likeness? Where is the reverence, the foundational gift of the Holy Spirit?

What a gift to fully notice the full existence of the other, especially those on the streets raggedly disguised as refuse, or the unborn sometimes found in trash cans. Such a light gesture — simply a glance pointing to such a different world. "Blessed are the pure of heart, for they shall see God" (Matt. 5:8).[69]

In Kristi's hospitality to others, it was not so much what she did, but how she did it. Hers was a special touch, the sacrament of the present moment. In so many instances, it was only others who always had the special gifts — tongues, healing, and so on.

As Kristi's years drew to a close, she was less interested in special gifts and in the more charismatic Masses we had sought out beginning with Fr. Barham's 1995 visit. The charismatic is but one path of devotion: *"I do not need that now,"* she said as we began hospice. In our final year or two she settled in to the more ordinary and quiet devotions, another path. I see clearly now that Kristi's was "yet a more excellent way" recommended by St. Paul: "[Charity] is patient, is kind . . . thinks no evil, is not self-seeking, is not provoked; but rejoices with the truth; bears with all things, believes all things, hopes all things, endures all things" (1 Cor. 13:4–7).

Endures all things . . . this degree of attentiveness became a defining path for Kristi, beginning fifteen years after our wedding, in late 1989, and ending in grace in the autumn of 2001.

Chapter Three

In Good Times and in Bad

We are doing this to have a few more years together.

— Kristi

A Walk on the Beach

Nearly every year the summer months brought our family to a favorite refuge on the Oregon coast. This was Cannon Beach, thirty
miles below the mouth of the Columbia River. Especially at low tide,
the sandy breadth extends for miles north and south. Anchoring
this shoreline and the Pacific Ocean vista is the enormous Haystack
Rock. Rising hundreds of feet above the edge of the breakers, the
mostly vertical rock is a haven for many species of sea birds. Twice
each day as the waves are rolled back it can be approached on foot.

Here we always found the open freedom for running or for
strolling together. In the evening the cherry-red sun sinks into a
sea of pastels, the last liquid spot of fire always seeming to stop for a
second or two before sinking fully beneath the horizon. Sunsets give
way to star-filled skies lost to our cities. And after dark the distant
rotations of the lighthouse beacon a few miles to the north pin the
invisible horizon securely in place for the night.

During our 1988 visit we met another family of four from Wisconsin. Casual chatter led us to Garrison Keillor's popular radio
show and magazine articles drawn from his youth and placed on

the banks of a fictional Lake Wobegon in Minnesota. There, all of the children were said to be above average. Circled with our own children around a shared beach fire, we learned that their high-school-aged son, John, was considering a student exchange program for the following year. This would take him to Russia. Historic political and cultural changes, still not visible to any of us, already were in the wind.

John was politically inspired in the best sense, and early the next spring wrote for my advice about urban planning schools in the United States. I had lost touch with academic programs, but was happy to offer what I could. In one important detail, my letter reached beyond what he asked. I related a particular evening I had spent in the early seventies with a fellow graduate student in our urban and regional planning program at the University of Washington. My friend, Fred from Ohio, was an unusually serious personality. Although he was not religious, he accurately described himself as a rigorous Calvinist in his day-to-day disposition. In this way he personified a broader cultural obsession with "doing" over being, and he knew this of himself. He was a bit driven. Self-exoneration through compulsive work can be a symptom of pride or, for others perhaps, at least a degree of anxiety or despair.

After earning a master's degree in urban planning, Fred went on to successfully apply his intensity to law school. He eventually made his mark with a prominent legal firm for researching and building an intricate landmark case on the extent and limits of liability for contaminated blood supplies, specifically related to Acquired Immunity Deficiency Syndrome (AIDS).

On some Friday nights during our school years together, I would visit Fred in his University District apartment alongside the Interstate 5 freeway. By the end of the week, we looked forward to the simple task of feeding his goldfish. Fred's income was spartan enough that sometimes the fish ate before he did. We shared scrambled eggs and toast.

Fred did not disguise his disdain for the patchwork of government regulations, especially in his area of specialization. This was the set of federal programs governing federal freeway and transit projects for major cities like Seattle (and even the elevated freeway section outside his second-floor window). As he sorted through a stack of the *Federal Register* on his floor, I challenged him with this: "About government incoherence, think how much worse things might be if this 'problem' were ever solved." Also to be watched is coherent power. This seemed like a profound critique at the time. Fred's response was pensive silence, and then a chuckle, "Hmm, I never thought of it that way before."

On one evening in the spring of 1973, still a few months before I met Kristi, Fred and I walked on the forested University of Washington campus under a velvety purple sky. Our path was bounded left and right by two four-story brick and ivy-covered Tudor Gothic classrooms buildings. We were drawn forward by the distant silhouette of the snow-covered and dormant volcano Mount Rainier. Nearer in front of us was a broad clearing formed by a square field of roses surrounding the very large circular reflective pond, Drumheller Fountain.

At this point where the enclosure opened to the wider vista, Fred went silent. Stopping, he looked back as if searching for something. Was it a sound? What had he seen? What were the words that passed between us? "I just had a sort of vision," he said, "and I saw what a real human community is supposed to be like. . . . I felt close to all human beings, as if even time did not matter." He paused again, and then concluded, "You Catholics, I see what you are about, I finally see what St. Augustine was getting at in his *City of God*. I have wondered about this for years."[1] And then he nearly begged, "I want some of that."

This struck me as one of the most unvarnished and genuine prayers I had ever heard: "I want some of that." And yet I was at a loss for words, hesitant. Incompetent to respond to his simple petition, I said nothing. During my navy years I had been drawn to St. Augustine. I knew his *Confessions* and *City of God* and how these express and capture for us a truth larger than ourselves, but one that also seems to claim a place deep within ourselves. The truth is larger than any or all of our actions and points toward an eternity that in some way holds in its hands even our sense of time and space. Augustine's thought frees us from being digits — possibly even well-fed digits — within the calculus of the earthly city. The horizon no longer bounds us; it welcomes us to a higher city.

In my 1989 letter to John about planning the human city I recounted this moment with a friend under a purple sky. Yes, I encouraged John to look into urban planning schools as I had done, and I gave him some leads. But I added that he should not forget the deeper human (because also more than human) city. Keeping one foot in each of these two cities is a greater challenge than simply becoming a better urban carpenter, or an economist or politician, adjusting investments and trends on a piece of geography. It requires faith beyond mathematics and even beyond trendy optimism and natural good will.

Augustine's perspective turned out to be most timely. In the following year, in an event equivalent to the decline of the Roman Empire in his time, history was to witness the collapse of the atheist-dominated Soviet Union, the last and most repressive empire in our period of "modern" history.

As for Fred, my response to him fifteen years earlier always had been totally inadequate. His silence and the opening he left me — "I want some of that" — passed me by, but our friendship continued. In the coming years after Kristi and I married, Fred visited and confided in me from time to time. During one of these visits he delivered an assembled and painted model reconstruction of my ship, the USS *Hornet*, together with a well-researched and typed history. We were very touched by this surprise gift and the thoughtful effort that went into it. Kristi was always caring toward Fred and made sure we had sandwiches if he dropped in at noon. She knew that beneath his rigor was a vulnerability and gnawing loneliness. Her conclusion was accurate enough: *"What he needs is a girl to bring him out of himself."*

The year after meeting the Wisconsin family, the summer of 1989 again found our family at Cannon Beach. The sands are usually washed clean, but I still kept my eyes open for a stray shell or two to offer Kristi for the kitchen windowsill back home. We strolled north of the Rock, surrounded by the constant drumming of the incoming tide.

At a break in the light talk, my girl tugged gently at my right elbow: *"Peter, I have been waiting for the right time to tell you something . . . I think we're going to have a baby!"* Kristi's cheerfulness at this was magical and so familiar, and after a step or two I caught up with her spirit. The light flashed in her dark eyes; and here again was the same unique smile. It had been a long and unexpected wait, those many years since our second, Mark, had been born. And his older sister, Laura, was now fourteen. As I caught up with this news, we stepped together into thoughts about our enlarging future.

But a few weeks later, back in Seattle, our smooth beach at the edge of an abundant sea became a desert. From the garage I heard the awaited sound of the car docking as Kristi returned home from another visit with the doctor. How was the checkup, I thought, as I reached for the doorknob. But my angel pushed it open and slipped quickly past me into the kitchen, with eyes turned away.

Below her breath, *"It's cancer."*

My God, my first thought was how did she drive home all alone with this shock? Is it not enough to first be lifted by the joy of a long-awaited new child, then to lose not only such a hope, but to have it replaced by cancer?

Cancer. . . .

I caught up with Kristi in the living room. The davenport backs toward a large window and our solitary hawthorn tree in front. The facing opposite wall is decorated with our family pictures — our wedding picture, school portraits, and an early family picture of the four of us on Easter morning seated in front of our 1895 burled walnut piano as a backdrop. I remember some of what we said as we sat there together. I asked the deliberately distracting question when the next appointment might be. In the times ahead, there would be more moments. Over the years I would often simply rub Kristi's feet, and wisely say nothing.

Cancer treatment is disorienting. It is both a cure and an abuse, and for Kristi it was to be especially severe in its side effects. Eventually, in the years ahead (all of the nineties), our way through it always came in three shared steps that we discovered and remembered together. First we would find and agree on "the path," which was to be our immediate future. With the medical team, we would pick through the possibilities and then settle on and accept a particular treatment. A decision helps to fence in the wandering mind and the panic; it gives a calendar. Small steps are possible. We had a direction and were not in free fall.

Then, second, we took this path together "one day at a time." It is quite enough to get through the day without guessing at more than you need to know and with the good chance of being wrong. There are a lot of little steps to fill the days and weeks. But there was to be no jumping ahead or looking back with "What if?" Cancer victims come to understand this. For us it would be a radical right mastectomy and twenty-six weeks of chemotherapy, followed by a short break and then a final eight weeks of radiation. From the chemo there is a 60 percent chance, we were informed, of sterility. But one day at a time. . . .

And our third and special step was "to not look down." And what did we mean by this? We recalled from Fr. Breslin that in another storm St. Peter had actually walked on water (Matt. 14:28–32). Now, this is what we had to do. Held up by the eyes of his Lord, Peter had been able to do this until the fragile moment when his own eyes drifted independently away from the eyes of Christ. He looked down. He looked down at his feet, and only then noticed too much the splashing and rising of the waves. To be distracted by the waves, nothing more complicated than this, is to be overwhelmed and to sink. To keep the eyes fixed is to trust, over and over again, very much on the edge, but no longer alone.

We prayed a little. We prayed as we had learned from Barham and others, in small bits, but for particular protection and deliverance. Not long prayers, not even undistracted prayers, but a reaching from where we were toward a power and gentleness outside of ourselves. Over the years we prayed for this particular outcome, or that particular test result. And we moved on, one day at a time. We actually continued to trust that such prayers are heard, sometimes even before they are whispered.

And we marked on the calendar upcoming events that we might be able to do. Always something more to look forward to, something positive to fix our minds. Still, in late 1989 and early 1990 this was our first cancer experience. At the start we looked forward to Christmas one month away. Kristi chose to postpone an early surgery for one month, so that our family celebration with Laura and Mark might be normal. We knew the possible risk in this. As always, there were the Christmas tree, the colored lights in a darkened room with carefully selected music, and a special seasonal novena prayer: ". . . Through the mystery of the Incarnation we have received a grace beyond our power to comprehend or fully imagine. . . ."

The surgery came four days after Christmas, on December 29, 1989. For the hospital stay Kristi selected a bright new light orange bathrobe. (I thought it was coral, but we often had a different eye for the in-between colors.) And looking ahead to the chemotherapy, I mail ordered a little surprise for Kristi to find later in a package on the porch. This was a wall plate depicting a doctor making a house call to a doll held up by sweet child. With his straight white hair combed back, the doctor looked a great deal like pictures I had seen of Kristi's grandfather.

At the hospital the evening before the operation, we stood together in the silent hall watching the nearly full moon over the sparkling city skyline to the south. Later in the week, I arrived early in the afternoon to find, already, that our new pastor had made time in his schedule for Kristi. Our very warm Fr. Jim was sitting beside Kristi in quiet and friendly conversation. So many times we are lifted by those who have totally dedicated themselves to be available to us, as ordained priests without biological families of their own.[2]

The twenty-six weeks of chemotherapy followed, one after the other. We began to learn a new medical vocabulary.[3] After the first month the treatments became increasingly difficult. We broke the path into manageable pieces. Thirteen weeks is the halfway mark, something like the midpoint of a twenty-six mile marathon. Perseverance requires that we locate ourselves in some way along the path. After these six months there came a full month off followed by the relatively easy eight weeks of radiation.

In all of this, we were a short four miles from the hospital. Kristi wanted to make most of the trips for weekly treatments on her own, usually on Mondays. At first things were relatively easy. But as the weeks rolled by, the recovery took until midweek or even longer, and eventually Kristi was not really well until the weekends. The weekends were good for special outings, and we always made a point of not looking ahead to the following Monday.

Seasoned cancer veterans had advised us to keep the routine as normal as possible for younger family members. Laura and Mark were at school during the day. While Kristi was drained by each treatment she bounced back enough to watch and enjoy many of Mark's team basketball games in the evenings as she had done with his older sister. While we were successful in keeping things at home as they had been, cancer is still such a detour.

Our wife and mother was mostly upbeat, but sometimes was saddened that so much might be slipping away. Life is changed and lost. There is a melancholy to be resisted. I would try to remind Kristi that the secret revealed by Christ overcomes this loss. We would notice together that total fulfillment — including fullness and completion for the very moments we saw slipping past — will be given. It is our total selves who will be healed and, as Fr. Barham had insisted, we are healed even now by the resurrection, which is both in front of us and already achieved. This certainty is solid encouragement against the deception of either despondency or too vaporous a spirituality.

It is the complete person who is healed by the Lord of All History and who is the Soul of our souls. We would return again and again to this: "Eye has not seen or ear heard, nor has it entered into the heart of man, what things God has prepared for those who love him" (1 Cor. 2:9; Isa. 64:3).

It is not only that the tears are replaced by joy, that each tear is *turned into* joy (John 16:20). Nothing is lost at all, not a hair on our head is left uncounted. If love is infinite, then this total transformation is not an exaggeration. We would often repose together in this central hope that all of the incomplete moments of the past, all of them fragments, are each returned to us with the fractures fully restored. Healed in the sense of being brought forward intact *and* a hundredfold. This, rather than in any lesser sense of being only forgotten or replaced by something else. To not see this is to not understand the resurrection. Joy does not enter us; we enter joy. This awaited gift includes the stuff of our lives. It is totally disproportionate to any suffering that we accept with trusting *surrender* (quite different from submission). The tears are turned into joy. "Every drop of earthly bitterness will be *changed into* an ocean of heavenly sweetness."[4]

At the beginning of our life with cancer and shortly after the end of the final radiation treatment, Kristi felt much better. It was now that she tried her hand at part-time work in a small travel office. Near the end of the first year, in September of 1991, she even took a one-week training tour to Aruba. By now she was mostly recovered. I enjoy the small tour diary she kept. On her final day a scheduling error had her and another trainee rushing by taxi to the airport to catch the return flight to Seattle. The tanned driver breathed only the relaxed island air. Kristi wrote. The driver "assured us we had plenty of time — don't worry, be happy — I should work on that!" I see now, so late, that while she often worked on *that,* her anxious husband in so many ways continued to check his watch whenever we left the house.

Through all of this my professional work was on our side. While we still felt some financial stress each month, we always had enough. Our medical insurance was exceptional and covered nearly everything. And my schedule only rarely took me from home in the evenings. When I needed it, I was eligible for time off during the day. We were so much more fortunate on these points than are many others, and we counted our blessings. As a family we were not mutilated by our overall economy that too often divides unwilling families into two full-time income producers. I always told Kristi that if she found something she had the stamina to do, and wanted to do it, then this would be wonderful. But she was never to feel that she was falling short for not being in "the work force" —

yet another modern label designed and perhaps intended to keep us in line.

We remained a family first. Kristi's chosen first vocation was that of mother and wife. Still, her stamina was down, removing her from any full-time job track and increasing the feeling sometimes of being "useless." She remained most conscientious about her special housework and enjoyed cooking for her family and extending hospitality to visiting friends. The long path for her was to put up with, and finally even to embrace, cancer. And more than this, it was to be a wife and mother, to be a friend to others — and with the departed saints she loved.

The "Little Way" of St. Therese and the prayers recommended by Fr. Thomas were always with the family at our evening meals. Each day for the rest of our lives together, Kristi and I deepened in Thomas's novena to the Holy Spirit, which he hastily penned during one of his many visits.

> *Soul of my soul,* I adore you.
> Enlighten me, guide me, strengthen me, sanctify me, heal
>   me, and console me.
> Tell me what I must say; tell me what I must do.
> Give me your beautiful fruits and gifts.[5]
> I promise to subject myself to you, to accept all that you will
>   allow to happen to me.
> Only teach me your Holy Will.

I have finally discovered these lines that might serve as a definition of the "Soul of my soul": "There should be *in us* a kind of spiritual paradise where God may walk and be our sole ruler with his Christ. *In us* the Lord will sit at the right hand of that spiritual power which we wish to receive. And he will sit *there* until all his enemies who are *within us* become his footstool, and every principality, power, and virtue *in us* cast out."[6]

Stay with Me

From the first cancer surgery and treatments in 1989 and 1990 Fr. Thomas dropped in at our home whenever he could. These visits were for us a sanctuary of peace not captured by any efforts of mine now to find suitable words. Even as Kristi's remission stretched into years, his prayer to the Holy Spirit and his favorite novena to Therese of Lisieux were always with us. The dinner table afforded a brief but fairly routine and dependable centering for us, and for Mark and Laura during their high school careers. The novena begins: "O little Therese of the Child Jesus, please pick for us a rose from the heavenly garden and send it to us as a message of love. . . ."

Before our eyes, over these last twelve years, Kristi *grew into* these prayers. From these and her devotion to the Eucharist and closeness to Mary came a deepening gentleness and acceptance. And in her disciplined handwriting, learned from Sr. Deodata at St. Gertrude's Academy, on a pink recipe card was this additional Prayer of Family Consecration to Jesus and Mary:

Most holy Virgin, Mother of God and of the Church,
To your Immaculate Heart we today consecrate our family.
With your help, we entrust and consecrate ourselves to the
            Divine Heart of Jesus,
In order to be with you and with Him in the Holy Spirit,
Completely and always entrusted and consecrated to the will
            of the heavenly Father. Amen.

Cancer checkups in the first years were regularly spaced and routine, usually three months apart and sometimes a glorious six. And so the uninvited guest fell into the background during those first five years, but still we lived more for the moment than otherwise. Life was a bit more precious, and was touched from time to time with grace. I was always with Kristi for the hospital visits, especially for the CAT scans (computerized pictures built up from sets of x-ray images) and the more revealing MRI checkups (magnetic resonance imaging).

The MRI is a tunnel and can be claustrophobic and intolerable for some patients. After a careful start, we did better. Kristi became more relaxed and secure when I was on hand to rub her feet. Over the years these routine visits became one of our togetherness outings. The technicians got used to seeing both of us. I would leave work early to meet Kristi roughly half way as she came four miles south in the opposite direction to Northwest Hospital.

During the nineties, Kristi's medical history began to add up, but most of our time by far was spent in living more or less like everyone else. For most of our time together, cancer and hospitals were in the background. Yet for both of us and the kids, hospitals kept coming into our lives for one reason or another. Ten years before, in the early 1980s, Kristi had been injured in an aerobics class. From this she had suffered periods of recurrent and severe back pain. This hung around for over five years.

The lower back muscles were "frozen" for much of this time. Many evenings Kristi ate dinner standing against the kitchen wall while the rest of us sat at the table for the dinner she always prepared. Along the way we had confirmed that codeine spinal injections brought too many complications. During one family visit in Seattle, my physician father-in-law caught me alone in the living room and asked me if I really understood. "You may be dealing with this for the rest of your life." "Yes," I said, this possibility had crossed my mind.

But even as I write this, I know that the more accurate tone — the picture I will remember after more time has passed — is all the much greater good times. Kristi's back finally healed. I have a snapshot of my girl in 1985 crossing the finish line for the parish five-kilometer race. She came in third in the women's division and glowed with that inner delight that was so much of how she did things.

The late eighties, before the cancer in 1989, were especially good to us. But in 1992, and two years after the mastectomy, Kristi remained held down by fatigue. This was finally traced to Graves' disease, a thyroid deficiency, rather than to any lingering effects of the treatments. By the time this new disease was suspected it had been active too long, masked as it was by the early tiredness of cancer recovery. Driving the four miles home after the new diagnosis, I weighed the warning and the distinct possibility that Kristi might now lose her eyesight within a week or two. The thought of my wife learning her way around the house in the dark shook me to the core. Our "path" in this instance was nothing better than to wait. At work I distracted myself from the fear that I would receive a morning call from Kristi telling me that she could not see. But we were lucky, and after successful radiation treatment, daily thyroid tablets (synthroid) simply became part of the routine. Life for Kristi was normal again. Much later, when I looked back and openly admitted to my fear, I found that Kristi had barely considered the danger. She said at least that she did not even remember the problem.

There were other things to notice. It was during the early nineties that Kristi told me for the first time of a recurring experience that might have been only physiological, but I am not sure. This happened possibly two or three times since our marriage, and more frequently before. Kristi spoke of fully waking at night and finding herself facing up toward a visible dark cloud within the bedroom, and more than this, an ominous sense of evil.

"Kristi, you should wake me if this ever happens again."

"*I cannot,*" she said, "*when this happens I am completely paralyzed and cannot move. I pray until it goes away.*"

My own medical dunking came in late 1991. During a Columbus Day windstorm I fell from a ladder to the driveway and landed tangled in the unforgiving hickory rungs. On the inside, my right leg was nearly broken off, The femur was separated and widely displaced from the still intact socket and ball joint. Muscles were broken loose and the surface layer of the hip was shattered off. In the emergency ward, a familiar place by now, Dr. John was brief with me. Of the extensive damage, he said "We cannot put that in a cast." With wires and pins I might be immobilized for six months. At the hospital emergency center Kristi prayed, and I suspect her trusting prayer was answered in a specific way. My doctor decided to try something that he had never done before. Surgery was postponed overnight while a precision stainless steel device (an interlocking two-piece "Gama nail" a little less than a foot long) was flown to Seattle. The consulted medical team included the inventor in Pittsburgh and a third colleague in Miami. The disconnected bones in my leg were hollowed and then bolted back together.[7]

The prognosis was that I would walk again, but for the rest of my life this would be with a swaggering limp and probably a cane. Kristi interpreted this as a cross for me to humbly accept. *"Do you accept this?"* she asked a few weeks later as I balanced for the first time in a chair at the dinner table. I was not interested in being steered by misplaced piety when I wanted to walk and to run again. "Only after I fight this thing and cannot beat it — only then will I accept it as His will for me."

I was irritated and typically impatient, but also confident in my understanding of what Christian meekness actually means and what it does not mean. One surrenders only after the struggle and after it is clear that it is He, and not our passiveness, which has closed all other paths.[8] This was the view I always presented to our high school students during the annual Confirmation preparation classes.[9] Any normal young man should be put off by the saccharin Christ portrayed in too much pasty artwork. It was a moment of moral strength and righteous anger, not weakness, when Christ whipped the moneychangers from the temple.

I did learn to walk normally and then to run again with a padded right shoe, with one leg shorter, but without a limp. Coming off of Kristi's surgery only the year before, it was important for me to show Laura and Mark, then sixteen and thirteen, that Dad was well enough to stand and shoot the basketball. Kristi was so supportive and, looking back later, she was a bit amazed. *"You just did it!"* she blurted. This is good incentive for any husband. I came out of the experience feeling closer to Kristi in her recent cancer ordeal, and I think she took some mental notes that were to help her in the future. Our experiences nudged us a few steps closer toward our future path and the deeper trust that both of us would need. In this way I was even thankful for my permanent injury and thick-soled shoe. And maybe the kids could trust a bit more that at worst, normalcy is always just around the corner.

With other bumps along the way, Kristi and I learned a little how to recognize and defuse the communication thing — surely heightened for us by the extra stress in our lives. The trick was to short-circuit the occasional spiral passing through quick words to apparent disrespect. With a helpful light touch, the English writer G. K. Chesterton says to all couples, "The combination of a man and woman may be, indeed is, a dangerous chemical combination; frequently resulting in an explosion."[10] It is good to remember that it is only because of the *closeness* of marriage that the friction is even possible. We named this spiral (aggravated a bit by my irritability) "the worms." When this intruder showed up, we learned to go for a walk. Not entirely joking, a close relative offers this: "A long walk has saved many a marriage!"

One year after my injury, and not long after Kristi's bout with Graves' disease, Kristi suffered a freak fall a few steps from our back door. It was September 1992 and we were on our way back from my first doctor-approved outing to the neighborhood track. Kristi's left foot and her right kneecap were broken. This meant six weeks in two casts at home in another leased hospital bed. For the second time the ground floor recreation room became our infirmary. I slept on a mattress on the floor at Kristi's side. I learned precisely where to place the pillows and how to adjust them. Neighborhood strolls in the autumn sun were done in the wheel chair. The breaks healed, but the knee recovery was never total. We did continue our regular walks down the forested side streets in our neighborhood. Kristi usually used an elastic knee brace, which I artfully cut to reduce the pressure on what remained a sensitive kneecap.

The next year, in the summer of 1993, Kristi came to terms with the permanent effects of her medical situation. The chemotherapy had done its worst. There could be no more children. On a sunny day we walked together at the neighborhood track. Thinking also of her reduced stamina, Kristi arrived at this: "Maybe God knows best. . . ." Fifteen years had now slipped by since Mark came along, and Laura was now nearly eighteen and ready for college.

There came the solemn resignation, under an indifferent pop-corn cloud sky, as we saw the future narrowing itself into apparent predictability. The empty nest was around the corner. We had sometimes considered adoption, but had not really pursued it. We continued our regular monthly support to a few selected organizations such as the Catholic Near East Welfare Association. Kristi continued to donate modestly every month to a center for homeless teens in Manhattan and a new pregnancy aid center in Seattle. She visited the nursing homes on a weekly schedule, and with her urging I became active for a few years in the weekly events of our parish's St. Vincent de Paul Society.

For the family, special events included a trip to the Finger Lakes area of New York in late 1993. This was part of dropping Laura off for her first year at Franciscan University in Steubenville, Ohio. (It had been the healing of memories at a conference here that so moved our visitor Otto early in 1988.) And late 1994 brought Kristi with me to a work-related conference and special trip together to the magic of New Orleans and its French Quarter shops and restaurants. After returning to Seattle, Kristi wrote back to a dealer to order a delicate gold cross pendant that had caught her eye. From this point forward, this gossamer cross was around her neck every day of her life.

Six years after the first cancer, a CAT scan and MRI revealed a new cancer site in the sternum (February 1996). For there to be a recurrence after such a long remission is not the usual pattern. Now, each cycle of treatment found a way of becoming more pre-occupying. Kristi was visibly uplifted by this thought: "Your cancer is something you have, but it does not have you. Cancer does not define who you are."

We were dealing with a spreading "Stage IV" bone cancer, the most advanced category (there is no Stage V). My dearest Kristi, what is our path? We found our place together on the davenport. The possible treatment was borderline "experimental" and possibly not eligible for insurance coverage. Kristi's first reaction was that she did not want to be a financial burden. (As if saving the house, but having it empty, would not be a burden.) My response: "No, we will sell the house if we have to . . . we will find a way." It turned out that the steep costs of the treatment — an advanced bone mar-row replacement called a "peripheral stem cell" transplant — would be covered by insurance. An anonymous voice on the telephone reported this good news. We continued to live one day at a time without looking down.

As the big date approached to begin the hospital sequence, Kristi's father in Idaho took a turn for the worse. He was dying and was under Jeanne's care at home in Cottonwood. Torn between extending a quick visit with him and the gathered family and her already rescheduled preadmission to the hospital, Kristi felt forced to return to Seattle. She returned without burdening "Daddy" with the reason. This awkward departure broke her heart. He would die a few days later on March 8, 1996. We stood with the extended family as he was buried with military honors alongside his own father (and medical partner) in the Cottonwood cemetery at the north edge of town. In our remaining few years, Kristi sometimes remarked to me that she never again would organize family visits around hospital schedules. In the following few years she lightly confided to me, *"Oh, I talk to Daddy all the time; we are closer now than we have ever been."*

As always, our friend Fr. Thomas was in touch and wrote to us, "Part of you has died with him, and part of him lives on in you to make you the beautiful person you are. You have my prayerful sympathy that the Lord who comforted and consoled Martha and Mary at the death of Lazarus will so console you now with His Presence and Power and the hope of your faith in Him, the Resurrection and the Life."

This heavy loss and the new and demanding cancer treatment would overlap other and happier family events. But how does a family organize around cancer? Mark's high school graduation came first on the calendar. Later in the spring came Laura's planned wedding. She and her fiancé, Rob, were to exchange their vows in St. Mark's Church in Seattle on June 8. One great consolation in Kristi's mind was this timing. The dates fell together with the wedding only three days before we would begin the workup for chemotherapy and the transplant. For a couple of months the wedding preparations kept us busy and distracted our attention from what else was coming.

For her maids of honor Laura selected friends she had known at the neighborhood St. Mark's parish school and then at Bishop

Kristi's home: her father's clock and chair. "Part of you has died with him."

Blanchet High School in Seattle. Reviewing the list I was amused and asked Laura if she noticed anything special about her best friends. A light finally went on, followed by laughter: "Oh, my gosh! Am I the only one who's white? I never noticed!" Many of Laura's longtime friends were only partly Caucasian, and I am certain she had never thought about this detail. Each was either partly Hispanic, black, or Cherokee, and one was fully Filipino. The dresses were all the same color, forest green.

The Hutchinson Cancer Research Center (the "Hutch") is located on the historic Capital Hill overlooking downtown Seattle. Immediately following the wedding Kristi entered the Hutch to begin treatment in advance of the actual transplant. We already had waded page by page through the thick protocol description and the intimidating release forms. One rises from the table feeling that all of this is a flattery to researchers and a stiff dose of highly specialized vocabulary to the patient (but precise enough to guard against spurious litigation). Signatures are needed; the medical world is inherently risky and, sadly, a big and complicated business. Medicine has come a long way since the days of general practitioners, a nurse or two, and their patients.

During this transitional period before the actual transplant on July 24, we gathered in the downtown hotel room where twin Kerry and her family were staying. I happened to glance at the obituaries in the morning paper. Listed on a single line of fine print was our friend Fred, dead at the age of fifty-one. No cause was given. Only a few months before, I had regained contact with Fred after losing touch for a few years. During a special lunch on the waterfront we had caught up with each other and before parting we had explored a few stores in the Pioneer Square historical district. While he was turned the other way, I bought and wrapped a copy of John Paul II's *Crossing the Threshold of Hope*. It was a hunch that he might enjoy reading this. I was also thinking that this might be some kind of response to his fascination with St. Augustine and the Communion of Saints fifteen years earlier on the university campus. I expected that we could challenge each other at a later outing.

The book is an interview or dialogue between the pope and a prominent journalist and had been a recent topic of dinner conversation during family visits to the Camas Prairie. At one point John Paul II begins with this, "From a human perspective, can (and how can) one come to the conclusion that God really exists?" John Paul II also writes:

> The event at Calvary is a historical fact. Nevertheless, it is not limited in time and space. It goes back into the past, to the beginning, and opens toward the future until the end of history. It encompasses all places and times and all of mankind. Christ is the expectation and simultaneously the fulfillment. There is no salvation through anyone else, nor is there any other name under heaven given to the human race by which we are to be saved. (Acts 4:12)[11]

With a spring in his step and his wrapped gift in hand, Fred made his way through the stoplight and up First Avenue into the downtown office center. That was the last time I saw Fred.

Leading into a bone marrow or stem cell transplant, an amount of chemotherapy is given sufficient to kill the cancer without also killing the patient. This treatment attacks the growing cancer, but also any other growing part of the body, including even the hair and sometimes the eyelashes. The first step is to shrink the tumor. For us this involved two unfamiliar forms of chemotherapy.[12] Heading into the actual transplant, Kristi was given three more heavy doses of chemo.[13] Finding tolerable medicines for Kristi was to become a tricky step because of her well-known susceptibilities and allergies.

The letter from the Hutch to my employer read, "Transplantation is a very critical and arduous therapy that carries a high risk of serious complications. However, it is the only treatment that offers Mrs. Beaulieu the possibility of cure."

In the transplant procedure the life-restoring step follows. For Kristi's transplant, we were lucky that identical twin Kerry was available and, of course, eager to be the stem cell donor. Healthy bone marrow or stem cells from either a donor (if possible) or the patient, are restored to the patient. The basic idea is to stimulate recovery of normal new growth after subtracting the cancer. During this critical period the patient's immune system is reduced to almost zero. The day that the new growth begins, perhaps three weeks after the transplant, is lightly referred to as the first day of the rest of your life, a "first birthday." And it is. Kristi's first birthday came pretty much on schedule on August 11.

Working the numbers in earlier consultation, we had been told that our chance was barely one in five that Kristi would live more than a year or maybe two, even with the transplant. With prayer and the knowledge that every case is different, we hoped for more. In my mind I had factored in Kristi's age and her freedom from any organic weaknesses that are statistically more common to older transplant patients. I convinced myself our chances were fifty-fifty. Responsibly, Dr. Lee, our oncologist, declined to give me a number. My God, work the numbers until they come out right!

A few days into the actual transplant sequence, Kristi suffered her first coma. This was finally attributed to either chemical interaction or to medical allergy, or possibly to both. On a handwritten sheet for Kristi's file I find for this day an antiseptic summary alongside four of the listed medications: "Possibly interactive, causing catatonic anticholinergic reaction including delusions. . . . " The team had known to avoid certain individual medications, but now there were the medical combinations. Even some of the relatively harmless premedications were unknowns for us. However cautiously, we entered more trial and error.

In August, two or three weeks after the transplant, Kerry and Kristi's mother continued to take their turn staying with Kristi at the hospital. I was rushing Mark to the airport. Both of us were booked on a flight for his first autumn semester registration at Franciscan University in faraway Steubenville, Ohio. It was impossible for me to be personally at the hospital with Kristi and on the plane with Mark at the same time. Under a dark early morning sky, a light band of sunrise silhouetted the Cascade Range to the east as Mark and I headed southbound on Interstate-5 into Seattle. The airport was twenty-five miles ahead, and downtown Seattle and the Hutch were still in front of us. Passing on the left was the Gothic Blessed Sacrament Church, a landmark to so much of Kristi's and my life together. The steeple slid past the stable background of the Cascade Range and Mount Rainier.

Kristi had slipped back into a coma. In total dependency my mind turned to the *Memorare*. This is a simple petition through the Mother of God to her Son who is one with the Father. No one who asks, we believe, is left unaided. Again, I found the conviction that one must pray without questioning, without looking down. Ask quickly, and then leave the prayer suspended with no lingering afterthoughts. Faith and reason, both, with neither diluted. The petition escaped into the air and I glanced at my watch. It was six-thirty in the morning. We did have time to visit the hospital again for a few minutes. Soon we were on the too-familiar seventh floor racing to the end of the hall. Ahead at Kristi's door was yet another suspicious early morning gathering of the medical team.

From inside the room, Kerry broke through and rushed toward me, "We don't know what happened, but Kristi just woke up!" Not the news I feared. (On one of several similar occasions a nurse took me aside with this: "We have another 'situation,' but don't worry, this time it is not life-threatening!") I edged inside and searched past the half-drawn curtain. Kristi had been such a wasted and motionless figure, and we had not known when or if she might ever regain consciousness. But here she was, sitting up and beaming! She actually glowed with her dark-eyed dynamite smile. This picture so totally contradicted the medical situation. With a fresh breakfast tray delivered already at her side, Kristi looked so bright that all of these surroundings simply looked strangely out of place.

In front of all present, I fell onto the bed at Kristi's side and we held each other, and cried together. (Oh God, Kristi, I miss you so much!) It was 6:45 in the morning. "When exactly did she wake up?" I asked. Kerry looked closely at the clock. "Fifteen minutes ago." This was the same moment that on the freeway I had made the petition with the expectation of being heard. A coincidence, many might say. But John Paul II has reminded us that "Christians have no right to believe in coincidences." We love such coincidences and were learning to count on them.

In the coming days and then weeks, other traumas and surprises found us. In September we spent an entire Saturday sinking into perplexing symptoms, first at home and then back in the outpatient center. With the uncertainty still eluding diagnosis I was asked at closing time if I wanted to take Kristi home for the night. What kind of night might this be? I reversed the burden of proof. I challenged whether the remaining nursing staff, given the same growing uncertainty, wanted to be responsible for *not* admitting Kristi for continued close monitoring. In a flurry of activity, we entered the hospital, and I was given an extra roll-in bed for my use in Kristi's room.

We watched through the night. Not knowing what was happening, I recall thinking and possibly casting off a prayer that what we needed was someone like Dr. Alex. I had heard of this cancer specialist from my longtime friend, Eric, from high school and college years. Eric was a laboratory researcher for the Hutch. I knew from him that Dr. Alex was the world expert on transplants between identical twins, but I did not know yet of his empathy for those with medical allergies and sensitivities, based on his own personal understanding.

Imagine our amazement and delight on Monday morning when a new doctor presented himself at the door. "Good morning, to keep in touch I work at this hospital for two weeks each year, and I am assigned to this floor and to this room. You are my patient. My name is Dr. Alex." Kristi's symptoms were diagnosed. We were dealing with one of two kinds of blood infection. Blood infections are always fatal without special antibiotic treatment. Of the two treatments that might be used, we hoped Kristi could tolerate the one she needed. Surprisingly, this time Kristi showed none of the side effects expected from even the least sensitive of patients (alternating chills and overheating referred to as "shake and bake").

After only four or five days of hospital recovery, Kristi suddenly and violently threw herself back onto her pillow and rolled her eyes upward. The nurse had left only seconds before; I was the only one in the room. Before Kristi sunk, she got this out: *"I'm on fire . . . I'm burning up, from the inside out!"* Momentary unconsciousness, back and stomach cramps, clawed hands, an extended tongue and bugged and rolled-back eyes.

This time I was losing her.

My voice could be heard far down the hall. An echo hollered "Code Blue" and instantly a crisis team exploded toward me from three directions. In a few seconds, not more, they had Kristi hooked up to a new cart full of monitors, and she was injected with emergency drugs.[14] The second hand was ticking, and we waited. Of cardiac arrest, we would know in thirty seconds or a minute at most.

Four doctors and nurses surrounded the bed, and I found the fifth, the pharmacist, skillfully easing me away from the bed and out of the room. I ended up standing along the wall in the hallway, with the pharmacist between me and the entry. "My God, is she going to die?" I wondered. "What happened," and, "why am I standing here in the hall?" *Kristi was my wife more than she was their patient.* I pushed back into the room and to the head of the bed. Cradling Kristi, I lifted her forward even as she still arched her head back and resisted my hold.

"Stay with me, Kristi, stay with me!" I blatantly recited the Christian and always strange Catholic prayer, the *Memorare,* into her right ear. Loud enough for her to hear, however far away this might seem to her, I was also quite loud enough for all in the room to hear. What is this strange incantation, they must have thought? "Stay with me, stay with me!"

It was the (designated?) pharmacist again who tugged at my shoulders from behind trying again to guide me away. But behind him I heard the instruction of the wiser (and Jewish) Dr. Alex; "No, leave him alone . . . he is doing the right thing." As I pleaded into her ear Kristi seemed to relax slightly. I guided Kristi with a voice in her darkness — the antidote, I told her, would cause shaking, but to not be afraid of this, "The shaking means that the medicine is working." Someone needed to talk Kristi into not closing down. Someone needed to talk her through the crisis and her darkness and simply reassure her, second by second, that this time her reaction was to this cure and was normal, and not to be feared.

The trembling and the crisis drained away and fully subsided after forty-five minutes.[15] The grand mal seizure had come only seconds after a treatment of vitamin K, a very routine daily treatment for all patients. We were coming to understand that one danger in hospitals is the routine treatment of non-routine patients. Here again was cumulative error. For Kristi's medications an infusion line, a semi-permanent shunt called a "Hickman line," had been inserted near the collarbone. This line for receiving medications and daily hydration was crimped internally and so had been a problem for the past three months. We had declined an optional second surgery to fix it.

The pinched line already had made the weeks of home hydration very difficult, and now did not accept the vitamin K infusion. With a syringe the distracted nurse then injected the fluid too rapidly into an alternative tube. We did not know until a later interview that in this instance we were probably dealing with a potentially fatal medical error rather than an allergic reaction.

Days after the event and safe at home again in our own bedroom, my dear Kristi told me that she had heard my voice in her ear so far away. This alone, she said, is why she did not let go.

I think now of where I was positioned, at the right head of the bed. Was this the moment shown to me at our wedding rehearsal (see chapter 1)? Was this the moment I saw then, when the "20" (years) over the hospital bed was extended to a "23," and then a few years more? It is certain that Kristi was on the steep slide into cardiac arrest and probably would have died that minute — if our "extra pair of eyes" (which happened to be mine) had not been there. She surely would have died if the alarm had not been called. Was the prayer at the bedside the reason, and had Mary interceded again for us with her Son?

At the wedding feast in Cana, Mary once interceded with Christ over empty wine jugs. Our Lord said, "My hour has not yet come," and yet at the request of his mother He performed an unlikely first miracle, at that moment rather than at any other (John 2:1–11). He changed the water into wine and even His own path was changed from that moment forward. Perhaps it was the prayers of others that placed me at Kristi's side at that time. I have long suspected that the autumn before, in late 1995, our Fr. Ed Norris offered his last days of cancer for "a particular cause," for Kristi. Grace is everywhere, but we do not see it. And we do not see it in each other.

We often defer to God's "plan" for us as if it is a fixed blueprint (and rationalists rightly reject such fatalism as this). But nudged by our shared memory of Christ's response at Cana, we might suspect that "His plan" is love, and that part of *this* plan is to change the design itself if we but ask with total trust and self-abandon. Perhaps this in the design. Looking back from wherever we are, we usually see trends in the past ("history") and think we understand, but looking forward the future remains undetermined and always open to freedom, and to graced intervention so easily stirred by prayer. He works from within the situation, not from a frozen blueprint or what we too often imagine to be a fixed situation. If we but say yes, grace is almost genetic in its closeness, perhaps even more so.

The medical tone and technical terms in Kristi's record simply fail to convey what she endured through all of this. Medical sensitivity runs in the Orr family, but Kristi was by far the most extreme case. At one point, Dr. Alex paused at the foot of Kristi's bed to stress for us that the bedside teams always do look out for medical sensitivities, especially for the one patient in one hundred (the 1 percent) who demonstrates very severe reactions or allergies. For at least two very different drugs, Kristi was far off the chart, "one in ten thousand," he said. All told, he estimated as he washed his hands, "You are probably one in a million. To show where you are on graph paper, we would need to roll out a sheet running down to the end of the hall."

After many years of giving Kristi special scented soaps on special occasions, I found all of them neatly stored in a hidden place. All these years she had been appreciating the thought, but had been using special order facial soaps that did not contain troublesome additives. And for a period in the 1980s we did not subscribe to newspapers, because of the vapors given off by the printer's ink. When I called the distributor to cut off deliveries, I gave two excellent reasons, "My wife is allergic to the newspaper ink," I said, "and I am allergic to news!" I tracked down a small fan, and a transparent plastic sheet that Kristi needed to cover and read even ordinary books. This particular allergic reaction lasted a year, but thankfully was not permanent.

Our confidence in questioning all of Kristi's medications was emboldened by the memory of an earlier experience within the extended family. This came with Dr. Orr's heart attack and open heart surgery in the early 1980s. Reading the fine print and now suspecting that the medications were the cause of his severe disorientation, the family intervened forcefully to terminate the doses. (This was at a Spokane hospital.) It was only then that he recovered from all of his severe symptoms. The very routine and false diagnosis had pointed to dementia triggered by the combined stress of illness and age: "They often go downhill." This obtuse attitude remained unquestioned in the particular physician's mind at least outwardly, even as Kristi's father (also a doctor) faced him down eyeball to eyeball and strode out of the hospital into the light of day and the many remaining and normal years of his life.

At one point during Kristi's first hospital stay, and with this family episode starkly in mind, it was clear to me that the night desk simply did not get the picture. Back in Ohio I had received a despairing telephone call from Kristi's mother and twin sister (the extra pair of eyes during my four-day absence). Routine medications, so many times prohibited, had routinely slipped into the room when Kerry briefly stepped out.[16]

Having prepared for the unthinkable, a serious communication breakdown, I had thought to bring a key phone number with me on my flight with Mark to Ohio. My direct call to the home number of the primary physician reached her at two o'clock in the morning, Seattle time. "How is it," I quizzed, "that I can be in Ohio and have a better fix on what is going on in Kristi's room than your night watch, only fifty feet down the hall?" Here was communication, and there was no argument. To a most responsive, "What do you want me to do?" I laid out a simple plan: "Visit the hospital ward immediately, instruct the night watch *in person* on your rules for Kristi's medication, and then convince my vigilant family to their satisfaction that the team fully understands and has fully corrected the situation, and that you are fully in charge." Above the system, above any system, exercise direct personal accountability — this was my suggestion from two thousand miles away, and this was accepted. From my days as a naval officer, I knew clearly that the rule is you can delegate authority, but you cannot delegate accountability. Everyone knows this, not least of all medical teams. Turn away for a second, and routine takes over.

So many risks must be weighed by even the best medicine. So much uncertainty and so many patients. And for us, the confusion of surprise allergies or sometimes only medical intolerance, a fleeting disconnect in medical steps, or something so simple as a pinched shunt or catheter.[17] In all things human, there is such a fine and costly line dividing professionalism from distraction combined with pride dressed up as professionalism.

A patient in a numbered room is still a detail that matters. Do we end up playing the averages? Protocol over patient? With Kristi's regimen of treatments, it was once explained to me by yet another new physician on the overloaded floor, "We follow the *rule*, not the exception." To which I retorted without a second's pause, "Why not follow the *patient* instead of the rule?" It must have been the Spirit speaking through me. A thoughtful silence followed as if a light had gone on, and then a "yes" of agreement.

By now the chart at the foot of Kristi's bed was too thick to be read and *this* was the message. From this point onward the summary message was red-lettered by hand onto the outside cover. Finally, and again, "No medications." *None.* Hospital organizations — even prestigious research centers like the Hutch — consistently go out of their way to be more than organizations, but we still had quite a time of it.

In a hallway discussion while Kristi slept, I discovered with surprise that one of the doctors was reading the *Philokalia*.[18] I also was reading this, and even had a copy with me. What are the statistical chances of that? This book is a remarkable collection of meditative texts written by Orthodox Christians between the fourth and fifteenth centuries. It is the path of contemplation, much akin to the inspiration of St. Benedict in the West and St. Gertrude's Academy. The "philokalia" is the inner stillness that enables the deep listening — perhaps even between patients and doctors in modern hospitals. I was asked, and had to admit that, no, I was not reading it in the original Greek. Here for me was a needed and well-deserved prod toward humility.

I felt and knew again that we were on the same team and on the same page. A balanced look back on our hospital turmoil, deeper than pretending to assign blame, would show the heat turned up on at least three ingredients for miscommunication. Yes, there were disjointed medical steps, but there was also Kristi's delicacy, and my own agitation. These were not easy times.

We now read of the far too many patients who are reported to die each year from medical errors, including allergic reactions. A report by the Institute of Medicine[19] links medical errors in the United States to as many as ninety-eight thousand deaths each year. In 1996 Kristi was spared.[20] She again was an exception, this time *not* one in ninety-eight thousand.

I begin to wonder about the missed connection on a grand scale between what isolated specialists see at so many bedsides, and the separated decision to place medications on the stock market and then to stock them on pharmacy shelves, fine print and all. There are also the trial medications withheld from the market for too long. At best, this is an imperfect world.

On the way out the door for the last time, we contacted the most informed registered nurse who had helped us. From the records she assembled a list of some seventeen medications to be avoided in case we might ever have to return. This list included everything from morphine and codeine, as we had always known, to routine nonprescription drugs. The medical surprises extended to premedications, to preservatives in medications, and even to very minute amounts of plastic leached from infusion bags. In this last instance of leachate, this unlikely explanation had been suspected by Kristi's younger sister Lori. As an alert dental technician she had heard of *one* such case and connected the dots.

When the possibility of a reaction to the plastic itself came under suspicion, we confronted the routine and some of the self-assured team members. Admittedly, it did sound bizarre. There must be some other more reasonable — more familiar — explanation for the symptoms. But, as a benefit of the team approach, again there was the universally respected Dr. Alex. Gathering the others around the bed one more time, he was sufficiently confident in himself to listen to the patient. He offered the guidance that sometimes the patients actually know things about themselves that medicine cannot see. Further infusion of nutrients was delayed (the trial removal for a day or two would not matter) and the symptoms left us.[21]

During the long summer of the transplant and repeated outpatient visits and inpatient confinements for treatment, we shared the halls with Carl Sagan, author of *Cosmos* and the popular followup television series. He flew in regularly from New York for his own series of treatments and checkups. At one point I found myself speaking briefly with him in the outpatient waiting room. He was reading two books at the same time, one on race relations in the United States and the other, I think, on the Nixon presidency. An obviously thorough reader, he seemed particularly attentive to the footnotes and fine print. A worthy habit.

Much might be said about his naturalistic theology, and the apparent transplanting of the transcendent Creator fully into finite creation as if there were no difference between the two. But speaking one on one in the stark simplicity of a cancer ward waiting room, I found in Sagan's few words a sovereign kindness. While we would have differed on the unique incarnation of Christ as the divine intimacy and the Word made flesh (more than simply one manifestation among many), we did see eye to eye on the presence of cancer within families. Deeper than all of the complexity we can uncover by science, there lies hidden a universal humility within each of us.[22] We really can find simple ways to talk to each other, and to listen.

On balance, over the intervening years I finally see how the medical system and its professional teams went out of their way to openly invite outside watchfulness. From the beginning at the Hutch, the family and I had been urged to be with Kristi as "an extra pair of eyes." Pioneered at the Hutch, this safeguard is more and more recommended. I stayed with Kristi day and night, relieved regularly by other family members. Without this as part of the overall medical system, Kristi and I would not have enjoyed the extra five precious years together following the successful transplant. In all, we knew even then the good fortune of our access to the best medicine in the world, and we counted this as one of our many blessings.

What, then, of the vast many who have no medical insurance? And the millions of children worldwide who are beyond the reach of even simple medications, and who die each year from very preventable diseases? All of this is incomprehensible; out of sight, and out of mind. As an equation, presumably an ethical equation, the human predicament simply cannot be fully "solved." Discovering this boundary to any human effort, Blessed Mother Teresa found her place with the forgotten in the gutters of Calcutta. She tells us that it is enough to take each other one at a time. She encourages us to not despair at "the multiplicity of His presence." It is a mystery more than it is a management problem. And most certainly, we are not a math problem to be solved by subtraction, by deliberate and direct deletion of the unborn and of the elderly among us.

Kristi's "Poem"

With Kristi's treatments and her medical reactions came an unusual inner trial. For good reason, we called these allergic reactions "medication hell." Kristi's special words give a glimpse. The separate thoughts are gathered here from a period of several weeks during and following the transplant. From Kristi's experience all of us might be struck how in our most personal suffering we are still and especially not alone. We take part directly in the suffering of Christ, Who by our free conversion is the deepest center of ourselves. We are invited not only to imitate Him, but to *identify* with Him.

We should not have done this.
Don't let them give me the wrong medicine...

> Forgive them, for they know not
> what they do. (Luke 23:34)

My mouth is so dry, I'm so thirsty.
I'm so dry, help me.

> I thirst. (John 19:28)

Nothing makes any sense,
Everything is distorted. Everything is backwards.
Am I dying?
Am I dead?
Am I in hell?

I want to be free.
I want to run and play.
I want to be back with my flowers.
I want to go home.

> This very day, you will be with me
> in paradise. (Luke 23:43)

I can't remember. . . .
I'm disconnected . . . from my body,
I am dissolving.
The hospital is melting, and they want me to stop it.
Does Jesus want me to die?

> My God, my God, why have you
> forsaken me. (Mark 15:34)

Am I fighting too hard?
I must get up.
"It" is starting again. . . . Am I in hell?
I don't remember despairing against the Holy Spirit. . . .
I don't think I can find my way back.

I'm so dry.
One drop of water on your fingertip for my tongue, . . . one, not more.
I am choking! (this after an accidental two drops). . . .
Did I doze? If I sleep . . . I will die.
It keeps on going, over and over, and over, and over.

Will this ever end?
Help me . . .
I feel so miserable.
Jesus, Mary, and Joseph
Have mercy on me.

> Into your hands . . . (Luke 23:46)

Oh. Ohh! I'm on fire!
I'm burning up . . . from the inside out!!!

I had a dream that I was flying.
There were three of us. . . .

I don't know who they were . . .
Maybe they were just . . . friends.
. . . Can I . . . help you?

Oh, look at the geese!
I really do want to get back into life!
What a glorious day,
See the sunflowers over there.

. . . Peter, it's really true,
You really do love me as I am,
God has given us so many gifts.

> I do not pray that you take them out of the world,
> but that you keep them from evil. (John 17:15)

Am I dying? Am I dead? Am I in hell? Only inches away from my eyes, my battered spouse stares vacantly and motionless from her pillow. And with all seriousness, out of some inner desolation, she asks in terror and wonder if she is dead. I am barely able to guess at the unseen void that separates me from her. I thought to myself, Kristi has been chemically pistol-whipped by cancer medications. I reassure her, "No, it is only the medicine; this will pass."

Everything is backwards. What does she mean when she says everything was "backwards?" I sense it, but cannot define it. I sense where she is in the abyss and say that I understand, just enough. After all, what does hell look like from the inside?

Even later, Kristi is unable to define her darkness except by this single word — "backwards" — and it is still frightening. I now can venture a guess what might be going on spiritually. Kristi was always nurtured in and took for granted (a fitting word) the fundamental goodness of things and the friendship of people. I think that with her extreme intolerance for drugs this footing is unraveling, and she sees our universe for the first time as alien — from the outside.

(Perhaps she sees the Cartesian universe that has so misshaped our times.) *"I don't think I can find my way back,"* she says.

I suspect the medical team might have some insights into psychological disorientation, but this — the spiritual? I am informed that Kristi is likely slipping into possible permanent dementia. She might always be this uncomplicated and helpless. There is the serious specter that she might need to be institutionalized. We ease down the hall together to yet another room. Kristi does not do well on the diagnostic quiz.

I suspect that the quiz is too much "inside the box," and that maybe it is the routine quiz itself that is failing a larger test.... I search: would any additional medication be a self-fulfilling prophecy locking Kristi permanently into medication hell? With Kristi seated at my side, I most carefully face the two doctors and propose that they are missing something. I suggest that Kristi is suffering from the combined effect of current medication and hospital-related sleep deprivation. If so (I suggest for their review), then sleep — uninterrupted and *without* medication — could be the answer. In the worst case, I nudge, a weekend at home will make no difference. Within myself I restrained a growing rage, my and our worst enemy. With their consent, but no longer needing it, I bundle Kristi and we find the door and go home. I teach Kristi how to sleep again, and to sidestep her learned terror of dying if she dozes.

Help me . . . I'm choking. In the familiar surroundings of home and bed, I sit by Kristi's side. She asks for a single drop of water from my fingertip. A second *drop* falls accidentally to her lips. She swallows and begins to choke. A single drop of water? How dry must she be! (*"Peter,"* she pleads, *"I said only one."*) We cannot see beyond the visible as the hospitalized lie motionless before us. What happens, really, to so many of our silent people in rest homes?

Am I dying? Am I in hell? I don't remember despairing against the Holy Spirit. . . . Again, those frightened dark eyes stare out of a vacancy. The second question is most serious, the sin against the Holy Spirit. Kristi fears that she has been unfaithful in some way, and that she has despaired. She fears that she might have fallen into total despair about herself before God.[23]

The sin against the Holy Spirit is to completely turn away from Mercy itself. It is to do this under the fearing notion that while I might still believe in His mercy in general, I am particularly beyond the reach of a kindness that in this one case is less than infinite.

Of course this is a false fear. "No," I say as calmly as I can, "it is only the medication." Will this terror ever stop? Later Kristi tells me that while she *knew* that she was in hell, she still *believed* my reassuring words. In all our lives, we do well to use reason, but without neglecting faith.

I'm . . . disconnected . . . from my body; I am dissolving. We drift in and out of comas. The bewildered look on my Kristi's face. She is somewhere else altogether, and when it passes, instead of forgetting, as is the normal pattern, she remembers all of this. She confides to me later that in her dreams, mine was the only face that was normal, not mutilated and not "scorched and melting."

If I sleep . . . I will die. The problem is clear to my extra pair of eyes. This is not dementia, but could become so if more medication is given.[24] To correct sleep deprivation more medications — always with the risk of interaction — should not be added. Repetitive error, if done by a patient instead, is labeled as neurosis.

There can be so many bedside interruptions from so many different technicians. In the quiet of our home I rub Kristi's forehead slowly with a circular movement of my thumb. This is one little gesture that always relaxes my bride into sleep. Eyelids close and then flicker in the pattern of deep REM sleep (rapid eye movement), the first evidence of real sleep in two weeks. I stay seated by her side, not daring to stir. Kristi sleeps for two hours and forty-five minutes with no new team member to wake her to check pulse or to question if she is resting well. As she wakes the risk of dying is disproved to her, and more sleep follows. At the beginning of the week we are able to return to the hospital with the clear beginnings of a new Kristi.

I'm burning up, from the inside out! Later in the hospital again, this point in the "poem" marks Kristi's seizure and such a close call with cardiac arrest (the bedside episode is recounted above).

What a glorious day! And then, free again from the hospital, we walk in various parts of Seattle, to the beach, to a park, through the neighborhood. Two or three months of vigilant home care begin. Kristi sees the late season flowers and begins to live again. We join each other back on "the path," one day at a time, without looking down. It is a time to take short drives, to rediscover normal scenery, to visit the Seattle beaches and Whidbey Island in Puget Sound.

Of the transplant, Kristi said that one possible long-term effect she might not be able to bear would be a possible permanent loss of hair. We had already weathered a few rounds of chemotherapy, but now the repeated cycles had their way. We shopped again for wigs, together. For nearly a year Kristi still hoped and was light hearted, *"Is it getting any thicker?"* But then just as lightly, *"Just think of all the hair appointment money we're saving."* And, *"Think of all the combing I used to have to do."* This loss, so important to a woman, was a burden carried totally on the inside and revealed most completely only to her mother. I became the barber for Kristi's severely thinned hair. Clippers, kitchen chair, towel, simply another one of the little things we did together.[25]

Someday the slash-and-burn approach of chemotherapy will be replaced by more targeted treatments.[26] Partly due to research and experience — especially the experience of the patients! — chemo might become only a bad and fading memory in medical history. Racing from home to an outpatient center trying to outrun a spike in body temperature will be less frequent. And the complication of pneumonia will be less likely to cancel an otherwise successful and well-aimed treatment. There will be fewer quiet moments (as I witnessed) outside hospital room doors.

In a letter to the Hutch, following our last hospital episode, Kristi and I recorded our picture of missed connections by the ever-rotating medical teams. From the bedside vantage point, we told our experiences clearly enough, but in a constructive tone. Kristi wanted it this way. It was true that the Hutch was severely overloaded in the spring of 1996, and that with her allergies and medical intolerance Kristi was a highly unusual case. But there was more.

Responding to our letter, the Hutch reconstructed at one time and on one table our months under their care. The review team assembled and went through the written records thoroughly and then sent two letters back to Kristi and me. As advocates, we were respected and treated as members of this team. How to excel at both research for future patients and at the care of patients today who are no less real? There would be expanded procedures, they said, to protect rare patients. While continuity of care is carried out extremely well in most cases, they wrote:

> The points you raised have to do with many of the details that come across daily management of individuals who, as you well note, vary individually from one person to the next. . . . I would like you to know that in the coming calendar year we are beginning to make changes in our attending schedules such that attending physicians will have a thread of continuity from inpatient to outpatient service greater than has been held in the past by going sequentially from an outpatient service to the inpatient service in subsequent months and vice versa. . . . This extends not only to the attending physician level but also to the primary providers. . . .

Tatoosh Range, Mount Rainier National Park. "*Together we escaped to Mount Rainier to walk a short trail....*"

This sounds bland, but it directly met the challenge even as we saw it. Unbroken one-on-one familiarity with the patient is more consistent, even if case overload remains unchanged. Doctors and nurses are more in step as a team at the bedside of each patient. This effort was already under way even before our writing. Steps now were also under way to line up the patient's countless hospital visits — one for each specialist — into continuous time slots less disruptive and painful to outpatients. Patient care rather than health care....

But, finally, the problem is not limited to medicine. In all the modern world, how might the *person,* not the patient, remain more than a detail on the factory floor? In medicine, as in all things human, the elusive big picture must always be the transcendent human person in front of us. Not the research protocol and not the system. This is a challenging prescription for medicine and elsewhere (even my field of urban planning!). My surgeon father-in-law prayed each time before the first incision. First, do no harm.

A report from the Institute of Medicine (a follow-up to the earlier report cited above) leaves an opening for this kind of refocusing.

On the list, but not yet at the top of the list, treatment should be "patient-centered."[27] But even here, it seems to me, the patient is still seen as part of management and not as transcending all system management and all systems. Finally, the chasm is not a "safer health system." The chasm is the marginal last 20 percent of this system, the need for more coherent diligence at the bedside, not the 80 percent management down the hall.

In retrospect, I find myself asserting, probably unjustly, that while medicine may be *in* business, it still is not quite *of* business. The solution is cultural, not managerial. The need is for a less *distracted* sense of vocation to the patient. There is no system, or system of systems, that is equal to even one human person. Patient-centered medicine awaits a person-centered culture.

As Kristi's father detected thirty years before, we missed a turn when we redefined ourselves. It's all in the labels: "health care providers" and "health care consumers" (and "terminated pregnancies").

Yet Another Path

Less than two years after the transplant, in September 1997, a new cancer was found. Again it was bone cancer and again in the sternum. Kristi and I were nearly sure that this time it would be terminal. Together we escaped to Mount Rainier to walk a short trail above the timber lodge and enjoy again and for the last time the alpine slopes and flowers. It seemed that we would have a few more months. We were together, living the "sacrament of the moment" as if time did not exist. There was so much to bear. The heaviness had suddenly moved up into plain view. I casually snapped a picture of Kristi in a sun hat sitting beside the trail and searching the ridge crest to the south. Later, I thought, I might frame this remembrance shot for Mark and Laura.

When Laura was still small enough to carry on my back we had hiked up the trail visible on the peaks to the south, and then farther around the south side of the largest, Pinnacle Peak. And from there, in the far distance, we had seen the still intact Mount St. Helens (the eruption was a few years later in 1980). I had always dreamed of returning again, Kristi and I, with two crystal glasses and a bottle of wine. Now we were at least in the neighborhood.

Was this really happening again?

With the medical team we decided on another path. We went back to a treatment tolerated earlier and to more radiation. Thinking for the long term, Kristi also continued regular infusions of a bone hardener.[28] Over a period of two or three months Kristi eased toward the decision to undergo another unusual treatment clinically termed a "sternal resection." This is sanitized wording for cutting away and removing the affected bone, and then reattaching the disconnected ribs to a substitute synthetic pad (Gortex). Kristi had heard of one such case, and we asked for information about this possibility. At first our oncologist, Dr. Doug Lee, was opposed to such a radical procedure. But after his personal research and consultations he changed his mind, and Kristi cautiously decided to go forward in this way. I supported Kristi in her decision, and agreed that it was the right thing to do.

And so we entered another horribly anguishing path, but still a path. A close team of specialists was assembled from the Seattle area. Such decisions are so intricate, so vulnerable to the amateur views of patients and the easily fragmentary views of specialists. And the implications of any path that might be chosen can be so enormous. Should we do nothing? We did have the likelihood that the recent stem cell transplant was protecting us against any other cancer sites, and this weighed in the decision, which finally was Kristi's alone.

During the quiet moment of decision, Kristi said to me, *"We are doing this so that we might have a few more years together."* The only cancer site, we hoped and thought.

Heading into this huge unknown, we thought about the front yard, something we could handle. What else is there? For an empty spot we selected a dogwood tree. We had always enjoyed the blossoms on our walks together. Kristi was attracted to the flowers and now asked for nothing more than *"to live long enough to see it bloom."* Imagine her delight when the new tree did come into bloom and then, after it lost its flowers, fully bloomed for a second time only two months later.

In early April of 1998, a few days before Easter, the lower two-thirds section of Kristi's sternum was surgically removed.[29] Immediately following the operation, our close family surrounded the hospital bed. Kristi opened her eyes. The pain was severe. She was unable to inhale even slightly: *"I'm suffocating...."* A medical oversight — the more important pain medication, the antidote for "deep cutting pain," had been overlooked. (Overlooked!) This must be administered three hours early at the beginning of an operation. It takes this long to begin to have any effect.

This picture became clear as I stood beside the bed holding Kristi's hand, and she mine. I felt a slight squeeze, and her meaning to me (even now as in normal settings) was to be patient. Poised and motionless with her eyes closed, she was guiding me away from a very likely and disruptive demonstration of outrage. I asked the oxygen rate to be accelerated and coached Kristi to have confidence in very shallow and frequent breaths, to avoid even the slightest chest expansion. Breathe without really breathing.... This would be work, I hoped and promised. If she could escape any rib motion, she might also escape the deepest pain. The dose was given, but the unrelieved pain would continue for hours. This breathing technique seemed to help as we began the three hours of crucifixion. We continued, shallow breath by shallow breath. Finally, of the delayed pain killer, we heard, *"I think it's beginning to work."*

Placed on Kristi's pillow and then in her gentle hand was a special family crucifix. This was the same Benedictine cross that her father had held during his final days at home in Cottonwood two years earlier. It shows both faces of the Christian mystery, the crucifixion on one side and, on the other, the crucifix held high as a symbol of the resurrection. These are inseparable. With the resurrection are these words: *"Ejus in obitu nostro praesentia muniamur* — May we be strengthened by His presence in the hour of our death." This double image reminds us of His mystery within our very selves — that we are to be as He is when we finally see Him face to face.

On Easter morning, still in the hospital, all of this found a lighter tone. Light laughter in the hospital ward. Removing the food tray was a young high school volunteer. He returned to the room a second time and looking again at Kristi he felt safe to announce quietly, "Alleluia, He is risen!" And Kristi glowed that special dynamite smile and then repeated his words, *"Alleluia, He is risen!"* We all repeated his words, and then this teenager — his name was Joshua — actually knelt at the side of the bed and led us in spontaneous prayer. We learned that he regularly gathered before classes to pray with his classmates. They did this outside and next to the high school's flagpole, because to do so inside could be highly disruptive. The Creator of the universe does not have a hall pass.

The mystery on the Benedictine crucifix is that the Lord's real resurrection comes *through* real death, not simply after. This was a reminder to Kristi and me of the unusual visions experienced by the mystic Julian of Norwich. Julian lived in fourteenth-century England. At a point when she was very near death, she received over a brief day and a half a sequence of sixteen distinct visions. These "shewings" (showings) combined the suffering and the earlier transfiguration and resurrection of our Lord, these luminous events somehow contained *within* the first.[30] Before Julian, the face of the crucified Christ was suddenly transfigured into wonderful beauty, such that her own preoccupation with suffering was replaced with "an inexpressible joy and sense of absolute assurance."[31] Sometimes it is only through pain that we come to the deepest joy and absolute assurance. After her unlikely recovery from her illness (attendants thought Julian had died), she was so deeply affected by what she had witnessed that she spent the next forty years in a relatively solitary life as an anchoress.[32] The first twenty-five of these years were spent writing of her most gifted experience.[33]

Sometimes inside and through our pain we find the mystery of divine grace. It is to heal the troubled and lost heart that Christ came fully to us *through the veil,* at a single point in human experience (under Pontius Pilate in Galilee). Our inclination to turn inward to self and to recoil from pain and grace is a result of the primordial sin, original to each and all of us. This reflexive pride and its twin, fear, pervert and obscure, but do not eliminate, the gift of a still deeper and more original innocence. The enduring center of this innocence suspects, even now, that we are still in an enchanted and gifted universe. We are reassured of this by Mary's response to a messenger from the infinite Lord, in her "fiat": "Be it done according to your word" (Luke 1:38). We can be guided by the testimony of the saints. Mary's "Oh, yes [fiat]" even sounds a lot like the delighted response my future bride had given to a special proposal of more earthly marriage.[34]

The question presents itself: As part of this mystery, can ordinary people also suffer willingly and mystically for others? Are there some who do this in a way that makes a concrete difference to others? Are we "persons" only by being in communion with others, more deeply so than we can fully know in this life? Not by what we do here and now, but by what we are to become and by what we are already from the beginning? A little more free, might we see that our suffering truly and literally is part of His universal suffering for each and all of us, the Soul of our souls?

Some suspect that Kristi was such a "victim soul," one who chooses to suffer with Christ and for others. Kristi's prayer intentions do fit this two-sided pattern of self-abandonment. It seems that there really are some through whom healing is given to others. And then there are some, possibly including Kristi, through whom donated suffering is accepted for others. If any of this is true, then this truth possibly about Kristi is part of a larger mystery:

> Insofar as man becomes a sharer in Christ's sufferings — in any part of the world and at any time in history — to that extent *he in his own way* completes the suffering through which Christ accomplishes the Redemption of the world.[35]

At least something of this can be seen in the way Kristi endured and even accepted and embraced her given path of cancer. Through it all, she continued to identify with her "dear Lord" and with the unborn. Saturday vigils in front of the selected abortion clinic were more regular than the weather.

And along the way, Fr. Benedict Groeschel's visit to a street corner in the Pacific Northwest was another of Kristi's special consolations. In early 1999, he joined two hundred others in a Saturday morning street vigil in Everett, some twenty miles north of Seattle. In his writings, I now find that Groeschel has this to say about human suffering, and possibly about Kristi:

> [Christ] cries out and suffers still in his members. This mystery of Christ's continuing suffering in his members is obvious if anyone visits the Carmel in Dachau concentration camp; it confronts you in the chapel of Calvary Hospital in the Bronx, where the Stations of the Cross symbolically show *the suffering Christ manifesting the symptoms of advanced cancer.*[36]

Chapter Four

Interlude:
A Return to France

The love of God shatters every order established by man.
— Spoken to us at St. Gildard Convent, Nevers, France

Paris

In the spring of 1999 Kristi was in apparent remission. Again, we were free, and Kristi's family had surprised us the year before with shared donations enough to help us take a trip to Paris and other parts of France. Kristi's certificate and training ten years earlier in the travel field would be a big plus. This trip was to be an early twenty-fifth anniversary gift. We would include a pilgrimage to Lourdes in the foothills of the Pyrenees. Laura was now with her own family in Florida, but we were able to arrange for Mark to catch up with us in Paris during spring break of his junior year at Franciscan University.

As important as this return to France was for our Kristi (after twenty-six years), she still put others first. While our tickets were bought far in advance, we had one other step before our actual departure was certain. Kristi had to assure herself that my eighty-two-year-old mother in Richland (eastern Washington) was recovering successfully from a recent hip replacement. With her family background in medicine and her own high school experience as a hospital volunteer, Kristi wanted to help nurse and coach the recovery.

But with this done, in May Kristi and I boarded an early east-bound flight in Seattle. First on the list to visit in Paris was a street address Kristi had unknowingly walked past many times during her year at the Sorbonne (1971–73). This site was on the Left Bank, the Chapel of the Miraculous Medal at 140 rue de Bac. It was here, on November 27, 1830, that Catherine Labouré sat attentive in the presence of Mary the Mother of God. This most exceptional event lasted two hours. As is the pattern for many Marian apparitions, this was the same year as a revolution, also in France.

To the left and forward of the altar is the seat used by Mary, and to the right on the other side is her statue. The statue was completed at Catherine's request shortly before her death in 1876. The embrace of the spiritual world of eternity throughout our world of space and time is captured in this statue and a special symbol. Mary is portrayed as she appeared in a vision cradling a small sphere in her hands. During her last visit with Catherine, Mary explained that "this ball represents the whole world, especially France, and each person in particular."[1]

The transcendence that this symbol suggests of the truly human struck me — our exemption from the limits of time and space, length, width, depth, and geography. I mentioned this to Kristi and she politely tolerated my monologue. Only a few months before we had come across the writings mentioned above of the English mystic Julian of Norwich. As part of Julian's series of visions, she also beheld a simple "hazelnut." Despite its smallness, similar to the sphere, Julian was given to know that this hazelnut represented all of creation. Like the hazelnut and the sphere, the world as we know it has such smallness compared to the greatness of God and His action as maker, keeper, and lover. In this and other visions Julian understood God to be truly active in every point in space and time.[2]

As we had already learned, there is no circumstance beyond His reach. Fr. Barham had even wondered at the infinite worth of a single drop of Christ's blood. And Scripture tells us of the "pearl" of great price, greater than an entire field, and of the final dimension achieved by a single mustard seed. This deflating of the immensity of our physical universe within a "larger" spiritual reality was both fascinating and healing for me. The vastness of the soul within, this capacity for God, is larger than the desert wind or a vacant sky randomly scattered with distant stars.

But my particular conceptual need to see through the size of things was never part of Kristi's less distracted psychology and inner life. At rue de Bac she was simply with one of her special friends. In her travel journal, Kristi writes of our daily visits to the chapel. "*I wanted to go to confession, so I sat in back in line, but went up to sit with Peter and Mark for communion.*" And then, "*After Mass, I went up to bid adieu to Catherine Labouré. I love this chapel; it is a holy place. . . . A we were walking out I saw a pilgrim priest near the door, so I asked this dear priest to bless my [religious] medal. After blessing it, he asked me (in English) to pray for him. St. Catherine, please pray for this dear priest.*"

Before crossing the Seine and l'Île de la Cité, we also visited the Musée d'Orsay art museum. Dr. Orr had long been interested in painting and had done several watercolors and oils. His sense of color and hue variety was highly refined, as one might expect from a fine physician who could easily distinguish one tissue or subtle symptom from another. On one wall was a small framed field of green accented by a pattern of orange flowers. Kristi thought of her Daddy and wrote, "*We saw Monet's Les Coquelicots (The Poppies) done in 1873, which Daddy loved. . . .*"

At Notre Dame Cathedral I was again taken by this entry into another world. This is a world in which human continuity and our wonder before creation are larger than mathematical space. Symbolically this is expressed by the replacement of the rose windows of Notre Dame and other early cathedrals, with clock faces on more recent church towers. Translucence is replaced by mere measurement.

While I was quickly drawn into the cathedral architecture, Kristi was drawn to a single candle. She wrote, "*We went to the adoration chapel in back behind the choir and prayed and lit candles for the family and friends. It was so beautiful and quiet back there . . . we bought a Sunday missal in French for me.*"

This soaring architecture of light is an excellent place in time to reflect on the reason for a series of monthly sermons delivered there by the cardinal archbishop himself, Jean-Marie Lustiger.[3] Tracing at least to the Revolution, the rupture in the heart and mind of France has led to two opposed appetites for power. These appetites, he says, are felt either by those seeking a restoration or by the Christian Marxists. Standing free of both, the cardinal would rather restore the Church's role as one of service rather than either or any kind of power. The symbol of the priesthood is Christ washing the feet of others. Lustiger is a leader in planting a new and deeper culture in place of both factions.[4]

Stepping from Notre Dame to the opposite side of the Seine, the Right Bank, we visited a museum — the Musée de Carnavalet. Kristi found a new journal she liked and began to record her daily impressions of our special trip. And here we inspected a collection of relics of the Revolution of 1789. The ambiguities of the Revolution were not lost on Kristi. She long had been interested in French history, especially following her earlier studies in Paris.[5] The serious flaws of the ancien régime exacted a terrible price. Revolutionaries desecrated the Notre Dame Cathedral, which had embraced us only moments before. Conscripted by the forerunners of modern rationalism as a temple of Reason, the cathedral served as a chamber for a recruited goddess of Reason who displayed herself in lurid ceremony on the central altar. Here for certain and for all to see were the excesses of any human construction based on passion masquerading as reason and unleashed to stalk human victims on an unbent knee.

Kristi, always attentive to the personal, recorded this detailed journal entry: *"I found the French Revolution rooms the most interesting. We saw paraphernalia. . . . These included a reliquary with articles of St. Peter and St. André belonging to Louis XVI as well as a leather pyx, map reading instruments, his spoon and fork, a lock of his hair; also a ring belonging to Marie Antoinette and a lock of her hair."* To Kristi, the loveliness of the world was in the details, and she was always rescuing me from myself with her special way of seeing. Her attention rested finally on an oil portrait of the standing ten-year-old Louis Charles (the Dauphin, or heir) at the time of his imprisonment by the revolutionaries. I had glanced already at this piece, but had not seen his eyes the way Kristi did.

Kristi was transfixed, *"His eyes are so sad."*

She recounted to me how this young boy was torn away and separated from his imprisoned mother, Marie Antoinette. Although a child, he was also heir to the throne and therefore eligible for special abuse. (With the modern-day erosion of the family itself as an institution, child abuse has become more widespread, ever more "democratic.") From her readings Kristi told me how this mother and son had been much maligned by modern historians. In many respects the rise of the new powers fed on the desecration of the family and religion as much as it did on the destruction of the old political powers. Von Kuehnelt-Leddihn once quoted to us the insight of a living French diplomat that the slogans of liberty, equality, and fraternity are based on "murder of the father," and here the king.[6]

Lourdes

After five days we left behind the streets of Paris on our way south, attracted by the more rural landscape. Historians tell us that the rupture at the cultural level in France between the logic of reason in the urban north and the logic of faith more in the south helped feed the cultural split that reinforced the Revolution. This difference and then divorce between two worlds seemed to be still visible on the landscape in the numerous scattered countryside shrines. In the village squares we thought we saw more spires free of clocks.

Our first destination was Lourdes. Kristi's family intended our trip as a pilgrimage to this site for consolation if not for healing. The Grotto at Lourdes is the place on the map where Our Lady appeared to the fourteen-year-old Bernadette Soubirous eighteen times during the first half of 1858. I had lit candles many years before at a replica of this shrine in Immaculate Conception Church in Seattle to celebrate the births of both Laura and Mark. And another shrine on the grounds of St. Gertrude's Academy in Kristi's Cottonwood, Idaho, also depicts Mary as we see her statue at the Grotto of Lourdes.

Besides Lourdes, many other shrines and apparition sites are still remembered in this region of France, perhaps dozens. But Lourdes is the only one judged to be authentic and formally recognized by the Church. Here the figure of the apparitions identified herself as Mary, the Mother of the Christ, the incarnate second person of the single triune God. In a moment of immense respect, Mary was asked and gave her free consent to be mother of the incarnation.

And this moment, which is at once outside of time and within time, grace worked in both directions. First, with the coming of Christ the future was altered forever. Second, His coming even transfigured the past. Mary's "fiat" (yes) affirmed her free surren-der: "be it done to me according to *your* Word" (Luke 1:38). This acceptance of her role as the Mother of Christ is reflected *retro-actively,* in a sense, in her preservation at the moment of her own conception from the inner fracture and separation so original to ourselves (rather than to God), the original sin. Mary's original innocence is in no way turned away from Him who made all of us from the beginning. At Lourdes, Mary identified herself to Bernadette in her own dialect: "Que soy era Immaculada Conceptiou" (I am the Immaculate Conception).

In 1999 we were among the six or seven million visitors who are drawn to Lourdes each year. Among the visitors are nearly a million sick and handicapped from all over the world. They are attended by volunteers. The year before we had shared lunch in our Seattle home with one such volunteer. Ed was fully converted from his bout with religious indifference by what he saw with his own eyes at Lourdes. He told us that as a result he stayed as a volunteer stretcher-bearer for much of the following six months.

In our confirmation classes at St. Mark's Parish, in the early 1980s, Kristi and I sometimes referred to a book, *The Miracle of Lourdes,*[7] by Ruth Cranston, a Protestant researcher. Cranston describes several of the most documented cures. These are organic healings rather than psychiatric, although she also points to frauds who have tried to gain entry into the official record. In the investigations, the Medical Bureau develops case files over a period of a year or more. Then these are much more fully developed by the International Medical Commission that was formed in 1927 for this purpose. In each case the line of research must demonstrate a real and sudden cure to a real illness that prior to the visit to Lourdes showed no tendency toward improvement. The role of the commission is to find evidence of cures that are permanent and for which there are no natural or scientific explanations. Validation also requires a third step, separate acceptance by a Canonical Commission of the Church.

Of the thousands of apparent cures at Lourdes, the sixty-sixth fully documented and accepted case was completed in May 1998, only one year before our arrival. The cure took place eleven years earlier in 1987 and involved a man crippled with multiple sclerosis. Volunteers lowered him into the waters of the bath, but he soon moved fully on his own and had no further need for helpers or for his wheelchair. The cure has been permanent.

During our visit to the Grotto, we recalled Dr. Orr's table talk about Alexis Carrel at Kristi's childhood home on the Camas Prairie. Carrel witnessed and documented the earlier healing of Marie Bailly, a bedridden victim suffering from advanced tuberculosis and abdominal inflammation (peritonitis). And of prayer, Carrel later wrote in his small volume simply entitled *Prayer,* "Everything happens as if God listened to man and answered him. The effects of prayer are not an illusion." God both speaks to us and listens. As Kristi and I had learned together, we are to pray with expectation for our concrete needs.

In her appearances at the Grotto, Mary spoke these words to Bernadette: "I do not promise to make you happy in this world, but in the other." (There were one or two times when Kristi seemed personally attentive to this message.) Bernadette, the privileged witness, was canonized in 1933. She was a favorite among Kristi's special sainted friends. Kristi saved a brochure on the secret of happiness found at Lourdes. It tells us that we find at Lourdes: "The gospel, the poverty of an unencumbered heart; the prayer, which opens us to God; the conversion, which changes our life; the Church, which gathers us together as brothers and sisters."

We loved this place and were happy to visit several times during the next four days. Of the Grotto, Kristi wrote, *"We sat and prayed here — it is such a peaceful spot, a little piece of heaven!"*

On the third afternoon we turned west into the magic of the snow-peaked Pyrenees and then returned to spend a special evening in a small village restaurant facing these slopes. Our head chef spoke very little English but said he had been trained in Indianapolis. He also had worked for a few months in Washington, D.C. We were the only ones at table, and the several courses he sent out to us seemed to go far beyond what we had ordered. From our seats it was not difficult to almost hear the advancing army of Hannibal during the Punic Wars. With his elephants he passed somewhere between the snowcapped peaks above on his way from Carthage to test the gates of pre-Christian Rome.

After several walks in town, Kristi sat at the writing desk in our hotel room: *"My knee is so much better; Mary I think has blessed me with a little miracle!"* She concluded her diary entry with this: *"Another beautiful grace-filled day! Mother of Lourdes and dear little Bernadette, please pray for us. Bon Nuit."*

The following day we paid one last visit to the Grotto and then found our way east and then northward to the thirteenth-century citadel of Albi. A massive brick cathedral marks an important site of the Albigensian war, the first internal crusade in Christendom. Here is a history with at least enough complexity and blame to go around. As part of this puzzle, Christian marriage — as a concrete and fruitful union of physical and spiritual persons — was threatened seven hundred years ago, as it is again today. The Albigensians explained the existence of evil by pointing to two different gods. One of these is good, and the other is evil *and* the real source of our earthly and bodily existence. The human person is not both body and inward spirit together; rather the spirit is trapped in a physical cage.[8] In the most devoted adherents, contempt of the body was to be expressed through unfettered choice of starvation, suicide, and abortion. Total renunciation was most convenient on one's deathbed, oddly reversing the opposite practice by many early Christians (the Emperor Constantine in the fourth century comes to mind) who postponed their baptism until an imperfect life was clearly at an end.

Marriages in general and each marriage in particular, and *our* marriage — and the beauty of conception — these were directly threatened by this aberration in the human family of families. Christian marriage does not divorce grace from nature, nor the reverse. In Catholic thought eros, the "theology of the body,"[9] is not rarified Platonic eros — eros as a thirst for beauty, but still confined to the world of concepts and ideas. The physical and the spiritual are inseparable this side of the veil and inseparably graced in marriage. The alternative is dualism, and even a rejection of the incarnation. The physical and the spiritual are not like oil and water but graced in a harmony and covenant that mirrors and is mirrored by the intimacy of Christ and all of creation.

It was largely the politics of Albigensianism that was fatal. Rejection of loyalty oaths finally invited a broadened counterattack from the hilltop castles across much of France. In time these new power centers would evolve in the West as "the state" *fully* apart from reverence (equated with the church), which in our day would undermine marriage. Marriage becomes neither a sacrament nor a covenant, but a state-assigned hall pass. Some also see a direct line between the spirit of negation that bubbled up at Albi and our devaluation of the most vulnerable in our culture today. In the post-Christian and radically secular state, abortion and euthanasia have also found in the courts a new host organism not unlike the cult at Albi. In time this resuscitated cult might market cloned body parts for some while openly harvesting the same parts from others whom we choose not to recognize because they are so small. If we are not willing to bow our heads, it seems everything we might do runs the risk of being only a caricature of service to others.[10] The revelation to us in our technological age is not so much that there are two commandments (love of God and of neighbor), but more precisely that one comes before and enables the other.

Beaulieu sur Dordogne

North of Albi we stopped at Souillac for the night where the roadway crosses the Dordogne River on its course west to the Atlantic. The next morning, instead of following it downstream to the well-known castle sites of Sarlat and Begnac, we decided to turn upstream. On the map we had discovered a village with the family name, Beaulieu sur Dordogne. This upstream path took us through Martel. Here we recalled how the grandfather of Charlemagne rallied the Merovingian kingdom at Poitiers in 732 to repel the Moorish invasion of Europe from the west.

A few miles farther we discovered our special destination — the village of Beaulieu. I believe this is the village of origin in the history of my father's family, as partly researched by a genealogist for my grandmother. I believe that it was from here that my father's ancestors set out for Quebec in the early nineteenth century.[11] The name Beaulieu means "beautiful place," and this is accurate indeed. For very good reason Beaulieu is also known as the "Pearl of the Dordogne." A deciduous forest drops down toward a mirror-like stretch of the river. Church bells ring on the hour from the octagonal central tower of the abbey, where it has stood for nearly one thousand years. Here was a vantage point in history for viewing, as from the outside, many of the shallow preoccupations of our admittedly vibrant times.

The Benedictine and Romanesque Abbey St. Pierre, completed in AD 1140, is the site of an earlier monastery begun at the founding of the town in 855. Part of the abbey, the restored sacristy with its uneven stone floor, dates from 860. This was more than a century after the battle of Poitiers, but followed by only a few decades the death of Charlemagne. During the continental religious reforms of the late eleventh century the abbey was placed in the hands of the monks of Cluny. Later still, during the Hundred Years' War and on the heels of the Black Death, the foreign English armies made their way as far south as the surrounding Dordogne Valley (1356). The episodic history took another turn when the Huguenots, French Calvinists, took Beaulieu in 1569. The monastery was damaged but later restored and then was totally destroyed in the Revolution of 1789.

Only the abbey and its hourly ringing of the bells have survived from their early beginning and persevere to this day. In the surrounding silence, the forested hills seemed to almost breathe and to remember so much. I was reminded of this same silence as I found it in the Idaho forests at Kristi's home on the Camas Prairie. We are too quick to see nature as only a setting for the little things that we do or as a resource pool to support the little spot in time that is our present.

A very short stroll east from the abbey led us to our hotel room, a third-floor garret framed in generous heavy timber. From here the abbey tower met us at eye level and filled the opened west window. The river sparkled directly below the opposite east window. Our *"great adventure"* — Kristi's term — was our canoe trip on this river the following morning, eighteen miles down the Dordogne. This had been a season of especially heavy rain, and our daring adventure was only one year after the operation to remove most of Kristi's sternum. Yet she was the most eager to test the waters. A lot of spunk, there.

Less than a minute after our launch the swift current caught us sideways and we capsized. The water was shallow enough at this point for us to regain our footing, and for me to rescue Kristi with my right arm and her wig with my left. Mark dragged the canoe toward the nearby island.

Taking inventory, we found that we had lost nothing except one paddle and, much more interesting later, the channel map. With a fixation on methodical foresight, I had made sure we launched with an extra paddle, three instead of two. But Kristi wanted to eventually return all that we had rented and was intent on finding that which was lost. *"We will pray to St. Anthony."* Every now and then, this would be Kristi's answer to my forgetfulness, while I would begin a typically anxious search for whatever had been misplaced. Then in the very same breath Kristi completed her remark: *"Oh, look, there it is!"* Far on the other side in an eddy under a steep embankment was the glint of orange striping on an orphan paddle.

We made our way downstream in segments, stopping and looking and then advancing, and portaging where necessary. At times Mark caught sight of his mother standing at the water's edge in her white coat soaking wet and looking a bit apprehensive. He egged her on in the special little way he had with her: "Come on, Mom, this builds character." After three hours we were overtaken by a flotilla of five boats paddled by an experienced German group. One member spoke English, "I am from Hamburg, he [pointing] is from Munich, and these others, from Heidelberg. We like this river. It is less quiet than the Loire last year. This, you know, is white water. It is very important to listen," he added, "because you can hear the dangerous water before you see it."

Five hours after our launch, six boats drifted together into the deceptively placid stretch of controlled water shown in tourist photographs of Beaulieu sur Dordogne. The slipping sun painted only the tops of the forested and enfolding hills, and here and there a half-hidden hillside chateau.

In his book *Surprised by Joy*, C. S. Lewis mentions another special valley like this, in his English countryside. His valley had brought enchantment to Lewis in his youth. After his intellectual concessions to narrow rationalism and materialism were found wanting, he again recalled this early experience of deep "delight." This sense of delight was inexplicable to his "Lucretian" mind-set — the modern and cramped presupposition, shared with the long-ago Lucretius, that existence is fully defined as a complex swarm of atoms.

Lewis questioned his own atheism. This materialist notion offered no explanation for Lewis's delight. This kind of delight is a gift, not a phenomenon. A delight because it certainly comes from an "other," and this other is a giver. Human existence has a face at its heart, and a name, and Lewis as a complete person was becoming free again to feel truly loved, because he was *not* fully at home here. He was more than an estranged observer on an alien rock pile in space. He found himself to be a Christian.

In the valley of the Dordogne this testimony came back to me, carried by a gentle breeze sweeping from the hillside into my own soul. During a morning outing I had turned and was looking back from the foot of the hilltop bastion of Castlenau.[12] We were still in sight of distant Beaulieu. On the hour the bells of the Abbey St. Pierre lifted up from the valley and mingled with the singing all around us of the birds.

This precise moment spoke to me. This was my valley! This was my delight. Each hour, year after year and over the centuries, the chime of distant bells is carried up by a cool breeze from somewhere far away and deep within. And mingled with this is the singing of birds, and it is one harmony. I announced to an unsuspecting son, "Mark, no one has a right to live in a place so beautiful as this."

On this last full day at Beaulieu, the country roads led us to Rocamadour, a shrine and pilgrimage site clinging to the side of a canyon wall a few miles south. Viewing the *vertical* construction still from a distance, I was startled by a new and refreshing sense about all of our humanity. Everything we do is molded by the landscape and natural world in which we have lived from the dimmest beginning. And yet, we really are "pilgrims in a strange land" here below, passing through, and equally free in whatever period of history we might find ourselves. The inner compass points and draws us beyond any horizon. The human person, and especially one's wife, is the greatest adventure and a holiday from the weight of history.

Past visitors here have included Queen Blanche and her son, the king St. Louis IX. When the men of Beaulieu leveled the nearby castle of Astaillac in the thirteenth century, it was these monarchs who disciplined the band and exacted restitution for the widows. And Louis, even as king, routinely served with his own hands the hundreds of impoverished subjects he invited each week into his residence. As our friend von Kuehnelt-Leddihn reminded his audiences, it is against monarchies of this mold that we might measure occasionally the table served up by some mass democracies of our times.

On our final morning, we made one last visit through the heavy wooden doors of the abbey. Inside, this empty Romanesque cave — a witness to nearly one thousand years of history for the French people — was filled with the powerful organ music of Bach, a German with a universal art. Shafts of morning light cut through the notes from high window openings. Our very new and dear friend, the organist Jean Grivel, sat cradled alone in this enormous setting. Nearly deaf now, he was transported as his hands practiced their gift.

Jean was now seventy-six, and his varied career included sixteen years as a banker in Senegal. Home now for many years in his place of birth, he donates his time and musical talent. He was one of the very few town residents who spoke at least a little English. Kristi immediately loved this dear fellow. And since her death Jean has written to me each Christmas. He is another who was touched by Kristi's indefinable quality. "As you, we are sure that she is now with Christ and watches over you, your children, and surely over us who met her." And the following year, "Receive our best wishes and our prayers for you and Kristi your wife who is near God now."

Breathing the air of our village on the Dordogne, I felt so much at home, or nearly so. I am exactly one-half French, but the other half is German. As a teen I asked my father, only once, if my blue-green eyes were blue or green. "French green," he snapped and grinned. My mother's blue-eyed family also came to the United States in the mid-nineteenth century and traces its history back to Hanover (Northeim), Lippe (Detmold), and Bavaria (Langenzenn). The family tree on my mother's side (Hattstaedt and Brauer) includes a Lutheran minister in every generation for five centuries back into the 1500s.[13] Catholic priests are in each earlier generation for another two centuries. Probably the watershed was the dividing of turf under the Religious Peace of Augsburg in 1555: *Cuius regio, eius religio* — the ruler of a region determines its religion.

The crossing of these two European paths in America and in my parents, in God's mysterious way, was an intended challenge and grace for the family. During my high school years I sometimes felt that through the generations the deeply divided cultural and religious map of Europe hovered above our family of five. The three worldviews for us at my hometown were our own more or less Catholic and Lutheran roots, with both of these overshadowed by the very dominant scientific hubris of a twentieth-century nuclear boomtown, the Manhattan Project. A sign of eternal hope, my parents, German and French, married on September 2, 1939, the day following the Blitzkreig invasion of Poland and the full-scale start of the Second World War. Even friends predicted to them that the marriage would last not more than a year, but they did not really know my father and mother.

Looking to the future and to Europe, Kristi and I thought sometimes about the emergence of a person-centered, and therefore Christian-rooted, culture on the Continent. This might stretch from the Atlantic to the Urals and might be barely possible again with the formation and expansion of the European Union. This large boundary harkens back to a time before the urban hinterlands were politically divided by state boundaries cutting across and reshaping so many complex human populations. And it looks toward a deeper and more culturally united future.

Pointing to and anticipating this larger cultural unit, in 1983 John Paul II elevated the Eastern saints Cyril and Methodius as co-patrons (with St. Benedict) of Europe. Recent history and the dismantling of the Iron Curtain offer the chance for people to breath again with both lungs, with the dynamism of the West rooted again in a deeper contemplation more intact today in the recently perse-cuted East. Our vision might again reach beyond the horizon of our own artificial endeavors. In his visit to Poland in 2002, John Paul II supported Polish entry into the European Union. But at the same time he reminded the European Parliament that if its charter does not clearly acknowledge its Christian roots — respect for the human person who is always prior to the state, and for religious institutions apart from the state — then this lack of foundation in a globalized world will almost certainly undermine any meaningful union within ten or fifteen years.

Less transient than politics and economics is the stone bell tower of St. Pierre Abbey. On the morning of our departure, Kristi caught the spirit of Beaulieu in her journal: "*This morning we woke up hearing the river, the birds and the abbey church bells from our garret windows. This is such a beautiful spot — I really do not want to leave this heavenly spot. The day is sunny so we went out for a while on the veranda to watch the river. . . .*" And thinking back to all of Paris and now to the deeply rooted charm of tiny Beaulieu sur Dordogne, Kristi also made this enormous statement to me, "*If we ever come back to France, I would rather come to Beaulieu than even Paris.*"

And in eternity the fully unfolded human memory will surely treasure the splendor of this exquisite valley. Through His eyes, we will see how it has been consecrated not only by the devout monks who discovered it at the sunset of Charlemagne, but also by the stroll under a starry sky of a devoted couple, more recent by a millennium and just passing through like the stream beneath our garret window. In the Great Springtime a thousand years are as a single day. Time does not exist.

Nevers

After Beaulieu sur Dordogne, Kristi, Mark, and I drove north to Nevers. Here we found the convent of St. Gildard, founded in 1680 by Benedictines, the same order that founded St. Gertrude's on Kristi's Camas Prairie in Idaho. St. Bernadette of Lourdes rests here in a glass-enclosed shrine. We arrived at the chapel and shrine in the early evening and Sister Margaret Mary offered to break her routine and give us a special tour of the convent grounds and buildings the next morning.

We began with morning Mass in the chapel. Other tourists were present, including a group of about twenty pilgrims from Germany. I find this entry in Kristi's journal: *"After Mass a German pilgrimage group surrounded us (in front of Bernadette's crypt) and sang German hymns so beautifully that I cried."* In my heart we still stand there together, and I love even more now the beauty and simplicity of those few tears. St. Augustine said it best in his *City of God:* "The tears of a single woman are worth more to me than all the emotions of the Roman people."[14]

For our special tour, Sister departed from the usual route and led us to the upstairs infirmary where Kristi's dear Bernadette died after a long illness. Our guide also told us about herself. Sister was Dutch born and had spent ten years in the jungle camps of Cambodia serving the refugees from the Khmer Rouge and Pol Pot (a Sorbonne graduate) and — some would say — from the abruptness of the U.S. departure from Southeast Asia.[15] Our guide spent part of each year at St. Gildard, while summers took her to Brighton, England, where she donated herself to one of only a handful of homes that care for patients with AIDS. Not cut out for the strictly contemplative life, she announced, "You have to *do* something." She had spent a little time in Japan and had heard of the Language Institute of Odawara where Kristi had taught for six months in 1971.

Standing together in the morning sun, we prayed that our Mark, now three years into the Marine Corps Reserves, and Sister's nephew, who is also named Mark, would be spared duty in Kosovo. (As I write in early 2003, Kristi is gone and Mark is deployed to another battle, in Iraq. Kristi, pray with me again for Mark.) At one point during our visit, Sister mentioned so off-handedly the entirety of the Christian message. With a matter-of-fact tone she turned the world right side up: "The love of God shatters every order established by man."[16]

In her diary Kristi entered this note to her special friend: *"Good night, Bernadette, please pray for us,"* and later, *"We bid our farewells to Bernadette — dear little saint, guide our steps toward our sweet Savior."* The following day we returned to Paris and were treated to a wonderful meal prepared by the family Kristi had served as governess over twenty-five years before (Françoise and Patrice in Noisy-le-Marly, not far from Versailles). The two children, now fully grown and conversant in English, joined us with a special hug and kisses for the gentle caregiver they remembered so fondly.

From Paris, our flight took us through London and then over the polar route to Los Angeles and then back to Seattle. Upon arriving home from our pilgrimage and special vacation, Kristi concluded her diary so priceless to me now: *"Peter and I are happy to be home. Thank you, sweet Jesus and Mary, for a blessed trip. We pray we can return again one day."*

In addition to Catherine Labouré and St. Bernadette, Kristi's other and most special friend was (and is) St. Therese of Lisieux (1873–97). Therese, the Little Flower, rests now in Lisieux, France. We were unable to visit Lisieux, but how happy Kristi was when

Therese came to us instead after our return to Seattle. The relics arrived on tour in January 2000.

Therese is the saint of the very simple path, a needed hint for our overly complicated and threatening times. She died at the early age of twenty-four near the beginning of the twentieth century (1897). The daily prayer is short and ends, "St. Therese, help me to always believe as you did in God's great love for me, so that I might imitate your 'Little Way' each day." We began this daily prayer in 1990 under the caring inspiration of Fr. Thomas.

When asked what she meant by the "Little Way," Therese answered: "It is the way of spiritual childhood, the way of trust and absolute surrender."[17] This smallness depends on trust. It is the freedom of humility, a fully human freedom of the moment dropped into a world so often organized to extinguish this spirit of the smoldering wick. There is a delight found in little acts of self-imposed freedom, as in fasting. Over the years Kristi found this prayer for the "Little Way" to be a powerful one in its smallness, capable of keeping even the fear of cancer in its place. The Little Way is the spirit of acceptance. Mother Teresa of Calcutta (beatified on October 19, 2003), too, reminds us that nothing is small in the eyes of God.

In the last line of her autobiography, Therese writes, "I beseech You to cast Your divine glance upon a vast number of little souls. I beg You to choose in this world a multitude of little victims worthy of your love!" Perhaps Kristi is one of these.

The path of Therese's traveling relics included a stop at St. Joseph Carmelite Monastery in north Seattle. The monastery is near our home and even within the boundary of our St. Mark's Parish. We were among the more than one million in the United States who visited the relics in churches, monasteries, and cathedrals across the country in late 1999 and early 2000. It was the morning of January 24 of this pilgrimage event that we found ourselves sitting quietly with perhaps a dozen others before the reliquary. We were part of the work crew for the day who were privileged in this way.

As we sometimes did, we caught the attention of an attending priest. We asked him to pray with us for Kristi's healing. This time the message nudged us toward a different path. He too seemed to have the special gift of healing, but was the first to guide us more toward courage than healing. Kristi and I, always together, paused without a word. No words were necessary. Within marriage, and especially between spouses sharing a danger, understandings can be woven from so many threads deeper in the fabric than any words. We stepped a bit closer toward what might be sent, but then simply looked forward to the day's events. We were present to the moment — one day at a time without looking down.

As I write, the renewed memory of this short silence together restores to me a fleeting but deep repose. I remember. There really is something, a direct kind of access, in a moment of silence. I am reassured again that in death Kristi did not simply leave me behind, but that at every step we did this thing together. And that this togetherness in its intimacy and solidity is indestructible.

Chapter Five

Into His Hands

Spending my heaven doing good on earth, like St. Therese.
— spoken on Easter Sunday, 2001

It's Starting Again...

"Just think, Peter, we made it to fifty!" It was Kristi's birthday, July 6, 1999, and together we had outrun the cancer for this long. Kristi had been keeping track ever since it first struck her at the age of forty, ten years earlier. A fiftieth birthday is something of a marker.

And then shortly after our return from France, we learned that the cancer had lodged in two tiny new sites in the pleura of the right chest wall, the same side as the mastectomy in 1989. We were thankful not to have known this before our trip. Our pilgrimage to Lourdes and our special vacation to Paris and other parts of France had been light and uncomplicated.

We did not know exactly how long we had and there was still a blessed vagueness about the future. We did know now that the disease was systemic and permanent. Another heavy phone call to Laura in Florida, a continent away. Mark and I took a break from shingling the back roof of the house, and over a cold beer this time I broke our news. In two weeks he would return to Steubenville for his senior year. He had absorbed similar news three times before, once in elementary school (1989), once coming out of high school

214

(1996), and then two years later. But this was different. Thoughtfully he asked the question: "How long do we have?" I gave a wide range, up to five years, but finally I answered the question, "Probably two years."

As the months passed, Kristi sometimes would notice someone less fortunate, perhaps a cerebral palsy victim confined to a motorized wheel chair. *"Compared to her, my cross is nothing."* Never had there been even one word of complaint. Not once in all twelve years. Once, near the end, on our way to the parking lot from a hospital waiting room Kristi did remark to me, *"Look at that person smoking, and he is healthy, while I have cancer in my lung."* This was more of a whimsical note than a complaint, and it was as close as my Kristi ever came to complaining about the cancer.

On March 21, 1999, Kristi left a seemingly harmless note for me next to the kitchen phone. *"I'll be right back. Doctor wanted me to have an ultrasound of my arm at Northwest Hospital. P.S. Honey, could you grate some cheese? Love you! Kristi."* (The final meaning of a series of checkups would be given to us one year later to the very day.) We took the new evidence and this new trial one day at a time. More trips to the MRI for a liver scan, and then the brain and the spine. Here we were clean, or as clean as we could tell. Because of past reactions to the dye used in these tests, we settled for the reduced 85 percent reliability based on test images not sharpened with dye contrasting.

Count the small blessings. Kristi liked the foot rubs while she was in the MRI machine, and we noticed and enjoyed the little things — even the shady boulevard to and from the hospital. We turned to a new chemotherapy agent[1] and entered a pattern all too familiar.

Sometimes in a quiet moment after still another visit to the hospital, I would propose to Kristi, "the Lord is good." This was a phrase she liked. And with heartfelt enthusiasm, Kristi would immediately proclaim, *"Oh, Peter, He is so good!"* Such a release of inner joy in response to my tentative words. The mix of daily notes in Kristi's handwriting on our calendar for that summer of checkups and day-to-day living is almost comical. July 29: *"Tumor smaller,"*[2] and July 30: *"Venetian blinds arrived."*

Friends came to the door with special dishes. Josie, with her husband, Luis, presented a special Filipino dish. She faithfully continued to care for all of the needs of her own family, even as she carried on with kidney failure and dialysis at home five times a day. After more than a decade, the Lord was to release her into His mansion only a few weeks later. Josie was always such an inspiration to Kristi and me.

As the days ticked by we approached our twenty-fifth wedding anniversary (October 12, 1999). This year our reservations were scheduled well in advance. The year before, we had taken the long-deferred hydrofoil trip north on Puget Sound for a three-day stay in Victoria, British Columbia, the site of most of our honeymoon trip in 1974. This time it was to be a simpler weekend at a Victorian bed and breakfast in Coupeville, a favorite village destination on the rural Whidbey Island.

The week before our escape Kristi became frighteningly disoriented from an anti-nausea drug.[3] She was pulled back into medication hell, an impossible situation. Kristi could not continue the medication, and yet, having been on it for weeks, she would have to ramp down as best she could. To stop such drugs abruptly is very dangerous, so a declining dose over a couple of weeks was prescribed. But Kristi simply would not hear of it. It was not tolerable.

How to endure both the drug and its sudden withdrawal at the same time? I gathered Kristi into the car and judged that what she needed was more time for the worst of the medication to wear off a bit more. I reassured my girl — fear is also an enemy — and we headed for the country in the opposite direction from the hospital. (In looking back, I see that this was as reckless as it was desperate, but I at least checked in advance that Coupeville had an emergency room.)

As autumn rains fell from a solid gray sky, we spent the entire afternoon in our quaint bed and breakfast second floor bedroom, me with Kristi in my arms. *"You just stayed with me and held me, all afternoon,"* she would recall later. This new trip into severe medication hell did finally pass us by. In the late and drizzly afternoon, Kristi was not well but asked for a short ride.

Was the church nearby? We wondered where we might find a refuge and visit the Eucharistic Presence who asks so much, but who also gives so much more. The country road led us for a few miles past the water's edge and inland fields, and then back again. Returning to the town, we impulsively turned right. Was it more than coincidence that the church appeared around this particular corner? And that the locked door was kicked open for a second or two by the cleaning lady, precisely as we parked at the curb? We felt welcomed. Inside we found our solitude together and a place of peace. We simply sat quietly facing the tabernacle and He surely looked back at the two of us.

The new medicines had seemed so promising, but were a disaster, too debilitating to continue on even a reduced dose or cycle. The ever smaller and widely spaced chemo doses could not be effective. We were down to one-third of the recommended weekly dose, and this was on alternating weeks. But even at this rate it was not tolerable. The last dose came a few months later on March 8, the fourth anniversary of the death of Kristi's father. Kristi's decision to discontinue this final treatment had come over a period of several months and even years. We would also dismiss the most experimental protocols offered to us and available in other parts of the country to patients willing to be part of a test. What would happen if Kristi had a likely severe reaction during the monthly airplane trip, and this for a medicine whose benefit to any particular current patient was likely nothing more than statistical information?

After these many good years, the cancer and its treatments finally brought us to this: *"Peter, is it all right with you if I tell [the] doctor I cannot take anymore . . . ?"*

We had reached this point. Was I willing to let my precious wife go, for her sake? Was it over? The effects of some cancer treatments are very tough and unpredictable for the one in a hundred . . . but for "one in ten thousand or one in a million?" From all of our years of past experience, we knew where our line was. In my heart I knew that when Kristi was clear about her absolute limits, that this in itself would tell me that she had gone as far as she could — physically, emotionally, and spiritually. I would simply remain at Kristi's side and accept the fact that now she would slip away from me.

We were coasting. There is a communication without words. On the surface my answer was yes, it was okay. And I did mean this, and even now would not hesitate. We always had been on the same path together, and I knew the truth of it.

In his familiar office, Dr. Lee turned to me after Kristi so calmly reported her decision. Such composure, even in this. Looking me in the eye, he asked what I thought. Beside me was sitting the love of my life. "Whatever Kristi wants on this, I can accept. We are together." We were totally together on this, but this was also beyond my ability to fully absorb. As always — one day at a time, and do not look down. It is as if I was anesthetized within my mind and my heart, or was I sharing in Kristi's trust in her "best Friend"?

"There is no one here," he said, "who could find fault with this decision. You have given this the 'old college try.' And you know as much about what we can do here as we do. You have done everything, more than anyone else." Our case file covered surgery, chemotherapy, radiation, a very difficult stem cell transplant, and most of these more than once, and then all of the medical intolerance and allergic reactions, and constant MRIs. Kristi's file came in three stuffed folders instead of one.

At first things went as usual, but month by month Kristi became more tired and I was to know that my wife was slipping away. Our children, now grown, would lose their mother. Mark was twenty-one, and Laura was twenty-four and with her own family. This would add to other losses in their young lives. In the autumn of 1995 a traffic accident had taken Jeff, Mark's best friend from early grade school onward. And later this year, Laura was to lose her best neighborhood friend, Amy. She would die of an inoperable brain tumor at the age of twenty-four.

Thinking now of Kristi, I do remember noticing that this turning point must be one of the first places where distancing by a spouse might begin. In little things perhaps not even fully deliberate, the survivor might begin to plan ahead and alone about the future, a little here and there. All of this to reduce the blow. Without need for reflection, I decided and knew with certainty that I would never set foot on this path of separate thoughts toward a separate future.

Kristi, for her part, remarked, *"People say that I have courage. Even our doctor says that, but he doesn't know. I am not courageous at all, I am nothing."* But at other times Kristi found consistent support in a favorite verse, "I can do all things in Him who strengthens me" (Phil. 4:13).

Unable to consider morphine or even codeine, we would need to discover another pain medication. We simply trusted that this could be found. Sufficient for the day are the troubles therein. And still we were blessed. At first Kristi felt very well. In December of 1999 we invited her mother to travel with us to visit Laura and Rob and our three grandchildren in Florida.

On one sunny Sunday morning it the beginning of 2000 we were in our Seattle living room. Kristi rose from her chair and looked

over the davenport into the front yard past our hawthorn tree and
the new dogwood. Bathed in brightness from outside, she spoke to
me now of her other world:

> *I worry about you.*
> *I don't want to leave you alone.*
> *And Laura and Mark.*
> *But for me, it's a win-win.*
> *From life to greater Life.*[4]
> *I know this with a certainty.*
> *I've just had a long talk with Jesus —*
> *my best Friend.*

Oh, to know *this* with a certainty. I was so lifted by this profession and window of true hope. I preserved Kristi's words that day
on a scrap of paper and still carry it like a picture in my wallet.
(This particular fragment, this relic, is the nucleus for writing this
book.) Over a year later I would read these words back to Kristi,
and she was so surprised, *"You actually wrote down something that
I said?"*

In spring of 2000 we enjoyed a wonderful event at Franciscan
University. It was Mark's graduation in mathematics with a minor
in theology, with much of this work under an inspiring and evangel-
ical convert.[5] And in the summer we drove once again the familiar
path across eastern Washington and into central Idaho for a family
gathering. Along the way we stopped at the wheat country community of Uniontown. In the late 1800s the Benedictine nuns had
stayed here for a few years before selecting their permanent location at Cottonwood. Kristi entered our names in the guest registry
of St. Boniface Church on July 2, 2000. This was a pilgrimage site
for the global Jubilee of the new millennium.

Our home in North Seattle. "Bathed in brightness from outside, she spoke to me now of her other world."

The church building was begun in 1904, and in 1910 it was the first to be consecrated in Washington State. The noble brick Romanesque design is distinctive from the outside, and the interior is a world apart from the surrounding wheat fields of the Palouse prairie. Two rows of freestanding Corinthian columns support the vaulted interior, matched by five stained-glass windows shaping either side-wall. The interior character is dominated by the richness of the statuary and fourteen evenly spaced Stations of the Cross and carved woodwork. Across the front, standing vigil, are the life-size Joseph and Mary, then St. Francis and St. Boniface, and St. Patrick and St. Anthony of Padua. Several figures stand above and on either side of the central tabernacle. On the right is Kristi's favorite St. Therese and then St. Francis Xavier, the first missionary to Japan. Even with three aisles and seating for maybe five hundred, its aesthetic character was a little like our simpler Holy Cross Church on the Camas Prairie in Keuterville.

On the front façade, I discovered a consoling symbolism that I have seen nowhere else. Here again is the rose window, a glimpse of the translucent and eternal, but above this is also a nod to the here and now. The clock *with* the window, neither excluded by the other. And then higher still, silhouetted against the blue prairie sky and seeming to embrace both time and eternity, I was greeted by Mary with open arms, the "queen of heaven and earth."

Not long after this visit to St. Boniface, autumn brought the first real sign of new trouble. There was a hoarseness in Kristi's voice. Probably a virus, she thought. It continued for several weeks and then months. Yet another appointment and MRI finally detected a new cancer site. This new site was in the very upper apex of the right lung and this happened to be pressing against the right radial nerve near the collarbone. The new site finally explained Kristi's mild and then increasing arm discomfort of the previous year, and now it was paralyzing half of Kristi's vocal cords. Her right eye was dilated. A neurologist recognized this set of symptoms as a classic case of Crohn's disease, but from an uncommon cause.

The loss of voice continued into the first months of 2001, but symptomatic therapy did bring slight improvement. Textbook cases of the disease are uncommon, and the neurologist cautiously asked if Kristi would agree to be interviewed by three or four medical students. With the unruffled calmness of her childhood, of course she said *yes*. During high school Kristi and Kerry had worked as volunteers in the Cottonwood hospital, and early in his career her father had even delivered a paper on thoracic surgery at an annual meeting of the American Medical Association. I know she did it for Daddy as much as for the students.

In the coming months Kristi would be interviewed again. A media team in Seattle became interested in her story and the serenity with which she was handling her terminal disease. Interviews were not the kind of thing Kristi was inclined to do. But she was asked, and so she agreed. A television crew visited the house. Kristi was only slightly nervous about this, but composed herself and must have bewildered them with her answers. I was at work on that day, but know that she must have mentioned unfamiliar things like the value of suffering and acceptance of the will of her "dear Lord," whatever it might be. The footage was not aired, but our girl was at peace with the whole encounter and it could have been a wonderful consolation to many viewers. (What more correct kind of response would have been accepted by the clipping table editors?)

In a better year (probably 1985) Kristi had been interviewed by another camera team. This was during one of the bus trips to the state capitol building to mark and mourn the anniversary of *Roe v. Wade*. She was disarming to this team as well, and as I sat beside Kristi on the bus I was proud as always to be her husband. She spoke in such a non-political and unguarded way. Then the interviewer turned and asked me how long these annual events might continue. A moment of silence, and finally I answered accurately into the microphone, "As long as it takes." This footage, mostly of Kristi, was prominent on the early evening news. The camera panned back from the excited newscaster to reveal the capitol dome behind and an even more monumental rainbow sweeping a complete arch overhead.

Now, in the spring of 2001, Kristi paused for a minute in our Seattle recreation room. She looked out the window toward the evergreens in our backyard and of her lost voice she whispered:

You know what I miss?
It's the singing.
But I'll be singing soon.
The Lord's going to give me a new voice.
I'll be singing again in heaven!

There it was again, her unusual degree of freedom in letting go, and her eager anticipation of new things to come.

But soon anxiety symptoms crept up on us, and we did not think these were emotions only, or something simply in Kristi's head. We took short afternoon drives — to a park, to the waterfront restaurant, and one or two times to Alki Beach in Seattle. We had gone here five years before to help Kristi walk off the devastation of her stem cell transplant. *"Peter,"* she said, *"You have always been here for me."*

During this period Kristi unexpectedly called me at work from time to time. It was the unexplained anxiety symptoms: *"It's starting again."*

These signs seriously worsened on Ash Wednesday, February 28, 2001, and the day of the first large Seattle earthquake since 1965. There were other signs of reduced stamina. Walking up the flight of stairs to the bedroom sometimes left our girl breathless. More trips to the hospital and more tests.[6] This cycle showed that the left lobe of the liver was probably affected, and the right scapula and the pelvis. The medical record comments that "we believe she needs systemic therapy at this point in time."

The cancer was out of control. It had begun.

The goal now was not a cure, but relief from rapidly advancing symptoms. Pain control. The right scapula was radiated to shrink the tumor. We continued, as best we could, to hold down the recurring anxiety and the nerve pain throughout the right arm. Several new medications were carefully considered, but even the few we could risk triggered severe reactions.[7] Kerry and her mother made the first of several trips from Idaho to our home. Kristi and Kerry, always soul mates, still thrived in each other's company.

The final period began on a Friday afternoon, March 16, 2001. Kristi had taken a particular over-the-counter drug to ease the nerve pain. New disorientation took over, but subsided over the weekend. On Monday morning (March 19), the Feast of St. Joseph, Kristi called me at my office, this time at an early nine o'clock. The anxiety symptoms were now looming. I came directly home and by midafternoon Kristi was nearly immobilized in our darkened bedroom, and each half hour she was noticeably weaker and farther from me. More calls from the bedside phone to the hospital. The seizure during the transplant five years earlier flashed before me, but this new meltdown was "*worse than anything at the Hutch,*" she whispered. Oh God, I cannot imagine how this could be so. How many times had we known this sinking from moment to moment?

Kristi was clear that she wanted no "extraordinary" treatment.[8] It was not morally required. It had been a year since we had discontinued our ineffective treatment, and with full justification. The minutes and half-hours passed, and in our darkened bedroom we were sure that our Kristi was dying today. She simply wanted to accept the Lord's will, and to stay clear of either pharmaceutical heroics or euthanasia. She chose graceful surrender and hope over willful presumption or despair. Her life was still very much a gift to protect even now, and in no way her own possession.

So many times over the years it was nearly impossible to see clearly what was happening. Too much medication? Or too little? Or some other unknown interaction? And the clock was ticking. Is it an allergy and dangerous, even life threatening? Or is it sensitivity only? So often we had run into such in-the-dark decisions. This time the physician on duty felt that an emergency room visit would involve only the standard anti-allergy drug (epinephrine), and not again such fearful and now futile interventions as the ventilator. I was to be vigilant about Kristi's temperature and ready to make the move.

Finally, and so very weakly, Kristi said to me, *"I think my system is closing down. . . . "* Again in bed, she turned her eyes up to me and asked, *"Promise me that this time you will let me go."* She feared the possible full battery of pointless treatment at the hospital, and now she seemed beyond the point where I could even move her.

I promised.

But there was the doctor's telephone advice. As Kristi followed me with her eyes I picked up the phone. I called the emergency number. To my wife, so weakened, I now had betrayed a promise and a trust. Excitable and always needing to be in control, she must have thought. "It's too hard," I agonized and looked away. Totally alone I hoped that I was taking care of my spouse who was also so totally alone. I trusted that by this phone call I was saving her rather than dooming her to indefinite medication hell, the very thing we had guarded against for so long.

Our pastor, Fr. Kemp, arrived almost as soon as he was called. He gave the last rites. The emergency team was with us, and their equipment remained scattered across the bed. Minutes later Fr. Kemp stood aside in the downstairs kitchen and gave his reassurance as we hurried from the house to the waiting ambulance. Mark and I were nearly certain that we were losing Kristi, perhaps even within the hour.

In the emergency room we sat quietly by Kristi's side and together prayed the special prayer we had learned along the way. St. Matthew teaches and assures us that where two or three are gathered together, there too is the Lord in our midst. This is a great mystery. But we had been guided to the extraordinary and less familiar next line above this one, "I say to you further, that if *two* of you shall agree on earth about anything at all for which they ask, it shall be done for them by my Father in heaven" (Matt. 18:19–20).

Medical allergies can be fatal, but for us the effects of the suspected painkiller passed their critical twelve-hour point and began to dissipate. A set of x-rays was canceled. In this wrenching episode Mark and I were emotionally inoculated a little against Kristi's postponed death. Everything from this point forward seemed such a glorious reprieve. At midnight the three of us stepped together under the stars and into the crisp night air. Kristi, mostly recovered, thought back on the day and said what I needed so much to hear: *"Peter, you did the right thing."*

On Monday, Dr. Lee ordered a full battery of diagnostic tests. On his clear instructions these were conducted even beyond the laboratory closing time. At home again, we waited two days for the results. Kerry and Jeanne arrived again from Idaho at seven o'clock on Wednesday evening (March 21). We sat together on the davenport. Twenty minutes later the phone rang in the kitchen, and I rose to answer it. It was Dr. Lee. Listening to his forthright report, I finally asked Mark's question to me from two years before: "How much time are we talking about?"

"I could be wrong," was his answer, "and have been in the past, but it is between one and seven weeks. Do you want me to talk to Kristi?"

"No," I answered, "I will talk with my wife."

The soup of cancer cells in the pleura of the right lung had finally joined and rapidly spread to form a kind of shell. This had wrapped itself entirely around the right lung "like an orange peel." Kristi was being strangled. Her body was working on one good lung. In addition to the weakening caused by the cancer itself, she was being deprived of oxygen. Small wonder that walking up the stairs sometimes could take her breath away or that the nervous system was sending panic signals back from all parts of the body. This invasion was the organic source of her growing anxiety over the past several weeks.

Kristi's anxiety suppressant could continue to mask this symptom. On the phone Dr. Lee and I already had touched bases on future dose levels, which now were to be ramped up with caution. Possible addiction and kidney involvement were no longer realistic concerns.

In the living room I found Kristi sitting quietly where I had left her a few minutes before, beside her mother and her dear identical twin sister, Kerry. But in the phone call the entire world had changed. "Kristi, that was Dr. Lee." They might have overheard, and surely in her heart Kristi already knew the message.

I simply said what Kristi already knew, "Dr. Lee says that we have between one and seven weeks." I paused and then gave the details. Kristi turned so serenely to her mother. They were sitting so close, hand in hand. Her first thought was compassion. *"Mom, I'm so sorry. . . . Just think, I will be with our dear Lord and with Bernadette."*

Jeanne had lost her husband, the doctor, in 1996. Now she was to lose a special daughter. In a handwritten note Dr. Orr was still very present to his family for times like this. Kristi had treasured her copy in recent years. It reads: "Dismiss all anxiety from your mind. Present your needs to God in every form of prayer and in petitions full of gratitude. Then God's own peace, which is *beyond all understanding,* will stand guard over your hearts and minds, in Christ Jesus" (Phil. 4:6–7).

I have violated this truth so often. I have left open the door to inner torments ever eager to gain entry and to multiply themselves. They are legion. But there has also been a beacon in something Kristi had said, and this has given me intermittent peace. I am lifted by Kristi's own view of all that had happened to us over the past twelve years. She had been standing in the kitchen when she said these words:

> *I would not want to do that again....*
> *But I would not want to have missed it either.*
> *The grace...I would not have known.*

This is not a passing remark. Through it all, Kristi treasured most the grace given, and the grace Giver.

On the Edge of Eternity

Written on the wall calendar for March 21, in Kristi's calm way, I find this matter-of-fact note: *"Dr. Lee called about tests."* In a way, it seems so simple.

In the coming days I roughly noted in a tablet a few of our daily events. These notes grew into a small journal that I would eventually photocopy to give to Mark and Laura. I hoped it might help them in coming years to remember their mother as she really was (and is). The idea for this book came later. The remainder of this chapter is based on this journal and tells our story of nineteen weeks of hospice care in our home. Some is priceless sweetness, light moments. Consolations, even special consolations, came our way in the final weeks that Kristi was with us and even afterwards.

As before, the unbroken thread through these five months (longer than the predicted few weeks), and the source of Kristi's serenity, was her inspired devotion to the Real Presence of her "dear Lord" in the Eucharist.

This devotion imprinted from within everything in Kristi's life — the sadness, but much more the joy and delight in so many ordinary things. Every day at first, and then each day that she was physically able, we received communion brought to our home. Kristi was now the shut-in. She knew that at each Mass, all members of the Mystical Body are present, within the truly present Heart of Christ, unbounded and undiluted by physical distance or the passage of time. As Fr. Steckler had taught us at the beginning of our marriage, there is no distance in the Communion of Saints. In this communion our very selves are incorporated into the one Christ with something of our original innocence as at our baptism. And we are insepa- rable from each other — connected to all those nurtured by the same saving image of God within.[9] And the self-abandonment of Christ calls for a similar self-abandonment from those who receive. Everything that we love will endure, in truth and not only in imagi- nation, and will not be taken away. Each day, Kristi was falling into His arms.

And now, at each Mass, Kristi is truly beside me. To some this is denial, but to others such presence challenges us to a much deeper affirmation.

The stillness of Kristi's inward prayer after reception of commu- nion was uncommon. Unknown to us, this unselfconscious and yet visible devotion had become a great inspiration to others in our parish. At home after a long pause Kristi would stir and her eyes would open, and she would emerge to help conclude the final group prayer. Our friend Colleen, who came to us each day, took me aside in the driveway a few days after Kristi's death. She confided to me that it was by simply watching Kristi that her own faith — then pos- sibly slipping away — was restored. Here was a conversion without a single spoken word. I am told there were others.

March 25. This is the Feast of the Annunciation of Mary. On this special day and at my side in the dining room, I felt a familiar nudge against my right shoulder. Here was the same surrendering smile and tilted head Kristi showed me on the day when she said *yes,* that I was the one she chose to marry. *"This is a new experience, Peter. Dying. And I don't know how good I'm going to be at it."* A shared private second for us with a lightness greater than the burden — me and my most vulnerable flower petal, overwhelmed at the imbalance between helplessly dying and still wanting to get it right.

In the first few days, Kristi scanned the obituary page of the newspaper. *"Look at all these people, every day, and we don't really notice."* And then later, *"Why make such a big thing out of dying? People do it every day."*

March 26. *"Just tell them some days are not as good as others. Who knows, after lunch I may be up dancing on the table."* The hospice care team was fully assigned and started on this day, only five days after Dr. Lee's call. Bev was to be the hospice team leader from Providence Hospice of Seattle.[10] She would visit at least once a week at first and more as needed. We were entering something new.

Kristi wanted to never, ever, leave home again for treatment. We had always intended that home hospice care would be the path. We knew little about this, but favored the home over the anonymity sometimes found in hospitals, and like a growing number of others, we were learning on the job. Hospice care recognizes dying as more than a medical process (*hospis*, a resting place on a journey). Help is provided where the patient is, rather than collecting the patients where the hospital investment is. The hospice concept actually traces back to medieval monasteries, but in modern times began in England in the late 1960s.[11] Nearly two thousand hospice programs exist in the United States. Physicians are free to recommend hospice for patients who are not expected to live longer than six months, and our remaining time together was measured in weeks.

Oxygen cylinders were delivered to our door, and I was trained in their use and in the use of a separate and nonportable oxygen compressor for the bedroom. The compressor came equipped with a lengthy plastic tube and nasal piece. With these aids Kristi could come down the stairs as far as the recreation room. We would have evening movies, and Kristi already had several in mind. In the bedroom we found that the hum from the compressor worked like a lullaby each evening when it was time. Kristi's growing tiredness and a repetitive cycle of day and night medications — periodically adjusted — became the routine.

Death was imminent.

Under hospice we would be sure to respect Kristi by letting nature take its course, without actively intervening in any way to cause death. Academically we had bumped into the ethics of this boundary years before at the table on the Camas Prairie. Once or twice I had even found reliable documents on medical ethics and sent them to my father-in-law.[12] I had known at least obscurely that my need to clearly understand these questions might someday be more than academic. Now, in our society we have a widening hole in the dike — physician-assisted suicide (PAS) first in the Netherlands and Belgium, and then in Washington's neighboring state of Oregon.[13]

With Kristi, the ethics of dying was personal and finally upon us. We were familiar with "living wills" and had gone through this drill five years earlier at the time of the stem cell transplant. This time we chose not to sign any of the available forms. Now, as the primary care giver, I would always be present to respond directly and to make specific decisions if Kristi could not.

Part of the path before us was to deal with pain and with possible depression, which too often can predispose patients toward short-cut decisions. But with Kristi's devotion to her "dear Lord" we always kept moving in a more graced direction. Our path would be one of acceptance and of trusting dependence on additional pain medications that we had not yet identified. Together we mapped a course day by day for the girl I married. The possibility of facing these days without morphine had always been over the horizon and carefully out of mind.

Was all of this really happening?

We raised up a short prayer to find a pain suppressant that might be tolerable. The phone rang the next day. Eileen was a friend from several years earlier, and is a widely respected hospice nurse. She offered herself as a volunteer assistant to Bev. Twice blessed. Eileen is uncommonly gifted in being intently present to each patient as a whole person, and then in remembering obscure medical details that matter to the particular person in front of her. She recalled immediately an older painkiller that might work for us (Levorphanol).[14] She explained that the molecular structure is different from the more recent and common pain suppressants — morphine and codeine — which Kristi could not take due to her allergies. We would have to find and try it. We had a chance of being lucky.[15]

As we eased into hospice, there were still the everyday quips and the bantering. I remarked to Mark and Laura that "I don't want any noise in this house. I want it silent!" And it was Kristi who quickly answered in their place, *"Okay, I'll try to be quiet."* She agreed with Laura that even light makeup was an unneeded distraction: *"This isn't a beauty contest. Remember when I used to keep my nails painted. . . . Oh vanity of vanities."* And of the wigs so carefully selected over the past five years, *"When I'm in heaven, I'll have the prettiest hair. Curly! And all natural."*

March 27. *"I wish we could just get there. Sometimes I feel that my faith is so weak. But I know God uses our weakness to make us strong."* Kristi grew eager to make the final transition. One day at a time . . . Kristi's attention on new things to look forward to was now fixed on "the Last Things." This was actually happening.

Each day we learned important details. Water by itself is tasteless and becomes difficult for patients to swallow. I would like to have known this from the beginning. A touch of lemon or mint or anything else will help. We did happen upon watermelon chips; these were attractive and the season was right. Family arrived, Kristi's and mine. My two brothers, John and his wife, Kath, and their three grown sons, and Tom and his wife, Janet. Over the years our visits between Seattle and California had been so few. Friends and parishioners lined up several times each week to deliver wonderful dinners. This gift may seem so little, but such thoughtfulness and daily contact helped to change totally the tenor of what was happening, and this can never be repaid. Each evening the new and special tastes maintained Kristi's appetite and willingness and ability to eat and drink. Yet with each week and then each month this capacity tapered off. We were warned to expect this as Kristi's overall health and digestive system closed down from the cancer.

March 28. "*So, there are no more doctor's appointments. That's actually a relief... after all these years.*" Kristi brought a moment of laughter.

Fr. Steckler called. He was our Jesuit friend from my graduate school years. He had attended our wedding in Keuterville and in more recent years had visited us from time to time for lunch when passing through Seattle.[16] His call came from his parish on the Oregon coast, and he spoke the thoughts of many when he said, "I will always remember Kristi as effervescent, ebullient, and alive!" (Two years later he added, "The thing about Kristi was that she always listened intently to what others had to say, whatever it was. So self-effacing.")

This date also marked the end of the first week of hospice care. We were now inside the one-to-seven week period that had been given to us. Kristi spoke of flowers and crosses: "*You know, this could drag on for a long time. That would be really embarrassing, after all these flowers.*" And later, on waking from her daily nap, "*All the dreams have been good ones.*" And then, "*I asked Cherie [her sister] to ask [pray] that this goes fast... but maybe I want it too easy. I know that He does not want us to choose our own crosses.*"

March 30. We began thinking about having more time together, maybe seven weeks rather than only one or two. We took a short walk in the sun in the back yard. Mark and I decided to plant four climbing roses. Kristi had long wanted climbing roses in the back yard to fill the gap along the fence left by the removal of a row of matured evergreens. From left to right these roses, all shades of pink, are Collette, Compassion, Pearly Gates, and then my favorite, Angel Face. I expected that I would care for these each year as part of a severe emptiness and a moving-on that I could imagine only dimly.

April 2. *"There, now we've done a few things. We've trimmed the bouquets. They look a little better now. Don't they?"* And that evening Mark discovered a rainbow outside his upstairs bedroom window. Kristi made her way upstairs and saw this as a silver lining as she always did, *"Oh, a sign of hope!"* Several months after the death of his mother, Mark would confide to me that these declining months were even harder for him in some ways than the later fact of actually losing her.

April 3. *"If you get the laundry out of the drier, I'll fold."* Kristi continued to do the very ordinary little things around the house that she could. Throughout our marriage she had been conscientious about the routine needs of the home — cleaning, laundry, cooking, and gardening. There is in all of us such a deep need for even routine accomplishments, whatever they might be. As Kristi's paralysis of the right arm rapidly advanced, she still wanted to fit new family photographs into an album. These simple moments were almost more poignant than I could bear — I held the album and opened the plastic sheets as Kristi struggled to nudge into position selected pictures that she would never look at again.

At some point during hospice, perhaps in early April, Kristi faced me from her chair near the living room fireplace, and said, *"Peter, after I'm gone, if you find another person to marry, you must know that it is okay with me."* I turned away. *"I have to know that you hear me,"* she pressed. In all that we had been through during the past twelve years especially, even in my most solitary moments I had never said "what if?"

This discussion was short, "Yes, I hear your words, but *you* are my wife." I had always decided to never even begin to imagine a sort of exit strategy for myself. To me, this would be the first step in distancing and, it seemed, a sort of infidelity. And, it would make the ordeal solitary and impossible. It would leave me spinning in space in a way that would come soon enough. For my possible good, Kristi knew that her message was delivered, but I — also for my good — left the message unopened.

On this day a second small supply of our painkiller (levorphanol) was located. Only a few days earlier an unclaimed sixty tablets had been found by a neighborhood pharmacist. A regular supply of this discontinued drug would be hard to find.[17] In the first instance, a prescription had been pushed to the back of the shelf and left there for six months. Now, after a dragnet search, an additional ninety tablets were located at the hospital of our hospice provider. Enough for a couple of weeks at least. The onset of possibly uncontrollable pain was pushed farther out.

To be careful, we had started with one-fourth of a single tablet. Even this put Kristi into a very deep sleep for over four hours. At this unlikely daily rate — maybe a quarter of a tablet each day — we calculated a hypothetical two-year supply. There I was, always calculating. From Kristi's pillow, a smile toward the Franciscan crucifix on the nearest wall to the bed. And another piece of light humor, "*Two years is too much.*"

April 4. A beautiful sunny morning greeted us through the open bedroom curtains. With her hair (a convincing wig) and a little light makeup in place after all, we headed by car to the bluff in Edmonds five miles to the west. As far south as we are in Puget Sound, we had been lucky to see a whale in January. We thought we would take another look. The oxygen tank rode in the back seat.

Kristi was lighthearted, always more buoyant than I. Of all the possibilities for short trips, this vantage point toward the sound was the only destination she wanted in these final months. What did she see, quietly peering out to the west? Was Kristi, so silent, looking back with me or looking ahead to her "best Friend"?

The Olympic Mountains formed a majestic half of the horizon, and fading westward at the north edge was Hurricane Ridge. To the right and directly ahead was the horizon separating us from the strait leading to the vast Pacific. And wrapping farther to the north were the southern bluffs of Whidbey Island, and the more distant and permanently snowcapped Mt. Baker. Nearly twenty years earlier, when Laura and Mark were only six and nearly four, we had made our first special trip to the Olympic Peninsula. Now the carefree memories drifted back across the water. Each half hour a ferryboat, sized to carry up to two thousand passengers and over two hundred cars, slips out of sight against this nearly permanently snowcapped silhouette, sometimes dwarfed by a silvery fan of sunlight cutting down through broken clouds. In the evenings the views were always different, but now our visits would be in the afternoons, timed to match Kristi's declining energy level.

On the drive home I asked in an offhanded tone, "Would you like to see our cemetery plot?" I had been tending to details. The Holyrood Cemetery is only a mile from our home. It offers generous grounds under a scattered cover of mostly evergreen trees, accented with birch and flowering cherry. Looking north from the selected plot we have a tunnel-like view slightly downhill under the trees to a large urban lake. Our plot is on the higher ground to the south, with a mausoleum on its west, and bordered on the east by a second small section reserved for infants. On a few occasions over the years we had visited the children's section, and I knew Kristi would like being nearby.

Such a peaceful moment and, again, from Kristi came that special smile: "*What a peaceful day. This is beautiful. Thank you so much.*" Kristi saw her new ground through angelic eyes. After all this, here

The "Quad," University of Washington. "In the afternoon we strolled among the famous flowering cherry trees on the University of Washington campus."

was my wife, radiating a beauty without shadows, saying that her burial plot was "beautiful." And with these words forever in the air, for me and for the family, it is.

April 7. "I'm excited; let's get out. We've planned the funeral. Let's go!" We had spent the morning with Kristi's visiting family and worked our way through the funeral arrangements. Kristi was careful and sure in what she wanted — every detail from the readings, to pallbearers and music, and especially a procession of nieces and nephews, each carrying a single rose before the beginning of the Mass. Now Kristi was excited at the prospects of dropping her completed planning task and taking a ferry ride across the Sound to Port Gamble. This was to be another special day trip topped off with treats on the way home.

April 10. "When you're young, and growing up, you think you are going to accomplish great things . . . but we did accomplish great things — Laura and Mark. Laura and Mark are great things. Such beautiful children!" Kristi had summarized a good part of our life together. What does one look back on that runs deeper than worldly routine, or success in one form or another? Family, it was a very good feeling, but for the same reason, also deeply melancholy. Mortality and eternal life come harnessed together, and the timing for family members to slip from one to the other is not of our choosing.

April 13. On Good Friday we were perky: *"Oh look at those clouds, can you just see Christ returning in His glory!"* And later in the evening, *"Just think of the suffering Christ went through even before the actual crucifixion. And this without narcotics. And we, with tons of narcotics, can endure so little pain."* Oh my Kristi, do you not know that our free offering of this ordeal, especially from our side of the altar at each Mass, *is* His suffering? The cancer now, and my broken heart later. This is the secret of the eternal Mystical Body of Christ as it unfolds through time in us: "The sufferings of this life cannot be compared to the glory that will be revealed in us in the life to come."

April 15. *"Alleluia, He is risen!"* Kristi awoke with a smile on Easter Sunday. This was the same sense of delight she had showed in the hospital three years earlier on Easter morning after her sternum operation. Kristi and Mark and I attended Mass at our parish together and then ate brunch at a classy restaurant we often reserved for special occasions.

In the afternoon we strolled among the famous flowering cherry trees on the University of Washington campus. The timing of our visit was poetically perfect. The fragrant blossoms clouded loose and free in breezes otherwise too slight to be detected. Fitted in a lacey and loose white dress a young girl, perhaps ten years old, danced beneath the enormous branches and delicately caught with outstretched hands and in midair a few of the blossoms. One and then another, and another. She was enthralled by the white blossoms and, for us, she became one of them.

"*We will have to come here again next year . . . who knows, maybe I'll be flying around up above somewhere.*" And then Kristi made this remarkable comment,

> *Spending my heaven doing good on earth,*
> *like St. Therese. I'd like that.*
> *Maybe I'll ask the Lord if I can do that too . . .*
> *at least for my family.*

St. Therese, again, is the saint of simplicity sent as a gift for our times. She is remembered by millions and is asked especially to intercede for our concrete needs in this world. Not long before her own death in 1897 at the age of twenty-four, Therese asked her Lord to be allowed to reach through the veil to do good on earth: "After my death, I will let fall a shower of roses. I will spend my heaven doing good upon earth." We already ask the Father that His will be done "on earth as it is in heaven." Only a small stretch is required to find a saint or two tagging along. It was consistent simplicity in this contact that inspired Kristi's springtime prayer.

April 18. Kristi was strong enough to take an hour-long drive to the world famous tulip fields in the Skagit Valley an hour north of Seattle. For a few weeks each year the expansive river delta blooms into rich bands of color — red, yellow, pink, white, and others. Artists and calendar photographers never tire of seeking new backdrops of snowcapped ridges or nearby barns for this pallet. After this brilliant display the bulbs are harvested for shipment to the Netherlands for global marketing.

"*Who knows, if I had a miracle, I don't know what I'd do. Because our energy would come back, and we'd want to do all of these things — to help people.*" Earlier in the year Kristi had called Blessed Sacrament Church to volunteer for kitchen work on the Sunday afternoon dinner. Very common guests come by the hundreds. This is the volunteer program begun in 1969 under our friend Fr. Fulton and has operated every week without interruption ever since. But Kristi's special intention was blocked by the growing paralysis of the right arm and the different path now before us.[18] She felt more than ever the need to do small things for others, but could do nothing.

By now we had a routine for medication. Our homemade notebook guided a daily symphony of six pills on different cycles. These began with the familiar synthroid tablet, and an over-the-counter headache tablet. The others were a white pill for the nerve pain in Kristi's right arm, the pink pill for physiological (oxygen) anxiety, our special substitute for morphine, and another proven tablet for nausea.[19] The oxygen tank was always in the car with us. Thankfully, this combination was working, but with hospice permission the doses were inching upward. *"You know, it takes a good deal of organization being sick. Can you imagine not being organized?"* Kristi watched as I was arranging another sequence of nighttime doses.

April 21. This was another sunny day with another short trip to the bluff facing Puget Sound and the Olympic Mountains. Mark felt free to fit in an afternoon of commercial pilot training, and Laura made her dependable phone call from Florida. There followed a steak barbecue in the back yard and a rented movie, this time Audrey Hepburn in the 1965 version of *My Fair Lady.*

April 22. *"I really feel good today; the Lord has given me a gift on Mercy Sunday."* Side by side we inspected the rose buds in the back yard. Mercy Sunday responds to the clear message of Christianity. It celebrates this deepest message of divine mercy, especially as it was intimately revealed in the early twentieth century to the now St. Faustina.[20] Ours is a God first of mercy from the very depths, the Soul of our souls. This is also the message of the evangelist St. John — God is love — and it was the message of our friend Fr. Fulton, who valued John's more mystical fourth Gospel over any of the three Synoptics (Matthew, Mark, and Luke).

On this special morning we managed a restaurant breakfast with Kerry and then shopped for dresses. Light banter masked what we all knew to be true, that this was another "last" together. During the proceedings and in a typically husband fashion, I hid and dozed in a generous wicker chair between the clothing racks. I awoke forty-five minutes later in time to make out a check.

April 24. The first month of hospice was behind us. The prognosis of only one to seven weeks looked too pessimistic. I faced the trees and roses in the back yard and had a long talk on the telephone with Dr. Lee. It was clear that we would be able to enjoy Kristi for more time than we had hoped. Kristi had known best her own body. Some of her weakness of the past several months had been due to only a virus, as she thought, and this had finally passed.

Still, it was only a matter of time. Dr. Lee gave this new guidance: "Find that space where time does not exist. Build up the treasured moments. Set and achieve realizable goals each day — because there is no way of estimating just how much time we actually have. There are no books on how to do this — to simply forget about time." To some degree we had already been doing this — living the moment — for the past several years. This is the secret we had at least touched, the life of the present moment, not encumbered too much by fear of the future or remorse for the past.

April 30. "I feel melancholy, low, and teary. It's sad, dying. It is such a letting go . . . but, I think I'm beginning to feel better now. It's nice, hearing the birds. . . . " (Kristi at least seemed to pass through this darkest wasteland in one day; for me it was to take two years and more. . . .)

May 3. On this date, a recruited out-of-state pharmacist with Internet skills located a fully adequate supply of levorphanol. This painkiller, now known to be a discontinued product, was found in Arizona in one of four regional medical warehouses. We heard that this was possibly the only remaining supply in the country "or even the western hemisphere." And even this was scheduled for shipment on the same day that it was found — to be destroyed by the manufacturer. A coincidence? This was clearly a concrete and Marian answer to a specific prayer.

May 5. "*What I'd really like to do is just get up and putter. I think I'll go out and pinch those flowers. There is a sadness. Not being able to watch our grandchildren. And yet, I know this is what Our Lord wants of me.*"

May 7. Standing in the dining room, my Kristi edged up to my right elbow. Looking down into her eyes I cradled her face between my hands and kissed my girl, first on her left cheek, then her forehead, and then her right cheek, one-two-three, and those lips reduced so long now to a whisper. So fragile, so vulnerable, so very beautiful, as if no time had passed since we first met. "*You held me and kissed me and told me how beautiful I was, just like that, on our honeymoon. And I wasn't sure whether to believe you.*" One of those golden moments that is infinitely larger than terminal cancer. One must finally affirm either time or love — and Kristi and I know (if it can be stated this way) that there are times when time does not exist. Eternity is one of these.

May 9. After breakfast the doorbell rang. I opened our home for an unscheduled visit from Kristi's very special friend, Jan. She sat on the davenport next to my chair while Kristi rested upstairs in bed. Before long she told me a remarkable story.

During the most recent Sunday Mass, at a point during communion, Jan sensed very powerfully Kristi's presence in the church standing before the open tabernacle. Yet Kristi and I had stayed home on that day. Light flooded outward from within the tabernacle itself. Jan turned to her husband, John, at her left and told him of this powerful experience.

Jan said that a tear or two slid down John's face. "Yes," he said, "I had the same experience, but there was something more." John related how he had opened his eyes and looked up to see the same light from the tabernacle. But then he also saw Kristi. She was facing and approaching the tabernacle. He saw three figures in all. Kristi was escorted on either side by two other figures who stood beside her arm in arm. The faces were turned away. On Kristi's left was a woman in a blue veil and robe. From the blue John concluded that this was Mary, the same Mary who had appeared to Bernadette at Lourdes in 1858 and to Catherine Labouré in 1830. And on Kristi's right and robed in a brown Carmelite habit was surely St. Therese.

John lowered his eyes for a second and then looked up again. The momentary image was gone. Kristi's hair had been "long, dark, and full," he recalled later when I asked specifically about this. He had seen Kristi not as she was at that moment, but as she was to be. And a full three months later at the interment, John recalled and added this, "Peter," he said, "there was something more. When I saw Kristi for that short moment, she was wearing the same dress that she wore at her funeral" — a dark floral dress with coral flowers and with a bright pink sweater. John had seen Kristi in a church and at a time when she was at home with me, and in a funeral dress that she and I had not selected for several more weeks.

A Gift of More Time

May 10. "I feel good today, a little weak, but it isn't as it was. Maybe we are being given another little gift." The seven weeks were now passed. Each day was a gift, and we were to have more time to be together. The first chickadees visited the new feeder suspended from the pine tree directly out the back door. A new dress — "peach sorbet" — arrived and looked fine for a possible Mother's Day outing in a few days.

On our way home from a very short daily drive, we stopped at a mundane and crowded intersection along the fully urban and sign-cluttered State Route 99. This route is legendary in the Seattle area for its traffic and auto sales brand of urban sprawl. What good can come from such a place? I turned to Kristi amid our shared tiredness with all that was happening and the heat of the day. And I posed the question. As I sometimes did at humdrum moments, I repeated the words I had written on a flower petal a few months after we first met: "Marry me!"

And Kristi's answer came as a beacon flash from a distant star:

> *I'd like to . . .*
> *I think Our Lord meant you for me —*
> *from the very, very beginning.*

From the very, very beginning! To this, Kristi heard from my innermost self: "I'll hold on to that!" Larger than the brief times we might have been out of step in day-to-day things, our marriage itself, "from the very, very beginning," is an eternal moment.[21] Yes, it is surely vaster by far than the sweep of sightless planets, and all of history and of time itself. Made as we are for eternity, what a curiosity it is to exist within time. A lifetime together to choose freely, or not, a universe larger than what we see with our eyes and more intimate than we can imagine. From the beginning, we have such a calling for simplicity and total fidelity equally in little things and large and to each other. In each passing moment it is the little things that open into personal lifetimes. My "peewee," my "plum."

This conviction of "the beginning" has only increased. "In the beginning was the Word, and the Word was with God: and the Word was God. . . . All things were made through him. . . ." (John 1:1–3). In a mysterious and concrete way, our marriage, all marriages, partake in this *origin*-ality of God. After Kristi's death I was to discover that John Paul II consoles us with these words: "In the Christian view of marriage . . . the mutual and total bond, unique and indissoluble, is part of God's original plan . . . *from the beginning.*"[22] Compared to marriage, all of time is only a point in eternity.

Later on the phone my mother on hearing of Kristi's words, confirmed all of this to me, "Oh, Peter, a marriage made in heaven!" It would not be much of an exaggeration to say that all of these pages are my effort to begin to grasp what it means for one spouse to say to the other, "from the very, very beginning."

May 13. "That's a pretty busy morning, especially for someone who isn't even supposed to be here." On this Mother's Day, Kristi enjoyed flowers from Mark and pictures from Laura and her family in Florida. A new dress, Mass, and French toast at a familiar restaurant. Kristi also enjoyed Laura's note in her beautiful card:

> Dear Mom — I can't begin to express what you have meant to my life. It wasn't until I had my own children and saw a lot of you in the things I said and did, that I fully realized this. I know I still have much to learn and can only hope to live up to your example. I miss you terribly and hope to see you in June. With love and prayers — Laura, Rob, Robby, Anthony, and Kristina.

May 16. Dr. Lee wrote back: "I would be honored to serve as a pallbearer and I appreciate very much the opportunity to honor you in that way. It has been a major privilege for me to know you and to take care of you." Kristi felt a growing tiredness, and by now her appetite had diminished. Ours were gentle and quiet moments often too deep for tears, but not always. We turned together to the bird feeder — chicadees and towhees and finches. In the late afternoon an unusual lightning storm hit north Seattle — a translucent lime green hue painted everything out the back door except for the garishly contrasting redness of our azaleas, the sequoia redwood, and the cedar. The darkened cloud cover broke here and there for royal blue patches of early evening sky beyond. These contrasted with the light ochre cloud linings. The storm gusts came after dark.

Our prayer, sometimes conscious and verbal but mostly not, was being distilled — that Kristi's passage through the veil would be quick and gentle, and then that we would be together again in the twinkling of an eye. Kristi: *"Oh, yes. . . . I am ready. I would welcome it."* In reading this so many months later, I marvel at how close Kristi had come to the untainted inner peace explored in readings I had studied years earlier shortly before the first cancer and then at the time of the transplant:

> If you are untroubled by passion; if your heart yearns more and more for God; if you do not fear death but regard it as a dream and even long for your release — then you have attained the pledge of your salvation and, rejoicing with inexpressible joy, *you carry the kingdom of heaven within you.*[23]

If Kristi is not welcomed directly into heaven (which she already carries within her), then there is no God. . . . In my later grief, this instantaneous demand consumed my mind. It came more as a compact certainty than as a doubt or anger.

May 19. "Maybe I should go in back to smell the flowers . . . do the ones in front need water? Help me go to bed. I don't know if I'm up to this, dying. It seems a little dark some times. I'm so very tired. I just wish it would come." The weakness was advancing, and Kristi's appetite was nearly gone. Her digestive system was closing down.

We paused on the meditation by an early and obscure saint (St. Theognostos) in Kristi's monthly *Magnificat* prayer booklet. He wrote, "You have received a sure, unequivocal pledge of salvation when your heart no longer reproaches you for your failings . . . when you await death, which most people dread and run away from, calmly and with a ready heart."[24] While reading this to Kristi, I discovered that we spend most of our lives seeing things backwards.

Salvation is not so much to transcend ourselves, but to transcend an accretion and the only thing that we do own, our false selves. The real self fully within, and not outside or awaited from elsewhere, is gifted to remain and live forever. But the flawed layer, the next layer out from this center — where does this impostor come from but as an abuse of our freedom for the truth deeper within? Our origin and center is in the creative act of love who is the eternal One, the Soul of our souls and the source and eternal Spouse of our true selves.

Eternity is not longer than time; it is outside of time altogether and has a name and a face. Christ is the Logos — intelligent reason and the knowledge of the Father, in person. Is it possible to imagine ourselves unclaimed by such a sovereign intimacy? But then our imagination alone is not the path we should follow. Imagination by itself is the false path leading from estrangement to idolatry and, in our day, to ideology.

Is it by a lack of will, a failure of truly free will, that we become blind in our hearts and minds to Wisdom? We should marvel at Christ's choice, at Gethsemane, to endure the crushing introspection of our convoluted hiding, or our promiscuous pride of life. To endure this burden rather than to diminish by one iota our radical freedom to choose wisely within His Wisdom — or not. It is the vastness of *this* radical freedom, undefiled, that lifts us above all nature to be "in His image."

I suspected that Kristi's humility and gentleness breathed this air. And of such uncomplicated freedom for the truth, women I suspect are generally superior theologians to men. This is because real and potential mothers know, in a way men too often do not know, that the only really convincing argument is self-sacrifice. It is from the heart, not by the fragment reason alone that we are "saved." God is intelligent self-donation. God is love.

May 20. Jeanne and Kerry arrived again from Idaho. Kristi was not sure she would live even until June 3. We held an early birthday party for Mark. Failing to notice the author, I was consoled by this: "Faith is the patient waiting for what we cannot control, so that when it comes we are able to receive it as a gift."

May 21. We awakened to another beautiful summer day and we again joined the birds and the squirrels in our back yard. Family visits always restored Kristi. More listless now, Kristi retired into the house for a needed nap. But half an hour later the bed was empty and she was not to be found. Searching the house and then pulling Mark's bike from the garage, I soon discovered the twin sisters in the lustrous five o'clock sunlight strolling back from a nearby neighborhood park. As with the stem cell transplant, another transfer of energy from Kerry to her twin.

May 25. "I worry about you... you'll get a haircut when you need one? Promise me." Laughter, my heart is lightened. I recalled an incident nine years earlier in our front yard, when Kristi had asked me to get a haircut, and I declined. There was an edge to this detail, the memory of imperfect communication. To Kristi, my attitude was a cutting disrespect, to me the moment to be respected. The little things that matter. Oh, yes, I promised to get a haircut when I needed one and even when I did not.

After four days of visiting and uplifting activity, silence returned to our home as family members departed again for Idaho. Kerry and Jeanne, especially, were regularly on the road for the day-long trip between our house and Cottonwood. Kerry's family needed her. The family included husband Chuck and eight children, many of them still young enough to be at home.[25]

May 27. "I've lost the use of my right hand. I miss being able to express myself through my little notes. Pray for me that I can simply offer this up... like [the loss of] my voice." Over the phone Jeanne suggested finding a wide-grip pen. My special trip to the store was successful, and we found that this would work. Such a simple thing brought back the familiar and undemanding smile to our angel's face.

Our back yard birdhouse. "... we again joined the birds and the squirrels in our back yard."

May 30. "*Oh, look at all of the beautiful flowers! God really does love us!*" Again we were at our favorite vantage point of Puget Sound on the Edmonds bluff. The vista was in front to the west, and the flower-lined walkway bordered the lawns and picturesque fences behind. The comments by Fr. Fulton from forty years before sparked back to me. On that spring evening in Seattle, he had awakened me to the simple fact that if we have eyes to see at all, each flower is not a piece of greenery in a rock garden, but a symbol of God's universal love for each of us. Here again in my lovely wife was the larger truth of symbolic vision.

Kristi sometimes had seen herself not only as a flower, but as a specific flower. From her teen years she had felt however vaguely that she was to be a rose of Sharon — a fresh bloom for only a short time that then passes away. And, yes, there was my dear mother's motto: "Be sure to smell the roses along the way." My Kristi — identified at a prayer session eight years earlier as "the flower that the Lord is pleased to crush."[26]

May 31. "*I feel a sadness. I feel a sadness, that it's all over.*" The weightiness of Kristi's short remarks, especially this one, is impossible to capture on a written page. On this quiet day the stillness held us as we sat with the birds and flowers in the back yard. Each and every uncut blade of grass pointed upward and stared separately back at me. We tried again to notice the path that Kristi had found looking out the living room window the year before: "*From life to greater Life.*"

Looking back, all of us see trends in our lives as also in history, but this is not how life is lived. Life is lived in the moments that reach to us from in front. These are open — shaped by decisions and actions of either self, or of self-donation to a surrounding and active presence. History is biography, and the best biography is not fully defined; it is religious in this way of openness.

The pain, I was learning, is part of the openness. It rises from a deep well and will never fully go away. The coming loss cannot be filled simply by new and arbitrary things, by some fleeting and more-or-less useful layer of distraction. The breadth of the whole world, good as it can be, really does not count for much compared to the depths. It was at the brink of this abyss that Fr. Barham, years before, had counseled our parish to breathe with both lungs and to seek first the Healer, even above the possible healing. And reading my heart, he prayed for "Peter in his perplexity." (Perhaps it is from this prayer that there comes now the cleansing, from this book.)

June 1. "I feel so useless." Here is the kind of thing that a husband instinctively and inadequately wants to solve by "doing" something. Practical solutions so often show that we do not hear what our wife, stirring at a deeper level, is actually saying to us. It would be good to listen.

Impaired stamina, from the early nineties, had kept full-time work out of reach for Kristi. So many times I had reassured her that in our family she was never to be harnessed as a necessary second source of family income. As a family we would not be shaped by a hostile or indifferent economy. Anything Kristi might want to do should be for personal reasons. Paid or volunteer work, either one, must be a personal fulfillment. And yet it was this ordinary kind of engagement and usefulness that Kristi had seen slip away and that she missed so very much now.

Is it ever possible for any person to *be* useless? In our suffering generously embraced — another kind of doing — we mirror St. Therese and even Christ. *"But I have so often thought so little about those poor people in the nursing homes."* This was coming from Kristi, who had visited the shut-ins with a special touch that caused others to "marvel."

Is it useless, Kristi's given path of vicarious suffering? The density of the Communion of Saints — if we could see how closely we are tied to each other in good and in our weakness (and sometimes by a suffering fully accepted), we might not be able to go on living.[27] We linger on the promise of a New Springtime waiting to lift up our sinking and tired world.

After helping Kristi to bed, I scrambled for something to muffle the panic and clicked on the television (the universal anesthetic). I hit precisely this sentence: "I have found that there is a higher Gospel, the Gospel of Suffering, that paves the way to the Third Millennium of families, of every family, of all families."[28] Maybe we will survive our current Dark Age only as families, one by one, rediscover themselves and each other. Each marriage: a personalized icon of infinite togetherness. Together, families will stand higher than whatever intrusive or deformed political or economic gangrene hammers at their door. Something like the Amish, but not so few, and a network not nearly so isolated. And rooted in the Word — the Real Presence in the Eucharist — as well as the words of Scripture that tell us about this presence.

This awakened family of families, each a window to grace in the world, will spring forward from the same inner life that inspired an earlier and alternative network. In a few centuries, historians might compare such an awakening of solid families to the monastic awakening, the taproot of Europe planted by St. Benedict across another crude landscape in an earlier era. Might this flowering of the family, existing prior to any state,[29] be the delayed fruit of the Second Vatican Council and the seedbed of the New Springtime of the human spirit? The council saluted families as "domestic churches."

Is it really useless for Kristi to witness now to these awaited candles in the stretching shade? I was losing my wife, the heart of my family, and she means so much more to us than all the world.

June 3. Mark's birthday. The daily routine now called for a morning nap and another in the afternoon as well, added to fifteen hours sleep each night. We viewed the concluding part of a favorite movie,

Anne of Green Gables, based on Montgomery's novels about growing up on Prince Edward Island in eastern Canada. From this idyllic
distraction came the hour or two of relaxation between evening
medications and the familiar hum in our bedroom of the oxygen
compressor.

June 6. "I'm so excited, I can't take my nap now!" The chance
to work with flowers gave a shot of new energy. And so we completed light work in the new rock-bordered flower pad encircling
our Sequoia tree in the back yard — geraniums, pansies, cosmos,
heather, and lobelia. Color out back visible from any window, under
the magic of the bird feeder. This was a very good day.

*June 10. "It's really something how the body keeps trying, even when
the end is close and there is no [physical] hope. It keeps trying to eat and
to keep going."* Such growing detachment. The daily routine had us
reading together each night while Kristi waited for the first nighttime
dose to take effect. From *Celine: Sister and Witness to St. Therese of
the Child Jesus*[30] we found this verse from the Song of Songs: "Winter
is past, the rains have ceased, arise my beloved, and come." Kristi
was getting closer to her "dear Lord."

Other readings close to Kristi's heart helped her make better
friends with Elizabeth of the Trinity, Catherine Labouré, and many
others of the graced life.[31] Most of all, and at the end with her limited
energy, Kristi asked for the short and uncomplicated readings. These
were entries in *Guideposts* supplied by my mother.

One evening during Kristi's final year she had paused on the
writings of Elizabeth Leseur (*My Spirit Rejoices*). I treasure now how
she turned to me, arrested by Elizabeth's reference to the *"indwelling
of the Holy Spirit."* This put words to her modest, very personal, and
unspoken experience of the God resting within. Here was another
echo from our daily half-minute prayer together for so many years
to the Soul of my soul. Words that cracked the door for me, and
that I had resolved to think about more, always later. Elizabeth's

Blessed Sacrament Church. "The St. Peregrine novena opportunity is offered each year..."

writings reveal a purified spirituality especially in the face of her own suffering during her final months. She is described as a "married St. Therese Lisieux," the example of trusting simplicity through the "Little Way."

June 11. During the previous week a friend, Sally, completed the annual novena to the patron saint of cancer victims. The St. Peregrine novena opportunity is offered each year at our familiar Gothic-style Blessed Sacrament Church. Even Sally now accepted that Kristi was dying. Instead of praying for recovery, she prayed simply that there might be for her a "special consolation."

Two or three days later the phone rang. Yet other friends, Matt and Georgene, were calling to tell us of a traveler from Thailand. Archbishop Lawrence Khai had unexpectedly changed his travel plans through California and would be with them in Seattle. This visit had been suggested over the phone by Msgr. Reilly in New York, founder of the Helpers of God's Precious Infants. We had met Reilly and others for dinner three years earlier during his visit to Seattle.

June 12. In Seattle the archbishop stood with the weekday vigil group outside the tucked away and busiest abortion site in the state of Washington, one mile north of our home.[32] From time to time Kristi had been a witness here on weekdays. The archbishop was also eager to visit our home. He wanted to pray over Kristi with the relics of seven Thai martyrs of this century. These seven were beatified in 1989, the first step toward a declaration of sainthood. They were executed at the hands of the government in 1940 for their refusal to renounce their Christian faith. Now the archbishop sought through them a miraculous cure. A medically documented case is a necessary condition for possible canonization.

By this time Kristi was looking forward more and more to being released into heaven, but she considered again the possibility of a longer sojourn this side of the veil.

> *Lord if this be Your will, I accept,*
> *or if Your will is a quick passage, I also accept,*
> *either way with my whole heart.*

In white robes with thin scarlet trim and sash, Archbishop Khai entered our home. He had finished praying at the clinic on our neighborhood street corner — in place of Kristi, I choose to think. Obscenities had been yelled his way from a passing car, and he seemed a little dismayed. This happens from time to time. I always count it as a plus since it probably shows that Old Scratch is power-less and scraping the bottom of the barrel.[33] This observation made some sense and lightened the moment.

The visit went quickly, but by the clock lasted nearly and hour. The archbishop told how as a Christian teenager, he had been forced by a Muslim-led internal security bureaucracy to attend a Buddhist school. Buddhism was the official religion of the state. He was severely beaten for refusing to lead his class in prayer be-fore a statue of the Buddha. The district police chief faced the boy squarely and demanded that he open his mouth, "so that he could shoot his gun through my head." Here was something I had seen in my youth.[34]

In another village, the seven martyrs were also threatened repeat-edly with guns. On Christmas Day they were told: "Stop praying or we will kill you!" And all of them were shot to death the next day. Their last request had been granted — time enough to dress well because they were going home to their Lord and Savior (a reminder to me of Fr. Fulton's wish to be buried in white). The seven included such dangers to the state as two religious nuns, four teenaged stu-dents ages thirteen through sixteen, and a cemetery worker. Years later the police chief and others involved sought forgiveness and were baptized into the Catholic faith, one of them on his deathbed.[35]

Archbishop Khai told us that intercession by these seven had produced already the miraculous cure of a wretched woman three years before. "Six different diseases" had reduced her nearly to a fetal position on the floor. (This calls to mind the pitiful figure I had seen in Hong Kong on that Sunday morning in the autumn of 1968.) In prayer she was enlightened to visit the site where the seven were martyred and where, she was told, she would "witness the power." With help she visited the site, and as part of a group of sixty others she saw in the sky the dancing sun (as Kristi had seen in 1999), and in front of this, a vision of the seven martyrs. She was cured over a period of only a few days and "today is a healthy farm laborer." People still ask of this woman, "Are you the one we used to see curled on the floor?"

The attending doctors admit to the evidence, the archbishop said, but as Buddhists are unwilling to sign the paperwork necessary to advance the case toward canonization by Rome. The archbishop, with the relics — fragments of bone and particles from the burial site — offered prayers in our home for Kristi: our mother, daughter, sister, and spouse. He left small relics with us. Thank you, Lord, for answering the trusting novena by a friend for a special consolation for Kristi.

June 13. On this date Archbishop Lawrence Khai dated a letter to Kristi handwritten on beautiful multicolored stationery. I framed it for the entryway wall:

My dear friend, Kristi,

I visited you with the Relics of the Seven Blessed Martyrs of Thailand. May our good Lord give you strength and shower upon you a mighty healing power through the intercession of our beloved Seven Blessed Martyrs whose bones you possess now. You will be kept close to my daily prayers. You are a wonderful soul with great faith and patience. God love you.

Your friend from Thailand,
L. Khai (Archbishop Lawrence Khai)

June 17. On waking in the morning, my Kristi turned and reported to me, "*I had a dream last night that you were [in a duel] in a bullfight ring.*" After a pause, I risked asking, "Did I win?" "*Yes,*" she said, "*I think so... the other person was Sean Connery.*" I was a bit smug about this, secure in the thought that I claim an uncontested place even in Kristi's subconscious. Connery's regal eyebrows probably arch in the back of the minds of many husbands.

Kristi was still able to maneuver the wide-grip pen to write her little notes. This was Father's Day. The selected card carried a message about love increasing through difficult times, and then Kristi added: *"My Peter dearest — I will always love you. Your Kristi."*[36] In the months to come this simple and very unsteady script, written under such exquisitely fragile circumstances, would become a life ring for me. The card is a most valued possession and is framed over the mantle in our recreation Room which has become so empty and quiet. For Kristi and me, time is diminished, and I wait.

The evening before Kristi's dream, Mark departed for his two weeks with the Marine Corps Reserves unit in California. We were torn by the timing, but felt that if Kristi slipped into a rapid decline the Red Cross could get Mark back with us. So many uncertainties to navigate. We were a little encouraged: *"The pills seem to be working. I'm just so tired of the pain; I try to offer it up, but I'm just so tired."*

June 20. "I feel better today . . . 'the Lord loves a cheerful giver.' That's one of the readings. I'm going to try to keep that for my motto today." This piece was from the daily calendar on the kitchen counter (a gift from a friend in 1997) displaying simple prayers from Blessed Mother Teresa of Calcutta.[37]

After three days of more frequent medication, Kristi repeated again that she felt so very *"useless."* On this point, the very active St. Augustine encourages us, "To be faithful in little things is a big thing." The big thing is to let the Lord have His way in our small lives. This is the mystery of both Mary and Martha waiting on the Lord in their very different ways, one deeply present and the other, though a bit distracted, usefully serving.

All things considered, this turned into a honeymoon-type day. We made a small dessert together and were able to make a normal visit to the grocery store. We talked to friends over a display of apples and oranges. Then there was energy enough for milk shakes and

time in the sun at the Edmonds marina and Puget Sound shoreline.
Always there was the backdrop of the Olympic Mountains far to the
west. From a catalogue we ordered a pink dress for Kristi's birthday
on July 6. Not much, but this was another little family event to look
forward to, always one day at a time.

June 23. Our daughter, Laura, arrived on her flight from West
Palm Beach. More quiet and golden moments on the small beaches
nearby. I wandered a distance at the water's edge while mother and
daughter rested together on the driftwood for a special visit. So
much to say and so little help from words.

June 25. In the early morning before her flight home, Laura sat
quietly hand in hand with her mother on the living room davenport.
Three months earlier, Kristi had sat here hand in hand with her own
mother to receive Dr. Lee's telephone message. These were to be
Kristi's and Laura's last few minutes together this side of the veil.
How do we ever get through such times? A few smiles, quiet words,
restrained tears, and then for Laura the shuttle ride to the airport
and another long flight to her family in Florida.

After a later nap, Kristi turned to me in the yard: *"You are always
there for me. This dying thing is a lonely business. . . . I don't like leaving
you behind."*

But you aren't leaving me behind, I thought. Christ is the secret.
In Christ it is revealed to us — each of us and all of us — that
everything we think we leave behind is fulfilled a hundredfold, in
front of and above us, and really. Not behind. I thought to myself,
but failed to say, "I will carry you in my heart, and you will be carried
in the Sacred Heart, which excludes no one."[38]

I scribbled in the journal, "I hurt on the outside, and on the
inside." There is no place undamaged where I might rest. (God, I
do miss her so.) Perhaps in the larger design — is there a design? — I
was meant this time to remain silent. Maybe in this silence — which
continues until we meet again — Kristi is to take the lead. It might

be she who gives me hints as to what the words of my unspoken thoughts really mean. Kristi leads and I listen.

Somewhere during the final months of her hospice care in 2001, Kristi raised her eyes to me from across this living room. With such a childlike and total simplicity and vulnerability she asked, *"Was there ever a time that I ever did or said anything that hurt you, without saying I was sorry?"* Here was the final cleansing, remorse over exaggerated fears. Why did I not smother her with kisses? Or at another time, *"I am so self-centered,"* and *"I have not respected you as I should. Let's pray for the times we have not loved one another as we should."*

And with urgency she leaned forward, *"I have to know that you forgive me. I was not there when you needed me."* Passing before Kristi's memory must have been the period of two years when I was most severely stressed by job insecurity, and she did not really see how precarious it really was for us. And yet this was ten years past and near the time of the first cancer treatment, and it was my duty to be there for *her.*

Of her wish for unnecessary forgiveness, "Of course," I offered, without needing any time at all to think. Whatever it was that troubled this refined conscience, I did not want Kristi to linger now on any imaginary obstacles. In front of me was such whitened innocence. Heaven will include this transparent moment, transfigured like every moment touched by love or pain. Is there a difference? Is it not I who should be asking for forgiveness?

Back again at our vantage point toward the Olympics to the west I also confessed. It was my patented irritability, so frequently awakening beneath the surface, but more of a family joke than a secret. I might also have mentioned failings known of all husbands — and known especially to their wives — inattentive listening, and always pushing too much, too driven by the clock. Marriage, the translucence of a stained-glass rose window competing with the ticking of a clock. *"Oh, I forgave you for all of that — long, long ago."*

June 30. Our girl stood at the front door as the car drove away. Kerry had been with us again, but in the early afternoon began yet another eight-hour trip back to Idaho and her own waiting family. Throughout all their lives, Kristi and Kerry had been so close. "*I miss her. I just miss her cheerfulness. I miss her strength and energy. She does so much . . . and for me. I wish I had that. I feel so useless.*"[39]

Was it "useless" to love so much, to so totally offer up this ordeal, and to have such true devotion to the Eucharistic Presence so much at the center of us all? John of the Cross gently instructs us on this matter of uselessness: "One little act of pure love is of more importance than all other good works together." A headline hydraulics project is not required, only a single cup of water — or a food coupon delivered on the Seattle waterfront — for the least of His brethren. This, we are told, is the measure.

I wish I had spent a little more time at the end reading poetry to Kristi. I at least mentioned John Milton and *On His Blindness:* "Who best bear his mild yoke, they serve him best . . . they also serve who only stand and wait." Of our being useless and apprehensive, we stopped together at this: "Be still, and know that *I* am God" (Ps. 46:10).[40]

July 3. "*Just think what we could do if I weren't sick. . . . We could take dance lessons, and then tour the country.*" Oh, the tugging memories I have now of the dances when we always saved "the last dance" for each other. . . .

July 4. The Fourth of July. The first of our four new climbing roses bloomed in back. And Mark was home again to treat his mother to some surprise holiday fireworks in the driveway. In earlier years we had visited the unrestrained neighborhood displays of vintage Americana on the west beaches of Whidbey Island, and then the much more ballistic undertaking on the Tulalip Indian Reservation a shorter distance north of Seattle. At the end of our evening Kristi offered this: "*I just wish it would happen, but then this may not be our*

Lord's will." These were ever more tired days, only partly due to increased medication.

July 6. On this special day, Kerry and Kristi celebrated their fifty-second birthday together. In an earlier birthday note Kerry had written, "...you have always been my dearest soul mate....I will be comforted by remembering your promise of always being near to me especially at the hour of my death." Mark's special card was typically concise, and offered reassurance to his mother, "We'll be all right." (Several months later as Mark and I sat at our infinitely diminished table, I reassured our only son how important his note had been. To which I added, "Even if you didn't have a clue what you were talking about!" The shared laughter was one of many very small steps in healing each other.)

What an agony, this life. The more beautiful it is, the more it hurts. To love a spouse more than all else is one thing, but still short of consistently loving such that no other things exist. To *be* the path for each other, together...and yet there are so many daily distractions. All of this is unbearable, except to know that the fragments made whole are ahead and beckon us. This rather than being lost. We are gently called forward to this gathering in. A quiet sunny day in the back yard.

"I don't understand how I affect all these people this way." Roses and meals continued to arrive from so many, several times a week.

July 14. After a very bad two days, we summoned our pastor, Fr. Dennis Kemp, to hear Kristi's confession and give the last rites. On leaving Kristi's upstairs room he passed me in the hallway. His eyes were turned upward as if fixed on something in the sky (even through the hallway ceiling). As he brushed by I heard, "Thank you." "Thank you for what?" I asked. He paused, and respecting the absolute secrecy of the sacrament, said, "Nothing, just thank you." With his gaze still turned up he reached with his left hand for the railing and then felt his way down the stairs to the living room. Of what he had heard, the very little that could be said would be heard four weeks later in his funeral sermon.

The next day a slight recovery followed, and Kristi's ability was restored to accept oral medication. But the coughing spells worsened. These were totally exhausting. Even a single cough left her trembling. And to clear the air passage, the episode sometimes took an hour or more. I simply held my dear girl with helpless care, sometimes patting her back gently as might be done with a very small child.

On schedule we continued crushing the several pills (white, red, and green), diluting them in watered applesauce. My mind drifted back to my childhood when our green pet parakeet was stepped on and seriously injured. Safe and returned to its cage, it lay on the floor of the cage barely able to move or open her beak. The vet could do nothing, "She will either live or die." My father, always direct and practical, was unimpressed. "Heck, I could have told you that!" A problem solver, he cracked the birdseeds between two spoons fitted inside each other. Our tiny pet was then able to eat, first only a few cracked seeds at a time, and then in a few weeks recovered fully.

I thought of this as I crushed pills in the same way for my dear Kristi. *"You look like an apothecary,"* she whispered in her weak voice. *"I think it's beginning. . . . That's why I want this birthday package in the mail."* She had selected for the grandchildren a video of *Anne of Green Gables.* Laura's twenty-sixth birthday was July 28. A phone message: *"You're a good mommy, Laura."*

We meditated a rosary together, and made a rare outing to visit the tiny chapel of Eucharistic Adoration at our St. Mark's Parish. To our modern world, the sacramental life is just so much ritualistic substitution for a more enlightened self-acceptance. But in the sacraments we have the added insight that insights alone are not enough, that our concrete self-donation is a personal response to

His Real Presence. Likewise, the sacrament of confession is self-revelation to the Other, an additional world above self-analysis or even therapy. To deal with the reality of death only in our heads is the most unintelligent thing we can do.

"*It seems like there's a lot of repetition.*" After the midday nap, now much longer than in the early weeks, "*I was having all these good dreams, but now I can't remember them.*"

July 16. Kristi struggled again with boredom, the inability to do anything. I wonder, How much of our agnostic culture is simply the rot spawned by boredom? This question opens a new angle on the repetition of the Creed. Despite its skeletal form as a set of propositions or beliefs, the radical convictions sheltered and expressed in the Creed restore us not so much from vagrant imagination and deception, but from flat-earth boredom and the numbness from being battered by one thing or another. This boredom comes from within. The Creed is a window from this cell, and as a summary of the Gospel it is *the* window. It is the key to final perseverance in a spiritual struggle that is real.

"*If I did not believe,*" Kristi admitted, more than once, "*I would want to end it.*" St. Therese — a saint! — said the same.[41] And even Christ said something about being abandoned by His Father, but as a prelude to greater hope.

The fiber behind the "I believe" of the Creed is even more in the I than in the *believe*. Because of Him it is an unstated and deeper courage to know that there is an "I." It is the courage that "I exist," that I am not nothing. It is a turning toward. Not Descartes' "I think, therefore I am," but more deeply — I am, therefore I believe and I think and am loved by Another. I believe in the Soul of my soul who is within me because He is above me. The Christian formula: I believe that I might understand. And the Christian revelation: that the Fatherhood of the Creator is both so vast and so close that the veil of death itself is only a passage. I thought that I was helping Kristi, but in truth, He was helping us. Not only that the questions are answered, but for a moment or two the questioning itself is calmed.

And St. John Chrysostom had this also for us:

For this is the sum total of Christian belief: to look for our true life after death; at the end of life, to look for its return. Having then taken to heart the words of the Apostle, let us now with confidence give thanks to God, Who has given us victory over death, through Jesus Christ our Lord, to Whom be glory and honor now and forever. Amen.[42]

Still, what can we do now to simply fill the time? In the dining room we opened the Scrabble word game for the first time in four months. At the beginning of the year we had played regularly as a way to suppress the unexplained anxiety symptoms. I now regretted all the times over the years that I had played so competitively — so uncomprehending — at even this family game. I really could have been less focused, more playful.

July 21. One day early, we held a quiet birthday party for me. I turned fifty-seven. I do not recall actually thinking then about the dialogue twenty-seven years earlier in Keuterville Church when I was shown that at the age of fifty-seven I would be parted from my Kristi.[43]

July 22. Before Sunday Mass, Fr. Kemp met Kristi with a smile at the door of the church, "My little saint!" After Mass the family gathered outside again before breakfast. This comment was recalled, and Kristi turned to me and muttered under her breath, *"Well, we know that isn't true!"* What a surprise, not so much her remark, but the muttering. This might be the only time in our marriage that I recall Kristi actually muttering in this way. It was so spontaneously common. Sometimes she might give a perky *"Zut!"* (French for "Darn it.") But I was the mutterer. Many families have one, and this one was more than enough on any one team.

Kristi knew the distance to sainthood, the path reserved for her special friends. She asked Kerry and me to pray for her every day after she was gone. And we both signed on. I found later that even Kristi's special friend St. Bernadette had made very much the same remark: "People will say: 'that Sister Marie Bernard was a little saint,' and I shall thus be left burning in Purgatory."[44]

July 23. After several weeks sharp hip pains returned. This time Kristi was simply standing in the back yard. She stood motionless and trapped. *"I can't walk."*

I took Kristi into my arms and carried my girl across the threshold and upstairs to our bed. We had been careful all this time. We knew that if spreading bone cancer were to open even a hairline fracture in the hip, that this would be "catastrophic" (Dr. Lee's term) for caregiving at home. And there were the vivid memories of my own injury from ten years earlier. Both of Kristi's legs were fatigued. Inching a few steps to the foot of the bed was too much.

Once back in bed, she sat up for watermelon chips to soothe her cough: *"Why is [all of] this happening?"*

The coughing was caused by dryness and by now had become a very heavy burden. And Kristi's right lung was long closed down. Of the very bitter taste in her mouth that she mentioned on an earlier occasion, I chose not to guess. My larger fear had been that the malignancy might migrate from the apex of one lung to the other and lead to slow strangulation. Dr. Lee reassured me that "this is not how it usually works." (And how *does* it usually work?) We knew the final path could include eventual fluid buildup in the lungs, and labored breathing. But so far we had been able to keep Kristi in a slightly upright and comfortable position during sleep. Her breathing, even with one lung, was smooth. And it seemed that her fading physical ability to eat or to drink fluid might actually simplify things for her.

July 25. "Am I just going to get more and more tired, and then die here?" Later, *"I'm just a little tired. It's all so slow."* And then, *"I'm a little scared, but shouldn't be."*

How remarkable, and yet unsurprising, I thought. Kristi had a good breakfast and then walked on her own, most carefully, down the flight of stairs from the bedroom to the living room, and up again. Three to five days, we were told.

We read the short prayer *Anima Christi* (*Soul of Christ*) ending with, " . . . In the hour of my death, call me. And bid me come to Thee; that with thy saints I may praise Thee; forever and ever. Amen." And then of our smallness and of His infinite grace, Kristi breathed this summary wisdom of a lifetime: *"He does all the work."*

Nothing remained now of the stoic: instead, total surrender and trust. And it was His action from within — this powerful gentleness — that so touched others: "She was always so kind." Through her special path, Kristi was discovering now with absolute simplicity the meaning of truths that are so often concealed by words: "I repeat, it is owing to his favor that salvation is yours through faith. This is not your doing, it is God's gift; neither is it a reward for anything you have accomplished, so let no one pride himself in it" (Eph. 2:8–9). As I think of this, two years after Kristi's death, I marvel at this simplicity. Most of the religious turmoil and spilled ink in Christian history has to do with this mystery. He does everything, and yet, do we do nothing at all? Do we not have sufficient stature as persons to also respond?[45]

Kristi's surrender through disease and medication hell, part of a larger gentleness, is her heartfelt response to *all* that He permits. Of the possibility of miraculous healing, or not, she had said *"either way, with all my heart."* For myself, the words "all of my consent" I can understand, but "all of my heart"? This was a more feminine path, more Kristi's path. She did not write scholarly tracts or found institutions. Such big things were simply beyond the reach given to her or to most of us.

Instead, prayer beads. *"I have not been very good about saying the rosary lately. Can you help me with maybe one decade* (a group of ten beads, each one not much different than the hazelnut revealed to the mystic Julian of Norwich)?"[46] Kristi, yes, but you are now living the rosary. You have Mary on one arm and Therese on the other, and He is inviting you home.

I look back to the many times when we drove to one vacation destination or another. Even before we were out of Seattle, Kristi would retrieve and begin her rosary. It might take forty-five minutes instead of fifteen or twenty for her to reach the end, her delicate fingers caressing each bead. And there were the other times that we would pray the rosary together while walking through the shaded neighborhood streets. It takes only a short walk. Sometimes we would reach the end of a decade of ten beads and Kristi would glance up in quiet surprise: *"May we have a few more [beads], I have not finished my meditation."* When this happened, usually three or four extra beads were needed. I could not help but turn and laugh inwardly as I kept track in my distracted and mathematical way. The record was seventeen beads in one decade.

This afternoon she said, *"Maybe I should go to confession...."* Kristi simply loved this sacramental way of turning to Him. It was another special way to talk with her "best Friend." (In some cases a refined conscience can get the best of us, but this is not a widespread affliction in our time.) Confession is not a gimmick to manage our involuntary imperfections, real or imagined. He does not bother so much with ordinary shortcomings.[47] "What could you possible have, still?" I questioned. Confession is not squeaky clean; it is *"the truth about ourselves."*

And then back to me came this moment of transparency: *"I haven't really thought of it that way before.... Then I'm okay."*

This might have been the point when Kristi saw, more clearly than ever before, the difference between mere fingerprint smudges and real failures, however small, in morality or in our living of the beatitudes. To be truly "okay" as well.... surely the complete sacrament must also bring a deeper healing of memories even here below.[48]

Kristi was finally at peace.

At this point in her journey, if not before, I think Kristi became totally free before my own eyes. I was there to see it. For many years Kristi had been close to St. Faustina and her message of divine mercy. (We first discovered the autobiographical *Divine Mercy* in the parish chapel in 1987.) She deeply knew the special message to our time that God is first, and before all else, a bottomless ocean of mercy. He is not hard-hearted in our image and likeness.

Sanctity, finally, is looking at ourselves with the eyes of others without finding reason for self-reproach. I took this as a very fine sign from my lovely girl. I sometimes felt that she was too inclined toward rigor in small things, too much the perfectionist. Her few words, *"Then I'm okay,"* told me that Kristi was now truly free and unencumbered. She was eager for her "dear Lord," to escort her straight home. "Blessed are the pure of heart, for they shall see God" (Matt. 5:8).

In our organized and anonymous world, the sacrament of confession, and marriage too, sometimes seem to be the only two truly personal things left. Otherwise, only cash machines and Social Security numbers. The quantification of indulgences in the sixteenth century, the flash point worked by Martin Luther, has become a kind of malignancy, fully secularized and multiplied. Addition, subtraction, and sometimes splitting of shares. One need think only of our ritualized attention to the gross national product and the New York

Stock Exchange. Everything is quantified; nothing is sacred. By this logic we even assert a right to solve the human condition by subtraction of others — through either abortion or euthanasia. Compared to this cult of quantification the arithmetic of indulgences that inspired Luther's indignation is child's play.

For those short moments when we were not in Kristi's room, she had a small crystal glass bell to ring if she needed help. But even this became nearly too heavy for her to lift. The bed routine was to help Kristi lie on her left side away from her fully involved right lung and right arm. I felt nearly as useless now as she had felt for so long. But Kristi always asked that I be the one to tuck her and especially her arm with pillows in exactly the right positions. A flashback to setting the pillows nine years earlier when we were dealing with a broken foot and kneecap. I like to think that in this "fluffing" business I have a special touch.

Other times we sat together on the bed, several times a day. It was during one of these especially quiet periods that I glanced to Kristi at my right. She was weak and yet half sitting up. Her eyes were fixed, silently interrogating the Franciscan crucifix on our wall.[49] People sometimes talk of the air being thick. This was such a moment. In the silence Kristi must have been demanding, probably for the first time, *What kind of Friend are you? What have I done? Why are you letting this happen to me?*

I turned away, anxiously suspended for at least ten seconds, not at all sure of the outcome at this turning point. I felt strongly that this encounter called for a very final degree of perseverance and surrender of any remaining self will. Even Kristi might settle, finally, for anger and resentment. We had never been here before, not in all the twelve years. It seemed that it was now, after so much, that Kristi might turn away from Him. Was her sweetness more like it is in the rest of us after all, not really touching the center now so exposed? I offered an urgent prayer that the center would hold.

Then came a low exhale and a turning downward of the eyes. I felt from Kristi an *"Oh, well,"* and a deeper surrender — not to be confused with mere resignation.

A charged moment slid past, and a stark bridge seemed to have been crossed. Several weeks after Kristi's death a parishioner was to say to me, "She was so resigned." Is this how it looked to others from the outside? I remained silent but did not at all accept these totally inadequate words. Perhaps they were spoken so that I might see with great clarity what had really happened. The term "resigned" simply distorts the different kind of surrender that was going on. Instead, in another passing moment, I revealed to Fr. Kemp, "Watching Kristi's surrender was like watching the crucifixion."

July 27. Pain medications were increased again, and we now were at the point when more sedation was needed. Kristi was losing her ability to take pills, and these did not come in liquid form for possible transfusion. The hospice team began to think in terms of morphine. After so much precaution for the allergies, I again vetoed this. "You think that because *you* do not see it [the medication hell within], that it does not exist!" We were not going to risk a repeat of "Kristi's Poem," that terror, now that she was so close.

"Don't let them give me the wrong medicine," she pleaded at the beginning of hospice.

From the intricate medical record the hospice team created a new and original path. As a sedative, we would substitute a pre-medication (a relaxant) for chemo that Kristi had tolerated well a few years before. This was a novel use of pre-medication. Infusion (of Versed) through the abdomen had never been done before.

Listless though she was, Kristi followed all of this, *"Oh, for the simple, good ol' days."* This involved a small pump and much finer almost string-like tubing than would be used normally with veins in the wrists. Even when she was up and around, finding a vein usually had been a challenge. A secret relief to me — if standard infusion into the veins had been possible for Kristi, in combination with the pills, there might have been a greater risk of fatal overdose.

But then with the novel infusion there was no way of knowing how much of the dose was entering the bloodstream. And by now I was crushing all of the pills and mixing them with water. Kristi slept and received the pill solution under her tongue from a small syringe. We felt that these doses were working to some degree. But again we had no way of knowing how much of these doses was actually being absorbed into the bloodstream. To keep up with the treatments, the small volume that could be given under the tongue at one time (one cubic centimeter) required a dose each hour.

To discontinue the pills and rely only on the Versed would be risky. If the infusion was ineffective there could follow a period of discontinued medication of any kind and *very* extreme discomfort. Working with so many uncertainties, we did the best we could. For the third time in as many days, the hospice team told us that we now had two to five days, or less. We applied a fresh medicated bandage to Kristi's right upper back and another to her arm to help sedate the nerve pain. Kristi's weight had dropped from one 125 pounds to probably 95. Her upper right arm was tiny now, a little larger around than a broomstick. In recent weeks Kristi had so tenderly cradled her diminishing arm, regarding it with a look of vulnerable bewilderment.

July 28. "Wish Laura a happy birthday." Then Mark sat with his mother. Very quietly: *"I love you Mark. Go get something to eat."* And then weakly on the phone: *"Hi, Kerry, how are you doing?"* Then, *"Oh, [I'm] just hanging in there."* The last of the four rosebushes in the back yard — Angel Face — finally bloomed. Kerry was torn between the needs of her own family and whether she should make yet another trip to Seattle, now rather than a day or two later. Considering the sedation and coming sleep, Kristi's comment was so calming, *"Oh, it's okay, I'll know when she gets here"* (and we know that she did).

July 29. "Let's . . . go . . . to . . . Mass." Kristi woke suddenly from the sedation and laboriously edged toward the side of the bed. She was completely and totally spent and yet wanted to go to Mass.

Wanting desperately for her to remain in bed, but seeing no way to gently keep her down, I followed Kristi's inching lead. How was she doing this? There was no strength left, and yet she had awakened and was moving again. How can this be? In her soft yellow gown, she rose with help, so slowly to a standing position. Life inside of death. With Mark and me on either arm, for the next minutes we found the path slowly to the foot of the bed, and then into the hall.

The three of us stood motionless and aimless. So weakly and pitifully Kristi finally asked and repeated: *"Can we go back to the start?"* Kristi desperately needed to be back in our bed where she started and where we knew she would remain. I picked up my girl, so light now, and carried her back. This rising from the bed for the last time was the most wrenching moment of all. It simply defies words. Kristi had been resting quietly and now was so suspended and distressed.

"Help me." As we rearranged the bed, and not knowing how to handle things, I said to my reclining wife, "You have to help me help you." I shall long regret this impulsive and confusing wording at this sunset moment. Another pill for the renewed anxiety and her startled eyes relaxed again into sleep.

Months later after Kristi had left us, Mark and I sat alone now at the kitchen table. "Mark," I said, "do you remember that afternoon when your mother got out of bed?" And, of course, he did. "It is best that she is home now. That can never ever happen again." And we both knew together and with a certainty that this was true.

I look about at all the little things. Now I noticed more and more, still in advance, that the hardest thing about losing Kristi —

a spouse — is that *everything* is hollowed. *Nothing is left standing.* The totality of life and death. St. Paul encourages us: "We do not lose heart, because our inner being is renewed each day even though our body is being destroyed at the same time" (2 Cor. 4:16).

I wondered again why more women do not write about our help-lessness, and the letting go, why more are not theologians. And then I saw again — they are mothers. They are not so confined to words. Women are theologians without paper. "The heart has its reasons, which the reason cannot understand." When our daughter, Laura, was only seven, she already captured all of this. She bubbled to me, "Sometimes when people do something good to me, like when they give me something...I feel like my heart is getting bigger and bigger, until it's bigger than I am!" What published and celebrated theologian has ever said more?

July 30. Kristi's sedated rest extended for fifteen hours and beyond. The syringe cocktail combined with the Versed infusion seemed to be protecting her from the horrendous distress of being dissolved from within. Her temperature dipped to 102 degrees. As for our inventive home protocol, our watchful hospice nurses simply said that "everything we are doing here is in new territory," and they confirmed that it was working.

July 31. Kristi had been resting easy now for thirty-six hours. A week or two before, hospice had suggested that we transfer her to a quite comfortable institution for the final period. Now, as I faced the back yard, Bev eased beside me and asked, "How long can you keep on doing this?"

I glanced back, also looking within myself. As long as it takes, I resolved: "Indefinitely."

The timing of dosages had reduced me to sleep segments of one or two hours. But I found that I was still able to fall into deep sleep and even to dream between alarms.

Kristi's pulse rose and her blood pressure dropped. We knew that hearing is the last sense to close down and began to trust that Kristi could still hear us. Laura talked privately to her mother through the bedside telephone held in position for this, sharing a neglected last thought known only to the two of them.

We love this mother and wife. She was not going through the valley alone. Surely, in the next room, our Father's mansion was already filled with welcoming friends gathering forward from beyond the veil. Could she already see her Daddy and Therese and Bernadette and Catherine and Maria? St. Therese says of the Communion of Saints that they "communicate grace to each other greater than that of a family, and even the most perfect family on earth."[50]

I was to hear later that the aged Msgr. Doogan at our parish prayed through this entire last day for Kristi. On an earlier visit he had heard Kristi's confession. Returning downstairs that day, he commented to Mark of his mother, "Now there is a holy woman. She should be hearing my confession."

Eileen, the second volunteer hospice nurse, visited and offered sweet wisdom for this moment. In the bedroom we showed her several tiny relics on the dresser, probably a dozen. These were loaned to us by so many families and friends. Among them were little bits from Kristi's friends: St. Therese and St. Maria Goretti. Others were from the American saint Elizabeth Anne Seaton, St. Francis, Pius X, and several more. There were the most recent relics of the seven beatified Thai martyrs given to us by Archbishop Lawrence Khai. Eileen was amazed: "There are more relics here than in most of the cathedrals of Europe!"

This evening we felt a special urgency to pray for Kristi, and with her that she might hear us. Kristi's sisters and mother again sang "On Eagles' Wings." A small tear formed in Kristi's nearly closed right eye. Bev, sitting now on the bed beside Kristi, bolted forward to kiss her on the left cheek. This was a good evening, a bittersweet moment as Kristi slipped undisturbed toward the special gathering now within her trusting reach and their awesome embrace.

August 1. It had been five years nearly to the day since the stem cell transplant. Throughout the night we continued to give hourly medication under the tongue. Mark privately said his good-bye, as did the others. Laura called again. Sitting alone at Kristi's side during the night, I again looked into Kristi's turned head and nearly closed eyes.

Such weakness and such strength. Clearly, before leaving she waited for me, her imperfect spouse "from the very, very beginning," to also let her go. Did Kristi, more than halfway home, linger at great discomfort to herself for me? This, so that in my slow way, I might find time to understand just enough to survive what was coming for me this side of the veil?

I do recall clearly that on my knees, it finally came:

> Kristi, I am the only one who has not said good-bye.
> Look at you, what are you still doing there?
> It's okay for you to sleep now. I want you to go.
> Go to Him, He will catch you. He will.
> Even now I am impatient. I am so afraid.

And then in a second breath:

> O sweet Jesus, this has gone on long enough,
> Take Kristi home, and please do it today.

Two hours later at eight o'clock, I awoke on schedule beside Kristi. This was not quite five minutes after Jeanne and Cherie had checked on us. A lightness and peace filled the room and met my eyes even before I turned to face my wife. . . .

It was over.

The moment before waking me as she left, Kristi's gently spaced breathing — down to five very weak breaths per minute — simply stopped. After fifty-two years, one of the breaths was simply the last. Our son, Mark, and I sat alone with our Kristi a few minutes. And then we guided Jeanne and Kerry from the end bedroom to the bedside. As I rewrite these lines from the journal (over two years later), the lightness of this moment, Kristi's holiness, floats me now above the crushing burden.

Oh, Kristi, you were so still, no longer breathing. There was no need to check for a pulse, I could see that your heart was still.

Yes, our prayer against any final agony was also answered. "O precious in the eyes of the Lord is the death of his faithful" (Ps. 116:15). There was, at least for now and for all of us, a tender sweetness, a completeness that calms the heart and that is sufficient for the moment.[51]

Still in Kristi's hands was the special Benedictine cross with the crucifixion and the resurrection bonded to one another back to back. And about Kristi's neck, the gossamer gold chain and delicate pendants — the cross from our trip together to New Orleans, a small gold medallion from the Chapel of the Miraculous Medal at rue de Bac in Paris, and another from Lourdes.

I later imagined and possibly even sensed from Kristi in the moment of final transition, *"Let me kiss my Peter dearest before I leave."* Is it this gesture of peace from her eternity that woke me?

Shortly before noon I lifted Kristi from the bed and carried her down the stairs to the waiting gurney in the entryway and to the threshold of a larger mansion than I could ever provide. The mortician saw in her even now something different as we started together toward the mortuary. On the way we stopped at the bluff Kristi loves so much, for a final view of the water to the west and of the flowers, and for another short prayer: " . . . I promise to accept all You will allow to happen to me, only teach me Your holy will."

At the driver's invitation, Kristi's smiling face remained unveiled. "We all, with face unveiled, reflecting as in a mirror the glory of the Lord, are being transformed into his very image, from glory to glory, as through the Spirit of the Lord" (2 Cor. 3:18).

Chapter Six

... A Lonely Business

> Precious in the eyes of the Lord
> is the death of his faithful ones.
> — Psalm 116:15

The Road to Emmaus

In late June, five weeks before Kristi died, we sat quietly together in the back yard near the newly planted memorial roses. Before us the neighborhood and the entire world seemed suspended. I recalled the bittersweet moment on May 23, 1997, when Mary sent a message through the veil. Kristi's suffering of the "thorns" (shingles) was as "fragrant as the fresh summer grasses." As we sat there the lawn of spring grasses divided in the sunlight before us into separate and suspended blades. Dear love, you said to me: *"You are always there for me. This dying thing is a lonely business. . . . I don't like leaving you behind."*

This was the fleeting moment when I could not speak my thoughts: "But you are not leaving me behind. Christianity is the secret revealed that *everything* good we think we leave 'behind' is really in front of us and above. I will carry you in my heart, and you will be carried in the Sacred Heart of Jesus, which excludes no one."

Today above the mantle in our home is the last Father's Day card given to me by my Kristi. This is the first keepsake I mounted after the funeral. The complete message lettered on the card reads: "How many can say they have a true partner, friend, and lover they can count on in good times and bad? How many can say their love is even stronger for all they've been through? Only a lucky few . . . like me, thanks to you." And then, while Kristi still could write, in her weakened hand she had added:

> *My Peter Dearest,*
> *I'll always love you.*
> *Your Kristi.*

After twelve years of both cancer and daily treasuring the moment, on August 1, Kristi was gone from me.

This loss is incomprehensible.

And so I wrap her in words. The funeral was scheduled for August 11, partly to enable more of the family to arrive. This would not have been possible, except that Kristi remained with us as long as she did. I think now she heard all of our conversations, and that she resolved to stay with us to help us let her go. August 11 was also the fifth anniversary to the day of Kristi's "birthday," when the stem cell transplant started to kick in. Her birthday, the first day of the rest of her life, which now found her in eternity.

Two days before the funeral, shortly before noon, Archbishop Alexander Brunett left a call from the Chancery Office on our recorder.

This is for Peter. . . . This is Archbishop Brunett calling, and I just wanted to let you know that I did hear that your wife, Kristi, died. And I wanted to give to you and all of your family my love and condolences at this time.

I understand that she was a marvelous lady, and heard wonderful things about her. In fact, your pastor there tells me that she was one of the most saintly women he's ever run into, and that is a beautiful thing.

I'd love to go to the funeral and be with you on that day, but the anniversary Mass of the Providence Sisters,[1] which was scheduled six months ago, is at eleven o'clock Saturday morning, and I cannot change that time. However I do want you to know that you will be in my prayers, and thought of very, very strongly on that day in prayer and [the] Mass that I celebrate.

I ask the Lord to bless all of you. I know you are very blessed having someone who is a saint praying for you and still being part of your life and touching all of your lives as she will certainly continue to touch ours.

My blessings to you, Peter. I know that these are difficult times, but they are times [in which] also, in the midst of our sorrow, we can discover the beautiful, wonderful gift that God has given to us in her. Have a good day, as best you can, and know that you are supported by our prayers and love. God bless you.

On the evening before the funeral, friends and family gathered before Kristi's covered coffin in St. Mark's Church for recitation of the rosary. At Fr. Kemp's unusual suggestion, this familiar devotion was combined with Exposition of the Blessed Sacrament "to which Kristi was so devoted." On the altar at the center of the church was the round monstrance containing the consecrated Eucharist.[2] From his place at the right of the altar, Fr. Kemp offered meditative opening thoughts:

We gather together this evening in the presence of the Blessed Sacrament, because Kristi taught us so often the joy of being in the presence of the Lord, by her own devotion and her own life of prayer. In her living and her dying she continues to teach us. And with little doubt she intercedes for all of us as we offer this prayer through our Blessed Lady to Jesus and to our Heavenly Father.

Some who hear the rosary for the first time are amazed by this repetitive prayer of the Catholic Church. But more than repetitive, it is really a prayer of meditation. By the recitation of the Hail Marys we invite Our Lady to draw us deeper and deeper with each Hail Mary into the great mysteries of Jesus' love for us that we celebrate in this wonderful prayer.

Quite different from alleged idolatry of Mary, the rosary is simply a Scripture-based prayer of meditation on events in the life of Christ. The entire Marian devotion even traces back to a single line in Scripture. This line is unpacked and deepened for limited minds meditating through the fleeting centuries. From the unapproach-able God an angel appeared to Mary, and his words are those still repeated in the rosary cycle: "Hail, full of grace, the Lord is with thee" (Luke 1:28). "Full of grace?" Surely this is the original in-nocence, and more. Mary is the Immaculate Conception now an advocate for us, and the Mother of Christ who is our eternal God incarnate.

At the podium to the left of the altar, I spoke very briefly. "For those of us who might be troubled, [we should] know that Kristi is totally, totally at peace with this." Then I repeated Kristi's most consistent rosary petitions. These intentions had never been written down, but were familiar and had been offered singly or in small groups before each decade. Sometimes it was some, and sometimes it was others. Often we walked through the neighborhood, sometimes sharing a single rosary, with these intentions from her heart.

For all of the sick and the dying — and those in rest homes who are alone and forgotten, or who have no one to look out for them,

For all of those involved in abortion, euthanasia, pornography, or satanic worship,

For families everywhere and for troubled marriages — and for each of the members of our families, and for those carrying special burdens unknown to us,

For tiny children who today are in immediate danger of abortion, and for their mothers.

For all of those at "the Hutch" — and especially for those in our parish dealing with cancer: for the family of Karen, and for Nicole, Michael, and Joan and their families,

For healing, and for perseverance,

For us, that we might forgive one another from the heart — and for those we have spiritually adopted, and for the conversion of sinners and the indifferent,

For the souls of those departed — especially for the most forgotten.

(and finally)

In praise and in thanksgiving — for Your daily presence in each of our lives, and for the many blessings received, and

In thanksgiving for the path that is given to each one of us, whatever it may be.

Kristi's funeral on Saturday, August 11, 2001, was as she had planned it with us in the first week of April. Cherie enraptured the large gathering with the *Ave Maria*. The choir, organist, and another soloist refused compensation for their talent and later declined to even talk about this. Fr. Kemp remarked that the large white bouquet had been sent by the bishops (Brunett and Thomas) who could not be present. Neighbors reported that they had never been to any Catholic event before and never had seen a funeral so resplendent as this. The fragrance of Stargazer Lilies was everywhere (and remains with me still). The presence of heaven on earth, in each Mass, transfigured our first steps into total grief.

The central reading told of the encounter between the grief-stricken disciples and the risen Christ on the road to Emmaus (Luke 24:13–35). Fr. Kemp used this opening to unveil what it was about Kristi that so touched us all. I was astonished at first by his very deliberate remarks, but have become even more convinced of their truth in the three years that have followed, partly from the consistently similar comments of others. Fr. Kemp carefully weighed and delivered his remarks:

> Today is a profound moment in the life of this parish family. Today is indeed a profound moment for anyone who knew and who loved Kristi. For she has embodied for us the very words of Scripture that have been proclaimed this morning. I could recount for you a history of a life, but it would not begin to capture the great story of a soul.
>
> Was she a great "proclaimer"? Not in words, or shouting from a pulpit. But in a gentle, ever-so-gentle life, she shouted the Gospel message. And [she] made Jesus visible and real and alive for all of us. As in the Scripture so carefully picked for the day. Because to know Kristi is to know the deep and abiding love that she had for the Holy Sacrifice of the Mass and an incredible devotion to Jesus present in the Eucharist.
>
> Sitting in these pews with us, week after week, we saw her not only receive the cross of Christ into her life, but to embrace it. To embrace it with the dignity that belongs to all Christian believers. She suffered, but her suffering was not in vain. She would ask only, *"For whom else do I need to offer these*

sufferings to Christ? I'm not ready to leave yet, Father, there are more people who need my prayers before I go to my Dear Jesus."[3]

We saw her when she had every right to simply be at home and wait — wait for others to bring the Eucharist to her. We saw her when she had every right to simply wait and be served.

And yet for our own building up in Christ and because of her own deep, deep faith, she would rally her strength and come and do what she thought was most important. To be here with us as we celebrated Sunday Eucharist — to be here like the disciples on the Road to Emmaus. To hear the words of Scripture that not only burned in her heart, but shined on her face.[4] And to draw close to Jesus Christ in this celebration of the Mass that it is too easy to take for granted.

In all of my years as a priest I have never stood before a congregation and said to them what I say to you this morning. Beseech her intercession, ask for her prayers, seek her guidance.[5] And in gentleness of heart, and love of God, and devotion to his Church, we might be graced to be just a little bit more like her.

Were the words that crossed her lips ever words that tore down? Did anyone ever walk away from her feeling anything but closer to the Lord? In the Cross that she embraced is there anyone, is there anyone among us, who ever heard a word of complaint? For her and for us, the dear Cross of our Lord is no symbol of sadness or human destruction, but it is the symbol of promise, and it is the hope of eternal life.[6]

On the day before her death, when the Lord had already reached out his hand and touched *the one I will dare call His beloved,* on that dear morning she was trying to pull together enough strength to get out of bed. Pete is questioning, "What do you need, what do you want?"

"I need to go to Mass." At eight o'clock she left us in this
world, and where did she go? She went to Mass — celebrated
in the presence of the angels and the saints. She went to Mass.

While the family visited with friends at the reception, Fr. Kemp
slipped away and quietly rode with Kristi in the funeral car. In the
coming days we were to receive so many cards and notes of sympathy. Donations to Kristi's favorite charities were generous. One note
was from Fr. Thomas, our friend who had often visited, especially
at the beginning of our special twelve years. It was he who had recommended to us the intercession of St. Therese and the Novena to
the Holy Spirit. These two prayers did so much to cheer Kristi and
shape her through our entire ordeal. He wrote, " . . . May Jesus who
comforted Mary and Martha at the death of Lazarus — now comfort
and console you, Peter, at the death of Kristin, beloved of God!"

Where Are You?

> *God will wipe away ever tear from their eyes.*
> — Revelation 7:17

Kristi's interment took place at the Seattle Archdiocese Holyrood
Cemetery on the Feast of the Assumption (August 15). Three or
four times over the years she had told me that she wanted cremation.
She hesitated in the final weeks only long enough to be reassured
by me that this would not complicate the resurrection. *"Will this
interfere with the resurrection?"* she asked. This was her only question.
My God, she trusted me in life and death, and now for access to the
resurrection. My girl, she preferred the simplicity and the neatness
and, in her humility, the economy.[7]

Kristi's stone was placed nearly three months after her interment,
on the Feast of All Saints (November 1). Engraved at the top is her
favorite line from Philippians (4:13): "I can do all things in him

who strengthens me." And at the bottom is the longer Novena to the Holy Spirit,[8] which carried us throughout nearly half of our marriage.

After a year and a half of visits to the site, I came to actually believe and accept a simple truth. As Kristi was gentle with all, so am I to be gentle with myself. Throughout the cancer and the final ordeal, Kristi and I were together. Our children, Laura and Mark, grew into adulthood. Their separation from so special a mother is an immeasurable loss. Mark was to ask of his special mother, "Does she remember?" A sweet light has passed from our lives and from the world. *"My last wish is to die in your arms,"* Kristi whispered.

Our thoughts during hospice opened more deeply into the Last Things. Hospice is such a sliding into finality. We had been told that we had very little time, one week, or seven at most. A reprieve gave us more time, nineteen weeks in all, 133 days.

Dealing with the death of a loved one comes in layers. Like peeling an onion, I was told by Dr. Lee, who always had time for us. Each wrenching memory and recovery is momentary, and then unveils a still deeper anguish. I found that the layers of the onion get bigger instead of smaller. Or, what is the same, our own vision narrows. Grieving memory becomes disconnected. Those who grieve speak of tunnel vision. I found this to be true. It would be eight months before I recalled again such an uncomplicated closeness as simply holding hands.

How had I lost the feel of so many familiar things? We were capsized again, this time in emotional white water as in our "great adventure" in the Dordogne three years before. But no bottom rose up for me to stand on, no rocks beneath my feet. I reached again for Kristi, but this time the current was too strong and she was not there. Not only our world, but the entire self-sufficient world of the past few centuries — so exaggerated and so amputated from the reality of the vast life within — finally blows away as in a desert dust storm, the "desert of despair."

This uncertain side of my inner self jumped to action upon Kristi's death. "Is Kristi still my wife?" I feared. And was our marriage only a cloud? For all of our modern-day frenzy and even success, are all of us simply spinning — meaningless — around the sun? Is the human will — freedom and promise — of any consequence? Are Sartre and the tribe of stiff-upper-lip existentialists the best there is? They would have us deflect hopelessness solely by spreading activity over the surface of things, one project after another (Sartre's *les projets*), and by reducing God to our own metabolism.

Or is there a ground beneath these individual and collective doings? An abyss in either case — finally either a circular wasteland, or the ground of infinite love. There is no third choice. In my mind I did not doubt, even for a moment. There are things we can know, even when feeling is gone. But how does one deal with spiritual amputation?[9] The separation of spouses cuts deeper than the separation of identical twins. Of this spousal separation, this loss of mutual belonging, it seems, is amplified by a dormant aloneness of the spirit from near the very beginning, and which was not meant to be.

Kristi and I sometimes realized together that human division and cruelty in the world is so boundless that it is actually a convincing proof of the spirituality in man. Only perversion of a spiritual sort, a twisting of something destined toward infinite good, could account for such mutilation as we have seen in recent history, so far beyond any violence in animal nature. Nature is violent, but it is not perverse. How can there be a God in a world of such evil? For Kristi and me this became, "Beneath a darkness so convoluted, how can there *not* be a deeper design that has been mutilated — and therefore God?"

Finally, in grief, one does not get to the last layer, for that would be to fully define the one lost. And the point, a religious one ever present, is that the other — and the Other — is a mystery.

The new temptation, then, is to impose a caricature on the one lost, to find at least one single memory that will hold. I thrashed out for a control and perhaps a distancing that could stop the endless wandering through the house and through the flying memories. But this use of imagination is a violation and a disrespect. The person is a mystery, not a mental image. Lost forever is our daily familiarity and mutual affirmation in so many small things, even within the most monotonous routine. Of the pills Kristi had said, *"There seems to be so much repetition."* Even this was gone. This is the way it is.

I usually held Kristi's left hand in my right with my little finger wrapped separately across the thumb of Kristi's smaller hand. A perfect fit. I recall again the spring Sunday morning, probably three or four years before Kristi's death. Our pastor watched, and then teased us as we came together toward him. "Look at you two," he grinned, "married this long and still holding hands." This moment, so simple, and so totally gone.

Death is so total, so relentless, so irreversible.

These feeble pages are a story of Kristi, a good and gentle heart. I say *a* story, because even a spouse does not really know all of the mystery of the other. My hope here is to let her cheerfulness shine through on these pages, and yet this portrait is only a sketch. In the total knowledge of God, where Kristi now is, face to face, she is whole. I have only the front edge, the fragments, although from the day we met we were barely ever apart. I am sure that Kristi recalls with me the lines from Guardini (a somewhat melancholy writer) we read together at the beginning of our courtship on the "loneliness in faith . . . [and] the more precious will that love be which flows from one lonely person to another."[10]

What is it about Kristi that touched so many people so consistently, in such an indefinable way? The same author puts his finger on it, I think, in another passage treating the Road to Emmaus — the special reading selected for Kristi's funeral Mass. He observes for us:

> He takes the bread, breaks it; they recognize him, and he vanishes. What did they recognize him by? Not by the mere act of bread-breaking (the customary right of host and honored guest) but by his particular manner of doing so: the gesture, glance and palpable kindness so unmistakably his have remained after death.[11]

Kristi did not do great things, she did nothing out of the ordinary, but she seemed to have found a way to live in the presence of *the gesture,* and to reflect the gesture of the One who both creates and then transfigures the ordinary. Hers was "the more excellent way," the Little Way of collectedness and of gentleness toward the person in front of her each day, and not forgetting our daughters and sons yet unborn.

The temptation now held out by grief is to distance, to protect myself, to adjust and to let go and move on, to find closure. And this is a temptation, in response to the one departing who sometimes does pass through a normal and final phase of distancing from us. Even before the hospice, Kristi seemed to be detaching from worldly events, even if not the little events of the day.

Are we still together? Does spousal love add something to our notion of the Communion of Saints — the unity of all souls, each distinct and yet together as in a marriage, within the eternal heart of Christ? These are realities we shared with each other and I dare to hope we continue to share, as Archbishop Brunett suggested in his telephone call.

And how is it that a wife can be so entrusted and donated to her "best Friend," and still be an instrument of his love in the lives of others, even in marriage and to a husband so lacking? Kristi seemed to fall into the Magnificat: "My soul does magnify the Lord." And yet, this is my wife. In some mysterious way, love is most universal and ever enlarging when it is particular and exclusive.

Despite our possible day-to-day failings toward each other, in marriage He invites us to be concretely Himself to each other, to stand in His place. This is partly why Kristi's growing and then total devotion to Him in our later years was not a distancing from me as one might imagine. At the same time she also saw me as her "rock," though she knew clearly from the Psalms that only He is our rock. For the feminine mind and heart, there is no contradiction in this. It is a mystery to me, each marriage within the other.

In the first month or two I suggested to Mark, across our diminished table, that our path now was "to move on but *without* letting go." "This," I said, "is surely the key." Not one or the other. I found that this is the right path, especially within families and between spouses. We needed now to know that what we had in the past still endures in more than the memory. Or that the one remembered still is, even as the past slips away. And that this permanence is not imaginary — that the one departed also moves on without letting go. Is loss and grief possibly an opening, and not a closure? Kristi, is your soul more real than time and death? And what of two souls who had been together — are we still?

In the months ahead, Kristi's death took me back again and again to the nearby oceanside vantage and beach we often visited in the final days of hospice care. The Olympic Mountains now looked so dull. Over the water, the ferryboats came and went from nowhere. Now, stunned with Kristi gone, I slid between the logs to read C. S. Lewis's well-known essay *A Grief Observed*. A guidebook, I hoped.

Ferry on Puget Sound. "*Over the water, the ferryboats came and went from nowhere.*"

Lewis also faced the loss to cancer of his spouse, Joy. A few years older than I at the time of his own total loss, he dreaded that he might revert back to being the hollow man he had been before. A fearsome possibility. "Oh God," he writes, "why did you take such trouble to force this creature out of its shell if it is now doomed to crawl back — to be sucked back — into it?" The inner unraveling dragged me to ask not only if Kristi is still my wife, but if Kristi and I had ever really been married at all.

Does grief always do this, take away one's past as well as the future? My evasion of this looming fear was abrupt, a totally arbitrary act of self-defense against shock and panic. It was a grace that stopped me from analyzing even this random notion. Had I tripped here, I wonder if I ever could have recovered.

Lewis's grief is fully contained in his opening sentence: "No one ever told me that grief felt so like fear." He adds the sense of wandering "suspense." Fear with a suspense that the familiar is discontinued.[12] This borders on panic. For myself, what I felt was growing panic, a claustrophobic panic. There is nothing, nothing at all, to hold on to. How long can one be held up by a book, even a book by Lewis? Only minutes. In the movie of his later life, *Shadowlands*, a Cambridge student challenges Lewis with a line I used to point out to Kristi: "We read to know that we are not alone." But this is not really enough, not now.

After Lewis, I turned to Sheldon Vanauken's *A Severe Mercy*. The agnostic Vanauken and his young wife, Davy, later were attracted to Christianity by their personal contact with Lewis. In his book, he also reflects on the early death of his young wife twenty years before the writing. This loss, again so total, came after a magical twelve years together. After outlasting two years of initial grief, he discovered what he calls a "second death." For him, this second death is "the disappearance of the sense of the beloved's presence," which was coupled with the grieving. As the grief passes, so too the sense of presence. For Lewis the second death would be to find perhaps that his marriage had left him unchanged from his former solitary self from before the marriage.[13]

In our fear and imagining, are we too trapped by our too-natural sense of before-and-after? Instead, is a *continued* presence revealed to us as in the two-sided Benedictine cross so often seen in the hands of Kristi and her father, despite and through suffering? This cross shows both the crucifixion and the resurrection at the same time. Is a continued presence of even spouses assured in the similar vision witnessed by Julian of Norwich? The crucifixion is transformed into the splendor of the transfiguration. Is the second death only an imagining?

Vanauken sees this second death as a final turning away — on his dear Davy's part. But do the departed really turn away, leaving us twice, once in death which is total and again later in rejection — an even more final separation? My God, I thought, is my total loss not enough? Did I have this second and even more absolute banishment to look forward to? Total separation first, and then . . . *nothing*? Kristi, do not slip out on me twice! I might be able to do this thing if I know that you are still with me. . . .

Each day, often each minute of each day, is enough. A year out, two years out? A second death? Despair? Even Lewis, near the end, hears Joy saying, "I am at peace with God." To which he concludes his book, "She smiled, but not at me." For us, the ones left behind, for us to find and hold moments when we feel less sorrow, Lewis says, is not desertion. We are not "killing the dead a second time." Lewis seems to sense that the later turning away might be something inside of ourselves, something that *we* do — and so, I thought, that we might control.[14]

Control?

Maybe the only way Kristi can fully love Him, I imagined, is through the eyes of infinite love, with the eyes of the heart totally healed. And so, is it by looking through His eyes that the departed might really look back to us, while only seeming to us to look "away"? Is this is the Communion of Saints?

The missing piece I sensed, for both Lewis and Vanauken at the time of their writings, was that neither really suspected the full truth of the Communion of Saints! This communion is the solid companionship that endures beneath our fear and our sense of fundamental solitude, and our sojourn within time. It is more real than our false sense of aloneness, our self-inflicted share of Gethsemane. The God within is a family, and it is from this divine and triune intimacy, not from a monolithic God, that we are called into being. And we — together — are in His image, in His creative and fruitful divine intimacy. Kristi is forever turned toward me, not away, and even more so now that she is home with her "dear Lord."

The holiness of the saints is given them to share with us. . . .
That is the path God himself wants us to take. The saints, of
course, always direct us back to God as the source of all that
is good, but God directs us to the saints. For the saints are in
God, and by turning to them we are plunged even deeper into
the ocean of his Trinitarian mystery.[15]

I wondered (a good word), instead of the second death is it
possible for us to even hold hands through the veil?

Are you in the next room? "Where are you? I can't find you!"
The neighbors must certainly have heard this moan. It escaped for
the first time seventeen days after you left me, from a vast nowhere
within. A howling from one void to another. Then days or weeks
later, more than once, it came again and without much warning.
"Marooned," I feared, morbidly pleased that I had found the right
word. More than a death, the loss of a spouse is also an amputation,
as Lewis says, but more, it is a spiritual amputation. A shared soul is
severed. At the same time one is half a marriage and half a person,
and even less. There is no refuge, no undamaged layer within the
soul to which one might escape and hide.

For the previous twelve years, following the first cancer, we had
lived more and more the deepening present moment. And there
were always little goals, but the long term was something we left
aside. This kind of pause, to not subordinate the moment, is out
of step with recent times. The times paint a cocoon world, always evolving and moving more or less in a line from the past
to present — toward us or what we can paint ahead of us with
our imaginations (nothing more). Drilling into the moment, getting
around time in a way, is a deeper path.

The silence brings a detachment, communion of two on one path,
and even a trust in Christ who so deep within the eternal moment is
"the same yesterday, today, yes, and forever" (Heb. 13:8). We catch

the silence so infrequently, but He is the center that holds. We breathed with both lungs — action within a deeper presence (even when Kristi's right lung was gripped by the cancer). We prayed for both healing and for perseverance. Always both. If this is a contradiction, let the Lord sort it out. Simple and short prayers, she asked of me, like those of Blessed Mother Teresa on the flip calendar on the kitchen cabinet.

Perseverance from one moment to the next is both an island of resistance and an embracing affirmation. Together we resisted a surrounding darkness that, I am sure now, was always maneuvering to get in. To not persevere, to despair, is not simply a mood. It is the sin against the most intimate source and center of all being, and the center within our selves, the Soul of our souls. For me to despair now would be a sin against every special moment we ever had together, and every single leaf and flower petal we had ever shared. To despair now would be to deny the infinite compassion within the crucifix on our bedroom wall. It is the failure to believe that infinite mercy is meant even for our failings *and* even for our reproach and our self-doubts.

How did others see Kristi? After Kristi's death, for a school project the teenage daughter of a friend fashioned a memorial for Kristi. The symbols Brigid identified begin with a rose "because Kristi had such devotion to St. Therese." Other symbols were the color coral — "it matches her personality because Kristi was a very uplifting person. She was a person who made you feel good and special . . . always smiling." Another was a heart because she "showed love towards everyone, no matter who it was. Her love and kindness towards others was very powerful and made people want to be around her and be more like her." Yet another symbol chosen by this young girl was sunshine: "Kristi reminds me of the sun because she was always shining with joyfulness, and also because she always had a glowing smile on her face. Kristi was truly a saint. She treated others as they want to be treated. We all can learn from her wonderful example."

In late November, well over a year after Kristi's death, a casual acquaintance introduced herself to me with this: "She just glowed, she radiated Christ." From her center Kristi was forgetful of self — for her family and her friends, for many in heaven, and for many others conceived but not yet born.

But at the edge of our life together, Kristi's and mine, there had lurked an enemy known to both of us. In 1996, during complications from the stem cell treatment, Kristi had been touched by this inner hell. Now, in her final days, she had remembered something I only saw in her eyes from the outside. Severely reacting to medications, she had feared despair, the great distrust, and had asked: *"Peter, am I in hell? I do not remember sinning against the Holy Spirit."* Near the end Kristi said so often, *"Peter, pray that I persevere."*

We returned to the solidity and freshness of the Creed.

Believe and "be not afraid." Simplicity. At Kristi's side and for her need, I added to our Creed only one word. This was a word of emphasis. We *do* believe . . . in the Communion of Saints. . . . This was simple and concrete, not intricate theology. It is a response of perseverance toward real grace. The Creed itself is the human mind, ever aided by the Spirit given at Pentecost, receiving and unpacking the mystery of His concrete presence among us — the incarnation of the infinite God. At their root, all heresies and much of the modern-day mind-set are a denial of the incarnation.

We arrive at our shared permanence within His eternity — this is the Communion of Saints. Is one to dismiss this special proof of God, the mystical experience of the saints? Might we join their friendship with Infinite Love who enters into His own creation to face us from the cross? What of these — witnesses?

Tucked away in the nearly endless words of the Second Vatican Council we also find this exceptional line about these witnesses, to console both the dying and the spiritual amputees left behind:

> God vividly manifests to men His presence and His Face. He speaks to us in them and gives us a sign of His Kingdom, to which we are powerfully drawn, *surrounded as we are by so many witnesses and having such an argument* for the truth of the gospel.[16]

To this, what can we give but amazement? From childhood Kristi's circle of friends had included the saints. Now especially Mary, who by her "yes" became the Mother of God, and those saints of innocence. Trust them now. To guide Kristi's prayer for perseverance, we would reach for enduring friendships, "We *do* believe in... the Communion of Saints...."

The saints are not the way, but they point the way. They are not fabricated to clutter our imaginations, but in them we can marvel at the varied multiplicity of His presence within ourselves. The miracle of the loaves and fishes is not myth; it is the lever that locates the universe within eternity and puts even space and time and number in their place. Kristi, to persevere simply hold hands with your friends. Hold hands through the veil with these witnesses. Without letting go or turning your back, move on.

My intuition of the moment was that this anchoring in the Creed — our thoughts of the Father ("Abba": Daddy) — would hold and sustain Kristi. But really it is also the praying together — two or more — that sustains the Creed.[17] Both of these persevere together, the belief and the believers, neither without the other. Together with the propositions, we find a feminine understanding of prayer, one more rounded and tender than the standard definition of "lifting of the mind and heart." Prayer, even the Creed, is "an intimate sharing *between friends* with him who we know loves us (emphasis added)."[18]

For us now, perseverance is a sharing between friends *on both sides of the veil.* In the final days Kristi's smallness was simply to fall from my arms and into His and theirs. I am sure she did this even this side of the veil, surrounded from within by her special friends, this Communion of Saints. Now Kristi is with them and yet surrounds me still. Is it possible to hold hands through so thin a veil?

I find Kristi not in memory, not even accurate memory, but in self-forgetfulness. Then, Kristi, I see you peeking in and reassuring me, and in such moments the heaviness lifts. In death, the one lost is not in the past, and is not in the memory or in the imagination. Kristi is not the memories about Kristi, however rich or intact these yet may be. As some memories are diluted by the passage of time, she does not recede farther behind me. Kristi is in front of me and within, and each day closer instead of farther away. As Christ is in the Eucharist more than He is in the scriptural memory that only tells about him, so too is Kristi in my own self-forgetfulness rather than in my memories about her. She finds me in the collectedness; I do not find her in the striving.

The very tears are not simply discarded or replaced: "Your sorrow shall be *turned into* joy" (John 16:20).

I see that Kristi is not only free of the cancer ordeal, but that the ordeal itself is transfigured. It is transfigured in a love that is boundless and unconditional. It is exclusive to each special person, to each one of us. We can barely guess at what this means.[19] Heaven is the resurrection in person, not simply the idea of resurrectedness in our minds. And it is total.

While I long each day and each moment of each day to be re-united, I am calmed to know that in the eternal present Kristi now is overflowing in her delight.

They shall neither hunger nor thirst any more,
neither shall the sun strike them nor the heat.
For the Lamb who is in the midst of the throne
will shepherd them,
and will guide them to the fountains
of the waters of life, and
God will wipe away every tear from their eyes.

(Rev. 7:16–17)

Where Am I?

*Wherever you are on earth, however long you remain on earth, the
Lord is near, do not be anxious about anything.*   —St. Augustine[20]

Long before I met him, Kristi's father, when he could, flew for recreation as a private pilot. Giving this up for health reasons was a real
penance. He reminisced with me once about another pilot and a
writer who had captured in a book the freedom of flight. His *Night
Flight* is about his service delivering airmail in Argentina in the late
1930s. In another of his works, the same Antoine de Saint-Exupéry
summarizes what all of us sometimes feel, and what I felt as a child
in even the partial desert of eastern Washington. And now I was in
the desert of Kristi's passing:

Why O Lord (I prayed) impose on me this journey through
the desert of despair? I am struggling amongst the thorns. Yet
a sign from Thee would be enough to make the desert blossom
like a rose; then the golden sand and the great open spaces
and the wind sweeping the desert would be no more a jumble
of incoherencies, but one vast empire wherein I lift up my
heart, perceiving Thee beyond it.[21]

It was only a week after Kristi's death that I found myself threatened by a "jumble of incoherencies" and in a bookstore, lost. Strangely, a book popped off the shoulder-high top shelf and fell to the floor in front of me. It must have been shelved carelessly. I picked it up and slid it back into its place. I turned away and moved on. At the same sound, I turned back and discovered the same book on the floor once more. In my disconnected state I imagined that Kristi was selecting something for me to read. I was curious enough to buy it.

Here was a very ordinary paperback (the title does not matter) dealing with deep emotional and spiritual stress. Those who grieve severely risk falling into such a hole. In a quick skim I found the message that seemed to hit the root of a rising fear of the future. The elementary message to me at that moment was that, before all else, one needs to know in one's bone marrow that one is not alone. Obsession, constant worry, is prevented not by activity alone. Activity and churning can become addiction, and is a symptom rather than a way out. We must look at ourselves, and at our times. I was on a sort of ledge, like the suspended book pushed from the shelf. I needed to know that even now I truly *belong,* rather than not. I need to know that mutual belonging endures in some way, that in her death Kristi and I are not separated forever.

How to hold hands through the veil?

Without leaving us, Kristi has joined Mary and her friends — especially the saints Therese, Bernadette, Catherine, and Maria. Another one she admired, at the time not yet a saint, was Blessed Gianna Beretta Molla (canonized May 16, 2004). Gianna was also a housewife, and a pediatrician. In 1962, when Kristi was thirteen, this Italian mother had foregone chemotherapy so that her unborn child could live. She opted instead for a highly dangerous surgery that would not endanger her unborn child. The resulting infection led to her painful death from peritonitis.[22]

With these friends in mind and nearby, Kristi persevered.

The question now comes to me: How am I to persevere? Am I alone after all? Solitude? Total solitude is total hell. Reversing Sartre, hell is *the absence of* other people. After the death of a spouse, to outrun the solitude of hell the amputee strains to recreate the one lost. The mistake, unavoidable at first, is to become totally trapped in one's loss, rather than to rejoice (!) in the total healing of the spouse. Amputated soul memories, these emotional convulsions, are something like the shadow pain of nerve systems still remembering a severed limb no longer there.

But the one lost cannot be conjured up.

There is no voice or gentle touch to ground the mind and save it from itself, from constant spinning. Images flood the mind, but float detached from the one lost. The imagination can play cruel tricks. Distorted and highly impressionable memories, on and on, and then self-reproach. Every grieving spouse must know this. Lewis groped for what he called the "resistance" of the real person, but his Joy was as gone to him as Kristi is to me: "The most precious gift that marriage gave me was the constant impact of something very close and intimate yet at the same time unmistakably other, resistant — in a word, real."[23]

Is this minute-by-minute longing and anguish the reason why Christ — the incarnate Other and the Word made flesh — gives Himself to us so concretely in the Eucharist? The Real Presence. Outside of him is only anesthetized routine or sometimes madness: "Our hearts are restless until the rest in Thee" (St. Augustine). Are we tempted to despair *because* He is hope? How can this be? But Kristi is my life. Does He care that I am lost? And then came this:

> ...In a sense I do love light and voice and fragrant smell
> and food and embrace...an embrace no satiety interrupts —
> this is what I love when I love my God....Truth says to

me: "Your God is not the earth, nor heaven, nor any corpo-
real thing" . . . and I tell you, my soul, you are certainly more
precious than your body. . . . But *your God is the life of your life.*[24]

Still, I was totally trapped in my total loss. A full year ground
by before I could see, somewhat consistently, that by far the most
of what we had together was not the final months. It was not even
the last twelve years and our intensely close visits together to the
hospital. It is the smallness of my own mind that locks onto these
most recent things. Yet the hard fact is that you are not here. And
where is "here"?

What others know so easily, I began to relearn so slowly. Grief is
not a problem to be solved. Yes, at first it is a bottomless crater that
never ends. With each convulsion and each escape the pain goes
deeper instead of away. But with time the scar, if not a healing, at
least begins to catch up. In grief there is a waiting, but finally an
acceptance set free by exhaustion.

The first year found me walking the beaches that we had so
often visited together. Remorse tracked me down, self-reproach over
thoughtless words or silences. Marriage is not being there; it is getting there together. It is this that the death of a spouse tragically
interrupts. When we were asked after ten years of marriage to be
mentors and prayer partners for an engaged couple, Kristi wrote
to them:

> It would be unrealistic to say that marriage is all sunshine. But with
> God's grace and your unselfish care and concern for one another,
> your marriage will grow stronger and more beautiful with each
> passing year.

At the root of my discomfort then was the totally irrational feeling — fear spawns disconnected impressions — that in the end Kristi
had abandoned me. I was expendable.

Hidden from me for so many months was the deeper continuity and familiarity of our ordinary and day-to-day closeness. For most of us our latent psychology is a bit ragged around the edges. Trauma brings this out: the disconnected impressions, the global fears, and sometimes even the need to punish oneself. Were we really happy together? I was in a zone where I could not remember. *Where* was the togetherness now?

It is to restrain the reproach, this reflex, that we treasure the emotional anchors provided by things physical. I returned to the little notes Kristi had left for me so often on the phone pad. These served almost as saintly relics: "*Could you grate some cheese? Love you! Kristi.*" Scripture, too, is a living relic. The scriptural reading selected for Kristi's funeral, the Road to Emmaus (Luke 24:13–35), held another clue to my distress. The *concealment* of the real by the mental image can be so great that even with the very person of Christ again beside them on the Road to Emmaus, the disciples did not and *could not* recognize him.[25] We find something very profound here about the connection between what we see outside of ourselves, and *how* we see from within. Finally, it was in something so simple as a gesture that they recognized the light of his Real Presence through their own agitated darkness.

We are surrounded by eternity but we are afraid, because we do not see. We long to strip away the veil. At the end, Kristi finally longed for this total healing of passing through the veil rather than for being healed to any lesser degree in this life. But still she said, "*Either way, with all my heart.*"

In an abstract way, I detect in grief a passage through a succession of three rooms in my soul. The first is to discover so painfully and with some surprise that the separation is not total, that, yes, I can find a way to hold hands through the veil. This is discovered within the panic. And the second room is to see, with greater amazement, that all along Kristi is already reaching to me. "Of course," we might say, but not at first. She has never left, even though I myself carried her to the gurney in the downstairs hallway. And then, third, I find that those of us who are still here are more truly with Him and with our rewarded loved ones than we are "here," even now. Our presence is more than being "here." These three steps and others come as gifts; they are discoveries, not merely deductions.

> For just as he remained with us even after his Ascension, so we too are already in heaven with him, even though what is promised us has not yet been fulfilled in our bodies . . . while in heaven he is also with us; and we while on earth are with him . . . and although he ascended alone, we also ascend, because we are in him in grace.[26]

It is only when I am inwardly still, numbed from thrashing about, that I sometimes glimpse Kristi. Surely she is now face to face with her "dear Lord." When I stop squinting, I sense her instead simply looking in on me, overly intense as I have always been. I know she is closer to me now than before.

But the death of a husband or wife catches the survivor incompetent to rest long in this certainty. And this incompetence can come in two ways, not one. First, and quite enough, is the trauma of loss and amputation. This is total. The primal scream, "Oh God, no! How could you do this to me? I love you. I can't find you! I want you back!"

> I opened to my lover — but my lover had departed, gone.
> I sought her but did not find her:
> I called to her but she did not answer me.
>
> (Song of Songs 5:6)

And then overtaking this anguish is the other assault — for me finding that I had been untested all of my life. "*This is a new expe-*

rience. Dying. And I don't know how good I'll be at it," Kristi said. I told her she would do fine, but of myself, I did not have a clue. All of my life I had managed, but by this very definition probably had handled poorly shocks of much lesser weight.

In marriage there is the constant and unconscious reassurance. And more, there is the presence of one who needs and receives our reassurance and little affections in return. All of this is gone, suddenly. For whom now does one hold open the car door? Part of marriage is the silencing of murmurs within one's self simply because the spouse sees past them. Marriage moves us toward the inner stillness that is bigger than even the answers to our self-doubts. The only real solution to all such churning turmoil is a larger silence, not merely better jousting with a better answer.

Many months would pass — at least a full year — for me to gain the consistent confidence that while still not in control or, better yet, healed, I was being left stronger rather than broken. Asked early on by a friend how I was doing, and standing opposite the tabernacle in St. Mark's, I hung there without words like the massive hardwood crucifix on the back wall. After a pause of perhaps a full minute, all I could manage was "This is huge. . . ." To the same question from another, again I was speechless, but finally found these words: "It is necessary to cross a vast desert," not suspecting then that the desert was still in front of me.

But, Kristi, are we severed so totally? "If Christ has not risen; vain then is our preaching, vain too is your faith" (1 Cor. 15:14).[27]

And since He has risen, might I anticipate total reunion? Is my confinement in time actually wrapped somehow within your exquisite sharing in His eternity? After all, the tomb was not hollow (like a skull); it was "empty," which implies a gathering up, and a Gatherer.

I was to discover a beautiful poem:

What tender, inexpressible delight!
To see them, greet them, grasp their hands once more!
O hours of purest bliss that well o'erpays
The pangs of separation! Now restored
To raptures of love's welcoming embrace,
While soul enfoldeth soul — how lovingly![28]

Lifted by the words of a poet? Such a clinging desperation. But of my imagined aloneness, I had to wonder again: Who (not what) was it on the day before our wedding vows that showed me *in advance* this path of rupture and overwhelming torment?[29] Who was it that then asked for my commitment and even my consent? A commitment and a consent that I gave: "I will find a way." How is it that we receive such attentive respect? And from Whom?

It must be possible that *nothing* is lost, even now, and that to say this is more than simply poetry. I looked out from my hollowed mind with the real suspicion that in death we move deeper. We move not away from each other, but deeper, and our tears are not shed into empty and staring space. Like the stars of the sky the tears are also counted. I clung to the notion that only the false self is cut loose in death, and that for the one transfigured, death is a burrowing into the embrace of the eternal moment of Christ, "the same yesterday, and today, yes, and forever."[30]

But the restlessness is as relentless as death itself. It is death in the living. Was it necessary now for me to fully digest alone all the trauma that had happened to us — and that we *did together* — over the years (all that is in these pages, and more)? By carrying Kristi through hospice had I at least protected her from this fragile dance with despair? Did it fall to me now to finally digest all of the bumps that together we had been able swallow? Did it fall to me — now alone still this side of the veil — to make peace by finally looking down into the waves after all?

Must I fully absorb it all first before I can really be at peace and
let go? Or does the One who carried both of us leave a way for us
even now to at least hold hands through the veil?

The Little Things

> . . . the Purity of those Motives, upon which he acted, stampt a
> Value upon Things, howsoever mean and little in themselves.
>   — The Life of St. Francis de Sales[31]

In the agony of the first days and hours, I scavenged almost franti-
cally for whatever special remnants of our life together I might find.
Wrapped in plastic and tucked in her Bible from home was a stem
with a single browned flower from the bouquet of early 1974. Beside
it was a single wilted petal with ink marks "Marry me!" still visible.
Time does not exist.

Kristi's soul, her sweetness, was so often at risk of being mauled
by cancer and then by her medical allergies. This is the cross Kristi
fully embraced, not with triumphant courage, but with a small and
ever purified gentleness. A small gentleness, crucified. But it was
the cancer that was annihilated. Without any defenses left at all,
and trusting His mercy, she surrendered, without any other layers
of meaning. Single-hearted.

"And if we are given to suffer, deeper shafts are sunk in us than
we thought we could contain, depths destined to become, in the life
everlasting, reservoirs of greater happiness." St. John of the Cross
tells us that "the purest suffering produces the purest understanding."[32] And Kristi said of her long and dense suffering, "I would not
have wanted to miss it. The graces I would not have known." Her final
rosary petition gives guidance to each of us: "in thanksgiving for the
path that is given to each of us, whatever it may be."

In the horrendous days following Kristi's death I also scratched for other things, anything at all to hold on to. Always she complimented my service as lector in our parish: *"Peter, I like the way you read today."* I remember this little remark now when I need her close. It's all in the conviction and inflections. The gesture. I know Kristi wants me to continue at this. To simply *act* on the little things that she would like clears my mind instantly.

Marriage is all about the little things of each day. And when we are marooned by the death of a spouse, any little castaway note becomes a treasured message in a bottle from across a vast ocean or desert. Our little notes recall for me uncomplicated memories of simply *being* together in ordinary ways. I need to be reminded of the obvious. Over the years we saved many of our holiday cards and notes for each other. I treasure all of the notes between us. They remind me that the universe is still a friendly place.

Shortly after we returned from Paris, two years before her death, Kristi surprised me with a card. She was only too aware of my raw sensitivity to stress in the workplace. I had quipped a few days before, that even a prize from a Cracker Jack box would be better than nothing. In the note: *"You are my 'Cracker Jack' husband, and you win the prize! All my love, Kristi."*

The cards moved in both directions. Much earlier, less than six years into our marriage, I celebrated the end of some major lawn planting with a carefully selected card. It was embellished with my own lyrical nonsense: " . . . and so verily I took thy hand gently and kissed it, then for each finger planted a tree so that birds might surround our dwelling and behold thy beauty." Such lighthearted and delightfully foolish times were to be a strength for me in my new solitude. That same year, on our sixth anniversary, we visited the historic and crudely constructed Cotaldo Mission in north Idaho. In the undulating cemetery, one leaning marker stone especially caught our eye (1848–1916): "Standing over me no sorrow take, but love each other for my sake. Martin." Under the overcast sky we had prayed for Martin and the others.

And there are Kristi's other notes to me. After ten years of marriage, she wrote: *"Thank you for being 'home' for me."* And later, *"You are a dear husband and a wonderful father to our little olive branches."* Throughout our marriage, I sometimes would introduce my Kristi with, "This is my girlfriend. We have been married for twenty-three years." At unexpected moments I enjoyed modifying barely audibly (I thought) the last line of the Litany of the Saints: "Blessed be God in his angels, and in his saints ... *and* in this special little lady!"

The image that finally holds me is a simple restaurant we visited the last summer before Kristi died. The restaurant is a plain one, built on pilings that reach a short distance toward the slack water and marshes of an unnamed Columbia River estuary. A few minutes before stopping here on our way home from our favorite Cannon Beach on the Oregon coast, we marveled at a herd of some twenty wild elk — majestic and ancient — roving across a large meadow in our same direction upstream, in the slanted and golden light of late afternoon. From this memory I feel so simple a harmony, the quiet space between the notes in the music of our marriage. We stopped for dinner and faced each other, hand in hand across a little table. The room was large enough for only four or five other tables, all politely empty. Our diminishing future this side of the veil was known and lingered as near as the next room but waited politely and did not intrude.

After suffering an enormous wasteland, I feel again what I believe and know to be true. I have a glimpse, barely, of what Kristi's heaven includes. Discarding our imagination, after all of the big things are wiped away, might we find that heaven, too, is a "little thing," something to be simply treasured? A single tear turned to joy? For now Kristi's heaven, her eternal dream is all of our little moments, and it even holds our two bookend moments along the

Columbia River — elk at dusk, and the beginning of our courtship near the remains of a solitary log cabin where the sky was "a little bluer and the snow was a little whiter."

Part of Kristi's dream is a paralyzed hand and voice abundantly restored: *"I'll be singing again in heaven!"* And part is each of our written notes, even those lost along the way. Her heaven is everything personal, resurrected in poignant and gentle joy and not simply replaced by any more abstract joyfulness.

I cannot see much of Kristi's dream. But I know that as a few of our shared memories sadly might slip from my grasp, they are fully intact, transfigured, and eternally held by Kristi. In time I might forget, but *we* remember. And I do trust, now, that little duets of married couples are to be found in heaven.[33]

August 2001

Two weeks to the day after Kristi's death, at the interment on August 15, I was consoled. It was a graveside remark from one of our friends. Surely Kristi heard him. Of her death, our friend John revealed this: "While I was still praying for her recovery, the Lord was prepared to give her a total healing much more than we imagined." Even earlier, on the day of Kristi's death — August 1 — the calendar prayer for the day from Mother Teresa of Calcutta is surely Kristi's most recent note to me. For this is how I have decided to take it:

> In the bottom of your heart,
> You must be convinced *that you and I*
> *are together co-workers* of Christ.
> As such, you must be very close to Him.
> You must share with Him.
> You must be at His complete disposal.[34]

Kristi, through the veil let me be the hands for your prayer intentions, and in this little way to be with you still, until we are together

again. The splinters on my new cross are the many years of waiting
that now remain. During hospice Kristi sighed at how long even
this was taking. In the final months Kristi sometimes said, *"I wish it
would just happen."* And I know now what this means.

September

One month after Kristi's interment, near midnight on September 8,
I fell into my darkest moment. With a dull yellow hue, a far distant
moon lit the upper edges of its peephole through scattered and
lumpy clouds to the east. Even the journal of my first notes from
which this chapter is written became a source of near panic. Under
this moon, the tabernacle was still there, at St. Mark's. And facing
Him with me was a friend who said he was never there at this late
hour. But he was there now, and we talked. So little do we notice
when *we* are chosen to be His presence in moments of special need.
And our Savior seems to have a sense of humor. My friend, in His
presence, had the surname "Lord."

    Late summer also brought the annual parish picnic, a reminder
of when the kids were young. People. Beside me in the shade,
Msgr. John Doogan, now nearly eighty, made time to talk with me.
Three points were offered — beacons to hold the torn horizon in
place. First, he said, I was not to wish away the next thirty years,
"because you do not know what God has planned for you. That is
not love." I could not even comprehend a duration of thirty years,
or even ten, or even the next day without Kristi. I would preserve
this notion, but had no idea what to do with it. Christ did not pray
that we be taken out of this world, rather that we be kept from evil
(John 17:15). And then second, I was to pray, "I trust what You are
doing in my life *at this moment,* Lord, even if I cannot see what it
is." And third, he said, "Kristi will tell you when to begin to write.
Remember, she is not only safe now from pain, but she is with the
Lord, and her judgment now is perfect."

Five weeks after Kristi's death, I joined others at the monthly vigil at the abortion clinic near the cathedral in central Seattle. For the first time, here I was, alone, no longer standing beside my wife. And yet, now I see that Kristi, dearest love, was still here, to receive and hold the traumatized little ones, without their mothers, as they arrived to her through the veil.[35]

September 11, 2001, one month to the day since Kristi's funeral, brought the terrorist attack on the World Trade Center in New York City.[36] The abruptness of the loss for so many is beyond my ability to handle, so different from the nineteen weeks of hospice that Kristi and I had together. I heard Kristi's guidance to simply be present each day to whoever might be sent in my path. So often the gentle reminder from throughout our marriage: *"Peter, you must be more present to others."*

Telephone conversations to Kristi's mother and sisters in Idaho were frequent. Kerry recounted Kristi's words to her that I had been "her rock." Kristi had said, *"There are only a few men who would do what Peter is doing,"* and that without me she could not have persevered. These were reaffirming words to hear, but they floated disconnected in space. I felt nothing. A bleakness settled everywhere.

The second month after Kristi's death also brought a special call from her older sister, Cherie, with another sort of note, another hinge for me. The veil separating Kristi and me really is gossamer thin. It is thin enough for Christ to pass through from the other side, to show us that our hope is not in vain:

> So it is that the union of the wayfarers with the brethren who sleep in the peace of Christ is *in no way interrupted,* but on the contrary, according to the constant faith of the Church, this union is reinforced by an exchange of spiritual goods.[37]

In no way interrupted! The interval is more of a parting than a separation, and more of a unity than a parting.

I am deeply touched by the words of a spiritual woman Kristi had been drawn to in the last five years of our life together. Elizabeth of the Trinity wrote this remarkable line to her mother: "I leave you without leaving you, for I carry you in my soul, close to the One who is all Love." And to her sister she wrote (October 10, 1901), "There, close to Him, I find you again, for there is no separation for souls."[38] *No separation for souls!* To not be separated — this is the *definition* of each soul!

I began to suspect that the purpose of the veil, which seems such an agonizing barrier of separation, is to protect those of us still here. The veil, like the physical dimensions of the Eucharist, protects created love from the full view of uncreated Love. The veil protects me from Kristi's now perfect love for us and for all else besides. Kristi reposes in the Lord and now beholds me through His eyes. This glance, who could possibly bear such sweetness?

October

In the first months of darkness — more like emotional free-fall — the first real thread into my future came to me. Already an eternity. I was driving west to Seattle. The slopes of Snoqualmie Summit pressed toward me from either side. On the car tape deck I listened for the first time in twenty-seven years to the recording of our wedding day. Here was my first real hope that *all* was not lost, the exact words of our marriage vow. My promise was to love and honor Kristi "all the days of *my* life." This rather than "until death do us part." Each of us promised, *"I will love you and honor you all the days of my life."*

Kristi's death does not cancel our marriage! Was such a possibility, such a hopeful thought, anything more than the desperate psychology of the grief-stricken? Am I in total denial?

Our togetherness is in no way interrupted; I am *not* expendable. We, together, take part in His permanence. For the cloistered mystic, the path is to be "alone with the Alone,"[39] but for those in marriage, can we not also say that the path is to be "together within the Together"? (If the vocation of Carmelites like Therese is to find solitude within the community of the cloister, might the vocation of spouses be that of finding community together within the solitude of the world?) Marriage is permanence, an icon of the *inner* life of the Trinity. My struggling to hold hands through the veil is so feeble, an almost untrusting need. There you are, already in your glory, looking in on me and us from the very second you left.

Our marriage, the reality, is not confined to my memories of when Kristi was here with me. And of moving forward without letting go — I see now that the only way to *not* let go is to move forward. I was deeply moved by this poetic vision: "We stand in front of our past, which closes and opens at the same time. . . . *The past is the time of birth, not of death.*"[40] The past is the time of birth! This certainty, this permanence, has the power to reverse all fears. ("Do this in remembrance of me," Luke 22:19.) Yes, the world as we know it is always passing away, but the two things alone that matter to me are God and Kristi. And so, two realities of our marriage are ever before me. I am anchored by the indissolubility — *and* by the indestructibility.[41]

And then, there it was again, the sneaking self-reproach — the worst form of self-indulgence. Where was this reflex coming from, this sin against the truth of our marriage? I was lured by those many occasions when I had brought to our dinner table the tensions of the workaday world. Of this, Kristi had simply turned to me and said, *"Look what it is doing to you. Peter, you must put it all in the Lord's hands . . . all of it."*

How does one do "all"? Of solutions alloyed with self-seeking, of settling for less than all, St. Augustine has the last word. We would use Christ falsely as only a model, but not more. Augustine announces to us: "This is the poison of your error: you claim to make the grace of Christ consist in his example and not in the gift of his Person."[42] Christ is not only the model for our efforts; sacramentally we are *incorporated into* Himself. He is a short-cut to the friendly self-acceptance, and this comes directly with donation of the *self*, beyond any of one's needed talents.[43]

I am not sure which layer is the deeper in Christ, His forgiveness or His healing. With God there finally are no layers at all. And not only do we have His Person, but we also have His saints. St. Aloysius Gonzaga consoled his mother in words I find consoling as well.

> Beware, dearest mother, of wronging this infinite goodness, by weeping for one as dead, who is living before God to help you with his prayers far more than he could do when here below. This separation will not be for long, for we shall meet again, and enjoy each other's society in the next life, never to be wearied of it, but to be united together with our Redeemer, praising him with all strength, and singing his mercies forever.[44]

Two months after Kristi's death, and the day before our twenty-seventh anniversary, I entered into my journal: "Treasured Kristi, beloved of our dear Lord, pray for us."

From the kitchen calendar of Mother Teresa, the collection of daily note-like prayers that so shaped Kristi, I found this for the date of our wedding anniversary, October 12:

> To be holy doesn't mean to do extraordinary things, to understand big things, but it is a simple acceptance, because I have given myself to God, because I belong to Him — my total surrender. He could put me here. He could put me there. He can use me. He cannot use me. It doesn't matter because I belong

so totally to Him that He can do just what He wants to do with me.[45]

I began to recall more. One year before Kristi's death, I had offered a spontaneous prayer. I can mark the spot in the neighborhood. I was passing alone under the leaves of a maple tree.

Oh Lord, I know that you can heal Kristi completely, that she can wake in the morning and find that she is totally healed and even restored. If you will heal her, she can watch the grandchildren grow up over the years. You, Lord, can transfer to me all of her burden. I ask you to heal her and transfer the cross to me.

Did I really mean it? I thought so. The evening following the prayer, I recalled to Kristi in our living room one of Fr. Thomas's lessons from years before. He had revealed that in vicarious suffering one might *actually* bear the burdens of another unbeknown to them. Before I completed the thought, Kristi interrupted, *"Peter, you must not say that prayer."*

"Of course," I said, rejoicing within that for that one minute in the afternoon I had been totally free. This is the path, to not let the one hand know the doings of the other. This is the freedom: self-abandonment regained in small steps, one at a time. Oh, dear Jesus, I do thank you for the veil, for so totally healing Kristi of our cancer, at whatever cost to me . . . and even because of this cost to me.

In the early weeks and months I lost my way again and again in photographs, a poignant agony constantly renewed. In the pictures of the year before the cancer we were so unsuspecting and happy together. I grieved now not only for Kristi, but also for so much else. And I sensed that I too might let go of it, "all of it." This would not be to abandon Kristi, for she is not "there" where I remember her. Even now it is she who invites me forward, not back.

November

After three months, on November 1, All Saints' Day, Kristi's stone
was laid on our cemetery plot. November also brought a dream, one
of so few, to rein the rumblings of my mind. In the dream I returned
home through the front door from another day at work. This is as it
had been each day for those over twenty years in our second home.
My path took me past the davenport and through the living room.
As I turned toward the kitchen there she was, this time so radiant.
She turned from the counter, and freed both hands from her work at
the counter. I fell to my knees at her feet, sobbing my unrelieved grief
of the past three months since her death. In a moment I recited all of
the conventions I had invented to protect myself — the walks, the
grasping for reasons (mere reasons?) to hope, the clinging to verses
here and there, the tortured mental gymnastics, the self-reproach
and the self-justification and the photographs.

And Kristi folded her hands over my back from above, and with
a higher and deeper gentleness and wisdom — these are one — she
simply said to me, *"Peter, it's okay."* A dream and not more, and yet
not less.[46]

On November 5, Cherie's husband, Phil, dropped from sight on
a routine business flight homeward. He was flying solo from a work
site location in rough west central Idaho, south of Cottonwood. He
was killed instantly.

How is it that family members, miles away, knew his last words
seconds before the fatal impact and then "saw him rising from the
plane"? We believe that Kristi may now be doing good things on
earth, the way Therese does, "at least for my family" and that she
was there for Phil. Over the coming year Cherie and I sustained each
other by telephone through the many hourly and weekly stages of
grief. And for me there were the always-dependable calls from family
and most especially my twin brother, John.

Toward the end of this fourth month I was on the Camas Prairie under a darkened sky. What was it that drew me away from this family gathering and from all the others in the yard? I stepped to the lawn's edge with my back to the last haze of late twilight and faced the rolling fields and the mountain ridge far to the east. My eyes were drawn up into the near blackness to see directly overhead the brilliance of a shooting star, nearer the brilliance of the moon than a star, as it streaked most of the distance to the horizon. Such liquid splendor in the infinite and absolute silence.

Kristi, did you see this? If a man and a woman watch a falling star together, it is said, they will be in love forever and always. It is death, not life, that is transient. St. Leo the Great in a sermon encourages us, "He did away with the everlasting character of death so as to make death a thing of time, not of eternity."[47]

December

After four months, as the Advent season neared, St. Mark's parishioners began to feel more comfortable telling me their own remembrances of Kristi. A male friend remarked to me, "From the way I hear the women talk, there was something special. . . . " An acquaintance from twenty years prior simply noticed to me, "She was always so kind." Yes, that was it, gentleness and humility. And from some of Kristi's friends, more than one: "She is the most like I imagine Mary to be." And our friend, John, offered this, "I know people who met Kristi only once, and only for three or four minutes — just long enough to swap names — and came away unduly influenced, by grace." A card arrived from one of our daughter Laura's good friends and bridesmaids.

Kristi was such an incredible inspiration. The two of you wore your love for each other for everyone to see, and I cannot begin to tell you how incredible and fascinating that was to me

Seattle area beach. "...the familiar stroll on the beach restored for several minutes a long absent sense of well-being."

as a teenager. Thank you for sharing that with us.... [Kristi] was a beautiful angel. I believe that she was here on earth to await her wings.

Five years earlier, at the time of Kristi's stem cell transplant, another of Laura's teenage friends wrote this of her difficult adolescence:

> ...the care you gave to me put me through some of the hardest times. I like to think of you as one of God's angels, because — because of you — I believe that I can survive anything with God's love and guidance. Thank you so much for giving me that gift.

I discovered on a shelf in the recreation room Kristi's four-volume *Liturgy of the Hours*. For a year or two in the early nineties we had met with Fr. Norris and a small group of six or seven on Thursday evenings. We followed this daily cycle of prayer of the entire Church. Her favorite lines were from the Magnificat of Mary: "My soul proclaims the greatness of the Lord, my spirit rejoices in God my Savior for he has looked with favor on his lowly servant" (Luke 1:46–48).

In the void where we had once been, I resolved to be with Kristi by reading at least a little each day from her *Liturgy:* "O death, You separate those who are joined to each other in marriage. You harshly and cruelly divide those whom friendship unites. But your power is broken . . . O Death! I shall be your death."[48]

Weeks later, the familiar stroll on the beach restored for several minutes a long absent sense of well-being. More so than in the entire preceding year. The evening before had squeezed from me the fleeting prayer for the gift of a dream, even a small one. And then, there Kristi was again, so radiant and free, like before life got out of control. All I could say was "just look at you, you're gorgeous!" But I awoke, and she was gone from me.

Chapter Seven

A Lasting Portrait

This hope we have, as a sure and firm anchor of the soul, reaching even behind the veil.   — Hebrews 6:19

The Last Dance

In one of Kristi's little notes from over the years, she claims me now, *"I'll always be your only dancing partner. . . . I feel so blessed you chose me to be your wife. You are my rock! All my love, Kristi."* And so now, on this new dance floor where we are parted, but not separated, we begin the last and eternal dance. And it is Kristi's turn to lead. We used to joke about how the new dances do not require the partners to even be in the same room.

I returned to where we often went together in good times and in bad. And before the tabernacle on December 30, I was nudged toward a certainty. Not in words, but in calmness I knew this: "I gave you a beautiful wife, and know you now that she will never leave you." We really are to be together again, though in a way that I cannot yet see. I need not fear so much nor try so desperately to reach through the veil. In the other world, the "world without end" that surrounds us, time does not exist, and space does not exist. And since heaven is also within, I already carry Kristi within my heart. And I am carried by her. She is also the sky and the sea and the whiteness of the snow. Both of us are carried together in the Sacred Heart, the innermost Soul of our souls.

Five days before Christmas (2001) I found the first relic and the last of our marriage. Such a little thing, it was one stem and flower from the bouquet I had given Kristi the day of proposal so long ago. Pressed in her Bible, the flower petal: "Marry me!" Soon after, the family arranged to fit the delicate locks of Kristi's hair into tiny engraved silver lockets, one for each of us. Together with this delicate lock of hair, mine also includes an early portrait from the year we first met, and the third treasure is the preserved single flower petal.

Nearly half a year after Kristi's release (January 2002), another parishioner approached me in the church entrance. "How is your wife?" she asked. I gave a simple answer. "Oh, I am so sorry. I did not know. We knew there was something wrong." I sketched what had happened, the nature of Kristi's path of abandonment and that she had simply followed it with an ever more open heart.

"My sister pointed your wife out to me — so lovely — and told me to look and watch, there is something going on there that is holy." The parishioner now prays with Kristi every day. I recalled to her the special sermon delivered at Kristi's funeral, and our conversation was lightened with the idea that we should pray *to* Kristi. "Oh, it is true. You are a lucky man."

I think I remember closing that this is a mixed blessing.

During this sixth month, I joined a very close friend, Andrew, for Mass at the Byzantine St. John Chrysostom parish in Seattle. Andrew and his wife, Nancy, have been very good friends from shortly before the first cancer diagnosis in the late 1980s. During the first month of hospice, Andrew had written to Kristi about the "indebtedness" of his family, already close-knit, to Kristi: "Since we first became acquainted with you, your influence, or I should rather say, your very presence has made each of us better persons and has made our daily relationships with each other immeasurably more positive and more holy."

My very intense need at this point was to *see* that a bit of eternity is here, not all so totally faraway or "there." With my eyes and heart I needed to see through the thickness of the veil, past "a darkened mirror" and beyond "a glass darkly." Is there a transparency at least around the edges? I needed to see that it is not brutal, more of a parting than a separation and amputation. How much of my desolation is cultural, rooted more in *how* some of us see, than in how things really are?

The mystic Teresa of Ávila tells us that the veil is a product of our imagination. In seeing *through* the eyes, not merely with the eyes, the Byzantine Rite complements the more familiar Latin or Roman Rite and culture in the West.[1] Here the spirituality of Marian transparency and self-abandonment, so woven through the Byzantine liturgy and the Eastern Churches, supplies the second lung so valued by John Paul II when he challenges the whole Church and the West to breath again with both lungs. (His mother was Byzantine Catholic.) The pastor occasionally reminds his flock that "tradition is the living faith of the dead, while traditionalism is the dead faith of the living."

Lord that I might see!

Yet both traditions spring from the path of resurrection *through* suffering. This is the suffering offered by Christ, in history, and our particular history is our part in His total presence toward us. But the expression in the East does center less on the passion, and more on the transfiguration and the resurrection. Surrounding me on the walls and ceilings were icons, just as marriage itself is an icon. Visual icons painted free of earthbound visual perspective, free of time and space, free of the minuscule present. Eternity seen through the moment, like the reality of marriage *"from the very, very beginning."*

Here our action in this world reaches from within a deeper prayer and silence. Also more fully intact is the Benedictine key I had found nearly thirty years before on the Camas Prairie ("to pray and then to work"), and the two-sided Benedictine cross of crucifixion and resurrection. In the Byzantine Mass, we see how in the consecration, this *doing* by the Spirit and this *remembrance* of ours are mysteriously contained *within* the same moment. Space and time are set aside.

And so it is with Kristi.

She is not the receding memory. Here the Song of Songs (2:8–14) had me peering through the "lattice" in my desire to hold hands through the "veil." And here is my Kristi, at this Mass and at every Mass. All of them open toward the same Presence who called her home. She too, and all of the Communion of Saints, so intimately face to face with Him, are "here" as well. Or rather, as even now we step into the self-abandonment of Christ, we are already partly "there."

With this tantalizing thought floating across my larger grief, I found myself after the Mass visiting in Andrew's house. His younger daughter, Susan — always so close to Kristi — melted into tears. Now a university student, she grieved the loss of so dear a soul. But it was more than this (if there can be more). She wept for our common mortality, which in her young world now loomed enormously and everywhere as it had with me. Everything, all of it, passes away. I asked, "You are afraid because things pass away?" and she said, "Yes."

"Two things last," I said. "One is inside of the other; first God, and second is his Communion of Saints. Each member is a tabernacle for Him in this world and made from within, in His image. And this is where Kristi is now. It is only all the rest — only the husk which does not matter — that is loss and that is pain."[2]

Near this time, a half year after losing Kristi, our family was consoled by a pilgrimage that Kerry and Cherie and Kristi's mother

made, in January 2002, to Betania, an hour or two outside of Cara-
cas, Venezuela. The first reported apparition of the Mother of God
at this site was in 1976, and the first public apparition was reported
in 1984.[3] Cherie and Jeanne returned with an insight from their
pilgrimage guide, a retired priest from their state of Idaho, and
the visionary Marie Esperanza. From their experience they learned
that each person's heaven is different (not even partly anonymous),
uniquely designed for that divinely cherished person. This is surely
accurate. Especially if in some real and personal sense the baptized
already carry heaven within.[4]

> The integration of the I into the body of Christ, its being at the
> disposal of the Lord and of everyone else, is not a dissolution
> of the I but its purification . . . that is why heaven is *different for
> each individual.* Everyone sees God in his own way; everyone
> receives the love of the whole body in his own unalterable
> uniqueness.[5]

At Betania an additional suggestion was made — possibly a genuine locution. We were told by the visionary that Kristi moved
gracefully from this life to the next, that she is "in her dream,"
and that she felt such joy here that she was not really eager to leave
and barely noticed the transition.[6] Such mildness. Kristi did love
her life here so very much: *"there is such a letting go . . . from life to
greater Life."* Is it possible that in some way some of us see Christ
here *nearly* face to face even before we are fully in His presence?

And of Kristi's dream now, is there a corner there for me? From
our piano bench I find a note card from her singing days here, the
words to "Deep in My Heart." The final lines read: "Deep in my
heart, dear, I have a *dream* of you. Fashioned of starlight, perfume
of roses and dew. Our paths may sever, but I'll remember forever,
Deep in my heart, dear, Always I'll *dream* of you."

In February, the seventh month, Archbishop Brunett visited our St. Mark's Parish for the laying on of hands in the sacrament of confirmation. He and I were already acquainted by my appointment to the Archdiocesan Pastoral Council. (Looking ahead even in early 2000, Kristi had encouraged me to apply.) In the vestibule the archbishop remarked to me, "Your wife was a kind and gentle lady, it is said." And looking out over the waiting congregation from behind, he added "She is going to help us."

As part of this help, I find this note in a condolence card from Michael, one of those on Kristi's prayer list:

> Attending Kristi's funeral was an especially profound experience for me. In my prayers over the last several months, I have often sensed that the veil separating those living in eternity from us still bound in time is very thin. This sense was very much reinforced on Saturday. I am very thankful for the prayers, yours and Kristi's, on our behalf during my own struggle with cancer, and also the friendship. I know that I now have in Kristi a powerful intercessor to rely upon, and for this I am most grateful. With heartfelt regards, Michael.

A Sweet Fragrance

As they go through the Bitter Valley, they make it a place of springs.
— Psalm 84:6

My early journal records that twice in the early months of November and December 2000, I brought the first of many dozens of roses to Kristi's plot at the cemetery. I placed them in the recessed cup at the foot of the marker stone. Both times, within less than a day, the roses disappeared. Stolen, I thought, but clearly not removed so soon by the gardener for maintenance. As he *always* does, the gardener empties the water and inverts the flower cup to its usual position in its recessed receptacle. With Kristi's roses, it was this detail, this little thing that also caught my attention.[7] The water cup was full and unmoved.

Alongside of my mixed turmoil and inner healing, I began a bit whimsically to keep track of the roses. I remember how Kristi's friend, St. Therese, is known for letting fall from heaven a bouquet of roses on those she has favored. A fantasy in our neighborhood cemetery, maybe, but I was lifted by Kristi's gentle and most trusting way. Four months before she left us, on Easter Day (April 15, 2001), Kristi had whispered to me:

> *Spending my heaven doing good on earth, like St. Therese. I'd like to do that. Maybe I'll ask the Lord if I can do that too . . . at least for my family.*

On an early Sunday morning I wondered again at a new disappearance of the roses. For the third time I had left a bouquet. This time only the evening before. In the morning these too were now absent. The light snow must have come late; there were no footprints.

For Kristi to *receive* the roses through the veil would be so unusual, more than one can imagine. Nonsense, hysteria! Except for the apparent facts. And it would be so backwards from the special sign of St. Therese, who once released actual roses to one asking her intercession in the dead of winter. But might the backwardness also recall, and heal a hundredfold, Kristi's darkest and most disorienting suffering during the worst of the cancer ordeal? Kristi had said only that *"Everything is backwards."*[8]

Is Kristi actually accepting these roses as a sign, a gesture? Is this the healed words she could not find for our ordeal? Is this like other *physical* healings? Is it her "voice" fully restored by a touch of the Divine Physician? Is she singing for me in heaven? I am watchful, Kristi. I want to think that you do receive the roses, just as you

Holyrood Cemetery. *"What a peaceful day. This is beautiful. Thank you so much."* (Kristi)

did when I entered the back door at least a few times with such a surprise after a day at work.

A sign of hope? This is not so grand as the movement of mountains. Against the total landscape it is peewee small; it is only roses. But is there a mystical tunnel through the veil, given to us by the holes carved in His hands and feet and in His side?

I see in the disappearance of the roses something of Kristi's gentle smallness. Here is the absence of roses and nothing more. I allow myself the lyrical luxury to notice Kristi's touch, through the veil. I do truly wonder, what is the alternative? How simple it is to accept that if all the laws of physics come through His wounded hands, then some of these rules — within our little hazelnut existence — can be set aside by higher rules. Our dear Lord is seen face to face by my Kristi, and surely he hears her sweet request to be "*doing good on earth, like St. Therese . . . at least for my family.*"

A few very long months later, in early spring, Laura visited, with our three grandchildren. Together we made our way across the water to look in on our special Port Gamble cemetery. This would probably be our last time here together for many years. Behind the white picket fence of the cemetery, at the spot where Kristi and I used to catnap, we buried the small capsule I had kept in my shirt pocket with her assortment of hospice pills. Now, for Laura, it held the funeral card with Kristi's radiant picture, together with a lock of her hair. Laura had been unable to fly up for the interment, but now here was this second chance.

Closer to home at our Holyrood Cemetery, Laura and Mark went together to our plot with another dozen fresh roses. They had selected white. Half an hour before the gates closed, I checked the plot. The water receptacle was intact, but now these new roses were gone. I rushed home. Laura and Mark made it through the automatic iron gate even as it began to swing shut for the night, to witness for themselves the *absence* of the roses. This June happening marked the eighth such event. And July was the next. I placed the roses in the evening and by following morning (on July 2, 2002, on the second anniversary of our special visit to the pilgrimage St. Boniface Church in Uniontown) these one dozen yellow roses with fine red edges, still not opened, had disappeared. As had been the pattern, as far as I could tell the bouquets on surrounding plots were intact.

After fourteen months, on Friday evening, October 4, 2002, more than one year after her death, Kristi's identical twin, Kerry, and her family placed roses at the cemetery for their first time. We prayed together. Nudged by an inkling and a hope, I followed in Barham's footsteps and risked out loud this petition: "Kristi, although it is a bit extravagant, it would be a nice consolation for your twin sister if you would do your little thing with the roses." So blatant, and so much like my loud prayer into Kristi's fading ear during the transplant and in front of the entire crisis medical team, a prayer that was answered.

The family left early the next day on the eight-hour trip to Cottonwood. It was a Saturday. I visited the cemetery after the opening hour, but still well before noon. The cup and water remained undisturbed at the base of Kristi's stone, and the roses were already gone. This was the tenth bouquet (out of the thirteen) during the year since Kristi's stone was placed.[9]

Even apart from the roses, I began to see that Kristi is "here," and more than this, that she is also "there" for us and for me. As for the concreteness of the missing roses... this is nothing. But for it to be not possible at all for Kristi to receive the roses — *this* is impossible. All things are possible with God, even something so little as this.

In January 2003, Mark's Marine Corps Reserves unit was activated for probable deployment to Iraq. In his gear was a dog-eared Bible from his college classes. "Mark," I said as we drove to his destination, "read a piece of that every day. Things will change a lot. This will remind you who you are, and where you came from." After delivering him to his base in Portland, Oregon, I spent a full day at a sheer rock wall formation and shrine known as the Grotto. This is yet another replica of Lourdes in southern France. It was a peaceful day, with only a small handful of post-holiday visitors. At the top edge of the cliff the meditation chapel overlooks a vista to the north. I worked here for several hours on an early draft of this book. On leaving the Grotto in the evening, I lit a seven-day candle for Mark. With Kristi in mind I placed it with dozens of other candles on the cast iron rack beneath the shrine. Every one of the other candles, without exception, had been burning down since the weekend. There had been very few visitors since the weekend. Our candle was new.

With a sense of completion, I found no need to return the next morning. But at midmorning I looked up from my writing, and an inner nudge changed my mind. Yes, the pattern of candles was still there as I remembered them — all except one. The receptacle (in the third row down and fourth column right of center) was empty. This slot was as empty as any flower vase filled only with water (as empty as a vacated tomb). As with the roses, did Kristi *possibly* leave me this sign for Mark's safety? How can one be so sure this side of the veil as to say "impossible"? Is it likely that thieves would collect roses overnight in Seattle for over a year, and then follow me for a candle in Portland? Our experiences are touched from the outside by something more than we know.

In February I flew to California to visit Mark at Camp Pendleton before his likely deployment. As if arranged from above, there with us was Fr. Thomas. In the shade of a solitary tree he prayed powerfully again, this time over Mark dressed in his desert camouflage uniform. Toughened marines happened by in small groups of two or three, and I think envied this moment.

One week later in March, Mark telephoned me in Seattle to report that he was being deployed. On this same day a dozen red and partly opened roses, placed at our plot in Seattle only the day before, disappeared. Of sixteen dozen roses offered over the past sixteen months, this now was number twelve. Was Mark protected? In June, after his return from Iraq, we drove together up the dramatic Columbia River Gorge on our way to Richland and then Idaho. In his casual manner, between descriptions of sandstorms and waving villagers, he dropped this: "Dad, snipers shot at *me*, but they missed." And later he was to recall to me with wonder a star-filled night when his convoy in Iraq passed within sight of the ancient city of Ur. They stopped and gazed up into the Milky Way, and Mark knew that he was looking from the same place and into the same stars that had so elevated Abraham nearly four thousand years before. A thousand years are as the twinkling of an eye.

And now, from a reliable nephew, I was informed of exceptional help given through our Kristi's intercession to a prospective first-time mother. The mother was twenty weeks pregnant when her amniotic sack broke three months before Easter. In this case of fluid loss the doctors had been clear that there was no hope. The call to me was followed by a written account of a single prayer offered in Kristi's presence, and the result.[10]

Two months later on Friday night, August 1, 2003, I placed another dozen roses at Kristi's stone. Two years to the day since Kristi slipped away *"from life to greater Life."* On Sunday, it was only my reflection that I saw in the flower container still filled with water, "as in a mirror darkly."

Perhaps Kristi is reminding me of a little event I had witnessed even before we met. I mentioned this event later to Kristi, more than once. Maybe it is more than coincidence that on a few occasions (not nearly enough) I brought home a dozen roses, through the back door.

It goes back to the year after I left the navy, early on a sunny spring morning in 1971, nearly three years before Kristi and I met. Out the side window of my second-floor apartment in Everett I noticed a figure on the sidewalk across the street. Here was a tall and elderly transient in a trench coat. He paused before a streetside rosebush near a simple neighboring house, and only a few steps from the back porch. I recognized the man as one who lived in a packing crate under a railroad bridge near the Snohomish River a mile away.

He snipped a rose.

Another pause, and then he made his way up the steps to the back porch. This stranger was met at the threshold by an unprepared elderly lady. She answered bundled in a bathrobe and with her hair still in curlers. Transforming his rags into an elegant dignity, the visitor made a deep Thespian bow, and then offered the rose. This gift was accepted with unguarded delight. He then took her aged hand gently into his and kissed it. Not a single word was spoken between these strangers. And then with a spring in his step, he backed down the steps and strode away into the broadening sun streaks across the lawns and street.

It was a glorious moment on a glorious morning. I do believe in the transfiguring sacrament of the present moment. Perhaps time is more of an unfolding, an unpacking like a rose, than simply a sequence from past to future. The calendars, simply another invention of ours, deceive us. I think so, and so I also believe in the eternity of the Communion of Saints. And I see that the eternal moment passes through the veil — not in one direction, but in both. Grace is everywhere.

On the waterfront before she died, facing another solitary beggar, Kristi remarked in wonder, *"Did you look into his eyes? That was Jesus Christ!"* We can listen when we are told:

> It was the Divine Master who said: "Blessed are the pure of heart, for they shall see God" (Matt 5:8). Hence, no Christian reading these words in a spirit of faith has any doubt that, when God is to be seen, it will be by the eyes of the heart. . . . God . . . will be seen in the spirit (*whereby each of us will see Him within ourselves and in one another*); He will be seen in Himself.[11]

The beginning of the thirteenth month, September 2, 2002, brought another dream, so infrequent. From our early years, Kristi again wore her red plaid skirt and white blouse and brilliant scarf. We made our way to the dance floor as we always did for the "last dance." But the setting moved even as we did, and then the floor lost its magic, already cleared as it was for some more common other use. For barely a second I held Kristi, but then she faded and was gone from me.

I shall always miss my Kristi. But by what smallness of soul do I doubt the indestructibility of *us?* I am simply struck by the thought that here below, each act of fidelity beyond oneself renews not only our marriage and my marriage proposal carefully etched on a flower petal, but every leaf and flower petal in the universe, which itself is an act of love. I trust Kristi's parting, and can trust myself, and trust our marriage and what the Lord is doing in my life at this moment, even if I cannot see what it is.

I stand at a threshold barely at the edge of Kristi's soul now transfigured. How true it is now what I often said to her for no special reason at all, "Blessed be God in His angels, and in His saints, *and in this special little lady.*"

Holding Hands through the Veil

One of the books on Kristi's shelf is the journal of yet another of her friends, Elizabeth Leseur. Elizabeth, regarded as "a married St. Therese," offered herself for the conversion of her husband, an agnostic. His disbelief involved the hostility some skeptics hold toward any simpleton who believes, in this case his own wife. But after Elizabeth's death he deeply regretted having tried to pry her loose from her humility toward the Other. He had discover her journal, and this became the cause of his conversion (and his eventual path to ordination as a priest). In one entry, Elizabeth wrote longingly for what Kristi and I did and do still share:

My God, wilt Thou give me one day the joy of this solitude for two, united in the same prayer, the same faith, and the same love?.... The perfect union of two souls — how beautiful a harmony that would make! With him I love best in the world, let me one day make this harmony, O my God.[12]

A husband loves the universe through his wife, not because she is a means to this end, but because, in her exclusiveness, she is the universe. And yet this created love need not exclude its Source from deep within, the uncreated Love that it mirrors. I have come to see that it really is true that Christ is within. He is the innermost Soul of our bonded souls in marriage. Within Him, and outside of space and time, we also find the entire Communion of Saints. Within Him I find Kristi, still. An amazing release from the smallness of our spatial and temporal imaginations — *this* release is the nature of revelation and the Lord's full self-revelation in the incarnation. Needed from each of us is not so much a blind faith, but a peephole through the strangely comforting darkness of our blindfold, the veil. We need humility, the foolishness of Wisdom.

> For us as He remained with us even after his ascension, so we too are already in heaven with him, even though what is promised us has not yet been fulfilled in our bodies . . . while in heaven he is also with us; and we while on earth are with him . . . and although he ascended alone, we also ascend, because we are in him by grace.[13]

Lead gently, Lord, and I will follow.

Now I miss being happy together in the most ordinary things, the little things, even our routine trips to the hospital under our canopy of changing leaves. I do miss Kristi's transparency, her humility and gentleness. I miss her single-heartedness in all of the new little nothings of each day, her resting in her "dear Lord" even as she did the laundry, her delight at the back door in a surprise dozen roses. Kristi's vocation was single-heartedness toward her family and her daily communion.

For the married who now grieve, many religious writers seem to leave incomplete their understanding of one Scripture passage especially, "When they rise from the dead, they neither marry nor are given in marriage" (Mark 12:25). Maybe so, but there are duets in heaven, not increased anonymity. Marriage is indissoluble and indestructible.

> Precisely because eternity and a heavenly Jerusalem exist, a married couple who love each other know that their communion is not destined to end with this passing world and dissolve into nothing, but that, transfigured and spiritualized, it will last for eternity.[14]

Surely in eternity (in Him) we become in a glorified way most fully human, not less so.

So often over the years I encouraged Kristi with this: that our very tears themselves are *turned into* joy. And as I learn the last dance with her, she now encourages me. I must permit our past to let me go. I know that Kristi and I shall be hand in hand together again. I have the testimony of the saints — increased by one. John Paul II lifts a corner of the veil on the fullness of our resurrection.[15] He calls it "a completely new experience," but also assures us that we will recognize ourselves and each other, totally. This brings to me a wellspring of consolation as I recall Kristi's words to me in the first week of hospice care when she tugged at my elbow, looked up into my eyes, and said to me: *"This is a new experience, Peter. Dying. And I don't know how good I'm going to be at it."*

There comes for me, even now, a peace with Kristi's very particular happiness. This is her total freedom, visible to me more each day possibly *because* of the intensity of terminal cancer.[16] Kristi's favorite line from Philippians is recorded on her stone, *"I can do all things in Him who strengthens me."* After so long, I see that this line is incomplete without the following line, *"Still you have done well by sharing in my affliction*" (Phil 4:13–14). Differently than the quoted apostle Paul, I am husband to this spouse given to me to travel a single path, to be a single path together.

I finally noticed, or admitted, that I too am "crushed."

In this single word and this moment my own desolation lifted another notch. This final release came with the very simple knowledge that if Kristi was "the flower the Lord is pleased to crush," He mercifully did not leave me uncrushed and alone. Part of my consolation is that we have shared this affliction. I was not left out, and now our being together in our given and shared path is not interrupted.

> The most complete unity between spouses is experienced not when they enjoy something together, but when they suffer together, each for the other, each with the other, loving each other in suffering and despite suffering. The first unity should serve to make the second possible.[17]

My role, I think, was to help protect Kristi from — the terror. Not much different from the many times I maneuvered between her and unleashed barking dogs of all sizes. But when will I let go of the pain, this last earthly possession we shared so deeply? In the end, trust was the air Kristi breathed each day. No resentment — none — ever attached itself to the random violence of cancer. With Kristi, the roses are lifted higher than the thorns. In a tiny volume given to Kristi by Kerry in the final days, I find this: "A simple soul, faithfully fulfilling its duties, contentedly obedient to the suggestions of grace and being gentle and humble to everyone, possesses knowledge worth more than the most profound intellectual penetration of the unknown."[18]

The gift really is contained in the little things, like a roadside flower, like little children born and unborn, like the sacraments and — nearly lost in the imagined sweep of history — like the resurrection of an obscure carpenter in Galilee. I am finding peace from an eternity that has a face and a name: "If you find your delight in the Lord, he will grant your heart's desire" (Ps. 37:4).

Table Talk in a Restaurant

The most holy saint in all of history was a housewife.
— Rev. Benedict Groeschel, C.F.R.

"So, Peter, what was it like being married to such a spiritual person?"

What was I to say of Kristi? This question was put to me fifteen months after Kristi's death, and still a week or two before I would begin writing our story, Kristi's and mine. Answering the question from Kristi's very good friend was the start of this story. So at the end, let us return to the summary at the beginning.

The question came from Linda as she was seated at my left. I looked up from the silverware and white restaurant linen. She had been under cancer treatment from time to time since her surgery in 1983, now seventeen years ago. She also had been severely tested but was a bit better able than Kristi to handle chemotherapy. Of Kristi she now privately asked, "What was it like . . . ?" Linda's question had been asked of me by others as well. It deserved an answer, even in this unlikely setting as we awaited the hors d'oeuvres and the main course.

The year before Kristi and I met in 1973, a longtime friend of mine married Linda. This was shortly after he had completed his tour of duty as a physician aboard an American cruiser and flagship stationed in Japan. I had served earlier (1967–70) on an aircraft carrier. Over the years we had now kept in touch with Lee and Linda, more frequently after Kristi's first cancer operation in late

My Kristi *reading. "I miss being happy together in the most ordinary things."*

1989. I was in an elegant restaurant with Lee and Linda and their family and friends.

Linda prodded, "Kristi was a woman of such faith. She always had such a glow." I listened. "I have prayed every night for fifty-four years. Although I am Jewish, I always include Kristi now. And I also know that I will some day be with both of my parents." Linda's parents had died nine months apart in 1988 while Linda was undergoing one of her many treatments, one from an HIV-contaminated blood transfusion and the other from heart failure. This must have been a period of massive darkness. Like Kristi and so many others, she had learned to endure each treatment cycle for specific and chosen reasons: first, to see the two children grow and finish school, then to see them graduate from college, and now to see them both possibly married.

Separated by hundreds of miles, during Kristi's twelve years with cancer she and Linda often shared thoughts on the phone and in seasonal notes. I thought about Kristi's simplicity and remarkable serenity and glanced at the bright and overly rich chandeliers overhead. "An afterlife is a misleading term," I offered. "It implies a time sequence to something that is really outside of time altogether. Is eternity a bauble caboose dangling 'after' time, or is it an ocean on all sides, above and below and even fulfilling itself within? Does this make sense?" I asked. This nostalgia for God — and its fulfillment — is both in and outside of time altogether.

What could I say about Kristi's present joy, and her fulfillment now? And how was I to explain my own stunned and surviving certainty about these things? "Everything that exists," I ventured, "comes from the hand of a Love who is infinite. Not quantum mechanics, but somehow prior and deeper, we face a huge and creative and totally personal intimacy. This infinite love is also exclusive and particular to each one of us. A mystery from within, and it has a name and a face."[19]

I then found myself following an intuition. Ours is a single God, but He is not an opaque God. The secret is that His giving and His gift are not an object in His hands; they are *His own most intimate and Trinitarian inner life.* Calling us into being is the inner life of God, not an impersonal creative power other than Himself and that He only possesses, as we might imagine. Kristi, I said, was actually in close touch with this *origin*-ality of God as Creator and Father.[20] Hers was the familiar confidence that one is a gift — that while one might be at peace here, "here" is a path to a home beyond our present selves. We sometimes catch a glimpse that — rather than a debate over different kinds of evidence and ways of knowing, faith and science — the human mystery involves a gift and a Giver, not extreme complexity alone.

Pretending to inspect the menu we noticed how we so often are estranged by our forced objectivity. This is the sin of (partial) knowledge, the notion that all that stuff "out there" — the universe — is fully detached and is seen only conceptually with the eyes, not *through* the eyes.[21] To see only with the eyes is to detect only meteorology when in fact we are bathed from within by a sunset and a springtime. To see blindly, only with the eyes, is to reduce God to a mere idea and probably the most recent and fashionable idea like "progress." Reason alone does have its limits and, in times more enlightened than our post-Enlightenment, reason knows this. The human heart is bigger than we are, and He is bigger than the human heart.

A glance, and then Linda went on, "Yes, but what did Kristi have that I would like to have?" What *had* I learned worth saying about this, in the many, many months since Kristi's death, or even in our lifetime together? Kristi's most used prayer is direct. It locates God within, and speaks intimately to this source — "Soul of my soul," it begins. I went on, "This is what gave to Kristi the serenity noticed by so many. Finally, it turns on what Kristi believed and knew to be the truth, as He comes to us in person." We find that Christ came for our trust, to "free those who through fear of death had been subject to slavery all their life" (Heb. 2:14–18).

"Kristi's secret and the Christian message," I said, "is that from the inner life of an infinite God, an equally profound intimacy comes toward us where we are, and *through the veil*. This vast intimacy shows us that your intuition about rejoining your mother and father is true. And then He invites us, 'Follow me'" (Matt. 9:9).[22] Christianity knows that the Jewish chosenness and expectation is on target, and then it is the added and sustained astonishment at the fulfillment "in the fullness of time" and in the resurrection. Christianity is this astonishment, ever new, and ever delightfully at risk of being out of step with an indifferent or mocking world.

"This is the path that Kristi followed," I said. And, it involves a mystery, the path of fidelity and joy even and especially through pain. Not alongside of or sidestepping or enduring pain as an interruption, but *through* pain. Kristi's secret, finally, was a tender and consistent devotion to her "dear Lord." In this, I venture, she stood quietly apart from the entire drift of our time, or any time.

The cancer was a mixed blessing, and Kristi knew this. She was a humble and gentle spirit. I see that her trials and the removal of distraction that they gave opened her toward not resentment, but an ever deeper gentleness. It is so simple and transparent. To all of this, to the most inward voice of the "Soul of my soul," Kristi came slowly to say yes, unconditionally. By the cancer she was led into gentleness that was larger than even this arbitrary and terminal suffering. Here was a calmness that was more than a response.

This calm dignity is not what one imagines when we think of "heroic virtue"; it is simply gentleness enlarged by vulnerability, rather than hardened.

Linda and I noticed our surroundings. Was this conversation in a restaurant out of place? "No," I added. "It is the restaurant and our distracted world that are out of place." I leaned closer and recited part of Psalm 103, Kristi's favorite, as it appears on her funeral card. I have gone over these lines every day since, to help keep from losing my own grip. In these lines I find Kristi's portrait:

Bless the Lord, O my soul, and all that is within me bless his
    holy name.
Bless the Lord O my soul and forget not all his benefits.
He pardons all your iniquities, He heals all your ills.
He redeems your life from destruction.
He crowns you with kindness and compassion.
He fills your lifetime with good.
Your youth is renewed like the eagle's.

As we sat a moment more, we relaxed in how we — a Jew and
a Catholic — had this in common, the Psalms. Toying with the
silverware, I was able to recite another of our daily prayers. This
was Fr. Thomas's novena to the Holy Spirit,[23] who mysteriously is
also one with the Father and the Son. As a family we had used it
for strength at our dinner table nearly every day for twelve years
since Kristi's first treatment. It is this prayer more than any other, I
think, that kindled and sustained Kristi's consistent serenity.

God is to be found within, but we are not He. There is a subjectivity, but He is more. His residency is gratuitous and attracts us
to the total freedom of unconditional submission to His own unconditional love. Pascal hit this note: "The Stoics say 'retire within
yourselves; it is there you will find your rest.' And it is not true.
Others say 'Go out of yourselves; seek happiness in amusements.'
And this is not true. Illness comes. Happiness is neither without us
nor within us. It is in God, both without us and within us."[24]

Much more than a theological conclusion, eternal life is seen
through an opening one discovers within, often through arbitrary
suffering.

In the evenings Kristi sometimes would cross my forehead with
a drop or two of water brought home from the spring at Lourdes.
So simple, so fleeting. I would do the same for her, a cross with my
thumb on her forehead. And now I think how this nuptial blessing

prefigured what is said to us in Revelation: "And they shall see his face and his name shall be on their foreheads." Eternity in a single drop of water; the light glistens through the veil even into our tired little world. "And night shall be no more . . . and they shall reign forever and ever" (Rev. 22:4–5). When one has lost a spouse such lines achieve a poignancy beyond all imagining. An emptiness will always weigh on my heart, as if one of my ribs is missing.

The key to everything is silent trust. And Christ is trust in the Father, in person. "The heavenly Father has uttered only one word: it is His Son. He says it eternally and in an eternal silence. It is in the silence of the soul that it makes itself heard."[25]

I see how *in each of us* is played out the entire biblical account of God's promise to His people. The covenant is always there, and it is fulfilled in His coming in Christ. We can trust the promise and the Promiser. It is all one. Marriage, an icon of Christ's relationship to His people, is cut from the same cloth. In our marriage we live within a promise. Now it is not only that I believe in marriage because of God, but I believe in God because of our marriage. The window is the gifts of faith and hope, and a charity that is as nuptial as it is personal or communal. The full glory of heaven removes the last trace of anonymity.

And, of the little things, I now find another little note from my bride. After well over two years since Kristi's death, in the margin of her college text of *Hamlet,* I find her handwriting to me: "*Advice: don't grieve so much.*"[26] After three years, here was another discovery. In the side drawer of our antique buffet, our first furniture purchase, I recovered the tape of Kristi's first vocal recital. To the laughter of the audience Kristi explains that I am not present because I am . . . "babysitting." Then she dedicates to her absent husband a song specially chosen, for my "encouragement and patience." Twenty years after this heartfelt performance I received the angelic singing of my spouse, now absent three years, in "This is my beloved — and when he moves, and when he walks with me, Paradise comes suddenly near."

And then the dream. In the dream I catch up with Kristi in a small walled garden. We hold each other, knowing that we are losing each other. There is only us — with no other meaning at all. Cherry blossom petals drift into Kristi's long dark hair. I wake in tears to discover this: "In the Lord's garden are to be found not only the roses of his martyrs. In it there are also the lilies of the virgins, the ivy of wedded couples, and the violets of widows.... Christ suffered for all."[27]

Unconditional intimacy and friendship, in person.

All of Kristi's story becomes, finally, a single memory of a totally certain and resurrected future that is already within, lifted up in an instant beyond the cross by His embracing glance from eternity. In a book Kristi once bought for me, I rediscovered the depth of this belonging in a way that spoke to my particular blindness and now removes the desert from my soul:

> Religion is in fact that which man does in his solitude, but it is also that in which the human person discovers his essential companionship.... Such companionship is, then, *more original to us than our solitude.*[28]

More original than our solitude! As Kristi had said to me: "*God meant you for me from the very, very beginning.*" This beginning is the original innocence that, by grace, survives our slightly less original sin of imagined self-ownership and then the imagined veil. Injured is a nuptial freedom toward the innermost Soul of our souls. A companionship deeper than our self-inflicted solitude from the sin of self-containment original only to ourselves. Our inner desert was evaporating before my very eyes. St. Francis de Sales says this of marriage: "The union is so strong that the soul must sooner separate from the body of the one or the other than the husband from his wife."[29]

Finally, His crucifixion and resurrection — innocent suffering — is about His respect, for us. We do *belong,* to Him and in this way also to each other — in a way deeper and more original than anything we might construct in any of our lives or in all of our history. I find that we can touch hands even through the veil. Kristi's words at least begin to become my own: "*I would not want to do that again . . . but I would not want to have missed it either. The graces I would not have known.*"

And then,

> *From life to greater Life. I know this with a certainty.*
> *I've just had a long talk with Jesus — my best Friend.*

Notes

Introduction

1. In the Mass, "the consecration is the moment of God's great *actio* in the world for us. It draws our eyes and hearts on high. For a moment the world is silent, everything is silent, and in that silence we touch the eternal — for one beat of the heart we step out of time into Gods's being-with-us" (Cardinal Joseph Ratzinger, *The Spirit of the Liturgy* [San Francisco: Ignatius, 2000], 212). And in the Gloria Patri we also find expansive praise for His presence within His own creation: "Glory be to the Father, and to the Son, and to the Holy Spirit, as it was in the begriming, is now, and ever shall be, *world without end*" (emphasis added). Hans Urs von Balthasar explores the transcendent beauty and glory of God (to be held alongside of His transcendent truth and morality) with this exceptional insight: "The entry of genuine eternity into time (the incarnation of God), the entry of time into eternity (the resurrection of Christ and of the creation in him)." Between time and eternity he sees not a veil, but mutual transparency, something like a marriage and even the Mass. *The Glory of the Lord*, vol. 6: *A Theological Aesthetic* (San Francisco: Ignatius Press, 1991), 412.

2. Cardinal Joseph Ratzinger, *The Ratzinger Report* (San Francisco: Ignatius Press, 1985), 53. The *Report* was issued shortly in advance to the Extraordinary Synod of Bishops on the twentieth anniversary of the Council. He wrote, "What the Church needs in order to respond to the needs of man in every age is holiness, not management."

3. Bridging between personal authenticity and an authentic world is a preoccupation of many, especially including John Paul II. "Solutions must be sought on the global level by establishing a *true economy of communion of goods,* in both the national and international order. This is the only way to respect the dignity of persons and families, as well as the authentic cultural patrimony of peoples" (John Paul II, *The Gospel of Life* [New York: Random House, 1995], no. 9).

4. Stratford and Leonie Caldecott, "Magical Realism," in *Catholic World Report* (San Francisco: Ignatius Press, December 1998), 30.

5. Kristi's sainted friend Therese of Lisieux said of her own illness, "I am not dying, I am entering into life." Quoted by Leonie Caldecott, "Second Spring," *Catholic World Report* (San Francisco: Ignatius Press, October 1997).

One: Our Vow to One Another

1. Even when they turned thirteen the revered grandfather, Dr. Wesley Orr, still referred diminutively to Kristi and Kerry as "the twins." An abrupt step to adulthood was marked now as Kerry's foot and Kristi's hit the flagstone entryway. With this, they announced for their grandfather and the whole world to hear: "I am not a twin; I am an *individual!*"

2. For me the nearest relatives had been in the Midwest, two thousand miles away. Every year we shared holiday meals with an indirect aunt and uncle. In Richland the families were close for the most part, but uniformly young and cut off from relatives. My older brother, Tom, at the age of four was shaken by his first sight of wrinkles and white hair. He was startled by what was simply a grandmother in any other town like Kristi's.

3. We refer to a photo collection in Sister Alfreda Elsensohn's, *Pioneer Days in Idaho County*, vol. 1 (Caldwell, ID: Caxton Printers, 1978). The author was known to the family and a welcome guest at our wedding in the autumn of 1974.

4. From a letter by St. Leo the Great, *Liturgy of the Hours*, vol. 2 (New York: Catholic Book Publishing, 1976) for March 25 (p. 1746).

5. Of Christ's nuptial presence to us, we have this: "And so, in the end, what is involved is a reciprocal vicarious vision: just as the angels of the little ones on earth always behold the face of the Father for them in heaven (Matt. 18:10), so too do men on earth behold for the angels the beauty of the God who has concealed himself in flesh" (Hans Urs

von Balthasar, *The Glory of the Lord: A Theological Aesthetics*, vol. 1: *Seeing the Form* [San Francisco: Ignatius Press, 1988], 677).

6. In the act of consecration, "the priest says these words, or rather *he puts his voice at the disposal of the one who spoke these words in the upper room* and who desires that they should be repeated in every generation by all who in the Church ministerially share in His priesthood" (John Paul II, *On the Eucharist in Its Relationship to the Church* [*Ecclesia de Eucharistia*, April 17, 2003], no. 5).

7. The Church holds that Christ is present in the assembly and in the Scriptures and the other sacraments, but of the Eucharist teaches something more. The eternal comes to each of us in time: "The mode of Christ's presence under the Eucharistic species is unique. It raises the Eucharist above all the sacraments as 'the perfection of the spiritual life and the end to which all the sacraments tend.'" Here "'*the whole Christ is truly, really, and substantially* contained.' 'This presence is called "real" . . . because it is presence in the fullest sense: that is to say, it is a *substantial* presence by which Christ, God and man, makes himself wholly and entirely present'" (*Catechism of the Catholic Church* [San Francisco: Ignatius Press, 1994], no. 1374 [emphasis in the original]). The Eucharist is not merely fellowship alone, but it is a total handing over to the other; it is nuptial. See Hans Urs von Balthasar, *The Glory of the Lord: A Theological Aesthetics*, vol. 7: *The New Covenant*, ed. Joseph Fessio (San Francisco: Ignatius Press, 1990), 470–84.

8. *The Confessions of St. Augustine*, bk. 7, chap. 10 (Garden City, NY: Image Books, 1960), 171.

9. Allergic to metaphysical reasoning, our age also dismisses its own scientific hints. While science, by its nature, cannot prove articles of faith, it also comes up short in disproving them. A case in point involves the Shroud of Turin, possibly the burial cloth of Christ. The discrediting of the carbon-14 dating process, one of dozens of inquiries applied in the 1980s, is itself discredited. Exposure of the Shroud over the centuries to contaminating fires and to bacterial growth, and the selection of a later date cloth patch for the testing, all fatally compromise the

carbon-14 findings. Professional medical interpretations of events captured on the Shroud include one given to me by Kristi's father. See William Edwards, Wesley Gabel, and Floyd Hosmer, "On the Physical Death of Christ," *Journal of the American Medical Association* 255, no. 11 (March 21, 1986).

10. "This victory of meaning over being had its ultimate illustration in the shift from the Eucharist of Being, the Catholic doctrine of transubstantiation — the formula of Trent — to the Protestant insistence that the Eucharist *means* Christ but is not his very Body and Blood" (Frederick Wilhelmsen, "Death of the Age of Analysis," *Citizen of Rome* [La Salle, IL: Sherwood Sugden, 1980], 128). The Council of Trent was the late sixteenth-century rallying point of the Catholic Reformation. In harmony with Trent is this from a treatise on heresies by St. Irenaeus, bishop in the second century: "The Lord, coming into his own creation in visible form, was sustained by his own creation which he himself sustains in being."

11. From Karol Wojtyla, "Shores of Silence," in *The Place Within: The Poetry of Pope John Paul II,* trans. Jerzy Peterkiewicz (New York: Random House, 1982), 11.

12. Cited in Hans Urs von Balthasar, *Bernanos: An Ecclesial Existence* (San Francisco: Ignatius Press, 1996), 556.

13. The story of Marie Bailly is presented in Alexis Carrel, *Voyage to Lourdes* (New York: Harper, 1950).

14. T. S. Elliot assures us that this lesson does not point to a split between reason and unreason; rather the "heart" is meant to be the whole personality, including but not limited to reason alone (Introduction to Blaise Pascal, *Pascal's Pensées* [New York: E. P. Dutton, 1958], xviii).

15. Romano Guardini, *The End of the Modern World* (Chicago: Logos, 1968), 132. Today we are crowded by the instrumental and managerial approach to the world as we find it in the market and the professionalism of medicine, academics, and even some parts of the clergy. Too lost to us moderns is the deep sense of wonder and reverence.

16. Under the Manhattan Project, Hanford became the production site for plutonium (rather than uranium) used in the second atomic bomb, dropped on Nagasaki at the end of World War II.

17. See C. S. Lewis, "Dogma and the Universe," in *God in the Dock: Essays on Theology and Ethics* (Grand Rapids: William B. Eerdmans, 1976).

18. In later years I recalled to my parents this childhood feeling of discontinuity. For my birthday my father brilliantly selected a small edition book recording the earlier days of my hometown: Martha Berry Parker's *Tales of Richland, White Bluffs and Hanford 1805–1943* (Fairfield, WA: Ye Galleon Press, 1979).

19. "A world of nice people, content in their own niceness, looking no further, turned away from God, would be just as desperately in need of salvation as a miserable world — and might even be more difficult to save" (C. S. Lewis, *Mere Christianity* [New York: Macmillan, 1977], 182).

20. On this general question of chaos and design in the universe, Albert Einstein found that in the laws of nature "there is revealed such a superior Reason that everything significant which has arisen out of human thought and arrangement is, in comparison with it, the merest empty reflection" (cited from a German source by Cardinal Joseph Ratzinger, *In the Beginning* . . . [Grand Rapids: Wm. B. Eerdmans, 1995], 23).

21. Charles Moeller, cited in Vincent Micelli, *The Gods of Atheism* (New Rochelle, NY: Arlington House, 1971), 209.

22. This interest in Church social encyclicals continued. In 1994 I was privileged to deliver a paper at the annual meeting of the Society of Catholic Social Scientists (SCSS) on Pope John Paul II's encyclical marking the one hundredth anniversary of *Rerum Novarum* as well as the collapse of the communist Soviet Union (Beaulieu, "Notes on *Centesimus Annus:* "On Growing Younger as the World Grows Old," *Catholic Social Science Review* [1999]).

23. In what must have been a guided moment, my father gave me at the age of twelve a tiny gilded-edge edition of Thomas à Kempis's *Imitation of Christ*. During my high school years, often on walks along the Columbia River, I worked my way through this volume three times.

24. The *Hornet*'s moment in the sun came later in the year (July and November 1969), when she served as the Pacific recovery ship for the Apollo XI and XII lunar missions, when astronauts first set foot on the moon. Unreported was the spiritual blessing from Pope Paul VI in response to a "gesture" by our commanding officer, later Admiral Carl J. Seiberlich: "The Secretariat of State is graciously directed by the Holy Father to acknowledge receipt of the special philatelic envelope from the captain and crew of the USS *Hornet* . . . and in expressing His sincere appreciation of the loyal filial devotion which prompted this gesture, has the honour to convey, in pledge of abundant divine graces, the paternal Apostolic Benediction of His Holiness."

25. Some five hundred cubic miles of water rushed to the sea — in each of forty or more repeated events over a period of twenty millennia — carving the many landforms (coulees) we see today in the Columbia Basin landscape scoured across eastern Washington. Exploring the exposed hillsides, my family found several animal fossils dating much farther back.

26. Here began William Wordsworth's "Perpetual benedictions . . . / for those first affections, / Those shadowy recollections, / Which . . . Uphold us; cherish, and have power to make / Our noisy years seem moments in the being / Of the eternal Silence: truths that wake / To perish never; / Which . . . all that is at enmity with joy; / Can [never] utterly abolish or destroy!" ("Ode on Intimations of Immortality").

Two: Into His Presence

1. In a nutshell, at issue is the ambiguity of his "synthesis of the created Universe and its Creator" (citation from *Mon Universe* [1918] in the sympathetic Henri de Lubac, S.J., *The Religion of Teilhard de Chardin*

[Garden City, NY: Image, 1968], 237). In time, does the Word become flesh in widespread creation, or uniquely and personally in the incarnation?

2. A message to all of us: "God desires the least degree of purity of conscience in you more than all the works you can perform" (St. John of the Cross, "Sayings of Light and Love," in *The Treasury of Catholic Wisdom*, ed. John A. Hardon, S.J. [San Francisco: Ignatius Press, 1995], 490).

3. In the 1980s this complex was selected as the idyllic setting for the movie *Somewhere in Time.*

4. Pope Paul VI, *Evangelii Nuntiandi* (*Evangelization in the Modern World*), December 8, 1975, nos. 20–21.

5. In 1597 twenty-six Christians were martyred by torture and crucifixion at Nagasaki, which also was to be the target of the second atomic bomb, dropped on August 9, 1945. (The core for the bomb dropped on this center for Christianity in Japan was produced near my birthplace on the Hanford Atomic Reservation.)

6. Marx paused at this question — the premise that the human person, finally, is not a creator who invents himself totally. The question of contingency, he said, "is forbidden to socialist man" (*Writings of the Young Marx on Philosophy and Society* [New York: Anchor Books, 1967], 65–66; cited in Frederick Wilhelmsen, "Art and Religion," *Citizen of Rome* [La Salle, IL: Sherwood Sugden, 1980], 107).

7. I recall that in one of our kitchen table chats on the prairie, the family considered this piece from St. Augustine: "For they [the passions] are more easily mortified finally in those who love God, than satisfied, even for a time, in those who love the world" (*The Political Writings of St. Augustine*, ed. Henry Paolucci [Chicago: Gateway Edition, 1962], 285). To mark the collapse of the Soviet Empire, and the hundredth anniversary of the first formal definition of Catholic social teaching, John Paul II addressed the economic question within the context of a deeper degree of human alienation. In a lengthy and densely written *Centesimus Annus* (*One Hundred Years,* 1991) he included this: "It is

not wrong to want to live better; what is wrong is a style of life which is presumed to be better when it is directed toward 'having' rather than 'being,' and which wants to have more, not in order to be more but in order to spend life in enjoyment as an end in itself" (no. 36). The economic "alienation" behind Marxism is not radical enough: "The concept of alienation needs to be led back to the Christian vision of reality" (no. 41).

8. Aristotle comments on the (pre-Christian) relationship between reason and belief: "To believe is nothing other than to think with assent. . . . Believers are also thinkers; in believing, they think and in thinking they believe. . . . If faith does not think, it is nothing" (cited by John Paul II in *Fides et Ratio* [*On the Relationship between Faith and Reason*], September 14, 1998, no. 79).

9. In his commentary on Carmelite spirituality, P. Marie-Eugène, O.C.D., says this: "Starting with the principle that the theological virtues are engrafted in the natural faculties — faith in the intellect; charity, in the will; hope in the imagination and the memory — St. John of the Cross teaches us to discipline the natural faculties by exercising the theological virtues that correspond to them" (*I Want to See God: A Practical Synthesis of Carmelite Spirituality* [Chicago: Fides, 1953], 438).

10. Another response, both insightful and inviting of further thought, is the following: "Some Fathers of the Church . . . thought that if Adam had not sinned there would have been no marriage, with the sexual procreation that is now its distinguishing feature, because in the way in which it is now exercised, human sexuality is the fruit of original sin. However, from a more biblical and less Platonic perspective it must be said that *rather the reverse is true:* that, had there been no sin there would have been no virginity, because there would have been no need to question marriage and sexuality and subject them to judgment" (Raniero Cantalamessa, *Virginity: A Positive Approach to Celibacy for the Sake of the Kingdom of Heaven* [New York: St. Paul's House, 1995], 45; emphasis added). A further line of reasoning could stress that fully human

free will is not found in nature, that this freedom amplifies experience into binary choices shaped by the wholeness of the human heart — the call to single-heartedness. As a whole person, one chooses one human spouse or another, or by choosing none, the person anticipates with his or her entire being a less exclusive communion with Christ as Spouse, and all the Communion of Saints — past, present, and future.

11. Of Jastrow's treatment of the Big Bang and a beginning in time to the universe, the doctor was particularly delighted with this concluding remark: "For the scientist who has lived by his faith in the power of reason, the story ends like a bad dream. He has scaled the mountains of ignorance; he is about to conquer the highest peak; as he pulls himself over the final rock, he is greeted by a band of theologians who have been sitting there for centuries" (Robert Jastrow, *God and the Astronomers* [New York: W. W. Norton, 1978], 116). He also enjoyed the fact that possibly the first to propose a Big Bang (1927), a researcher named Georges Lemaître, was also a Dominican priest. Considering the Big Bang theory, which replaces the steady state universe, we might chuckle a bit now at the riddle "How many angels can stand on the head of a pin?" It seems now from science that our 100 billion solar systems, each with 100 billion stars, all fit on the head of a pin at that moment before the beginning of time. Scientists want to know the ultimate answers to questions, but philosophers and theologians and finally the religious want to live the answers to ultimate questions.

12. This earlier phase of post–Vatican II adjustment sharpened for Kristi and me when I took part in parish "listening sessions" hosted in our second parish in 1975. The sessions, curiously wrapped in the banner of the United States bicentennial, proved to be part of a dissident current nationwide, the stirrings of a church within the Church aimed to construct itself entirely from below. This would be a horizontal church replacing the ordained ministry that traces back to the hands of Christ (Matt. 28:18–20) with a new clericalism accountable only to itself.

Two corrective events in the Church included the Extraordinary Synod of Bishops, convened in 1985 by John Paul II to recall worldwide the original message of the Second Vatican Council in continuity with all of the previous councils. The purpose of the synod was for the Church to be deepened and only then more engaged with the world (the less familiar *ressourcement* and the more familiar *aggiornamento*). Thus, it was partly to avoid "a unilateral presentation of the Church as a purely institutional structure devoid of her mystery" (no. 4). The second event, directly affecting the Seattle region, was the Apostolic Visitation to investigate alleged irregularities in the Archdiocese of Seattle. Findings and fine-tuned instructions for Seattle were also issued in late 1985.

13. Whittaker Chambers, *Cold Friday* (New York: Random House, 1964), 226.

14. "A very simple person who bears within himself a sense of solid values and, thus, a sensitivity toward others, toward what is right and beautiful and true, is immeasurably more learned than the most experienced technocrat with his computer brain" (Cardinal Joseph Ratzinger, *Principles of Catholic Theology: Building Stones for a Fundamental Theology* [San Francisco: Ignatius Press, 1987], 341).

15. Existing *prior* to the state, the family is "a community of love and solidarity, which is uniquely suited to teach and transmit cultural, ethical, social, spiritual and religious values, essential for the development and well-being of its own members and of society" (John Paul II, Preamble, *Charter of the Rights of the Family*, October 22, 1983). Perhaps we would do better, as "conservatives," to see the family not as the cell of society, but as the DNA.

16. Only a few months after our conversation the rabbi was killed in a head-on collision on a reversible lane over Lake Washington during the peak of the Seattle rush hour. A car had veered into the oncoming traffic.

17. St. Augustine, *Confessions*, X, viii, 15.

18. This line is among the very few that I find underlined in the Bible Kristi owned from her youth.

19. Cited by Ratzinger, *Principles of Catholic Theology,* 66.

20. One of the most prominent theological advisors to the Second Vatican Council, Fr. Yves Congar, identified Therese as "one of the beacons that the hand of God has lit at the threshold of the atomic century" (cited in Guy Gaucher, O.C.D., *The Story of a Life* [New York: HarperCollins, 1987], 214).

21. Otto mentioned the special influence of Fr. John Bertolucci, author of *Healing: God's Work among Us* (Ann Arbor, MI: Servant Books, 1987).

22. The Irish Sister McKenna received the gift of healing during a celebration of the Mass. At the age of twenty-four, as the result of prayer, she was suddenly cured of rheumatoid arthritis and the resulting physical deformities in her feet. Since 1974 she has had a special ministry to those called to the priesthood. See Briege McKenna, O.S.C., with Henry Libersat, *Miracles Do Happen* (New York: St. Martin's, 1987).

23. Barham's education included a doctorate in psychology and a Canadian doctorate in theology. He taught at several schools and was vice president of the International Institute of Integral Human Services, a non-governmental organization of the United Nations, and vice president of the Institute's Council on World Religions.

24. One hope of the Second Vatican Council was that the Eastern Rite Churches (fully within the Catholic Church) might serve as a bridge toward the culturally similar but separated Orthodox Churches. Such a bridge could help enable both to dissolve complexities of separation dating back more than a thousand years to 1054 and before. The hope continues, and the past three decades have brought advances. Pope Paul VI and the patriarch of Constantinople removed from history the mutual (and personal only) excommunications fired back and forth so long ago by their predecessors.

25. At Lourdes the first investigation by the on-site Medical Bureau is followed by a deeper study by an off-site International Medical

Commission. The second favorable finding might still be rejected for non-medical reasons by a canonical commission.

26. As this manuscript goes to press, I am met by a friend of Kristi's who was prayed over by Fr. Barham during his visit at our St. Mark's Parish in Seattle. A victim of an aggressive cancer, she had been on an experimental "cocktail" of seven chemotherapies. After ten years the cancer has not returned. Perhaps this is due to the medications, but how does one explain her epileptic relative who stood with her to receive the prayer? He has suffered not a single seizure during the same period since that special evening.

27. In Scripture, Christ is recorded as performing healing in probably two dozen different events. These range from encounters with lepers and paralytics to the blind and dumb and to those possessed. The raising of Lazarus was more than a healing. Additional healing events are recorded in the Acts of the Apostles and much later, not in Scripture, as witnessed and carefully detailed for example by St. Augustine during his stay in Milan (*The City of God* [Garden City, NY: Image, 1958], bk. 22, chap. 8).

28. Scripture scholars might note the divergence of their scholarship in opposite directions: the political correctness of feminist theology and the rationalism of, for example, the male-dominated Jesus Seminar. In comparison, Vatican II attends to the living word, reaffirming the historical character of the Gospels and restoring a willingness to see both with and *through* the eyes. Responding to the direct indwelling of the Holy Spirit, and to living tradition as well as artifact, the Council reminds us, "For there is a growth in the understanding of the realities *and* the words which have been handed down. This happens through the *contemplation* and study made by believers *who treasure these things in their hearts*" (*Dei Verbum* (Dogmatic Constitution on Divine Revelation), no. 8; emphasis added).

29. Exodus 3:14, in John Paul II, *The Original Unity of Man and Woman* (Boston: St. Paul Editions, 1981), n. 26. The connection between the Hebrew revelations and the later classical thinking is also documented in St. Augustine, *The City of God*, bk. 18, chap. 37, 404–5.

30. C. S. Lewis, *God in the Dock: Essays on Theology and Ethics* (Grand Rapids: William B. Eerdmans, 1970), 66.

31. As is often the case, the Nestorians fell in step behind a heretical priest, Nestorius. He exaggerated Christ's humanity, making Him more of a messenger than a person of the Triune God equal with the Father and the Spirit within the divine intimacy of a single Godhead.

32. James A. Michener formulates things in this succinct way in his *The Source* (New York: Random House, 1965).

33. Erik von Kuehnelt-Leddihn, *Liberty or Equality* (Caldwell, ID: Caxton Printers, 1952), 85.

34. *Veritatis Splendor* (*VS, The Splendor of the Truth*), 1993. For the post–Cold War world we also find that "the Church's social doctrine is not a "third way" between liberal capitalism and Marxist collectivism.... Rather it constitutes a category of its own. Nor is it ideology...but of theology and particularly moral theology" (John Paul II, *Centesimus Annus* [*One Hundred Years*], 1990, no. 80). He writes that with the fall of Marxism there remains the *equally grave*" "risk of an alliance between democracy and ethical relativism" (*VS,* no. 101).

35. Erik saw a future for the Union, but as a confederation and not as a unitary state. As the European Union invents itself, Erik would be sympathetic to those features providing mediation and the Catholic social principle of personal responsibility, i.e., retaining decision making as far away as reasonably possible from all forms of centralization (the principle of "subsidiarity"). For Erik, one of the dismissed casualties of World War I was a non-secularized culture still surviving (in his view) in the multinational Austro-Hungarian Empire. In President Wilson's quest to make the world "safe for democracy," the model of multinational states was replaced by sovereign nation-states, democracies from below rather than mediated families of peoples.

36. Fulton belonged to the Order of Preachers, Dominicans devoted to scholarship and teaching. Albert Camus (see chapter 1) was in

sympathetic and close communication with the Dominicans near the time of his death.

37. Named after the nineteenth-century cardinal John Henry Newman, a convert from the Anglican communion. During this period I discovered Newman's classic, *The Idea of a University*. Newman celebrates the difference between a university of integrated thought and a shattered "multiversity" united more by administrators and a common dependence upon government grants. He wrote, "I lay it down that all knowledge forms one whole because its subject matter is one; for the universe in its length and breadth is so intimately knit together that we cannot separate off portion from portion, and operation from operation, except by mental abstraction; and then again, as to its Creator...we cannot truly and fully contemplate it without in some main aspects contemplating Him" (Garden City, NY: Image, 1959), 87.

38. Jack Fulton, *Love Grows in Brooklyn* (Seattle: Hillcraft Publishing, 1992).

39. In the mid-1800s Newman created a stir at Oxford when as an Anglican bishop and part of the academic Oxford Movement scrutinizing Catholic roots, he converted to Catholicism. Based on his years of published study he concluded that rather than being a branch in continuity with original Christianity, Anglicanism was more akin to the separated splinter factions of the early centuries.

40. Herbert Cory, *Enlightenment of a Freethinker* (Milwaukee: Bruce, 1941).

41. Improvised comments quoted on *Almost Biography* produced from John Paul II writings by EWTN television, St. Peter's Square, 1994.

42. For the Church, the silver lining in the record of sexual abuse by some priests might be the providential timing. The Church moves to correct the abuses, even as the United States and Canadian court systems more recently seem trapped and rudderless in the mire as they presume to redefine marriage.

43. Natural law refers to human nature and is not to be confused with natural science and so dismissed. "Of such [natural] laws the Church

was not the author nor consequently can she be their arbiter" (*Humanae Vitae* [*On Human Life*], July 25, 1968, no. 18). Part of this teaching has to do with contraception, but equally so is the priority of principle over pragmatism: "Though it is true that sometimes it is lawful to tolerate a lesser moral evil in order to avoid a greater evil or in order to promote a greater good, it is never lawful even for the gravest reasons to do evil that good might come of it" (John Paul II, *Veritatis Splendor* [*The Splendor of the Truth*], August 6, 1993, no. 79).

The moral question is often misunderstood as a rejection of responsible parenthood and natural family planning (NFP). This is incorrect. Instead, it is a finding that interventions sold on the market and imposed by some states directly contradict the nature of the whole human person and his or her fully human and free actions. Within the Church, this insight — that sexual unity and *openness* to fecundity must not be severed one from the other — is not set aside by secondary factors. Thinking more in terms of personalism than moral theology, John Paul II reminds us that direct intervention is inauthentic toward the depth of the human person, our very selves rather than simply an external code.

44. Cardinal John Wright, *Reflections on the Third Anniversary of a Controverted Encyclical*, Archdiocese of St. Louis, August 15, 1971. Note the term "controverted," not "controversial."

45. The prophetic minority said this: "It is, to say the least, suspicious that the age in which contraception has won its way is not one which has been conspicuously successful in managing its sexual life. Is it possible that, by claiming the right to manipulate his physical processes in this manner, man may, without knowing or intending it, be stepping over the boundary between the world of Christian marriage and what one might call the *world of Aphrodite,* the world of sterile eroticism? . . . Once submission to the given pattern is abandoned, all kinds of variations on the sexual theme which heighten satisfaction can appear to be enrichments of the sexual life" (cited in Wright, *Reflections on the Third Anniversary of a Controverted Encyclical,* emphasis

added). Anchoring more recent theological opinions in the Catholic
Church, we find this: "the commandment of love of God and neighbor
does not have in its dynamic any higher limit, but it does have a lower
limit, beneath which the commandment is broken" (*Veritatis Splendor,*
1993, no. 52). Being "at different points on the path" is one thing (as
in our observance of the Beatitudes), but being off the path is another.
History might eventually notice how Paul VI was dismissed by his critics
for seeing beyond the advice of his *Humanae Vitae* commission in 1968,
while bishops in the United States are criticized now for not rejecting
the advice of other secular panels of psychologists who reviewed cases
of clerical sexual abuse in the 1970s and 1980s.

46. George Weigel, *Witness to Hope* (New York: Cliff Street Books,
1999), 340–43.

47. A developed meditation on this line of thinking is David
Schindler, *Heart of the World, Center of the Church: Communio Eccle-
siology, Liberalism, and Liberation* (Grand Rapids: William B. Eerdmans,
1996), passim. "Our culture tends to marginalize the family. We need
rather to 'familiarize' ('domesticate') the culture" (p. 268).

48. The real enlightenment will come when women instinctively see
abortion as rooted in male dominance, and with Descartes and Pascal
in the subjection of "female matter to male mathematics" (Friedrich
Heer, *The Intellectual History of Europe* [Cleveland: World, 1966], 386).

49. Hans Urs von Balthasar, *The Glory of the Lord: A Theological
Aesthetics,* vol. 7, *Theology: The New Covenant* (San Francisco: Ignatius
Press, 1989), 84.

50. Georges Bernanos offers an extraordinary insight. "Purity is not
imposed upon us as though it were a kind of punishment, it is one of
those mysterious but obvious conditions of that supernatural knowledge
of ourselves in the Divine, which we speak of as faith. Impurity does
not destroy this knowledge, it slays our need for it. I no longer believe,
because I have no wish to believe. You no longer wish to know yourself.
This profound truth, your truth, has ceased to interest you. Insist as
much as you please that dogmas, to which yesterday you assented, are

still sole-present in your mind, that only reason rejects them. . . . You can only love yourself through God. You no longer love yourself, and you will never love yourself again either in this world or hereafter — through all eternity" (from *The Diary of a Country Priest* by Georges Bernanos, copyright (c) 1937, 1965 by the Macmillan Co. Appears by permission of the publisher, Carroll and Graf Publishers (2002), a division of Avalon Publishing Group, 126).

51. Hans Urs von Balthasar, *Bernanos: An Ecclesial Existence* (San Francisco: Ignatius Press, 1996), 305; emphasis added.

52. From Fr. Raniero Cantalamessa, O.F.M., cited in *Magnificat* (Spencerville, MD), June 2004, 31.

53. We are called to be "children of God beyond reproach in the midst of a twisted and depraved generation — among whom you shine like the stars of the sky" (Phil. 2:15).

54. Now that a full generation has passed, the presentation might stress more the incidental results of scientific research. Even in restaurants one now can overhear refreshing curiosity about the reliability of natural family planning (NFP) and the range of documented medical side effects from contraceptive practice. Predictably, the zero profit margin for NFP, which is not to be confused with the rhythm method, inhibits any information campaign by pharmaceutical companies.

55. On January 22, 1973, in *Roe v. Wade* (1973), the Supreme Court legalized abortion, and the companion *Doe v. Bolton* case extended this license into the ninth month. The Court opined that they could not "speculate" as to the instant when unique genetic life is distinct from the mother: "We need not resolve the difficult question when life begins when those trained in the respective disciplines of medicine, philosophy, and theology are unable to arrive at any consensus. The judiciary at this point in the development of man's knowledge, is not in a position to speculate as to the answer." Snuggling inside this halfway house definition of when human life begins, it was a cinch under positivist law for the court to gerrymander recognition of the human "person."

56. The "idealist" Immanuel Kant teaches us to think as if God does not exist. Other German philosophers are also involved, and the French, especially René Descartes in his use of doubt as the first premise — his famous "I think, therefore I am." In contrast, the Thomistic approach to truth is to not subordinate the *existence* of real things to our imagination and the rationalism of any particular era. This "realist" approach knows the difference between procedural correctness and a higher law. Even public debate between conflicting ideas is banned now in parts of the university culture as insensitive. Today one can stroll down university hallways and hear energetic assertions from students: "Society is *ideas* and to attack the idea is to attack the person." (One would think that the Nazi Holocaust and the current abortion holocaust would have taught us that it is unchallenged ideas that endanger the person.) Brought before the prefect of Rome on his way to martyrdom, Justin the Martyr was asked, "Do you have an *idea* [emphasis added] that you will go up to heaven?" And he responded, "It is not an idea that I have; it is something I know well and hold to be most certain" (from "Act of the Martyrdom of St. Justin," *Liturgy of the Hours,* vol. 3 [New York: Catholic Book Publishing, 1975], 1448).

57. G. K. Chesterton, *Orthodoxy* (Garden City, NY: Doubleday-Image, 1959), 20.

58. John Paul II contrasts the culture of death and the culture of life. And, not entirely unrelated, he speaks of the sexual scandal within the Church itself. He teaches that everyone " . . . must know that bishops and priests are totally committed to the fullness of Catholic truth on matters of sexual morality, a truth as essential to the renewal of the priesthood and the episcopate as it is to the renewal of marriage and family life" (John Paul II to the United States cardinals on April 22, 2002, cited in George Weigel, *The Courage to be Catholic: Crisis, Reform and the Future of the Church* [New York: Basic Books, 2002], 140).

59. Kahlil Gibran, *The Prophet* (New York: Alfred A. Knopf, 1987), 15.

60. Four out of every five women seeking an abortion are unmarried.

61. Gibran, *The Prophet*, 17.

62. Visiting our group was the founding volunteer of the Helpers, Msgr. Philip J. Reilly (Monastery of the Precious Blood, 5300 Fort Hamilton Parkway, Brooklyn, NY 11219). Reilly reports that he was in Manhattan and near "Ground Zero" on September 11, 2001. He also reports that when that part of the city was thrown into total darkness, one battery-lighted business continued without interruption. It was the nearby abortion clinic.

63. Bernard Nathanson, *The Abortion Papers: Inside the Abortion Mentality* (New York: Frederick Fell Publishers, 1983), 196.

64. This was Galileo's famous phrase at the end of his trial, not part of the official written record but perhaps verbally delivered: *Eppur si muove*. For Galileo, the significant fact was that the senses can deceive (the sun does not rise); for us the significant fact is existence over politics — the wonderful fact that a unique genetic code and person distinct from its parents is already present from the beginning at conception; that a fetus pumps its own blood in twenty-one days; that in four weeks the eye, ear, and respiratory system begin to form; that in forty-two days brain waves are recorded, the skeleton is complete, and reflexes are present; and that in eight weeks all body systems are present. The universe of the genome is no less real than that of solar systems and galaxies. (The genome is the forty-six chromosomes of the fertilized egg, a design of sixty thousand genes and over three billion base pairs of genetic code.)

65. The purveyors must feel that they are doing the Christian thing in marketing and offering this procedure, but besides the formaldehyde and modern currency, is there any difference, really, between this dainty collection and a scalp pole or shrunken heads not long ago in New Guinea?

66. The Marian apparition occurred on December 9, 1531, and involved the young Juan Diego (canonized as a saint in 2003). History tells us that tens of thousands were offered each year, men, women, and children (compared to the million plus each year in the United States

alone). Yet in the five-year period following the vision, already eight million had converted and presented themselves for baptism.

67. "The natural law always buries its undertakers" (attributed to Etienne Gilson by Heinrich A. Rommen, *The Natural Law: A Study in Legal and Social History and Philosophy* [Indianapolis: Liberty Fund, 1998], 237).

68. John Paul II, *The Gospel of Life* (*Evangelium Vitae*) (New York: Times Books, 1995), no. 73.

69. Blessed Elizabeth of the Trinity says it this way: "Our souls in his soul, and our eyes in his," cited in *Magnificat* (Buffalo, NY), January 2005, 129.

Three: In Good Times and in Bad

1. Informed of the sacking of Rome in 410, Augustine speaks to the makers of cities: "This is grievous news, but let us remember if it's happened, then God has willed it; that men build cities and men destroy cities, that there's also the City of God and *that's where we belong*." Then in *The City of God,* his masterpiece for the ages written between 413 and 426 AD, Augustine distinguishes two mystical cities formed around two different loves — one in which the love of God truly unites all men, and the other which is grounded in love of only the world.

2. Fr. Ted Sullivan preceded Fr. Jim at St. Mark's. Sullivan was the sole pastor for an unusual thirty-four years and was a bedrock priest chipped from the Rock of Peter. He did not mind facing into the storm that seemed to hijack parts of the Second Vatican Council (1962–65). Seemingly alone at times, Sullivan once said he was not sure that anyone would come to his funeral. In May 1988 his quick departure at the age of seventy-seven was marked by a funeral that drew a full house. This included a large majority (105) of his fellow priests from the widespread diocese covering all of western Washington. The entrance procession took over ten minutes, and together they chanted in Latin the songs many had not heard since their seminary days.

3. The first cancer chemotherapies were Cytoxan, methotrexate, and FU-5.

4. Blessed Henry Suso (died 1366) is cited in *Magnificat* (Spencerville, MD), November 11, 2001; emphasis added.

5. And what are the fruits and gifts of the Holy Spirit to which Kristi yielded day by day? Her friends found in her joy, peace, patience, kindness, generosity, faithfulness, gentleness, self-control, and perseverance.

6. From a notebook "On Prayer" by Origen, priest, in *Liturgy of the Hours,* 4 (New York: Catholic Book Publishing, 1975), 576; emphasis added.

7. A sign of the times, this excellent physician a few years later became one of the many to discontinue his practice due to the prohibitive cost of medical malpractice insurance.

8. Still, it is also true that God speaks to each of us by all of the little happenings of each day. Jean Pierre de Caussade preaches the "sacrament of the moment" (Caussade, *Abandonment to Divine Providence,* trans. John Beevers [New York: Doubleday, 1975]). My Kristi was sometimes too eager not to displease others and to be sweet. This disposition contrasted with my own, which too often was one of blustery indifference. Every marriage finds its rub point that needs some work, and I think this was ours, and Kristi continues to help me with it.

9. See Josef Pieper, *Fortitude and Temperance* (New York: Pantheon, 1954), 32. Some young men might be encouraged that meekness is the *readiness* to accept a cross, but it is not the passiveness as one often hears. Very much the opposite, coming from eternity it is most often quite out of step with the times, any times.

10. *Illustrated London News,* June 12, 1909, cited by Dale Alquist, ed., *Collected Works,* vols. 28–35 (San Francisco: Ignatius Press, forthcoming).

11. John Paul II, *Crossing the Threshold of Hope* (New York: Alfred A. Knopf, 1994), 68.

12. Taxol and carboplatinum.

13. Busulfan, melphalan, and thiotepa.

14. Epinephrine and then hydrocortisone.

15. Outpatient treatment for the blood infection continued for the standard month, and this was successful. The medication was amphotericin B combined with fluconozol. I asked if this could be administered without preservatives, which were another problem for us, and this was done. Instead we used Tylenol and hydrocortisone. The initial treatments were ramped up from an experimental 1 percent dose as another caution against possible allergy.

16. Our refusal of Benadryl, for example, became so routine as to be monotonous.

17. Continuous infusion of medication when combined with an obstructed catheter can result in recycling and cumulative overdose. In retrospect I realize we might have been dealing with this once or twice rather than more threatening allergies.

18. *Philokalia,* trans. G. E. H. Palmer, Philip Sherrard, Kallistos Ware (London: Faber and Faber, 1987).

19. Linda Kohn, Janet Corrigan, Molla Donaldson, eds., *To Err Is Human: Building a Safer Health System* (Washington, DC: National Academy Press, 2000).

20. Kristi was spared probably more than once. On two overly routine occasions the priceless stem cell extraction from donor Kerry was nearly mixed with that of another donor with Kristi's uncommon surname, Beaulieu. A mislabeled transplant also would have been fatal to the unknown patient.

21. Was this the placebo effect only? In 2001, five years after the transplant and this episode with infused nutrients, Kristi and I visited a new kind of specialist, a neurologist. We were referred to him to diagnose the spreading numbness in Kristi's right arm. My eyes wandered to a stack of medical journals on the desk before me. The top issue featured an article for the first time documenting the risk to some patients from even extremely tiny amounts of plastic leaching into solution inside infusion bags.

22. In a similar way in 1988 a friend of a family member in California found himself giving directions to the beach. The inquirer was a patient in a motorized wheel chair. An afternoon friendship unfolded. The native spoke his admiration for sharing the time with such a distinguished scientist from Cambridge. The reply came through a voice synthesizer, "Do not believe everything they tell you." Theologically, the speaker, Steven Hawking, has been classified by some media clairvoyants as a Deist; he is also a most respected member of the Pontifical Academy of Sciences. S. W. Hawking writes in *A Brief History of Time* (New York: Bantam Books 1988): "I've always wanted to know why the universe exists at all, and what was there before the beginning." In one form or another, this deepest human question resurfaces throughout the moment we call history. Fifteen hundred years earlier, St. Augustine also wrote: "My mind is on fire to understand this most intricate riddle.... In what space, then, do we measure passing time?" And preceding, we find this philosophical parallel to relativity theory: "The fact is that the world was made simultaneously with time..." (*Confessions*, bk. 11, chaps. 6, 22).

23. After Kristi's death, on the morning of July 21, 2002 (the day before my fifty-eighth birthday), a dream reminded me of Kristi's worst descent into medication hell. Kristi had asked in all seriousness, "Am I in hell?"

My dream showed me the *opposite* of love, as seen from within. I will try here to describe this intuition. The backwardness was the sense of being fully appropriated by an outsider, so totally that there was no particle of self from which to at least separately view the abuse and abyss as an intruder that is still other than one's self. In the total opposite of love, the self — as a being — is reduced from within by a foreigner, totally dissolved and turned inside out, into a total deformity. There is no form at all. Not solitary confinement, but foreign ownership through and through. Every relationship with others by which a person normally becomes a person is "backwards" from this. A surrounding darkness, but then a darkness even within the subject. There is no sur-viving viewer, only self-aware annihilation. It is not to have nothing, but it is to be this nothing, totally depersonalized. From the Creed we hear "He descended into hell" — in His eyes the fire of everlasting un-being for what-might-have-been. All of this in free fall forever, be-cause chosen by our innermost free will which is our very selves. Not necessarily that we choose evil, but that we choose our habitual self-sufficiency, that is, our own cramped definition and "knowledge of good and evil."

Kristi had said, *"everything* is backwards." In my journal I summarized the dream as one of "eternal and self-inflicted rape of the soul, *and* of the Soul within the soul." Is this mortal sin and is this hell? And is there a medical equivalent? Cancer, too, replaces and assumes the shape of the organ it attacks. In some way, had Kristi seen the cancer from the inside? Is hell the appropriation by cancer everlasting? "If the light that is in you is darkness, how deep will that darkness be" (Matt. 6:23).

24. Klonopin was the mentioned drug.

25. "Don't try to be beautiful by braiding your hair.... Instead, let your beauty be that of the person hidden in your heart, the imperishable beauty of a gentle and quiet spirit, which is precious in the sight of God" (1 Pet. 3:3–4)

26. At the time of this writing, Hercepton is reported as showing promise.

27. Institute of Medicine, *A New Health System for the 21st Century: Closing the Quality Chasm* (Washington DC: National Academy Press, 2001), 48–51. Absorbed with the near impossibility of delivering more with less, the study begins chapter 9 ("Preparing the *Workforce*") with the somewhat promising clarification: "Health care is not just another service industry. Its fundamental nature is characterized by people tak-ing care of other people.... The people who *deliver care* are the health *system's* most important *resource*" (207, emphasis added).

28. These medications, respectively, were intravenous Tamoxifen, Arimidex, and pamidronate.

29. Because of this radical surgery, Kristi's heart would be physically unprotected. Any sharp bump or blow could easily bring with it the likelihood of traumatic cardiac injury and quite possibly death. To protect against this, Kristi wore a baseball vest at first to protect against the steering column when driving and then was fitted with a molded quarter-inch thick fiberglass torso. Kristi soon declined to suit up and ignored the possible risk to herself while standing vigil on street corners in front of clinics. "Your only job," I instructed son Mark (in the Marine Corps Reserve), "is to stand between your mother and any hecklers who might protest the prayer group."

30. Brant Pelphrey, *Love Was His Meaning: The Theology and Mysticism of Julian of Norwich* (Salzburg: University of Salzburg, 1982). I believe that I had been led to this book. On one of my regular noon walks along the Seattle waterfront, a nudge led me to a particular used bookstore. On finding the book on Julian of Norwich, I was unable to find the price, but from a comparable volume I knew that this was beyond my price range. I decided that a completely unrealistic ten dollars would be my limit, a bare fraction of the sure value. The owner inspected the volume carefully, and also not finding the price, he offered it to me for exactly ten dollars.

31. Ibid., 4.

32. An anchoress lived a reclusive and meditative life but was also available to give counsel to visitors.

33. Her volume is available to us as her *Revelations,* or *Showings,* written in the same period as the works of Langland and Chaucer.

34. See chapter 1.

35. John Paul II, *Salvifici Doloris* (*On the Christian Meaning of Human Suffering*), 1984. Kristi noticed and recommended these thoughts to others, even in the early eighties at the beginning of her special path.

36. Benedict J. Groeschel, ed., *Augustine: Major Writings* (New York: Crossroad, 1999), 78; emphasis added.

Four: Interlude: A Return to France

1. Rationalists work mathematically toward a curvature of space and time with a different meaning. They seek a single equation showing that "space and time may form a closed surface without boundary.... What place, then, for a creator?" (Stephen Hawking, *The Theory of Everything: The Origin and Fate of the Universe* [Cambridge, MA: New Millennium Press, 2003], 126). Armed with this discovery we shall be able to find why the universe exists. This, Hawking says, would be "the ultimate triumph of human reason." And then: "...we would know the mind of God" (167). And, the divine participation in human suffering becomes a myth.

But God is more than the exiled watchmaker of the universe, and more than mind (rather, the Word made flesh, John 1:14). Even the mathematically closed surface is but a twinkling in His eye. And each new child, without exception, is also a new creation and a new universe, fully in His image and still *gifted* with an everlasting destiny to be face to face with the intimacy of the Beatific Vision. To us it is reported by Peter: "...do not be ignorant of this one thing, that *one day with the Lord is as a thousand years* and a thousand years as one day" (2 Pet. 3:8).

2. Brant Pelphrey, *Love Was His Meaning: The Theology and Mysticism of Julian of Norwich* (Salzburg: University of Salzburg, 1982), 112. Less mystical, G. K. Chesterton had this to say about the smallness of apparent bigness: "I was frightfully fond of the universe and wanted to address it by a diminutive. I often did so; and it never seemed to mind." And, "The cosmos went on forever, but not in its wildest constellation could there be anything really interesting, for instance, such as forgiveness or free will" (G. K. Chesterton, *Orthodoxy* [New York: Image, 1959], 62). Theorists of the Big Bang conclude that the entire universe, 100 billion solar systems, began in a dense cluster no larger than a single proton. Protons are found in the nucleus of an atom.

3. Lustiger's decision to convert was influenced by the actions of the wartime Pope Pius XII on behalf of the Jews.

4. See George Weigel, *Witness to Hope: The Biography of Pope John Paul II* (New York: Cliff Street Books, 1999). Lustiger's insight, in its varied forms, applies far beyond France, and even to the streets of Seattle. We can see it in the silent sidewalk sermons for a culture of life — the ongoing vigil by small groups standing on the street corners opposite our neighborhood aborturaries.

5. One favorite reading was Stanley Loomis's *Paris in the Terror* (New York: J. B. Lippincott, 1964).

6. See chapter 2.

7. Ruth Cranston, *The Miracle of Lourdes* (New York: Morehouse-Gorham, 1948), 45. Even at Lourdes a distinction is made between officially recognized events and a wider fringe of additional stories and cults that are simply tolerated or rejected. Sandra L. Zimdars-Swartz offers a phenomenological approach to Marian apparitions (including Lourdes, 57–67) that is neither apologetic nor antagonistic in *Encountering Mary: From La Salette to Medjugorje* (Princeton, NJ: Princeton University Press, 1991).

8. Like all heresies, Albigensianism was false because it was a distortion of a central truth. How wonderful to at least glimpse that the spiritual within *is* the person. And that what we see is also the person, but somewhat like a veil to this inwardness — this personal image of the "divine intimacy." This rich term is borrowed from a four-volume work so titled, by Father Gabriel of St. Mary Magdalen, *The Divine Intimacy* (San Francisco: Ignatius Press, 1987).

9. John Paul II, *The Theology of the Body* (Boston: Pauline Books, 1997), 378–80. In part, he writes: "The 'language of the body,' as in uninterrupted continuity of liturgy and language, is expressed not only as the attraction and mutual pleasure of the Song of Songs, but also as a profound experience of the *sacrum* (the holy). . . . This mystery sinks its roots precisely in the beginning, that is, in the mystery of the creation of

man, male and female, in the image of God, called from the beginning to be the visible sign of God's creative love."

10. A surprise to many, the Church finds only embryonic stem cell programs to be immoral. Stem cell research using other sources is supported (adult stem cells, umbilical cord stem cells, and embryonic germ cells).

11. The early family name in Quebec was spelled with "de" in front (de Beaulieu) indicating they were from a place by this name. And the remainder of the name, my father told me, had some reference to water (as very probably in sur Dordogne). Other details of this site also fit the verbal account I had heard as a boy. The point of debarkation is remembered by the family as Bordeaux, downstream.

12. After the heresy at Albi became a political issue as well by the refusal to take oaths of allegiance, thereby threatening the particular political order of the time, Hugh of Castlenau emerged as one of the military leaders against the Albigensians.

13. The reader met the most recent, my Uncle Otto, in chapter 2.

14. Bk. 3, chap. 14.

15. I recalled how months before entering the navy in 1967, I met another special person from the jungles of Southeast Asia. This was a tiny nurse of not more than ninety pounds. She too had spent several years in the jungle eluding capture with U.S. Navy doctor Tom Dooley. When I met her in a neighbor's home, she was returning to the United States to be treated for cancer of the jaw. For a long time this remained the closest that I came to cancer.

16. This proclamation is the absolute difference between the restricted and humanist *worldview* symbolized by the seven-sided temple we found in the forests of Puget Sound (chapter 2), and the Christian *vista toward eternity* symbolized, for example, in the eight-sided bell tower at St. Pierre in Beaulieu sur Dordogne.

17. *The Story of a Soul: The Autobiography of St. Therese of Lisieux* (New York: Doubleday Image Book, 1957), 159.

Five: Into His Hands

1. Gemcitabine.

2. This hopeful trend was only apparent. We were to learn with Dr. Lee that the MRI imagery would display a slightly different cross-section on each read. With small, irregular, or even spherical tumors the slight difference in size from one test to the next can be deceptive.

3. Prednisone.

4. Kristi's special saint, Therese of Lisieux, said in her own illness, "I am not dying, I am entering into life" (quoted by Leonie Caldecott, "Second Spring," *Catholic World Report* [San Francisco: Ignatius Press, October 1997]).

5. We had hoped that Mark could schedule some of Dr. Scott Hahn's classes. This was not to be, but Kristi prayed on it. A few weeks later Mark called to say that his senior year theology instructor was unable to cover his class and that Dr. Hahn had agreed to step in for the full year.

6. One specialist tried a relatively experimental test called a PET scan, positron emission tomography.

7. Xeloda and navelbine.

8. "Extraordinary" is to be understood as a moral term more than a technical one. The moral boundary of means burdensome, dangerous, and disproportionate to the expected outcome. This limit can be reached prior to the use of the most advanced forms of technology.

9. John Paul II, *Ecclesia de Eucharistia* (*On the Eucharist in Its Relationship to the Church*, April 17, 2003), no. 3: "The eschatological tension kindled by the Eucharist *expresses and reinforces our communion with the Church in heaven.* This is an aspect of the Eucharist which merits greater attention: in celebrating the sacrifice of the Lamb, we are united to the heavenly 'liturgy' and become part of that great multitude which cries out: 'Salvation belongs to our God who sits upon the throne, and to the Lamb!' (Rev. 7:10). The Eucharist is truly a glimpse of heaven appearing on earth" (no. 19; emphasis in the original).

10. The hospice program is operated by the Sisters of Providence and is not part of the Providence Hospital in Seattle. After the hospital was consolidated in 2002 with the nonreligious Swedish Medical Center, the independent hospice continued.

11. In England the publicity and use of hospice is much higher than in the United States (65 percent rather than 15 percent), partly because the patient is not required to forego curative treatment in order to qualify, as is the case with Medicare and most health insurance in our country (Wesley J. Smith, *Culture of Death* [San Francisco: Encounter Books, 2000], 220). After Smith's book, some hospice programs in the United States have added a "transition" program that enables patients to enter hospice without giving up curative treatment.

12. The protective moral principle is summarized: "Discontinuing medical procedures that are burdensome, dangerous, extraordinary, or disproportionate to the expected outcome can be legitimate; it is the re-fusal of 'overzealous' treatment. Here one does not will to cause death; one's inability to impede it is merely accepted. The decisions should be made by the patient.... Even if death is thought imminent, the ordi-nary care owed a sick person cannot be legitimately interrupted. The use of painkillers to alleviate the sufferings of the dying, even at the risk of shortening their days, can be morally in conformity with human dignity if death is not willed as either an end or a means, but only foreseen and tolerated as inevitable" (*Catechism of the Catholic Church* [San Francisco: Ignatius Press, 1994], no. 2279). Additionally, for co-matose patients nourishment and hydration through feeding tubes are normal steps of nutrition and are not classified as possibly problematic "medical" procedures (John Paul II, March 20, 2004).

13. In late 1991 our pastor asked Kristi to attend a conference in the Seattle area opposing a euthanasia initiative in Washington State. Kristi was not political and was relieved when I offered to go in her place. Attending in person, Bishop Thomas Murphy summarized the dangerous trend: "I fear in the depth of my being that the value of life will disappear from our society." He said this from the perspective of

having regularly attended his mother during her final three painful and bedridden years. Invited to a small dinner with us at the parish rectory a few months before the conference, Bishop Murphy heard of Kristi's cancer treatments and confided that he, too, had had cancer. Fifteen years earlier he had been cured of inoperable spinal cancer without medical explanation and possibly through the special healing prayers that were offered.

14. Levorphanol is a generic substitute for Levo-Dromoran, which had been developed decades earlier. We did not know whether this was still available on the market.

15. During hospice we even tried acupuncture, that is, no chemicals at all. This treatment may have done some marginal good in our case, but after two or three visits Kristi decided not to continue.

16. In 1986 Steckler had sent us an inscribed copy of his biography of an early bishop of the Northwest. "For our friendship over the years. May this reading inspire you to holiness" (Gerard Steckler, S.J., *Charles John Seghers, Priest and Bishop in the Pacific Northwest 1839–1886: A Biography* [Fairfield, WA: Ye Galleon Press, 1986]).

17. The report was that one of the ingredients was no longer available, but one might also wonder whether this product had been displaced by more expensive products, or simply more effective alternatives only for the more typical patients and the much larger market segment.

18. Kristi and I almost always knew each other's whereabouts. One troublesome exception I can recall was on a Sunday shortly after Kristi's first operation in 1990. I thought about car trouble or something worse and was a bit distressed. When she returned, I found she simply had stopped at the Blessed Sacrament kitchen to help serve meals for a couple of hours. Partly in memory of Kristi and partly to find a desperately needed routine, I now work at the kitchen almost every Sunday and find this a welcome part of my new life alone.

19. Listed in order, Neurontin, Ambien, levorphanol, and Reglan.

20. St. Maria Faustina Kowalska (1905–38), beatified in 1993 and canonized on April 30, 2000, was blessed with direct words from Christ on His message of Divine Mercy: "The greater the sinner, the greater the right he has to My mercy." His messages are recorded in her diary of over six hundred pages, *Divine Mercy in My Soul* (Stockbridge, MA: Marians of the Immaculate Conception, 2002), completed only in obedience to her spiritual advisor.

21. In his reflection *The Original Unity of Man and Woman* (November 7, 1979) John Paul II says this of Adam's sleep at the "beginning" (Gen. 2:21): "The analogy of sleep indicates here not so much a passing from consciousness to subconsciousness, as a specific return to non-being (sleep contains an element of annihilation of man's conscious existence), that is, to the moment preceding creation, in order that, through God's creative initiative, solitary 'man' may emerge from it again in his *double unity as male and female*." (*The Theology of the Body* (Boston: Pauline Books, 1997), 44; emphasis added.).

22. *Novo Millennio Ineunte* (Cambridge MA: New Millennium, January 6, 2001), no. 47; emphasis added.

23. G. E. H. Palmer, Philip Sherrard, and Kallistos Ware, eds. and trans., *The Philokalia*, vol. 2 (London: Faber and Faber, 1984), 361; emphasis added.

24. *Magnificat* (Spencerville, MD), May 2001.

25. Kristi was attached to each and all of the children. Ranging in age from twenty-seven to six, they are Greg, Paul (Kristi's and my godson), Dan, Matt, Christina, Mark, Jacob, and Rachel. Tragedy struck the family unexpectedly during Kerry's first visit with us at the beginning of hospice in March. Both of Chuck's parents, Ray and Hildegard, were killed instantly not far from their Idaho home in a head-on collision caused by another driver. Chuck (Uhlenkott) visited and consoled the elderly and uninjured driver of the oncoming car.

26. See chapter 2.

27. Georges Bernanos, *Diary of a Country Priest* (New York: Carroll and Graf Publishers, 2002), 166.

28. John Paul II, quoted on *Almost Biography,* produced from his writings and aired on EWTN television. In this selection from 1994, the pope was reflecting on his attempted assassination in St. Peter's Square in 1981.

29. Regarding the permanent rights of families, in 1983 the Vatican issued *Charter of the Rights of the Family,* which is grounded in many existing public documents. With reference to coercive regimes such as China, but also the politicized culture in the West, the Church asserted the right (by moral means) of each married couple for themselves "to decide on the spacing of births and the number of children to be born, taking into full consideration their duties toward themselves, their children already born, the family and society" (Article 3).

30. Stephane-Joseph Piat, *Celine: Sister and Witness to St. Therese of the Child Jesus* (San Francisco: Ignatius Press, 1997).

31. The books on Kristi's shelf include: Sister Aletheia Kane, O.C.D., *Elizabeth of the Trinity — Complete Works,* vols. 1 and 2 (Washington, DC: ICS Publications 1984); and Elisabeth Leseur, *My Spirit Rejoices: The Diary of a Christian Soul in an Age of Unbelief* (Manchester, NH: Sophia Institute Press, 1996). The reading stand also included these on Lourdes and St. Therese: *Some of Bernadette's Sayings* (Nevers: St. Gildard Convent, no date); Patrick Marnham, *Lourdes: A Modern Pilgrimage* (London: Granada Publishing, 1980); John Clark, O.C.D., trans., *Story of a Soul: The Autobiography of St. Therese of Lisieux* (Washington, DC: ICS Publications, 1976); Guy Gaucher, O.C.D., *The Story of a Life: St. Therese of Lisieux* (San Francisco: HarperSanFrancisco, 1987); and Rev. François Jamart, O.C.D., *Complete Spiritual Doctrine of St. Therese of Lisieux* (New York: Alba House, 1961).

Other readings at arm's reach were John De Marchi, I.M.C., *Fatima from the Beginning,* trans. I. M. Kingsbury (Cambridge, MA: Ravengate, 1980); Randall Garrett, *A Gallery of the Saints* (Derby, CT: Monarch Select Book, 1963); Fr. Jean Baptiste Saint-Jure, S.J., and Blessed Claude de la Colombière, S.J., *Trustful Surrender to Divine Providence: The Secret of Peace and Happiness,* trans. Paul Garvin (Rockford, IL: Tan Books,

1983); Kevin J. Wright, *Catholic Shrines of Western Europe: A Pilgrim's Travel Guide* (St. Louis: Liguori, 1997); and Abbe Omer Englebert, *Catherine Labouré and the Modern Apparitions of Our Lady,* trans. Alastair Guinan (New York: P. J. Kenedy and Sons, 1959).

32. Across the street from the clinic is a large parking lot embraced by two "big box" corporate outlets. One might notice the irony here, so symbolic of our times — the corporations are "persons" under the law, enabled in this way to outlive their members. They are even the ben-eficiaries of litigated Fourteenth Amendment protections. Meanwhile, real pre-born children under the same legal system are *not* persons with basic protections. We have contrived a comfort zone of disjointed legal fictions.

33. "Rejoice in the measure that you share in Christ's sufferings.... Happy are you when you are insulted for the sake of Christ, for then God's Spirit in its glory has come to rest on you" (1 Pet. 4:14).

34. See chapter 2.

35. This testimony is also recounted in *Global Family Life News* (Population Research Institute, March–April 2002), 12:2.

36. How much Christ's nuptial promise to His spouse the Church is echoed in Kristi's sacramental promise — equally nuptial — to me: "I am with you all days, even unto the consummation of the world" (Matt. 28:20).

37. Mother Teresa, *Loving God — Heart of Joy* (Edina, MN: Daily Blessings Pentagon Towers, 1996).

38. "We believe in the communion of all the faithful of Christ, those who are pilgrims on earth, the dead who are attaining their purification, and the blessed in Heaven, all together forming one Church; and we believe that in this communion the merciful love of God and His Saints is ever listening to our prayers, as Jesus told us: Ask and you will receive" (Pope Paul VI, *Credo of the People of God,* June 30, 1968). It probably was not by accident that this meditation was released only one month before the controverted encyclical *Humanae Vitae* (*On Human Life*).

39. In addition to caring for her family, Kerry was also the founder and for many years the very active and widely respected (on both sides of the issues) president of Idaho Right to Life.

40. "For those who have surrendered themselves completely to God, all they are and do has power. Their lives are sermons. They are apostles. God gives a special force to all they say and do, *even to their silence, their tranquility and their detachment,* which, quite unknown to them, profoundly influences other people" (Jean Pierre de Caussade, *Abandonment to Divine Providence* [New York: Image Doubleday, 1975], 60; emphasis added).

41. During her final ordeal Therese remarked, "If I had not faith, I would have taken my life without hesitation" (quoted in Guy Gaucher, O.C.D., *The Story of a Life* [New York: HarperCollins, 1987], 194).

42. *Sunday Sermons of the Great Fathers,* 4, ed. M. F. Toal, D.D. (Chicago: Regnery, 1964), 318.

43. See chapter 1.

44. *Some of Bernadette's Sayings* (Nevers: St. Gildard Convent, no date), n. 155.

45. After nearly five centuries we now have a joint agreement on grace, prepared over recent decades by Catholics and Lutherans. And yet, the riddle is not simple. It does not fit in the mind, and much hangs on the details. To this recent *Declaration on Justification* is appended the Church's clarifying "annex" clearly reaffirming the need for our active response, not once only as in being born again, but concretely in the specifics of our daily and more sacramental lives.

46. See chapter 4.

47. The transition from possible perfectionism to holiness is not a simple matter. Shortly after our marriage, as we were leaving a hardware store, I noticed a nail on the floor that was exactly right to help me hang a picture. Should I help myself by tidying up the floor? For Kristi it was an important matter that I not stoop to this level.

Now, thirty years later and in the new world of sweatshop globalization, we have the capability to bar code such commodities to help buyers decide whether to buy or not to buy. And consumer choice of medical "commodities" might require us in our "scruples" to distinguish between organ transplants derived from embryonic stem cells (involving both immoral harvesting and disposal) or instead from morally unobjectionable umbilical or adult stem cells. Even now we hear some in the medical profession asserting that "they" won't care, once all of this is available. "They made me do it . . . " is the original sin identified in Genesis 3:12.

48. And to be forgiven as we forgive . . . what does this really mean? Certainly more than superficial reciprocity. The ability to forgive truly depends *finally* upon the depth of one's own self acceptance. With fully healed acceptance at our very center, then we are able to accept *the other* in such a way that, as a sort of byproduct, his injury toward us is indirectly erased. The soul regards the soul of the other, *instead of* the injury: "Forgive us our trespasses as we forgive *those* who trespass against us." Penance is not morbidity, nor even a ritualistic way of moving on. It has something to do with memory, and our closed memory of anything but Him. Of the value of confession as a healing of memory, Francis of Paola give us this: "Memory of evil is an injustice . . . a sentinel who protects sins, . . . alienation of love, a nail that pierces the soul, wickedness that never sleeps, . . . a daily death" (cited by Cardinal Joseph Ratzinger in *Principles of Catholic Theology: Building Stones for a Fundamental Theology* [San Francisco: Ignatius Press, 1982], 212). "I have brushed away your offenses like a cloud, your sins like a mist; return to me, I have redeemed you" (Isa. 44:-22).

49. The San Damiano Cross (Franciscan) dates from twelfth-century Italy and is based on earlier icon crosses from the Eastern Church. It is called an icon cross because it is bordered by images of witnesses and others whose devotion is related to the crucifixion.

50. *Magnificat* (Spencerville, MD), November 1, 2002.

51. How peculiar, I thought, as my attention was drawn out the window to the suspended bird feeder in the back yard. As the family gathered within, three agitated crows dropped down and attacked the

feeder, scattering the small birds. We had never seen this weird violence here before, and I have not seen it since. It was almost as if evil had failed to enter our room, something like the spirits driven by Christ from a troubled soul into two thousand swine before they rushed headlong into the lake to be drowned (Luke 8:26–33).

Six: . . . A Lonely Business

1. The Providence Hospice of Seattle, which helped us so much, is operated by the same Sisters of Providence.

2. Kristi's grounding and faith depart essentially on this point from what we read in the Anglican C. S. Lewis, *A Grief Observed* (New York: Bantam, 1976). In his grieving the loss of his spouse, Lewis writes, "To-morrow morning a priest will give me a little, round, thin, cold, tasteless wafer. Is it a disadvantage — is it not in some ways an advantage — that it can't pretend the least *resemblance* to that which it unites me? I need Christ, not something that resembles Him. I want H., not something that is like her" (75–76).

With the Catholic understanding of the Real Presence in the Eucharist given through the hands of an unbroken chain of priestly ordination, this symbol also *is* that which it symbolizes. It is the Christ of Lewis's desire. This truly present Sacred Heart of Christ also gathers to Himself and includes the entire Communion of Saints, past and present. The Communion of Saints, too, is real — not an idea or a mere resemblance.

3. This expression can sound pretentious, but it is meekness. In a world deeper than our efforts to control, there are victim souls, those who really do voluntarily offer themselves — beyond their deeds — for the benefit and even the salvation of others. Kristi was surely one of these. Those who study this path of vicarious suffering refer to St. Paul in Colossians 1:24 and 2 Corinthians 4:12.

4. Even a year or more earlier, Fr. Kemp had mentioned that when he doubted the worth or impact of his homilies, he could always search

into the rows and there find Kristi at her usual place near the center, looking back with "such a glow" that he was always reassured.

5. This remark does not constitute a pronouncement by the Church. Kemp simply invites individual prayer.

6. I see the hand of Kristi's father in the triumph of his daughter. Around the family table on the Camas Prairie, he once read the lines quoted of Leon Bloy, the godfather of the convert and Thomist scholar Jacques Maritain: "There is only one sadness; it is not to be a saint." Maritain ventures a definition of a saint, the self-donation all should try to become: "Let us try, I would say, to imagine what takes place in the soul of a saint at the crucial moment when he makes the first irrevocable decision. . . . This act has to do with a fact, an existential fact: things as they are, are intolerable. In the reality of existence the world is infested with lying, injustice, wickedness, distress and misery; creation has been corrupted by sin to such an extent that in the very marrow of his soul the saint refuses to accept it as it is. . . . The only thing he has immediately at hand to oppose [evil] totally, and this intoxicates the saint with liberty, exultation, and love, is to give everything, to abandon everything, the sweetness of the world, and what is good, and what is better, and what is delectable and permitted, and more than anything, himself, in order to be free to be with God. To do this is to be totally stripped and given over in order to seize the power of the cross; it is to die for those he loves" (*The Peasant of the Garonne: An Old Layman Questions Himself about the Present Times* [New York: Macmillan, 1969], 246).

7. Prior to the Second Vatican Council the Church frowned on cremation, but the meaning associated with cremation is no longer one of assumed contempt for the spiritual and for the resurrection. See the *Code of Canon Law,* c. 1176, s.3.

8. See chapter 3.

9. Absent from these pages is any reference to grief recovery groups. This kind of shared conversation protects us from the caverns of self-doubt and reproach. I distrusted the misfit between techniques for coping — different than conversation — and my need to understand

in the depths of my own soul that Kristi's loss is part of a boundless and gentle Truth that is absolutely certain. From Kristi's Paris diary for 1972–73 there was this clue for me, however, which I had overlooked: "A precious thing...friendship." Beneath our feared solitude, we *actually* confer this gentleness and certainty upon each other, and it is in these gestures of genuine respect that we image the Father who sustains us. Regarding recovery groups, I simply missed the boat.

10. Romano Guardini, *The End of the Modern World* (Chicago: Logos, 1968), 132. See chapter 1.

11. Commentary on Luke 24:29–31 in Romano Guardini, *The Lord* (Chicago: Regnery, 1954), 420.

12. Lewis, *A Grief Observed*, 1, 55.

13. Ibid, 70, and Sheldon Vanauken, *A Severe Mercy*, epilogue (San Francisco: Harper & Row, 1980), 220–33. The term "second death" is biblical and appears in the book of Revelation.

14. "And, more than once, that impression which I can't describe except by saying that it's like the sound of a chuckle in the darkness. The sense that some shattering and disarming simplicity is the real answer" (Lewis, *A Grief Observed*, 83).

15. Stratford Caldecott and John Saward, "Second Spring: The Image of the Father," *Catholic World Report* (San Francisco: Ignatius Press, March 1994), 36.

16. Second Vatican Council, *Lumen Gentium* (Dogmatic Constitution on the Church), no. 51; emphasis added. More than a year passed after Kristi's death before I found this verification by the full Church of my words to Kristi. The term "them" refers to "those who shared in our humanity and yet were transformed into especially successful images of Christ." My original inspiration to point Kristi toward the saints came as a gift and in an instant. I recalled a reading from Jacques Maritain from my late teens. I have found the words: "An act of true goodness, the least act of goodness, is indeed the best proof of the existence of God. But our intellect is too busy cataloguing notions to see it. Therefore, we believe it on the testimony of those on whom true goodness shines in

a way that astonishes us" (*Approaches to God* [New York: Harper and Brothers, 1954], 107).

17. Some Scripture scholars might ask themselves what they would offer to a dying spouse, as in academic circles they discount certitudes handed down. "We must acknowledge that the books of Scripture firmly, faithfully and without error, teach the truth which God, for the sake of our salvation, wishes to see confided to the sacred Scriptures" (*Dei Verbum* [The Word of God], no. 11; cited in George Kelly, "A Pastor's Critique of the Critics," *The New Biblical Theorist* [Ann Arbor, MI: Servant Books, 1983], 154). Indeed, looking up from their lists of professional publications for each other, what do they offer to the dispersing flock of the Church, which is their spouse?

18. Therese of Jesus, cited in Otger Steggink, "The Doctorate of Experience," in *Carmelite Studies*, 4, Edith Stein Symposium on Teresian Culture, ed. John Sullivan (Washington, DC: ICS Publications, 1987), 285. Applicable equally to marriage and families ("domestic churches") after the resurrection, and to the nuptial bond between Christ and his Church, are these words on marriage: "[That] nuptial meaning of being a body will be realized, therefore, as a meaning that is *perfectly* personal and communitarian at the same time" (John Paul II, *The Theology of the Body* [Boston: Pauline Books, 1997], 248).

19. "Beloved, we are God's children now, what we shall be has not yet been revealed. We do know that when it is revealed we shall be like him, for we shall see him as he is" (1 John 3:1–2). " . . . life within God is not eternally the same, in a sense which would imply a kind of everlasting boredom. Rather, God's Trinitarian life is a 'liveliness' characterized by the always new and by 'surprise': in the words of Speyr, Trinitarian life is a communion of surprise (in the sense of an infinite ever-flowing fulfillment . . .)" (David L. Schindler, *Heart of the World, Center of the Church* [Grand Rapids, MI: William B. Eerdmans, 1996], 226).

20. Sermon 171, *Liturgy of the Hours*, 1976, 1823.

21. Antoine de Saint-Exupéry, *Wisdom of the Sands* (Chicago: University of Chicago Press, 1979), chap. 59. I discovered this volume

during my years at the University of Washington, and rediscovered and bought a used copy during our twenty-fourth wedding anniversary in Victoria, B.C., in late 1998. "He found them in a wilderness, a wasteland of howling desert; He shielded them and cared for them, guarding them as the apple of his eye" (Deut. 32:10).

22. By coincidence, the same affliction that was cured miraculously at Lourdes in the case often mentioned by Kristi's father, that of Marie Bailly and Dr. Alexis Carrel.

23. Lewis, *A Grief Observed*, 20.

24. *Confessions*, bk. 10, chap. 6:8–10; emphasis added.

25. Religious mystics such as St. Teresa of Ávila (sixteenth century) remind us that the spatial and temporal imaginations (physical) can get in the way of spiritual reality. The notion that death involves a separation from the one lost or from the full Communion of Saints, is an imposition of our imagination. *The "veil" of separation is imaginary.* Thus, in matters of both reason and faith, the human person is invited to set aside his own cramped way of perceiving. In tune with the thinking of Hans Urs Von Balthasar (*A Theological Aesthetic* [San Francisco: Ignatius Press, 1978]), we are to do this to the extent that the spatial and temporal imagination both reveals *and* conceals the reality and knowledge of creation — our presence one to another and to the Other.

26. Sermon of St. Augustine (for Ascension Sunday), *Liturgy of the Hours*, vol. 3 (New York: Catholic Book Publishing, 1975), 920–22.

27. For the Catholic, the Bible is more Church-based than the reverse. All of Scripture finds its center in the incarnation and resurrection as facts, not as products of migratory imagination or even scholarship. Inseparable from Christ is his Real Presence to us, too, from beyond time and through hands consecrated for this purpose by His hands and successive not without the Apostolic laying on of hands from one to another across the centuries.

28. John Walsh, S.J., *The Vision Beatific* (New York: Macmillan, 1926), 42–43. And later: "A great crowd of our loved ones awaits us there, a countless throng of parents, brothers and children longs for us

to join them. Assured though they are of their own salvation, they are still concerned about ours. What joy for them and for us to see one another and embrace! O the delight of that heavenly kingdom where there is no fear of death! O the supreme and endless bliss of everlasting life. . . . My dear brothers, let all our longing be to join them as soon as we may" (St. Cyprian in the *Liturgy of the Hours*, 4 [New York: Catholic Book Publishing, 1975], 603). One purpose of my writing is to clearly include *spouses* in a most special way to the listed throng of "parents, brothers and children."

29. See chapter 1.

30. St. Augustine, Sermon 171, *Liturgy of the Hours*, 1976, 1823.

31. Msgr. Marsollier, in *The Life of St. Francis of Sales: Bishop and Prince of Geneva*, vol. 2 (London: translated and printed in English for Thomas Meighan, in Drury-Lane, antique: 1737), 260.

32. Hans Urs von Balthasar, *Credo: Meditations on the Apostles' Creed* (San Francisco: Ignatius Press, 1990), 103.

33. The awesome idea of "duet" is not original. John Paul II applies it to the Song of Songs, in *The Theology of the Body* (Boston: Pauline Books, 1997), 369.

34. Mother Teresa, *Loving God — Heart of Joy* (Edina, MN: Daily Blessings Pentagon Towers, 1996).

35. Speaking to repentant mothers who have aborted their sons and daughters, John Paul II offers this: "You will come to understand that nothing is definitively lost and you will also be able to ask forgiveness from your child, who is living in the Lord" (*The Gospel of Life* [1995], no. 99).

36. Was September 11 preventable? As I write, intense debate continues as to why federal security agencies did not or could not talk to each other. Some of it is information overload and compartmentalization not much different from missed connections from time to time in a cancer ward.

37. *Lumen Gentium* (Constitution on the Church), no. 49; emphasis added.

38. Letter of September 17, 1901, in *Elizabeth of the Trinity: The Complete Works,* vol. 2 (Washington, DC: ICS Publication, 1995), 25, 29.

39. Teresa of Avila, cited in *Elizabeth of the Trinity, The Complete Works,* vol. 1 (Washington, DC: ICS Publications, 1984), 152.

40. Jerzy Peterkiewicz, "A Conversation with Man Begins: The Meaning of Things," Karol Wojtyla, *The Place Within: The Poetry of Pope John Paul II* (New York: Random House, 1982), 124; emphasis added.

41. Our late spiritual shepherd, Pope John Paul II, speaks on "the reality of the union with the person now deceased. *The value of the person, after all, is not transient, and spiritual union can and should continue even when physical union is at an end*" (Karol Wojtyla, *Love and Responsibility,* trans, H. T. Willetts [New York: Farrar, Straus and Giroux, 1982], 212; emphasis added).

42. *Magnificat* (Spencerville, MD), June 2003.

43. Even in personal psychology the true path is only partly to move outward in lesser steps, first from the solitary self to self-acceptance, then to believing, and then finally to belonging. While this is restorative, this modern and somewhat rationalist technique is possibly backwards. In truth, the well is deeper than we can ever think. And, in a world turned upside down (Augustine's times were much like our own), it is possible to go first to the bottom of the well: "In this is [the] love, not that we have loved God, but that He has *first* loved us" (1 John 4:10). God is the origin of all things visible and invisible, both the galaxies and the even larger inner vastness — the solitude and our nostalgia and capacity for God — and the original companionship to be reclaimed. The last is first. *The belonging is "there" first, as a gift.* With this deepest belonging comes belief and then compassion, and then the self-acceptance.

44. St. Aloysius Gonzaga to his mother on his own approaching death, cited in *Magnificat,* June 2002, 299. This was the entry for June 21, exactly one year following Dr. Lee's phone call informing us of Kristi's imminently terminal condition.

45. Mother Teresa, *Daily Blessings*. In our final months together, Kristi asked me to find our misplaced souvenir from Mother Teresa. Years before, we sent a donation and received in return a large book-mark with Mother Teresa's personal note. Now, over one year later I have found it. It includes a Prayer for Peace, followed by a handwrit-ten note, "God bless you, M. Teresa." Now you and Mother Teresa are together, and I have this relic to remind me.

46. Very near this same time our good friend Eric also had a vivid dream. Even weeks later he felt "compelled" to tell me. Eric described from his dream: "Kristi's hands and how she touched to heal [me]."

47. *Liturgy of the Hours*, 2:360.

48. *Liturgy of the Hours*, 1:1587.

Seven: A Lasting Portrait

1. The Creed, sacraments, and morality are identical, as is the special union through the succession of bishops from the beginning, to-gether with the pope and never without him. And all of this is centered on the singular Real Presence of the Eucharist.

2. "The world is passing away, the world is losing its grip, the world is short of breath. Do not fear. Thy youth shall be renewed as an eagle's" (Sermon of St. Augustine [Sermon 81, 8], in Peter Brown, *Augustine of Hippo* [Berkeley: University of California Press, 1969], 298).

3. These continue today, and while they are not endorsed by the Church to the same degree as are the apparitions at Lourdes, Fatima, and Guadalupe, they are likely genuine. Unlike so many such reports, Betania was thoroughly investigated. The "Pastoral Instruction on the Apparitions of the Blessed Virgin in Finca Betania" was issued after a three- or four-year personal investigation by the bishop, in late 1987. In cases of private revelations, clearly apart from the public revelations handed on by the Church, which are complete in the incarnation, Rome never interferes with the decision of a local bishop and clearly is not interested in needlessly disrupting popular piety in this vale of tears. Even the apparitions formally endorsed by Rome (these include Fatima,

Lourdes, and Guadalupe) received this recognition only after the local bishop first investigated and reported on the miracles.

4. In "heaven" space does not exist: "within" and "without" lose their meaning. This must be why we speak of being "face to face" with God, not to be anthropomorphic, but to avoid being geographic or spatial.

5. Cardinal Joseph Ratzinger, citation in *Magnificat* (Spencerville, MD), June 5, 2002, 86; emphasis added.

6. Summarizing from Marcius, who in the first centuries wrote of the redeemed, Hans Urs von Balthasar offers this: "He has an unshakeable trust, a certainty and a 'taste,' so much so that when he does enter heaven he will not at all feel like a stranger, but will find himself quite at home" (*The Glory of the Lord: A Theological Aesthetics,* vol. 1 [San Francisco: Ignatius Press, 1998], 274).

7. Of the resurrection, some attribute the disturbed tomb to the earthquake. But then there is the detail of the remaining burial cloth; we have yet to see an earthquake fold a napkin.

8. "Kristi's Poem," page 179 above.

9. I recorded most of the dates that roses simply disappeared, within not more than three days, and often within one day or less. In the first year these dates include twice by December 23, 2001 and then January 27, April 2 and 22, June 10, and July 2, 2002.

10. *This is the note:* "I came home one day, to have [his wife] tell me that her cousin had her water break at twenty weeks. With the trouble they had had getting pregnant in the first place, this was devastating news. I was troubled all evening, but also felt as if I was not powerless. I became convinced that someone was trying to get in touch with me, and I soon knew it was Kristi. I know she had a special love for unborn children, and I also know she could help. I suppose I knew this before she died, and that was a small part of why I came to Seattle to see her in the spring of 2001. I wanted to be in contact with her before she left, in case she might be inclined to help me if I ever needed it. I became aware that I would need to demonstrate faith for her to agree to save

this child. She made it clear to me that if I picked up the phone and called [the couple], and told them that their baby would be fine, that it would be so.

I fell just short of being able to do that. I asked for an alternative. I became aware that if [his wife] and I prayed together for this baby, that it would be healthy, for certain. As you know [his wife] and I found the courage to do this, which was not easy for us. I knew then that the baby would be fine. I never wondered again. The baby [name] was born at thirty-two weeks in April, and is now perfectly healthy." On first hearing of this I recommended reading Matthew 18:19.

11. St. Augustine, *The City of God*, bk. 22, chap. 29; emphasis added.

12. Elizabeth Leseur, *My Spirit Rejoices: The Diary of a Christian Soul in an Age of Unbelief* (Manchester, NH: Sophia Press, 1996), 59, 62. Toward the end, on one of our afternoon walks, Kristi confided to me: *"I guess it does matter that a couple is of the same religion."* For us this was a blessing. Real romance is not possible without the eternal. It is the eternal. Following is a short meditation on Leseur's desire and Kristi's comment to me, as these relate to the different theologies of different Christian communions, the "theology of the body" by which marriage is a direct source of grace and a sacrament to one another ("religious"), and the Communion of Saints.

In a more compassionate attitude toward "original sin," the Church distinguishes between deliberated sin and mere weakness. This is an enormous distinction. (See the Lutheran World Federation and the Roman Catholic Church, *Joint Declaration on the Doctrine of Justification* [Grand Rapids, MI: William B. Eerdmans, 2000], 21–22, *and* the Vatican "Annex to the Official Common Statement," 44.) In the Catholic view, sins by definition are of the free will and are chosen. Sin is the choice to call evil good. Or, perhaps, accepting the illusion that the good that we find about us comes from ourselves as the author. Sin is a deliberated perversion of the good: pride. Ultimately sin is a betrayal of the self, and therefore also a betrayal of the One who dwells within.

That sins can be shed through a deeper self-revelation (confession) is a celebration of redeemed human freedom, not subservience. Another Christian view holds that the person is less radically free and gifted, and instead is always divided, totally righteous and totally sinner — as a permanent condition under this non-Catholic view, we are limited to constantly starting over from wherever we are, but are never sacramentally embraced and set free as from the beginning. This is what is meant by the view attributed to Luther that man is "dung covered with snow." The Catholic view is more the reverse, that the eyes of the suffering Christ see us from deeper within and differently. And with the language of the body (John Paul II's "theology of the body") comes an original companionship deeper than our solitude, deeper than our aggression, and deeper than our inner dividedness. This wholeness gives us the sacramental nature of marriage (as well as the possibility of consecrated celibacy) and the discernment that the unitive and procreative dimension is not to be mutilated. In unity of "religion" Leseur longed for the unity of a personally unified husband fully together with a personally unified wife, without obstacles — single-heartedness.

Regarding the full reality of the Communion of Saints, the very broad Catholic teaching is that this is "participation in one common reality or else of entering into communication with others." The Communion of Saints reaches through the veil to the whole Church living and dead, without interruption. According to Emilien Lamirande, Luther reduces communio (*Gemeinschaft*) to community (*Gemeinde*), "making this article of the Creed simply a definition of the Church in the Protestant sense" (*The Communion of Saints* [New York: Hawthorn Books, 1963], 20; vol. 26 of the *Twentieth Century Encyclopedia of Catholicism,* ed. Henri Daniel-Rops [New York: Hawthorn Books, 1962]). Because of Kristi's and my unity in faith, I am not denied the consoling theme of our book expressed in the title — *Kristi: So Thin Is the Veil* — verified in Augustine's *City of God* (19, 13): "the peace of the heavenly city is the perfectly ordered and harmonious community enjoying God *and enjoying each other in God*" (ibid., 154; emphasis added).

In the Catholic Mass, the entire breadth of the Communion of Saints is experienced and often expressed by not holding hands in smaller congregational or even national circles.

13. St. Augustine, Sermon, *Liturgy of the Hours*, 2:920–22.

14. Raniero Cantalamessa, *Virginity: A Positive Approach to Celibacy for the Sake of the Kingdom of Heaven* (New York: St. Paul's, 1995), 9.

15. "Speaking of the body glorified through the resurrection to the future life, we have in mind man, male-female, in all the truth of his humanity.... This will be a completely *new experience*. At the same time it will not be alienated in any way from what man took part in *from the beginning,* nor from what, in the historical dimension of his existence, constituted in him the source of the tension between spirit and body, concerning mainly the procreative meaning of the body and sex. *The man of the future world will find again in this new experience of his own body precisely the completion of what he bore within himself perennially and historically*" (*The Theology of the Body* [Boston: Pauline Books, 1997], 248; emphasis added).

Then John Paul II adds: "*In the risen man, male and female, will be revealed, I would say, the absolute and eternal nuptial meaning of the glorified body in union with God himself through the 'face to face' vision of him, and glorified also through the union of perfect inter-subjectivity. This will unite all who participate in the other world, men and women, in the mystery of the communion of saints*" (p. 267, emphasis added).

16. Among Kristi's friends in a strange land was Fr. Breslin, a Columban missionary in Japan (chapter 2). St. Columban gives us this: "the more the soul loves, the more it desires to love, and the greater its suffering, the greater its healing. In this same way may our God and Lord Jesus Christ, the good and saving physician, wound the depths of our souls with a healing wound — the same Jesus Christ who reigns in unity with the Father and the Holy Spirit, for ever and ever. Amen." From an instruction by St. Columban, abbot (*The Liturgy of the Hours*, Twenty-first week of Ordinary Time), 4:174.

17. Cantalamessa, *Virginity*, 39. And there is this: "Rejoice, beloved, in the measure that you share in Christ's suffering" (1 Pet. 4:13).

18. Jean Pierre de Caussade, *Abandonment to Divine Providence,* trans. John Severs (New York: Image Books, 1979), 115.

19. John Paul II suggests that the wonderful Beatitudes Christ delivered on the mount are a "portrait" of Himself (*Veritatis Splendor* [*The Splendor of the Truth*], 1993).

20. At the time of my father's death in late 1988 I was enlightened by this experience of St. Augustine: "I entered into my inmost being . . . and by my soul's eye, such as it was, I saw above that same eye of my soul, above my mind, an unchangeable light. . . . It was above my mind, *because* it made me, and I was beneath it, because I was made by it. He who knows the truth knows the light, and he who knows it knows eternity. Love knows it, O eternal truth, and true love, and beloved eternity! You are my God, and I sigh for you day and night" (*Confessions,* bk. 7, chap. 10; emphasis added).

21. Malcolm Muggeridge attributes this familiar distinction between seeing with the eyes and seeing through the eyes to William Blake, *The End of Christendom* (Grand Rapids: William B. Eerdmans, 1980), 62.

22. Only later did it really strike me that in his full humanity Christ passed through the veil *from our side* into the darkness of our fear (not from the other side), consoled by not so much as a single celestial candle. He knows our abyss not out of sympathy alone, but out of a choking experience so much deeper than our own. We are saved because our suffering is His suffering, *not* simply like His suffering, and with Him is *fully* resurrected. It is His peace that He gives. Are we moderns still capable of the astonishment that leads to faith?

23. See chapter 2.

24. Blaise Pascal, *Pensées,* no. 465 (New York: E. P. Dutton, 1958), 130. "Lord, where do you live? My child, I do not live far from you, I am infinitely nearer to you than you think: I am called the unknown Guest, I live within you; seek me in purity of soul, and you will find

me" (G. Canovai, cited in Gabriel of St. Mary Magdalen, *Divine Intimacy* [San Francisco: Dimension Books, reprinted by Ignatius Press, 1987], 1:61).

25. St. John of the Cross, Maxim 307.

26. The adjacent lines from Shakespeare are those of the king to Hamlet grieving over his own father's death: "But to persever in obstinate condolement is a course of impious stubbornness. 'Tis unmanly grief. It shows a will most incorrect to heaven, a heart unfortified, a mind impatient, an understanding simple and unschool'd." And St. Jerome, the translator of the New Testament from Greek to Latin, actually labeled inordinate grief as a form of suicide.

27. Sermon by St. Augustine, *Liturgy of the Hours,* 4:1305.

28. Luigi Guisanni, *The Religious Sense* (San Francisco: Ignatius Press, 1986), 75; emphasis added.

29. St. Francis de Sales, *Introduction to the Devout Life,* trans. John K. Ryan (New York: Harper & Row, 1966), chap. 38 ("Instructions to Married Persons").

About the Authors

Peter Beaulieu and Kristi (Orr) married in 1974, ten months after they first met. Both are identical twins. Peter attended public schools and earned an undergraduate degree in Architecture and a doctorate in Urban and Regional Planning (1975), both from the University of Washington. Kristi, his treasured wife, is co-author, because her story was written with the help of her abiding presence, even after her death to cancer in 2001. Kristi attended the Benedictine St. Gertrude's Academy in Cottonwood, Idaho, and later earned diplomas with honors in English and French from Whitworth College (1972). In 1973 she completed a fifth year, in European Civilization, at the Sorbonne in Paris. Kristi was devoted to children, especially including the unborn, and shows us a consistent gentleness of heart, which was only deepened by her unusual ordeal with cancer. Peter and Kristi have two grown children, Laura and Mark, and three grandchildren.

Peter and Kristi Beaulieu, 1974

Kristi Beaulieu, 1995

Peter Beaulieu, 2000